A JEWISH PILGRIMAGE

BY THE SAME AUTHOR

Israel in Italien (Berlin, 1909)
Jewish Life in Modern Times (1st edit., 1914; 2nd edit., Revised, 1929)
The Ruhleben Prison Camp (1917)
The Journal of a Jewish Traveller (1925)
A Ghetto Gallery (1931)
Britain's Nameless Ally (1942)
The Jews in the War (1st edit., 1942; 2nd edit., Revised, 1943)
History of the Jews in Vilna (Philadelphia, 1943)
The Zionist Movement (1945. American and French editions, 1946. Spanish edition 1947. Italian edition, 1953. Hebrew edition, 1956)
The Progress of Zionism (8th revised edition, 1946. French edition, 1945)
Contemporary Jewry (1950)
Revised and enlarged edition of Paul Goodman's *History of the Jews* (1951)
A Short History of Zionism 1951. Braille edition, 1951; Hebrew edition, 1956)
Travels in Jewry (1952)
The Rebirth of Israel (Edited, 1952)

THE AUTHOR

A
JEWISH PILGRIMAGE

The Autobiography of
Israel Cohen

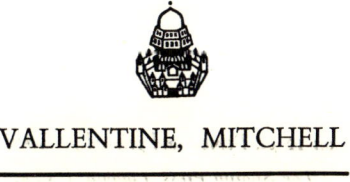

VALLENTINE, MITCHELL
LONDON   MCMLVI

All rights reserved
First published in 1956 by Vallentine, Mitchell & Co. Ltd.

Set in 11 on 12 pt. Bembo and printed in Great Britain by
The Sharon Press, London, E.C.4.

Preface

IN an age when an author of twenty-five can write his autobiography, and countless people in the forties and fifties have written theirs, it should not, I trust, be regarded as premature or presumptuous if I venture to present mine in the middle seventies. I have written it, not in emulation with the numerous autobiographies that now appear, but because I believe that I have an interesting and eventful story to tell, and also because I think it forms a useful contribution to contemporary history. It is based upon a great deal of material—diaries, press cuttings, letters, and miscellaneous notes—from which I have taken only what I considered essential, as well as upon a fairly reliable memory. Two momentous episodes in my life have already been described in previous books, my internment in a prison camp in Germany in the First World War, and my journey to Australasia and the Far East a few years later; but as the first of these books appeared as far back as 1917 and the other in 1925, and as they have both been long out of print and are probably unknown to the present generation, I have considered it desirable to summarise them at the appropriate places so as to avoid big gaps in the narrative.

In writing this book I have had the advantage of the constant and candid criticism of my wife, to whom I wish to express my gratitude for many valuable suggestions. I also desire to express my thanks to Dr. Oskar K. Rabinowicz, who read through the typescript, for his helpful criticisms on various matters of Zionist history.

LONDON, JUNE, 1956.   I.C.

For nigh on forty years we've been as one,
And thus shall be till either hence be gone:
To whom, then, shall I dedicate this *Life*
Save unto her — my dear, devoted wife?

Contents

CHAPTER I
CHILDHOOD IN MANCHESTER
1879—1895

Page 1

Birth and parentage—Home life conditions—Writing letters for grandmother—Sabbath observance—Festival ceremonies—School attendance—Religious education—A versatile pedagogue—Synagogue and "House of Study"—Public Library—Grammar School days—Henry Ospovat—"Lovers of Zion"—A Hebrew poet—Colonel Albert Edward Goldsmid—Manchester newspapers—Admission to Jews' College.

CHAPTER II
STUDENT YEARS
1895—1904

Page 22

Whitechapel in 1895—Orthodox lodgings—Hebrew authors and Palestine emissaries—The Jews' College staff—University College—Professors A. E. Housman and W. P. Ker—Queen Victoria's Diamond Jubilee—Theodor Herzl's first public meeting in London—A Zionist forum—Father Ignatius—A Hebrew-speaking society—Zionism at Jews' College—Conference at Clerkenwell Town Hall—Sir Francis Montefiore—Herzl's visits to London—Dr. Joseph Hertz—Introduction to Herzl—Offer of an editorship—First efforts in journalism—English and other studies—Professor David Woolf Marks—Solomon Schechter—Contributions to the *Gentleman's Magazine* and *Jewish World*—Experiences as teacher and preacher—Travels through Belgium and Germany—Herzl's last Zionist Congress—First meeting with Chaim Weizmann—Visit to Heine's birthplace—Ode on death of Herzl—Dr. Weizmann's first visit to London—Travels in Holland—Interview with Josef Israels—Graduation and departure from College—A Jewish Canon.

CHAPTER III Page 49
ADVENTURES IN JOURNALISM
1905—1908

Visit to Paris—Interview with Dr. Max Nordau—A Russian Socialist Club—A link with Nelson—Freelance journalism—Israel Zangwill and Lucien Wolf—The Seventh Zionist Congress—Rejection of East African scheme—The Bund centre in Geneva—Appointment on *The Tribune*—Proposed mission to Warsaw—Exposure of maladministration of Aliens Act—Sholem Aleichem in London—Investigating the Polish revolutionary movement in Cracow and the Ukrainian centre in Lemberg—First meeting with August Zaleski—Nahum Sokolow—The Hague Zionist Congress—A tour through Italy—Death of *The Tribune*—Return to freelance activity—Interpreting between Bernard Shaw and Reuben Brainin—J. L. Garvin and an Indian Prince—Speaking for Winston Churchill—Career and death of Henry Ospovat.

CHAPTER IV Page 73
IN ZIONIST SERVICE
1904—1914

Formation of London Zionist League—Ahad Ha'am's Cultural Zionism—Purchase of *Jewish Chronicle* by Zionists—Relations with Leopold J. Greenberg and Dr. Weizmann—A contract from Methuen—Parliamentary deputation from Turkey—Zionism in Constantinople—The Hamburg Congress—Appointment at Zionist headquarters in Cologne—Hans Herzl—David Wolffsohn in England—Weizmann's attitude to Wolffsohn—Visit to C. P. Scott—Zionist affairs in England—Meeting with Weizmann at Montreux—Wolffsohn as President of Zionist Organisation—Life in Cologne—Zionist headquarters in Berlin—Sokolow's political activities in England and the United States—Hebrew language conflict in Palestine—Shmarya Levin—The Vienna Congress of 1913—Weizmann's plea for a Hebrew University—Life in Berlin.

CHAPTER V Page 96
INTERNMENT AND IMPRISONMENT
1914—1916

Outbreak of First World War—A holiday at Schandau—Imprisonment in Stadtvogtei jail—Reporting to Berlin police-station—Visit to Dr. Matthias Erzberger—Arrest and internment in Ruhleben Camp—Stables as barracks—Segregation of Jews—Barrack VI—Religious worship—Anti-Semitic prejudice—Camp administration—Prisoners' Activities—Censorship of correspondence—Renewed imprisonment at Stadtvogtei—Nationalities and offences of prisoners—Convivial night gatherings—Return to Ruhleben—Mock trial and parliamentary by-election—Mental depression and moral decline—Exchange of civilian prisoners—Impairment of health—Release from camp and departure from Germany.

CHAPTER VI Page 112
INTERLUDE
1916—1917

Readjustment to life in London—Pestered by detectives—Recruiting a spy for Germany—Interview at Brixton Prison—Trial at Westminster Hall—Conveying an incriminating document—Articles on Ruhleben—Visit to the Rothschilds—Call on Zangwill—Book and lectures on Ruhleben—As substitute for Horatio Bottomley—Agitation for total exchange of civilian prisoners—Demonstration at Kingsway Hall—Sir Thomas Lipton's grammar.

CHAPTER VII Page 121
BACK TO ZIONISM
1916—1918

Zionism in England in the First World War—Weizmann's first approaches to British Government—Drafting a declaration of British sympathy—Antagonism of Anglo-Jewish leaders—Celebrating the Balfour Declaration—Raising money for land-purchase in Palestine—Public dinner to Weizmann—Successful interview with Sir Alfred Mond—Talk with first Marquis of Reading—Lecturing and writing—Marriage and children—Work in Jewish Department of Ministry of Information—Return to secretariat of the World Zionist Organisation—Entrusted with mission to Poland.

CHAPTER VIII Page 134
POGROMS IN POLAND
1918—1919

Interview at Foreign Office—Meeting with Mr. Zaleski in Berne—Journey to Vienna—Experiences in Cracow—Discussions with heads of Polish Liquidation Commission—Jewish self-defence militias—The pogrom at Chrzanow—Jewish conditions in Warsaw—Talks with Jewish leaders and with head of Allied Mission—Interviews with heads of Polish Government and political leaders—Interviews with Paderewski and Pilsudski—Visit to Lemberg—Origin and character of pogrom—A night at Jaroslau—Leave-taking in Cracow—Visit to Auschwitz—Return to Vienna—International Socialist Conference in Berne—Branting, Eisner, and Ramsay MacDonald—Peace Conference in Paris—Jewish Delegations and Minorities Treaties.

CHAPTER IX　　　　　　　　　　Page 149

PROTESTS AND POLEMICS

1919—1920

Continued excesses in Poland—Queen's Hall Demonstration—Attacks by *Morning Post*—Articles in *The Times*—Public protests in London and elsewhere—Meeting in Leeds Town Hall—British and American Inquiry Commissions—Jews and Bolshevism—Correspondence in *The Times*—"Verax" and the Chief Rabbi—Correspondence with Lord Northcliffe—Demand for manifesto by Anglo-Jewish leaders—Interview between Lord Rothschild and Sir Paul Dukes—Massacres of Jews in the Ukraine and White Russia.

CHAPTER X　　　　　　　　　　Page 161

THE ZIONIST HEADQUARTERS

1919—1920

The offices in Great Russell Street—Influx of Zionists from the Continent—Victor Jacobson, Shmarya Levin, Leo Motzkin, and Boris Goldberg—Max Nordau and the Executive—His critical attitude and dogmatism—His return to Paris—Justice Brandeis at Clerkenwell Town Hall—Professor Felix Frankfurter—Benjamin V. Cohen—Rev. William Hechler—Professor Patrick Geddes—James Malcolm—Cool reception by the Webbs—Return of Weizmann and Sokolow from Paris to London—Preparations for mission to Australasia and the Far East.

CHAPTER XI　　　　　　　　　　Page 175

MISSION TO AUSTRALASIA

1920

Extent and scope of journey—The "White Terror" in Hungary—From Trieste to Alexandria—A tour through Palestine—The Western Wall—From Port Said to Fremantle—Appeal campaign in Perth—Lunch at Parliament House—Campaign in Melbourne—General Sir John Monash—Sir Isaac Isaacs—Pulpit addresses—Interview with "Billy Hughes"—Jewish pioneers and politicians in New South Wales—Public meetings in Sydney—Civic reception in Auckland—Among the Maoris—Demonstration in Wellington Town Hall—Prime Minister Massey—Visits to Christchurch and Dunedin—Perilous journey through Rimutaka Gorge—Speaker Sir Daniel Levy—Meetings in Newcastle and Brisbane.

CHAPTER XII
TRAVELS IN ASIA
1920—1921

Page 192

Thursday Island and Zamboanga—Meeting in Manila—Hongkong's Jewish community—The Sassoons—Sabbath in Shanghai—Jews of Kai-Feng-Fu—Meetings in Shanghai—Arrival in Kobe—Experiences in Yokohama—A Jewish Bishop's grand-daughter—A link with Disraeli—Visit to British Embassy at Tokyo—The charm of Kyoto—Queen Victoria's Lady-in-Waiting—A meeting in Kobe—Through Korea to Mukden—Traders in furs—Origin and characteristics of Harbin Jewry—Chinese censorship of meetings—Experiences in Tientsin—Impressions of Peking—Singapore's Jewish community—Sir Menasseh Meyer—Travelling through Java—From Penang to Rangoon—Anglo-Jewish bookmakers—The Calcutta community—Sir David Ezra's "Zoo"—Agra and Delhi—Welcome in Bombay—The Bené Israel—Refugees from Persia—Carpet-dealers from Meshed—Lecturing in the Red Sea—Palestine revisited—From Brindisi to The Hague.

CHAPTER XIII
POLITICS AND PERSONALITIES
1921—1923

Page 217

Return to Zionist headquarters—Work as "Public Relations Officer"—"Ghost" writing—A tempting financial offer—Appointment as General Secretary—Arab campaign against Palestine Mandate—Balfour on leading Jews—The White Paper of 1922—Ratification of Mandate—Discussions about the Jewish Agency—Jabotinsky attacks Weizmann—Jabotinsky and Petlura—An indiscreet interview—Professor Michael Postan—Lieutenant-Colonel Frederick H. Kisch—Displacement of Ussishkin.

CHAPTER XIV
SOME SPECIAL MISSIONS
1922—1924

Page 229

Interview with Adolph Ochs in Paris—His impressions of Palestine—Article by Ramsay MacDonald—Zionism in Hungary—The British Legation in Budapest—Interview with Hungarian Acting Premier—Talk with Wilhelm Vazsonyi—A restless night at Timisoara—Visit to Bucharest—Interview with Rumanian Minister of Education—Return to Budapest—The *numerus clausus* in Hungary—Importance of Goldziher's Oriental Library—Negotiations for purchase of Library—Interview with Hungarian Minister of Interior.

CHAPTER XV   Page 240
JOURNEYINGS IN EUROPE
1924—1928

Journeys between 1924 and 1928—Political, cultural, and religious conditions of Jews in Eastern and Central Europe—The Free City of Dantzic—A mirthful Sabbath evening in Riga—Libau and the amber industry—Zionist refugees from Russia—Experiences in Estonia—Impressions of Prague—Official conference in Budapest—Interview with Count Bethlen—Jewish life in Yugoslavia—Synagogues in Belgrade—A call on the British Minister—Jewish conditions in Athens—Meeting with Sir Alfred Mond—Zionism in Bulgaria—Conditions in Plovdiv and Sofia—Interview at Ministry of Foreign Affairs—The Sofia grand synagogue—Winter at Rustchuk—Persecution in Rumania—Vandalism in Cluj and Oradea Mare—Professor Cuza, arch-Anti-Semite—The Jewish cemetery at Kishinev—A scholarly night-porter—Offer for a British passport.

CHAPTER XVI   Page 259
CONGRESSES AND CRISES
1925—1931

Scope and functions of a Zionist Congress—Preparation of Executive's Report—Vienna Congress of 1925—Military mobilisation against *Hakenkreuzler*—A promise of £1,000,000—Claude Montefiore and Rabbi Dr. Blau—Louis Marshall and the Jewish Agency—Opposition of Jabotinsky and Stephen Wise to enlarged Agency—Relations between Weizmann and Sokolow—Inauguration of Jewish Agency at Zurich—Einstein, Leon Blum, and other celebrities—Interrupted holiday at Rapallo—Arab riots in Palestine—Albert Hall demonstration—Shaw Commission of Inquiry—Report by Jewish Agency's counsel—Weizmann's talks with Ramsay MacDonald and Lord Passfield—Intervention of the (first) Marquess of Reading—Weizmann's indiscretion in Berlin speech—Meeting with Dr. Oscar Levy in Wiesbaden—Passfield White Paper—Jewish negotiations with Cabinet Committee—Justice Frankfurter and Harold Laski—Consultations with Baron Edmond de Rothschild and Leon Blum—Weizmann's telephone conversation with Ramsay MacDonald—The Prime Minister's Letter—Proposed Congress at Abbazia—The Basle Congress of 1931—Weizmann's indiscreet press interview—Sokolow succeeeds Weizmann—*A Ghetto Gallery*.

CHAPTER XVII   Page 281
A TRANSATLANTIC TOUR
1931

Professor Selig Brodetsky—Visit to New York—Stephen Wise as preacher—Settlement of Jews in Canada—Montreal Jewish community—Variegated conditions in Toronto—Traditional orthodoxy—From Windsor to Detroit—Cabinet Minister Croll—Visit to Governor-General in Ottawa—A lecture by Bertrand Russell—Meeting in Winnipeg—Calgary, Regina, Edmonton, and Saskatoon—A Yiddish play in Vancouver—A Russo-Turkish War veteran in Victoria—Visit to Seattle—Jewish farm settlements—Yiddish schools—Anti-Semitism—A prima donna in Chicago—Jewish claimant to Labrador—Return to New York—Talk with Dr. Cyrus Adler—Lunch with Jewish writers.

CHAPTER XVIII   Page 298
PRELUDE TO CALAMITY
1932—1935

Nazis in Berlin—Dr. Jacob Klatzkin—Mission to Poland—Palestine Office in Warsaw—Political and economic oppression—The Warsaw Ghetto—Slums and cellar-dwellings—Conditions in Lodz, Bialystok, and Czenstochau—Zionist enthusiasm in Lwow—Mediaeval Cracow—Vilna a citadel of Jewish tradition—Hitler master of Germany—Interview with Ambassador Masaryk—Article in *The Quarterly Review*—Jew-baiting in Rumania—Interviews with Duchess of Atholl and Eleanor Rathbone—The Prague Congress—Assassination of Dr. Arlosoroff—Loss of passport—From Prague *via* Vienna to Rimini—Talk with Chief Rabbi in Rome—Jewish community of Madrid—Memories of Toledo—Lisbon Jewry—The Gibraltar community—Impressions of Cordova—Visit to Barcelona—The Lucerne Congress of 1935—Weizmann's re-election as President—Palestine in 1935—"Tabernacles" in Alexandria.

CHAPTER XIX   Page 317
IN THE SHADOWS
1935—1939

Displacement, personality and death of Sokolow—Persecution of Zionists in Soviet Russia—Arab rebellion in Palestine—Twentieth Congress in Zurich—Visit to Padua—Cables about Arab outrages—Hitler's invasion of Austria—Goering's speech in Vienna—Visit to Herzl's tomb—Taxi-driver quotes from Daniel—Gestapo's "Black List"—Visit to Prague—Berlin Jewry's theatre—Conference at St. James's Palace—The Congress at Geneva—Hitler-Stalin Pact—A sorrowful leave-taking.

CHAPTER XX   Page 333
A VARIED CAVALCADE
1919—1939

Visitors at Zionist headquarters—Lord Samuel, Leon Blum, and others—Field-Marshal Smuts—Professor Einstein—Spanish Government's offer—Louis Marshall and Felix Warburg—Pinchas Rutenberg—Sir Elly Kadoorie—

Jacobus Kann—Dr. Alfred Klee—The poet Bialik—Mayor Dizengoff—A bevy of Professors—Alfred E. Zimmern—Hersch Lauterpacht—Sir Wyndham Deedes—Sir Gilbert Clayton—Sir George Macdonogh—Colonel J. H. Patterson—Lord Wedgwood—Mrs. Blanche Dugdale—Herbert Sidebotham—Sidney Dark—Miscellaneous callers—Emissaries from Transylvania—An actress in quest of finance—A revolutionary from Korea—A man from Scotland Yard.

CHAPTER XXI   Page 347

ON GUARD

1919—1939

Influencing public opinion—Countering anti-Zionist agitation—Zionism and Bolshevism—Attacks by ex-Government officials—Mr. St. John Philby and others—Contributions on Palestine to reviews—A lover of Sir Philip Sassoon—Addressing meetings—Near and Middle East Association—Challenge by Mr. Philby—Debates with Arabs—Speaking in Hyde Park—A talk on Radio Athlone—Earl Winterton's blunder—*Jewish Life in Modern Times*—Nazi persecution of German Jewry—Contributions to *Quarterly* and other reviews—Jewish Board of Deputies—Meetings at Chatham House—The Evian Conference—Letter from Professor Sigmund Freud—Mr. August Zaleski.

CHAPTER XXII   Page 364

IN RETIREMENT

1939—1945

Retirement from Zionist headquarters—Dr. Weizmann's tribute—A farewell luncheon—Press appreciations—Renewed fund-raising—Services for St. Paul's School boys—Proposed retreat to Canada—Sojourn in Droitwich—*History of the Jews in Vilna*—*The Jews in the War*—*Britain's Nameless Ally*—More articles in reviews—*The Zionist Movement*—Lectures on Zionism—"Anti-Semitism and Treachery"—"Economic Value of Refugees"—Hitler's policy of extermination—Jewish emissaries from Moscow—Booklet on *The Jews in Europe*.

CHAPTER XXIII   Page 377

POST-WAR EVENTS

1945—1956

The Zionist Conference of 1945—The Labour Government's somersault—Anglo-American Committee of Enquiry—London Jewish Conference—Preparing proposals for Peace Conference—Conference of Jewish organisations in Paris—Jewish interests in Peace Treaties—Ben-Gurion and Moshe Sneh—The Laski libel case—Zionist Congress in Basle—Dr. Weizmann's defeat—Lectures at Jews' College—World Jewish Congress at Montreux—Seventieth birthday in hospital—Conclusion.

INDEX   Page 397

Illustrations

Frontispiece: The Author   *Facing page*

Union of Jewish Literary Societies, Summer Assembly, Ramsgate
1904   40

Journalists at the Sixth Zionist Congress, Basle 1903   44

In the Ruhleben Prison Camp, 1915   102

In a Maori Village near Rotorua, N.Z., 1920   188

Welcome with garlands at Bombay, 1921   214

Conference for enlargement of the Jewish Agency, London, 1929 ..   266

Dr. Weizmann addressing the Twentieth Zionist Congress, Zurich,
1937   322

The Author's wife, Barcelona, 1950   394

Judaeus sum: Judaei nihil a me alienum puto.
After Terence

Chapter One

CHILDHOOD IN MANCHESTER
1879-1895

I

MY first glimpse of the world was from a frowsy nook in the Cheetham district of Manchester, called Red Bank, where I was born in the spring of 1879. It was within earshot of Victoria Station, to which my earliest memories are linked because of the shunting and shrieking of the trains, which often kept me awake at night. Shortly afterwards, however, we moved nearer to the heart of Cheetham, and in the ensuing years, as our family grew and my father's material position gradually improved, there were a few more removals, but all within the same district, and within convenient reach of school and synagogue. It was in Cheetham that by far the greater part of the Jewish community was then concentrated, and there my father settled in or about 1870 at the age of twenty. He had come from Lomza, a small town in Russian Poland, famous for its *Yeshivah* (Talmudical Seminary), which he had attended, not with a view to becoming a Rabbi but from the traditional desire to acquire Jewish learning. His emigration must have been prompted solely by the lack of any favourable economic prospects in the land of his birth, for the periodical pogroms which set in motion a steadily increasing exodus of Jews from the Tsar's dominions first broke out in 1881. My mother also came from Poland, together with her mother and three sisters, from the townlet of Kalvariya, much about the same time as my father; and although he belonged to a humble place of worship consisting entirely of recent arrivals from the Russian Pale of Settlement, my parents were married at the more imposing Great Synagogue, which was familiarly known as "the English *schul*."

Our home life was conducted in strict accordance with Jewish religious law and custom, of which my father was a conscientious devotee. If frequency and volume of prayer should have ensured perfect happiness, we were entitled to it in bountiful measure, for in addition to the morning, afternoon, evening and night prayers, and the long benediction after every meal, there were extra supplications for special occasions. Nor were these offered up only orally, for when my mother was expecting a child and took to bed there was pinned to the wall in her room a printed Hebrew amulet invoking Divine protection against the demon Lilith, who was credited with sinister designs against all infants. The recital of Psalms was believed to be especially efficacious both for averting misfortune and for securing good fortune, but it did not always produce the desired effect. For when, after a young brother of mine had become dangerously ill and was given up by the doctor, several Psalms prescribed by the Rabbi were intoned in Hebrew at his bedside but they failed to save him. On the other hand, my eldest brother recited a whole book of Psalms on the night before he had to sit for a Hebrew examination at school and won the first prize — a result that prompted me a few years later to follow his example, when I sat for a scholarship, with an equally gratifying sequel.

Although my parents fully realised that the conditions in which they lived were much better than those they had left behind they nevertheless spoke with a feeling of nostalgia about life "at home," as they always referred to the land of their birth. It was this emotion to which my mother, who had a musical voice, often gave expression when she sang Yiddish lullabies and other folk-songs at the fireside on a winter's evening. It was this feeling too that prompted my father to write regularly to his parents in Lomza and always to enclose a money order for them in a registered envelope. A few years after the first pogrom in Russia his mother came to Manchester on a visit, to see whether she would also like to settle there. But she arrived at an unfortunate time, for the city was enveloped in a thick clammy fog that lasted for several days. "*Choshech finster,*

CHILDHOOD IN MANCHESTER

finster choshech" ("darkness, dark"), she kept on muttering in a mixture of Hebrew and Yiddish as I guided her timorous steps to a friend's house in a neighbouring street. As soon as the fog dispersed she made up her mind to return to Poland, and did so a few days later.

In the following year we received a telegram informing us of her death. It arrived during the day, when my father was away, and he was not expected home until the evening. My mother therefore impressed upon us not to say anything to him about the sad news on his return, and held the telegram back until after he had eaten his supper in peace. As soon as he read the message he took off his boots and put on slippers, and he sent for the Rabbi and the synagogue beadle. The latter brought a low stool for my father to sit on, and made a rent on the inner part of his waistcoat as a sign of mourning. A number of neighbours were immediately summoned to make up a *minyan* (quorum of ten) for prayer, and my father said the mourner's *Kaddish* ("sanctification") expressing resignation to the will of the Almighty. For seven days the morning and evening services were held in our house, except on the Sabbath, when the mourner went to the synagogue and was greeted with words of consolation by the cantor in the presence of a sympathetic congregation. A small oil-lamp was kept burning on the mantelpiece the whole time, and my father, on his low stool, pored over the book of Job.

My paternal grandfather, whom I never saw, must have lived to a patriarchal age, for my father, after having corresponded with him for some thirty-seven years, decided in 1907 to pay him a visit. As my father (who had become a British subject some twenty years earlier) was unable to obtain a Russian visa owing to the anti-Jewish discrimination practised by the Tsarist Government, and as my grandfather could not or would not go beyond the Russian frontier[1], they had to content themselves with a talk in the waiting-room of the station at Grajevo on the Russo-German border. They found that they had become complete strangers to one another, and as all the people at Lomza about whom my father inquired had either

[1] Poland was then part of Russia.

3

gone to America or died, their conversation soon petered out. My father returned from his journey visibly depressed.

My maternal grandmother had a grateful affection for me because I wrote letters for her to her two sons, Moses and Aaron, who lived in Pittsburgh. They had emigrated to America at the same time as she and her daughters came to England, and they never saw one another again. The lapse of time only deepened her longing for news from them, and as they failed to manifest any of the virtues of their Biblical namesakes and she had never learned to write, she asked her various grandchildren in turn to compose letters for her to them. But unfortunately long intervals would pass before they elicited a reply, or they were left unanswered altogether. At last, when I was thought able and mature enough to take my turn as a letter-writer, I tried my hand at working upon the feelings of my callous uncles, who had shown such indifference to the repeated appeals of their aged mother. I upbraided them with the remissness of which they had been guilty throughout the years, admonished them to write to her about themselves and their families while there was yet time, and depicted the happiness that even a short letter would give her in her declining days. In response she received, a few weeks later, a long and penitent epistle, accompanied by a peace-offering of fifty dollars. This created as great a sensation as though I had won a mammoth lottery-prize, and from that time my grandmother would not have anybody else write letters for her but me.

II

The observance in our home of the Sabbath, and of festivals and fasts, was accompanied by a series of rites and ceremonies, which were honoured with punctilious exactitude. The Sabbaths and festivals had to be celebrated with fitting repasts, which entailed much baking, stewing, and frying by my mother, who had to look after a rather large family. Apart from many other tasks, she usually baked two twisted loaves, sprinkled with poppy-seed in memory of the ancient manna, for those occasions, and in accordance with religious prescription sacrificed a handful of dough (*challah*) upon the fire, a survival of the offering made to the priest in Temple times

(Numbers XV, 20). The candles that she lit on the festive table were stuck in brass candlesticks that had been brought all the way from Poland, and which were polished every week to a degree of dazzling brilliance. And though she expected no thanks, the vital part that she, like every Jewish housewife, played in the maintenance of a traditional home, found appreciation in the recital by all her men-folk, on their return from the synagogue on Sabbath eve, of the panegyric in the last chapter of Proverbs beginning:

A virtuous woman who can find ? for her price is far above rubies.
The Biblical prohibition against kindling fire on the Sabbath necessitated the weekly employment of a *Shabbos Goyah* (Sabbath Gentile), usually a charwoman living near-by, who attended to the lights and fire and did any other work forbidden to the Jew. The " fire-woman," as she was called, generally looked after a number of houses in the same district, and her charge was quite moderate. For a time we had an Irish woman, who, on Mondays, also did the family's washing, over which she smoked a clay pipe.

Passover was particularly welcome to the younger generation, not only because of the appetising fare that it brought, but also because of the games we were able to have with Barcelona nuts. The commonest game, called " Kupke," was played on the pavement. A little pyramid of five nuts was placed near the wall by one of the players, and then the others, standing at the kerb, threw nuts at it in turn until the little pyramid was upset. The provider of the pyramid pocketed all the nuts that missed the target, and the successful thrower became the owner of the pyramid, which was again subjected to the attack. Another and simpler game consisted of guessing whether the number of nuts that a boy had in his clenched hand was odd or even: it had the advantage that it could be played anywhere, even — surreptitiously — in the synagogue while waiting for the service to begin. Passover was also responsible for the creation of the *Kosher* wine industry in Manchester, for the need of wine for the *Seder* (family evening) service prompted a man of enterprise, who had at first been making the liquor for the requirements only of his family, to increase the supply for the benefit of his neighbours; and the display of three attractively labelled bottles in a parlour-window in Cheetham heralded the founding of what ultimately became an extensive and prosperous business.

The "Ten Days of Penitence," from New Year to the Fast of Atonement, were apparently not considered by my father sufficient to make amends for our countless iniquities, known and unknown, of the expiring year, as he insisted upon our going to synagogue also every day from the preceding Sunday to say *Selichoth* (propitiatory prayers), for which he got us out of bed before six in the morning. We therefore looked forward all the more eagerly to the Feast of Tabernacles, which, of all the festivals, has left the most fragrant and lingering memory, not so much because of the palm and citron which enriched the drabness of the northern climate with a touch of the East, as because of the songs of thanksgiving that resounded from every booth. No matter how humble the home there was a booth in the backyard, tastefully adorned by skilled and devoted hands; and as, in some quarters, the back of one Jewish street faced the back of another, there were often a score of tabernacles in close proximity. Since there was no risk here of provoking a Gentile neighbour to scoff, the *Kiddush* (sanctification) could be intoned with full-throated melody, and as the occupants of one booth were near enough to hear the benediction offered up in others, it was usual for each householder to wait until his neighbour had finished before beginning himself. There was thus not only a succession of sanctifications, but each seemed to be rendered, in friendly rivalry, at a higher pitch and with more vocal flourishes than those that preceded it, until we listened, in hushed admiration, to the last *Kiddush*, which was chanted by a beautiful tenor, whose benediction vibrated in the air in notes of dulcet splendour that soared aloft to the starry heavens.

The joyousness of the festival reached its climax on the last day, when the completion of the reading of the Law in weekly sections was celebrated with effusive gusto. It was an occasion for merriment, which, in the bethels of the Chassidim[1], found actual expression in dancing. But in the synagogue of which my father was a member the rejoicing was limited to the drinking of wine and whisky and

[1] The Chassidim ("Pietists") are a sect founded in the 18th century in Podolia by Israel ben Eliezer, who emphasised the emotional element in Judaism and enjoined observance of the Psalmist's precept: "Serve the Lord with rejoicing."

the consumption of sponge-cake. These refreshments were not partaken of in the synagogue itself, but in the *Beth Hamidrash* (House of Study) in the basement, where morning service began soon after six and was over by eight, as the lay reader did not indulge in all the elaborate trills and quavers of the professional cantor. I can remember that at one of these celebrations, when I could not have been more than ten, I was sent at an early hour to the shop of a baker who was an important member of the congregation to get a large sponge-cake. The shop was, of course, closed, as it was a holy day, but I went to the private door, and the baker's wife, on receiving my message, promptly gave me a rich brown cake in its tin, which I found rather heavy to carry. As I was struggling along with it I was stopped by a bearded policeman, who wanted to know what I was doing so early with such a big cake and where I had got it from. It took some time before I made him understand the nature of my mission, and he followed me until I disappeared down the steps leading to the scene of rejoicing. It was the only day of the year when quite respectable members of the congregation imbibed rather freely. My father would join a small party of friends who, after the synagogue service, trooped to one another's house in turn for a dram and a bite, their progress being marked by an increasing spirit of conviviality. But by the time they arrived at our house my father would prudently decide to go no further. As soon as dinner was over he lay down to sleep, and a few hours later had quite recovered from his annual indulgence. But as he grew older he gave up this habit.

III

Outside the home the main formative factors in my life were the school, the synagogue, and the library. I was at the Jews' School[1] in Derby Street for eight years, from 1884 to 1892, a period that was marked by two historic events. The first was the Golden Jubilee of Queen Victoria, in 1887, which was celebrated by a simple treat (for which we had to bring our own cups) on the morning of the great day and the singing of the National Anthem, in which we had been diligently rehearsed for weeks beforehand. We sang all three

[1] This school was destroyed by an aerial attack in the Second World War.

verses under the baton of our music master, and imparted particular zest and stress to the lines:

> *Confound their politics,*
> *Frustrate their knavish tricks,*

the meaning of which none of us understood. The other important event, which occurred a couple of years later, was the beginning of free education, when we no longer had to bring a penny a week, which used to be collected and entered into a register by our teacher every Monday morning. The abolition of that school fee, trifling though it was, brought relief to many poor parents, who found it hard even to provide proper clothing for their children. It often happened that boys stayed away for a day or two while their boots were being mended, because they had no other pair; there were also many who had no boots at all and came to school barefooted, both in summer and winter. The school committee eventually realised the hardship under which these boys suffered, and, from the late eighties, provided them every year not only with clogs and woollen stockings but also with a dark-brown corduroy suit and a muffler.

School attendance was affected in the winter by both fog and snow. Fogs were frequent and pitch-black and would have made the journey to and from Derby Street impossible without some adequate form of light, especially for those coming across the field (or rather what was then waste land) from Strangeways. The glimmer of the gas-lamps could hardly be seen for any distance on ordinary nights; in the fog it was completely shrouded. We had therefore to carry small oil-lamps, whose kindled wick gave enough light through the thick magnifying glass, although many a disaster befell cheap lamps, which smoked and sometimes flared up. Snowfalls too were frequent and prolonged, tempting the tougher boys to indulge in snow-ball fights. But while such combats in the playground were harmless fun, there were also miniature battles with the boys of a neighbouring non-Jewish school, which sometimes involved danger even for onlookers. On one occasion a snowball containing a piece of brick struck me on the forehead with such force that I fell to the ground. But fortunately the swelling that it caused subsided in a day or two.

IV

Although we had an hour's lesson in Hebrew and religion every day, including Sundays, few parents were satisfied with what they regarded as a mere smattering of Jewish knowledge that we thus received. Consequently most of the boys also attended a private Hebrew school, which was called *Cheder* or "room," for it was actually limited to a single room in the house of the teacher (or *Melammed*). It was an old Jewish institution that had been transplanted from the Russian Pale and flourished in most of the Jewish communities in the British Isles. The fee usually ranged from eighteenpence to half-a-crown a week, which was gladly paid even by parents who had grumbled at having to give a penny a week for secular education; and a teacher who had two or three dozen pupils was generally content, as he was usually able to supplement his income by other means. Instruction was imparted in branches of Hebrew and religious lore that lay outside the syllabus of the day school, such as the mediæval commentaries on the Bible and the authoritative code-book of ritual laws (*Shulchan Aruch*). We attended *Cheder* for at least an hour a day almost on every day of the year, for no *Melammed* was ever known to take a holiday; and a boy did not leave as a rule until he reached his thirteenth birthday, when he became *Bar Mitzvah* ("Son of the Commandment") and assumed the responsibility that had hitherto lain on his father for the fulfilment of his religious obligations.

My father was rather exacting in his choice of a *Melammed*. He would examine me every Sabbath afternoon in the lessons that I had learned during the week, and if he was not pleased with my progress or had any other reason for not being satisfied with my tutor he would send me to another *Cheder*. I must have attended over half-a-dozen of these little academies, of which the one that has left the most lasting impression was kept by a grey-bearded, spectacled pedagogue, a respected but crotchety character called Reb David. He lived in a little house at the corner of a small secluded street, which formed a blind alley; but he dwelt only in a part of it, as he was not on speaking terms with his wife, who also lived under the same roof.

He occupied two adjoining rooms on the upper floor, one of which served as his bedroom and the other as a school, and from the windows of both he could call down to his pupils who were playing with a ball or marbles in the street below and let them know when the time for their class had come. The reason for his estrangement from his wife was a mystery, but fortunately the household ran smoothly with the aid of two daughters, who contributed to the domestic revenue by giving lessons — one to girls and young boys in Hebrew and religion, and the other to girls alone in music and embroidery. It was under the guidance of one of these accomplished daughters that I was initiated at the age of five into the intricacies of the Hebrew tongue.

I can still see the little schoolroom, which was reached by passing through Reb David's bedroom. It was furnished with two long tables, each flanked by a couple of benches, and placed on either side of the mantelpiece, which was surmounted by a large Hebrew document in a glass frame. This document, written on white cardboard by Reb David himself — for he was a skilful scribe — displayed the blessings that were said on being called up to the reading of the Law in the synagogue, in alternate lines with the names and signs of the accents used for its cantillation. The recess on one side of the fireplace was filled with shelves laden with well-thumbed Hebrew books, and on the other side was a wooden enclosure containing a supply of coal, from which the nearest boy had to replenish the fire in winter. On the walls the sole adornment was a large announcement in English and Yiddish setting forth our master's professional activities, which included not only the teaching of all branches of Hebrew knowledge, from reading the prayer-book to the study of the Talmud, but also writing scrolls of the Torah and providing Hebrew inscriptions for tombstones. There was, however, one other object on the wall — a stout, black leather strap, with a menacing set of tails, hanging within easy reach of Reb David, and designed to act primarily as a reminder and a deterrent to any potential offender, though he did not scruple to use it, and with force too, even on the bare flesh, whenever he thought that the transgression was gross enough to merit such chastisement. "It shall not be said that the pupils of Reb David turned out to be *Goyim* (heathens)!" was his favourite admonition.

He had an inveterate passion for snuff, of which he took a pinch almost every quarter of an hour, followed by a resounding sneeze. He kept his snuff-box and a cane in front of him, at the upper end of his book, together with a small pair of scissors for trimming the candle-wicks (as candles provided the only light in winter), while his large red handkerchief, dappled with white spots, lay at his right hand. Beneath his book he kept a register, which he had made out of fine white butter-paper in a binding of brown cardboard, and in it he entered the weekly fees brought by his pupils. He had two pairs of spectacles, which he used constantly to change, and he wore below his round velvet cap a shade secured round his head by a narrow elastic band. As he was often liable to throat trouble he swathed his neck with a piece of red flannel beneath his collar, and he took a certain physic in the form of drops trickled from a little brown bottle on to a small cube of sugar, to which we gave the name of "stinking drops" owing to the odour that was diffused. His right ear also caused him frequent annoyance, so that he frequently used a rubber syringe, and he put cotton-wool not only into the bad ear but also into the good one. His ears thus being stopped and his eyes shaded, little incentive was needed for the spirit of mischief to break out among his juvenile disciples, especially if the lesson was dull, whereupon there followed an angry and abusive rebuke.

Occasionally Reb David would arouse our interest by telling us some Talmudic stories or Midrashic[1] legend bearing upon a Scriptural character or episode, to which we would listen with rapt attention, innocent as yet of any scepticism or rationalist tendency; and if any boy ventured to put a question that seemed to throw doubt upon the credibility of the story, he would glare at him and bite his lips. "You *Epikouros* (heretic)!" he would say, "don't you believe in the Oral Law? Don't you know it's just as important as the Written Law?" It was thus that we acquired our first knowledge of Jewish demonology, angelology and eschatology, of the machinations of

[1]The Midrash consists of homiletical expositions of the Scriptures, dating from about the 3rd century onwards.

Satan, and of the ceaseless feud between the " Good Imagination," which guided us along the right path, and the " Evil Imagination," which tempted us to err.

Reb David tried for a time to supplement his earnings by acting as sub-agent for a local agent of a Hamburg lottery. He would buy an eighth of a ticket and sell shares in it to those of his pupils who could wheedle a few pence from their parents for the purpose. He would paint an alluring picture of the prospect that lay before us if he won, of the fabulous wealth that would accumulate for us in the bank if our share in the prize were deposited at compound interest and left there until we attained our majority. But unfortunately luck never favoured his number, so he started trade as a knife-grinder. While rambling through an open-air market he came across a grindstone, which took his fancy. He had it brought home and placed in the schoolroom, where it formed a nine days' wonder. He invited us all to bring our knives from home to be ground, and several of us did indeed bring them, in addition to our own pocket-knives, and as we had to turn the stone ourselves while he merely held the blade, his charge was naturally small. But after a time he grew tired of the toy and it disappeared. Then he decided to become a pedlar in the suburbs in his leisure hours — " travelling " he called it, and as he was a scribe he naturally chose pens, pencils, and nibs as the most fitting merchandise. He arranged his little stock in a flat, black box, which he carried by a leather handle, but his commercial enterprise met with no success. For every evening he poured out to us a doleful tale of his adventures, how doors were slammed in his face and Christian boys called after him " Shylock " and " Smog " (an anti-Semitic epithet peculiar to Lancashire), so that after a while he sold his wares to his pupils without a profit. He then devoted all his leisure to the profession of a scribe, for he wrote Hebrew square letters that were as regular as print and more picturesque. He penned congratulatory verses for marriage couples, memorial cards bearing the day of the anniversary of a parent's death, and artistic book-marks with a florid border enclosing a Scriptural verse that began and ended with the same letters respectively as the Hebrew name of the pupil for whom it was intended.

CHILDHOOD IN MANCHESTER

After I had attended several little Hebrew seminaries, my father sent me to the Talmud Torah school, of which he had been one of the founders. This institution was intended primarily for the free education of poor children, but my father and other members of the committee, having had some difficulty in obtaining sufficient voluntary contributions for its maintenance, decided to supplement its funds by sending their own children to it and paying for them. The headmaster of the school in Derby Street was for some years a hostile critic of the Talmud Torah, which he regarded as a reflection upon the adequacy of his own Hebrew curriculum, and this attitude continued until he was persuaded to preside at a public examination of the Talmud Torah boys in his own school. A novel feature of this event was the performance of a Hebrew play dealing with the Maccabæan revolt, in which I took the part of Mattathias; and he was so impressed by this display that he wrote a letter to the Executive of the Talmud Torah, saying that he was now fully convinced of its " *raison d'être*." It is doubtful whether any member of the Executive understood the meaning of the French phrase, but it was regarded as such a tribute that it was reproduced in their annual reports for years later.

V

My father was also among the first members of the New Synagogue, in Cheetham Hill Road, the building of which, from its foundations, I used to watch in 1889. After it was completed a succession of candidates for the post of *Chazan* (cantor) began to arrive from the Continent, and their trills and tremolos attracted packed and critical congregations, until at last one was found worthy of the coveted appointment. Then there followed another series of aspirants for the more honourable and exacting office of Rabbi, all coming straight from the Russian Pale, with grey beards and long fur-lined gaberdines; and as, week after week, one of them entered the synagogue, the whole congregation promptly rose and remained standing in silent veneration until he took his seat. The trial *Derasha* or Talmudical discourse — for " sermon " would be a misnomer — was delivered (in Yiddish, of course) on a Sabbath afternoon, and seldom lasted less than an hour-and-a-half, so that only those who managed to keep awake all the time were competent to pass judgment upon its merits. The *Beth Hamidrash* (House of Study) in the basement was always a scene of studious activity, and there was no more edifying spectacle than the band of middle-aged and elderly students — business-men, shopkeepers, tailors, and other artisans — who, after the toil of the day, sat every evening at a long table, poring over a ponderous tome of the Talmud, while the venerable, skull-capped Rabbi at the top, whose own folio was illumined by two extra candles in tall brass candlesticks, expounded the intricate dialectical argument with the downward scoop of his right thumb and a spiritual glow on his face.

Next door to the Synagogue is a Public Library, of which I became a frequent visitor as soon as I thought I looked old enough, for there was a uniformed and red-bearded porter, familiarly called by the boys of the neighbourhood " Puggy Whiskers," who ordered out anybody who seemed to be under thirteen. I was an omnivorous reader of papers and periodicals of all kinds, which were then more numerous than they are today, and even Manchester was represented not only by the Liberal *Guardian* but also by the Conservative *Courier* and *Examiner*. It was there that I first became acquainted with *The Times* and other distinguished pillars of the British Press. I also dipped into such specialist journals as the *Scientific American* and *The Zoophilist*, and after I had my fill of the current press I would pore over reference works like *Whittaker's Almanack, Hazell's Annual,* and Haydn's *Dictionary of Dates*, from which I copied curious items of information into a pocket note-book. The proximity of the Library to the Synagogue had a certain advantage, for on the Day of Atonement and on other holy days dozens of worshippers would escape from the tedium of the reiterated confession of uncommitted transgressions to study the latest developments in the world's affairs.

VI

The school-leaving age in my boyhood was thirteen, and as my father could not afford to send me to a secondary school, I began to feel a little anxious about my future as my thirteenth birthday was approaching. The only two alternatives that seemed to present themselves were either to become a pupil-teacher or to go into some kind of business. But a few weeks before the crucial date I won a scholarship at the Jews' School which entitled me to three years' education at the Grammar School, and the problem of my future was thus deferred. The Grammar School was then situated in that dingy thoroughfare, Long Millgate, and as I first walked down Cheetham Hill Road wearing the school-cap adorned with the little metal owl, I fancied that all eyes were upon me. I felt transported into a new world, for only a tiny proportion of the boys at the school were Jews. We were assembled during the first quarter-of-an-hour every morning, while school prayers were being held in the Drawing Hall, in the room of Mr. Broadhurst, the principal Classical master, who kept a register of our attendances. I usually occupied the desk of W. P. Crozier, who afterwards became Editor of the *Manchester Guardian*. Among those who used to meet in that room in my time were Leon (later Sir Leon) Simon, who rose to the position of Director of Savings of the General Post Office, Isaac L. Kandel (now Professor Kandel), the authority on education, and Edward Isaacs, the brilliant pianist and composer[1].

Beginning from the bottom form on the Modern Side, I reached the Sixth in two-and-a-half years and picked up a prize in every form through which I passed. Two of my form-mates were James Agate[2] and T. C. Dugdale[3]. Agate was assertive and didactic and was made a prefect: he already gave evidence of the ready repartee and irrepressible critical faculty that afterwards made him famous. Dugdale showed outstanding ability at drawing. On one occasion, when we were doing " tests " together in the chemical laboratory, for which neither of us had any liking, we discussed our respective future. " I suppose that some day you'll be a B.A.," he remarked to me, whereupon I laughingly replied: " And some day I suppose you'll be an R.A." A few decades later, when he was elected a Royal Academician I wrote him a letter of congratulation and reminded him of that conversation, and I was glad that in his reply he said that he also recalled the incident.

Among some prizes for special subjects that I gained was one for

[1]Died July, 1953.   [2]Died 1947.   [3]Died 1952.

Hebrew, which had not been awarded for many years, as nobody had entered for it. I won it two years in succession, and on both occasions I was the only candidate. In the examination in one year I was required to translate Psalm xix from English back into Hebrew. As this Psalm was in the Jewish prayer-book and I knew it by heart, I had no difficulty in presenting a word-perfect version, complete with vowels. The examiner, a Classics master who was a clergyman, was so astonished that he asked me to explain how I gave such a correct rendering. He could not possibly have suspected me of " cribbing," as he acted as invigilator himself, and if he had any faint doubts they were dispelled when I recited the Psalm to him in Hebrew by heart until he told me to stop.

After my Jews' School scholarship expired I was awarded one by the Grammar School, tenable for a year, so that I had a little more time in which to decide about my future. I wished to remain at the Grammar School until I could get a scholarship for Oxford, as I thought of eventually becoming a master at a secondary school. But my father was strongly opposed to this. He wished me to go to Jews' College, in London, with a view to becoming a minister. He maintained that such a position would be better both socially and materially and would also command more respect. Another argument that he advanced was that as education at Jews' College was free, the only expense involved would be the cost of my keep, which he was prepared to bear until I could support myself by scholarships or giving private lessons. I was under the transient influence of Draper's *History of the Conflict between Religion and Science*, which I had just read, and parried his arguments with the objection that I felt no " call " for the ministerial profession, whereupon he resorted to entreaties, in which my mother joined. Eventually I yielded on the understanding that after I had finished my years of study at Jews' College I should be free to do as I wished. I thereupon wrote to the secretary of the College for particulars regarding admission, and on learning that it was desirable to have a knowledge of Latin (which was not taught on the Modern Side) I spoke to my master, Mr. Horsley, who kindly undertook to coach me in the subject for a few months before I left for London. I

CHILDHOOD IN MANCHESTER

therefore used the summer holiday in 1895 to do the first thirty exercises in Abbott's *Via Latina*, and when I presented my exercise book to him for correction, he drily remarked: "That's a nice way to spend a holiday." The fact is that until I was twenty-one I never had a holiday longer than a day's excursion to Blackpool or a week-end in the Isle of Man.

The three-and-a-half years that I spent at the Manchester Grammar School were, on the whole, a happy and fruitful period, in which I not only laid the foundations of my subsequent studies but acquired methodical habits of work. The bounds of scholastic life were somewhat broadened when I was given a humble part in the school performance of a selection from *King Henry IV*, at a rehearsal of which we had the honour of a visit from the Shakespearean actor, Sir Frank R. Benson, who happened to be in Manchester with his touring company and coached us through some difficult passages. I also had a fleeting contact with a more distinguished personality, when we discovered that the shabbily clad stranger, with dome-like forehead and reddish-brown beard, who acted as invigilator at a special examination, was the eminent philosopher, Professor Samuel Alexander.

VII

During the latter part of my Grammar School days I was a frequent visitor to the Reference Library, which was then situated in King Street. I usually went there on Sunday evenings, and as in those days we had no cinemas or radio, and in any case I had little money for entertainment, I also spent a good part of my holidays in that gloomy building. I pored over Burke's *Reflections* and devoured Macaulay's *Essays*, which fascinated me; I read through Stuart Mill's *Liberty* and dipped into Adam Smith's *Wealth of Nations*.

In the evenings I generally met there a youth with whom I had become very friendly at the Jews' School. His name was Henry Ospovat, and he had come to England as a young boy with his family from Dvinsk, in Russia. The drawing-master was struck by the speed and excellence with which he completed every piece of freehand drawing, whether a simple vase or a combination of objects.

One day he noticed some sketches sticking out of Ospovat's jacket pocket, and on examining them was astonished at the artistic skill that they displayed. One of them was a scene on the ship that brought the Ospovat family from Hamburg — a group of emigrants huddled together on the deck. When these drawings were brought to the headmaster he realised at once that here was a case of artistic gifts that deserved expert fostering. The school committee therefore helped to send Ospovat to the Municipal School of Art and also to apprentice him to a lithographer in a place off Market Street. At the School of Art he attracted the notice of Walter Crane, the visiting Master of Design, who formed such a high opinion of his ability that he gave him a letter of introduction to G. F. Watts, and a friend provided the return fare to London. I still remember the feeling of awe with which Ospovat described to me his interview with the great painter, who spoke approvingly and encouragingly of the work that he was shown. At the Reference Library he used to study text-books on anatomy and copy out in a sketch-book parts of the human figure, with the names of every bone and joint jutting out like tentacles. At about the same time as I was arranging to go to Jews' College he won a scholarship at the South Kensington School of Art, and as we plodded our way home after the Library was closed we used to discuss our plans and prospects in London.

I began to take an interest in Jewish affairs and political matters as early as 1891. I remember the year because it was then that *The Jewish Chronicle* (which was delivered in our house every Friday) appeared with a thick black border on the front page of the cover, which bore the heading "In Darkest Russia." It contained a detailed account of the pogroms that had again broken out in the Tsar's dominions and was the harbinger of a fresh influx of woebegone refugees (commonly called "greeners"), who began to pour into London and thence to Manchester and other cities. It was the hopeless plight of the Jews in Russia that had given birth in that country ten years earlier to the "Chovevei Zion" (Lovers of Zion) movement for the return to Palestine. There were branches in several countries, including England, and there was a constituent society in Manchester called "Dorshei Zion" (Seekers of Zion), whose meeting-place was

CHILDHOOD IN MANCHESTER

at the corner of Cheetham Hill Road and Carnarvon Street. The premises, two ground-floor rooms knocked into one, served the dual function of a rendezvous for Zionist enthusiasts and a place of worship, and the whitewashed front window was adorned with a sort of cornucopia bearing the fruits and flowers of the Holy Land. The moving spirit was a Hebrew poet and printer, Joseph Massel[1], bearded and bespectacled, who had translated poems of Milton, Longfellow, and Omar Khayyam into Hebrew. He was an intimate friend of my father and sought to stimulate my interest in modern Hebrew by presenting me with his poetical works, which he printed and published himself, and occasionally discussing with me his renderings of difficult phrases.

In order to arouse wider support the "Dorshei Zion" brought the "Commander" (as he was called) of the English "Chovevei Zion," Colonel Albert Edward Goldsmid (father of the Dowager Lady Swaythling), from London, to address a public meeting at the Jewish Working Men's Club in Exchange Street. He was a professional soldier, spruce and upright, and proud of his Jewish ancestry, although brought up in India as a Christian and ignorant of his birth until he reached manhood, when he was initiated with the traditional rite into the Jewish faith. He was distinguished among his Anglo-Jewish contemporaries by reason of his fervid enthusiasm and active propaganda for Jewish resettlement in Palestine, to which he devoted himself despite his military duties. But the audience in the gas-lit hall was scanty, the response was sceptical and feeble, and perhaps the principal outcome of the meeting was the suggestion that it gave to Israel Zangwill for the opening scene of his graphic sketch, "The Palestine Pilgrim," to be found in his *Dreamers of the Ghetto*.

Far different was the spectacle at a public demonstration in the Free Trade Hall addressed by John Morley, to which I was taken by my eldest brother. I have long forgotten the subject of his speech but remember being crushed in the dense crowd and craning my neck to see on the distant platform the impassive figure of the Liberal statesman. Having been born and bred in the city over

[1] Died in 1912.

which hovered the memories of Cobden and Bright, and nurtured from childhood on the *Manchester Guardian*, it was natural that I should be a Liberal, nor did I swerve — except for a day, after reading Blatchford's *Merrie England* when it first appeared. I met the editor of the *Manchester Courier*, Nicol Dunn, long before I met the more famous editor of the *Manchester Guardian*, for when Dunn was appointed to assume control of the *Morning Post* a cousin of mine took me with him to congratulate him and chaffingly warned him to be careful, as the *Post* was believed to be the favourite paper of Queen Victoria. I became familiar with political questions through attending the debates at the County Forum (in Market Street), and was an assiduous — though puzzled — student of the pamphlets on Bimetallism which I got from the local office of the Bimetallic League.

VIII

After an exchange of several letters with the secretary of Jews' College I was invited, early in December, 1895, to come to London to present myself to the Council. My father travelled with me to Euston, from where we went straight to the College, which was then situated at Tavistock House, Tavistock Square, long since demolished. The caretaker told us that the meeting of the Council would not begin for another two hours and suggested that we should meanwhile get something to eat. The nearest tea-shop was one of Lockhart's in Euston Road, which had not yet been supplanted in public favour by other more attractive establishments. Soon after we returned to the College I was ushered by the secretary into a gas-lit chamber, where a group of men, mostly bearded and partly bald, were assembled round a table. The secretary led me to the skull-capped, grey-bearded figure in the chair, who was the Chief Rabbi, Dr. Hermann Adler. The latter asked me a few personal questions, which had already been answered in my letters. He then handed me a book, from which I had to read a paragraph aloud. In it occurred the word " qualms," which he asked me to explain, and he was satisfied with my answer. That concluded my entrance examination. The secretary conducted me out to rejoin my father

CHILDHOOD IN MANCHESTER

in another room and asked us to wait a few minutes. Presently he returned to announce that I had been admitted, and told me to make immediate arrangements for living in London so that I could enter the College without delay.

Before leaving home my father had inquired of a friend of his, the Rev. Isidore Simon (father of Sir Leon Simon), who was minister of the South Manchester Synagogue, for the address of somebody in London who might be able to provide me with lodgings. Mr. Simon gave him the address of his father-in-law, popularly known as Reb Mottel Levine, in Great Alie Street, Whitechapel. We therefore took the train from King's Cross to Aldgate, and within half-an-hour were welcomed by the grey-bearded gentleman and his gracious spouse in the basement sitting-room of their old-fashioned house. Fortunately they had an attic which was free, and agreement was soon reached that I should occupy it and receive full board for three pounds a month. The following morning we took the first train back to Manchester, and I began to make preparations for returning to London.

Chapter Two

STUDENT YEARS
1895 — 1904

I

WHEN I began to lodge in Whitechapel in the middle of December, 1895, the district was inhabited by masses of Jews, who formed a very conspicuous and distinctive element of the local population. The great majority were immigrants from Russia and other parts of Eastern Europe, which they had abandoned because of the political oppression and economic distress which they had suffered so long. The ceaseless influx was increased periodically by the pogroms in the Tsar's dominions and was intensified by the Russo-Japanese War, from which able-bodied Jews, who felt that they owed no loyalty to a despot, sought to escape. For the first few months these victims of persecution continued to wear the long gaberdine, top-boots, and peaked hat of their native land, but as they became acclimatised they adopted Western dress. Intellectual and spiritual assimilation, however, was very much slower. They clung to their Yiddish speech, their religious customs, and their social habits for years. They felt at home in a quarter where the streets were lined with shops and restaurants bearing Jewish names and Hebrew signs, where the walls were covered with Yiddish posters announcing a Talmudical discourse by a Rabbi or the performance of a Jewish play. They were heartened when they saw newsboys rushing through the motley crowd, crying the names of Yiddish papers; or a stringed band at a street-corner playing a haunting Hebrew melody; or a pedlar offering for sale Hebrew prayer-books or the little four-cornered fringed garments prescribed in Deuteronomy. And if there was an unctuous missionary here and there who quoted the New Testament in Yiddish and sought to lure his hearers to apostasy, there were bastions of Judaism in synagogues and houses of Talmudic study, in little seminaries resounding with boyish voices chanting the Torah, and religious courts of judgment, which were impregnable against any attacks of mercenary conversionists. There were also libraries and clubs, asylums for friendless immigrants and for the poor and the aged. Moreover, the civil interests of the people of the district were watched over by a Jewish Member of Parliament, Sir Samuel Montagu (later the first Lord Swaythling), who gave convincing proof of his religious orthodoxy by being President of the Federation of Synagogues, and whose long patriarchal beard was of itself sufficient to inspire confidence.

The house in which I lodged formed an excellent vantage-ground from which to study various aspects of Jewish life and to become acquainted not only with local conditions but also with those abroad, for old Mottel Levine had visitors of all kinds. He was a venerable-looking figure, with white beard and upright bearing, whose appearance evoked deference. East End Rabbis, communal officials, refugees from Russia, scholars from Germany, cantors from Poland, and emissaries from Palestine, all found their way into his humble home and were given a warm, brotherly welcome. As he and his wife usually lived in the basement and wished to be spared the trouble of going upstairs to open the street-door, they had a cord attached to its lock and suspended through a hole in the ceiling, so that visitors had to stamp on the grid protecting the window from the pavement, and then the bottom end of the cord was pulled to open the door. Friends from the neighbourhood dropped in to exchange gossip, and there was seldom a discussion about religious conditions without a denunciation of Anglo-Jewish ministers, who were called " Reverendim," for their lack of orthodoxy shown in shaving their beards or carrying an umbrella on the Sabbath. There was hardly a Sabbath eve when Reb Mottel did not bring a guest home from the synagogue, a recently arrived immigrant in need of a meal, who would regale us with stories of his experiences and adventures since he had left his family in Russia or Rumania. Sabbath morning brought one or two pious callers (on their way to prayers) for a glass of tea, for they knew that Reb Mottel had a samovar (brought from Russia) in which water was kept on the boil over a small gas-ring from before the Sabbath, so that the teapot could be refilled whenever necessary without violating the sanctity of the day.

More interesting than these, however, were Hebrew authors who came in quest of a subscriber to their still unpublished book (recommended by a laudatory foreword by a well-known Rabbi), or others who stayed for a few months to work. One of the latter was Isaac Halevy, a notable Talmudical scholar, who was engaged on his monumental work, *Dorot Harishonim* (" Generations of the Early Ones "), in which he scarified the writings of Graetz and other eminent historians, and who, while being held in high esteem by his host, caused him serious concern by keeping the gas-jet burning until the small hours. Most interesting of all, however, were the visitors from the Holy Land. The most important was Israel Frumkin, the editor of a Jerusalem paper, *Havazzelet*, who had been imprisoned for six weeks by order from Constantinople directed to the Pasha of Jerusalem because of an editorial criticising General Lew Wallace, the American Minister to Turkey, and who came to London in search of new subscribers. Others who came for financial reasons were the messengers of Zion known as *Meshullochim*, whose business was periodically to collect the money[1] that had accumulated in little tin boxes in synagogues for the benefit of Jews in Palestine. Most of these emissaries kept records in Hebrew of their journeys and experiences, for they stopped in many cities between Jerusalem and London, and they let me read select passages here and there. After they had completed their mission in England they went on to America, and when they returned to London they again stayed with the Levines or at least called to see them. For the most part they were scholars, who comported themselves sedately and with some dignity. But in an old diary of mine, under the date January 16th, 1898, there occurs the following entry:

[1] The organisation responsible for collecting this money was called *Halukah*, which means " distribution," and it had a history going back to the seventeenth century.

Four bearded Jews were assembled, auditing the books of a society for the support of Jerusalem charities. One was the representative of an old society, who refused to comply with the demands of the others. A fierce dispute arose, in which they almost came to blows. The expressions and expletives used were below respectability.

The heat and fury then displayed were probably generated by fear of the young Zionist movement, in which the messengers of Zion rightly thought they heard an echo of the death-knell of their philanthropic régime.

My bedroom was an attic reached by a crooked staircase, and facing the street with its roar of traffic. It was very simply and sparsely furnished, the only concession to comfort being a wicker arm-chair in a corner. Besides my bed there was also a low, ramshackle bedstead against a wall, which I thought was put there because there was no other place for it, until I was told one evening that it was going to be occupied by a male relative from the country for the night. Such companionship was thrust upon me from time to time, and it was useless complaining as, in the circumstances, I had no alternative. There was, however, a more serious grievance to which I called attention — the fact that the fireplace was completely boarded across, so that it was impossible to make a fire, whereupon I was told that it was intended to keep out the cold and that, in any case, there was nobody available to attend to fires. The consequence was that during the bitter winter months I often kept the gas-jet burning at full pressure by day as well as by night, and that I sometimes had to wear my overcoat and (when not writing) even my woollen gloves. Before long, however, I found my way in the evening to the Students' Library at Toynbee Hall, where I was able to work in warmth and quiet, and there I was a frequent visitor as long as I lived in the East End.

II

Tavistock House, in which Jews' College was situated during the latter part of the nineteenth century (and which was pulled down early this century), was a large four-storied mansion, including an enormous basement, with a carriage-drive in front and a garden at the back. It enjoyed the fame of having once been the home of Charles Dickens, but I never found out in which room he worked. Besides lecture-rooms and a library, it contained living-rooms for the Principal, Dr. Michael Friedlaender, and the caretaker. Dr. Friedlaender, a native of Prussia, was a small, frail, white-bearded man, mild of manner and speech, and possessed of a vast amount of varied learning, ranging from the Talmud and Biblical commentaries to higher mathematics and astronomy. He seemed to have a particular fondness for geometrical progressions, and was in his element when chalking rows of figures and festoons of formulæ on a blackboard too high for him to reach without standing on his toes. His principal assistant for Jewish subjects was Dr. Samuel A. Hirsch, who came from Amsterdam. He was a portly, grey-bearded man, who always panted and puffed so much after climbing the stairs and reaching his room, that he was familiarly known as " Puffer." He taught the *Shulchan Aruch* and Jewish history, literature, and philosophy, and often surprised us by his apt quotations from Shakespeare. Our other Jewish lecturer was Israel Abrahams, burly and brown-bearded, who, apart from teaching homiletics, was mainly engaged in coaching the Preparatory Class for the London Matriculation Examination. He shared this work with a Christian colleague, George Washington Kilner, who was also a tutor in English and Classics at a Christian theological college. There were also teachers for French, elocution, and music.

After students of Jews' College had passed their Matric., their fees were paid for them to attend University College, to work for the Intermediate Arts and B.A. examinations, but they had at the same time to continue their studies at Jews' College. In the summer of 1896 I passed my Matric. and also won the Andrews Entrance Scholarship (in Modern Languages and Science) at University College, so that I had to take more lectures at the latter than my fellow-students of Jews' College. The simultaneous attendance at the two institutions entailed a physical as well as a mental strain, as I often had to hurry from one to the other at lunch-time and had to eat my sandwiches on the way. I must have done a great deal of walking in those days, as I often went on foot from Aldgate to Bloomsbury

STUDENT YEARS

and back so as to save a few pence; and I eked out my small pocket-allowance by giving some private lessons at eighteen pence an hour.

At University College some of my professors were men of distinction, and some are still famous. For Latin I had A. E. Housman, whose poetical work, *The Shropshire Lad*, had already won him a high and wide reputation. He looked anything but a poet as he strode into the College grounds in silk hat, morning-coat and high collar, although there was an air of shyness and even aloofness about him as he stood in front of his class, for he seldom faced his students but generally presented to us a sharp profile with a slight moustache. His colleague in the Greek chair, J. A. Platt, was a contrast in manner and temperament, for he always spoke to us directly and seemed light-hearted even about the most tortuous text or the most irregular verbs. More solemn than either was the great English scholar, Professor W. P. Ker, who also usually wore a silk hat, morning-coat and stiff collar. He generally arrived with a little pile of books under his left arm and walked with a slow, sedate step, and after he entered the room he went through a regular ceremonial as he deposited on the elevated table first his books and next his hat, and then lifted himself with a jerk on to the dais. He was clean-shaven, with a reddish complexion mottled with blue, and had the thin tight lips and sharp pointed nose of a medieval monk. Of all my Professors he was the slowest in speech, often repeating the same idea in different terms, so that it was easy to take full notes. He had a pronounced Scottish accent and broadened the vowel sound " a " in such words as " aspect " (a favourite of his), even lingering on it, so that it sounded like " ahs-pect." He had an immense range of learning and usually quoted from memory, but on one occasion he made a slight slip. In a reference to Gray's *Elegy* he quoted as one of the lines:

> The boding owl does to the moon complain.

As I knew the *Elegy* by heart from my Grammar School days I went up to Professor Ker after the lecture was over and pointed out that what Gray had written was " the moping owl." He immediately looked it up and " begged " my " pardon." At the beginning of the next lecture he generously made acknowledgment to me for having called attention to the error and told us that he had found

A JEWISH PILGRIMAGE

"the boding owl" in Book I of Cowper's *Task*. Although normally of dour visage he occasionally displayed a sense of humour, as when, after lecturing on Chaucer's *Canterbury Tales* and quoting at the end from the concluding lines:

And fareth now weel, my tale is at ende,

he faced us with a grim smile and slowly repeated the words:

And fareth now weel.

III

During my stay in the East End I had some memorable experiences. By far the most important was my view of Queen Victoria's Diamond Jubilee procession in June, 1897, which I saw at very close range at the corner of Lombard Street and the Mansion House. I stood there from half-past seven in the morning until half-past one, wedged in by a dense crowd, but thrilled as I watched the long picturesque pageant of pomp and Empire unroll before me, with the mistress of it all, a little majestic lady, borne along in her magnificent carriage, with its slow-stepping chargers and handsome outriders.

But to me personally the most significant experience was my presence at the first public meeting addressed in London by Theodor Herzl. The founder of political Zionism had already propounded his ideas several months earlier to a private gathering of Jewish intellectuals at the Maccabæan Club, of whom the most distinguished, Israel Zangwill, novelist and playwright, had acted as the chairman; but the cool and critical reaction with which he met determined him to appeal to the public at large. He therefore published his epoch-making pamphlet, *The Jewish State*, in February, 1896, and five months later, on July 12th, he appeared before a crowded gathering at the Jewish Working Men's Club in Great Alie Street. As I lived only a few dozen yards away I was able to get there early and secure a good seat.

It was a warm Sunday afternoon, and long before the hour fixed for the meeting the hall, which could hold only a few hundred people, was packed to suffocation and thousands were unable to gain admittance. The great majority of the audience were refugees from

Russia, who had not been in England many years and who still had vivid memories of the Tsarist persecution from which they had fled. They were all keyed up to a high pitch of expectancy, longing to see the man who, they believed, would lead them back to the land of their forefathers, and their hopes were fired by the story (which was unfounded) that Herzl had already spoken to the Sultan of Turkey. There was therefore a storm of prolonged applause when they had their first glimpse of the imposing and majestic figure as he stepped on to the platform and bowed his acknowledgments. An attempt had been made to induce Sir Samuel Montagu (uncle of Herbert [later Viscount] Samuel) to take the chair, but he was unwilling to risk his reputation as an esteemed City banker in connection with a political movement whose future then appeared rather dubious. The chair was therefore taken by Dr. Moses Gaster, Haham (Chief Rabbi) of the Sephardi community, who had been active in previous years among the Chovevei Zion ("Lovers of Zion") in Rumania. It was doubtful whether many were able to understand the elegant German in which Herzl spoke, but all were under the spell of his resonant voice and commanding presence. There were other speakers on the platform, but they did not form a harmonious chorus, for while Dr. Gaster gave his eloquent support some sought to damp the enthusiasm by pleas for caution. The loudest applause was aroused by a local Hebrew teacher, Ephraim Ish-Kishor, whose Yiddish speech, delivered with passionate fervour, swept the audience off their feet and evoked flattering compliments from Herzl himself. In the street outside the crowd patiently waited for a view of the man who was ushering in a new epoch in Jewish history, and cheers upon cheers followed him until he was out of sight.

The Zionist movement, which was officially established at the First Zionist Congress in Basle, at the end of August, 1897, deeply agitated the Anglo-Jewish community as it did all other Jewish communities. The Basle Programme, to create for the Jewish people a home in Palestine secured by public law, met with a twofold opposition — from those who advocated the Anglicisation of the immigrant Jews and from some of the leaders of the Chovevei Zion. The heads of all important organisations and institutions lost no opportunity of voicing their antagonism, and this was reinforced by the writings and speeches of the theologian Claude Montefiore, the journalist Lucien Wolf, and the scholar Israel Abrahams. One Sabbath morning, when I was at the Great Synagogue in Duke's Place (which was destroyed by an enemy raid during the Second World War), I heard the Chief Rabbi (Dr. Hermann Adler) deliver a sermon in which he stigmatised Zionism as " an egregious blunder." Few ministers under his authority had the courage to express a different view.

The Zionist problem was threshed out with heat and vigour at the King's Hall in Commercial Road, where there were crowded meetings every Saturday night, which I attended regularly. It was the only forum for Zionist discussion in London for many years, and thither came enthusiasts from all parts of the metropolis, although the majority were from the East End. Even Dr. Friedlaender attended a meeting there once when his son-in-law, Dr. Gaster, was the principal speaker. The strangest figure that ever appeared there was a monk, Father Ignatius, who thrilled his listeners with an inflammatory address on " The Reawakening of Judah." His monastic habit, theatrical manner, and zealous sincerity secured him a large and admiring audience wherever he spoke, or rather declaimed, and he was loudly cheered even by recent immigrants who did not understand a single word. His popularity brought him invitations to speak in various districts, and in the provinces too, until either a sense of the incongruous or the waning of the novelty led to his eclipse.

At one of these meetings in the King's Hall on January 2nd, 1898, the first Hebrew-speaking society in London was founded under the name of " *Hevrath Sfath Zion* " (Society of the Language of Zion). It was hailed as an immediate realisation of one of the ideals of Zionism. The inaugural address was given by Isaac Suvalski, a timid, bearded savant, who had already founded a Hebrew weekly, *Hayehudi*, for which he used to canvass subscribers by occasional trips to the provinces. He spoke in Hebrew, as did also those who followed him, but while their remarks met with general approval, there were mutterings here and there against their violating the holy tongue by speaking it bareheaded. These objections, however, were calmly ignored. At a lull in the discussion, when people looked round for the next speaker, I suddenly rose to make my maiden speech in the sacred tongue and suggested that a Hebrew library should be formed. My few remarks, coming trippingly from an English-born Jew, created a mild sensation, and in the following number of *Hayehudi* I read the editor's friendly comment: "Even in this wilderness there are grapes."

Among the lecturers at Jews' College there was no Zionist of the Herzlian school. Dr. Friedlaender was non-committal; Dr. Hirsch, as editor of the official organ of the Chovevei Zion, *Palestina*, adopted a critical pose; and Israel Abrahams was a declared antagonist. In one of his lectures on homiletics, "I.A.," as he was always called, spoke on the relation of the Messianic idea to Zionism. He said that one of the principal reasons why he was opposed to Herzl's project was because he was afraid that after the establishment of a Jewish State the position of the Jews remaining in Europe would be endangered. Some twenty-five years later I happened to meet him near the British Museum, when he again touched on the same theme. He was afraid that recognition of a Jewish State would affect the political status of the Jews in other countries, whereupon I called his attention to the special proviso in the Balfour Declaration which disposed of that objection.[1]

We enjoyed freedom of opinion at the College on the question of Zionism, and it was perhaps but natural that the students were divided in their views, some being supporters and others opponents, while a third category could not make up their minds (or perhaps had no minds to make up). It was at the College that I made my first speech on Zionism. The occasion was a public lecture on February 19th, 1898, by the Rev. A. A. Green on "Zionism in Modern Judaism," in which he expressed himself in favour of the re-nationalisation of Jewry. He was one of the rather small band of ministers who showed any sympathy with the movement in those

[1] The latter part of the clause:
"It being clearly understood that nothing shall be done which may prejudice the civil and religious rights of existing non-Jewish communities in Palestine, or the rights and political status enjoyed by Jews in any other country."

A JEWISH PILGRIMAGE

days. But a few years later, amid general wonderment, he turned his back upon the cause as he thought it would lead to the creation of a new Ghetto.

The discussions and negotiations between the Chovevei Zion and the followers of Herzl culminated in a Conference, which took place at the Clerkenwell Town Hall on Sunday, March 6th, 1898. I attended as a delegate of the Young Zionist Institute, an East End society which I had joined from its formation. There were about 150 delegates present from all parts of the country and also some distinguished visitors, including David Wolffsohn, of Cologne (Herzl's successor in the leadership of the movement) and Israel Zangwill. The three sessions were presided over by Colonel Albert Goldsmid, Joseph Prag, and Herbert Bentwich, the heads of the Chovevei Zion Association, who had convened the Conference, and there was a series of addresses, discussions, and resolutions. The main purpose of the majority of the delegates was to secure the creation of a body in England that should be affiliated to the Organisation founded at Basle, but such was the hostility to this object that it was not achieved until January 22nd, 1899. A gathering then took place at the Trocadero Restaurant, with Sir Francis Montefiore in the chair, to inaugurate the establishment of the English Zionist Federation, and a month later the first meeting of the Central Committee was held in the same place. The accession of the bearer of such a distinguished name as Montefiore gave considerable prestige to Zionism in England, and Sir Francis graced every public function by appearing in immaculate evening dress with white tie and white kid gloves.

Even after the creation of the Zionist Federation the Chovevei Zion still struggled on, although in the face of increasing opposition. In order to rekindle enthusiasm for the dwindling " Lovers of Zion " a public meeting, at which I was present, was held at the Jewish Working Men's Club on a Sunday evening in the summer of 1899, when Colonel Goldsmid presided and Major-General Sir Charles Wilson gave an address on Palestine. It was a crowded gathering, in which the number of Zionists far exceeded that of the " Lovers," but the strife was so acute that, after occasional interruptions, the

STUDENT YEARS

proceedings became very stormy. The Rev. S. Singer, whose English translation of the Prayer-Book has given solace to millions, was howled down, and one zealous Zionist was physically attacked.

But with each successive visit of Herzl to London his following increased and the Chovevei Zion slowly disintegrated. I remember in particular being present on three occasions when he spoke. The first was at the Great Assembly Hall, in Mile End, in the autumn of 1898, when there was a vast crowd both within and outside; the second was at St. Martin's Town Hall, in the summer of 1899, when Herzl read his speech in English; and the third was at a reception at the Hotel Great Central in April, 1900.

At the last of these gatherings Herzl was delayed, and as the people were becoming impatient an interesting visitor in clerical attire from South Africa was asked to step into the breach. He was the Rev. Dr. Joseph Hertz, of Johannesburg, who had been expelled from the Transvaal by President Kruger owing to his pro-British attitude (and who later succeeded Dr. Adler as Chief Rabbi of British Jewry). He gave us an account of the political struggle in the Boer Republic in a trenchant and combative speech, whereupon Leopold J. Greenberg (who later became Editor of *The Jewish Chronicle*) remarked to me: "No wonder they turned him out." When Herzl at length arrived, he gracefully apologised for his delay, which was due to the lateness of his train. At this reception I was introduced to Herzl by Jacob de Haas, who acted as his English lieutenant and addressed meetings all over the country in furtherance of the movement. De Haas was then assistant-editor of the *Jewish World*, which strongly supported the cause, as distinguished from the more influential *Jewish Chronicle*, which, under the editorship of Asher I. Myers, voiced the opposition of the communal leaders.

It was at Herzl's suggestion that De Haas decided to go to the United States in 1902 in order to help in the advancement of the movement in that country. He had brought out the first issue of a new monthly paper, entitled *Zionist Correspondence*, and the Zionist Federation was anxious to find an editor to succeed him. So one day I received a letter inviting me to attend a meeting of the Executive, in its humble office in Commercial Street, to discuss the matter.

I was offered what was considered the handsome honorarium of one pound per number, plus an indefinite bonus on sales. But as I was then working for a University examination, I had to decline the offer with thanks, and I am sorry to add that the paper died soon after.

IV

Towards the end of 1897 I reviewed my position and decided to begin trying my hand at writing. I had already contributed a short article to the *Manchester Evening Chronicle* in September, 1897, on " The Jewish New Year," for which I received seven and sixpence. Influenced to some extent by Zangwill's *Children of the Ghetto* and having become personally familiar with Jewish life and personalities in the East End, I felt an urge to commit my impressions and experiences to literary form. I had no intention of giving up my College studies, but thought that, as I finished my " prep." by about ten o'clock or thereabouts, I could, after a cup of coffee and cake in the Levines' basement, return aloft and sit down to write for an hour or two. The result was that in January, 1898, I wrote a sketch of a Ghetto character, " The Melammed " (Hebrew teacher), which I sent to the *Jewish World*. As students of Jews' College were expected not to engage in any work outside their studies, except a little teaching, I thought it necessary to adopt a pseudonym and chose the name of " Enoch Scribe," Enoch being an anagram of my surname. Within a few days I received a letter of acceptance from the editor, Mr. S. L. Bensusan, offering me a fee of one guinea. I replied immediately, agreeing to this honorarium. A week later came a proof. It was the first proof that I had ever received, and as, in the privacy of my attic, I took it out of the envelope and realised what it was, I literally jumped for joy. I felt a wonderful thrill, far keener than any that I experienced some years later when I was given my first commission to write a book.

Encouraged by this initial success, I wrote to Mr. Bensusan proposing to write a series of sketches of Ghetto characters, to which he agreed, provided that they were as interesting and full of local colour as the first. I therefore began to burn the midnight oil regularly, and after I sent him another two sketches he began to publish the series under the general title of "Ghetto Types." I also began to write short stories, some of which I contributed to a new monthly, *Young Israel*, which was edited by Leopold J. Greenberg. I wanted to have a story published in *The Jewish Chronicle* too, but as its editor, Asher Myers, was a member of the Council of Jews' College, I wrote to him over my pseudonym and from the Chelsea address of my artist friend, Henry Ospovat, who had settled in London shortly after me. The story was promptly accepted and I received a cheque for two guineas payable to Enoch Scribe.

I next ventured upon a sketch for the general press. In the course of a stroll one Saturday night along Mile End Waste, where there was a long array of stalls lit up by naphtha lamps, I came across a decrepit bookstall with a shabby owner, who was offering cheap paper-backed novels to the staring crowd. He called himself " a livin' monument of rags, a vendor of the gutter," and spoke in a croaky, lachrymose voice as he described the contents of each book that he held up for sale. The scene strongly appealed to me as worthy of portrayal. I therefore wrote a sketch entitled "A Disseminator of Literature," and sent it to the weekly journal, *Literature*, edited by H. D. Traill, and published by *The Times*. It was accepted and appeared in the issue of October 22nd, 1898. By the end of the year I had altogether seventeen contributions in different papers and felt that I was on the way to becoming a writer.

V

After nearly three years I left the East End for Dalston, as I could no longer bear the discomforts of my Ghetto garret and the incessant noise and clatter of the neighbourhood. I was disturbed not only in the day, particularly by the jangling chains of a flour-mill a few yards away and by the frequent din of a German brass-band, but also at night by the singing of a Yiddish amateur operatic society on the other side of the road, who rehearsed four times a week and gave rollicking performances at the week-end. There were, of course, compensating benefits that I derived from living there. I gained an insight into the life and problems of East End Jewry and the issues that divided it from West End Jewry; I found my way into the

A JEWISH PILGRIMAGE

dual realm of modern Hebrew and Yiddish literature by browsing in Mazin's bookshop; and came into contact with some brilliant minds of the time at Toynbee Hall. There, where I often saw Canon Barnett pacing meditatively across the quadrangle in his black sombrero and flowing cloak, I listened to lectures by the historian Dicey and the Positivist Frederic Harrison, the essayist Augustine Birrell, the English scholar Churton Collins, and the novelist Conan Doyle. I sought pleasant and fruitful refuge in the winter not only in the Students' Library at Toynbee, but also in the Whitechapel Reference Library and the Guildhall Library. But I wanted to be able to work in peace and comfort, as I had a stiff programme of work before me, and I found congenial " diggings " in the home of a schoolmaster who had once had Israel Zangwill as a colleague at the Jews' Free School.

My modest literary efforts influenced me in favour of specialising in English, and I therefore decided to take the Higher Senior course in that subject at University College, so that I might perhaps eventually become a lecturer in English and a literary critic. For the next three years, therefore, I attended lectures on various periods of English literature by Professor Ker and on Anglo-Saxon, Gothic, and Germanic Philology by Dr. Gregory Foster. Among my fellow-students were W. Wedgwood Benn (now Viscount Stansgate), the late John Henry Grafton Grattan (who later became Professor of English at the Liverpool University), and (in the Gothic class) the late R. W. Chambers (who was a successor of Professor Ker). At the same time I went to Professor James Sully for lectures on Logic, Psychology, and Ethics, to William McDougall for Experimental Psychology, and to Professor Foxwell for political economy. There was then no London School of Economics, and Foxwell, who was a lucid and interesting lecturer, always had a well-attended class.

In the summer of 1898 I won the Hollier Hebrew Scholarship, which was worth £60, and had in consequence to attend a weekly lecture by Professor David Woolf Marks (the Chief Minister of the Reform Synagogue in Upper Berkeley Street). For several years past Professor Marks had had only one student, the Hollier scholar, who was obliged by the terms of the award to attend his lectures,

STUDENT YEARS

and I was both his sole and last student. For in 1898 he was already 87 years old, and as in that year he celebrated his Golden Jubilee as a Professor (surely a unique event) he felt it fitting to retire, apart from the compelling factor of increasing infirmity. He used to be brought to College in a little horse-drawn brougham driven by his valet, who helped him out and supported him right into the classroom, where he assisted him into his chair. The valet then retired to the back bench and spread out his morning paper in which he studied the racing news until it was time to take his master home again. Marks was no scholar and I do not remember having learned anything new from him, but retain a vivid recollection of a lesson devoted to translating a Hebrew letter that he had received from a poor man in the East End. The latter bewailed the fact that his poverty had compelled him to pawn many things from his home and begged the Professor to help him to redeem them. He based his plea upon the importance that Jewish tradition had always attached to the virtue of *Pidyon Shevuyim* (" redemption of captives "), and the Professor was so tickled by this piece of dialectics that he sent him some money. After his retirement he lived on for another eleven years, dying at the age of 98.

The successor of Marks was Dr. Solomon Schechter, who was Reader in Rabbinics at Cambridge University and had leapt into fame by his discovery of the original Hebrew of Ecclesiasticus in a store-room at the back of an old synagogue in Cairo. He was the very antithesis of his ancient predecessor — alive, learned, and witty, a striking personality with a leonine head and shaggy beard. His introductory lecture in January, 1899, attracted a large audience, which included such intellectual luminaries as Israel Abrahams and Joseph Jacobs. I attended his class for two terms, during which it steadily dwindled. When he gave his introductory lecture at the beginning of the next academic year, it was held in the Botanical Theatre in the expectation of an audience of 500, but only twenty turned up. As eventually Schechter had only two students in London and two in Cambridge he felt frustrated and accepted the tempting appointment in 1902 of President of the Jewish Theological Seminary in New York. In this position, which he held until his death in

A JEWISH PILGRIMAGE

1915, he exercised profound and far-reaching influence.

While attending lectures at University College I continued all the time at Jews' College too, where, in addition to Rabbinics, I began to study Arabic under Dr. Hartwig Hirschfeld. I also went on writing sketches and stories for the Jewish press, and occasionally contributed poems, both grave and gay, to the *Jewish World*. I found an opening for some of my Ghetto sketches in that sedate monthly, the *Gentleman's Magazine*, which was published by Chatto and Windus. Old Mr. Chatto sent for me, and told me that, as the journal was declining in favour, he would not be able to pay me more than half-a-guinea for each article, to which I readily agreed, as I considered it a distinction to appear in its pages. In addition to this miscellaneous work I frequently wrote notes on current topics for the *Jewish World* and also reported for it public meetings and lectures. When I had to cover a communal dinner on a Wednesday evening I did not get back to my room until after eleven. I then had to transcribe my notes of lengthy speeches, which took me until about three in the morning, and I delivered my " copy " at the office some hours later before going to College.

As I had now become independent of my father and needed a little extra money I undertook to give five hours teaching a week at the Religion Classes of a local Synagogue for fifteen shillings. After several months, however, my engagement was brought to a sudden end owing to my interest in Thomas More's *Utopia*. I had a small edition of it, which I kept in a jacket-pocket, and one Saturday morning, when taking a walk across Hackney Downs, I sat down on a bench and began to read it. Presently there came along the black-bearded chairman of the Religion Classes, who gave me a scowl that could bode no good and passed on. The next morning, when I arrived at the school, the headmaster solemnly informed me that he had been instructed to give me a week's notice because I had desecrated the Sabbath. I expressed astonishment and asked for an explanation, whereupon he told me that the chairman had seen me the previous day on the Downs with a book.

" And what is wrong with that ? " I asked.

"Don't you know that carrying on the Sabbath is a sin ?" he retorted.

"But the book is so small that I can slip it into my pocket," I returned.

"That makes no difference," he replied. "You leave at the end of the week."

The fiat had gone forth, and there was no appeal. But I had no reason to regret the incident, as soon afterwards I was engaged to give private lessons to some boys in Hampstead at seven-and-sixpence an hour and later also to their cousins in the West End.

In the latter part of 1901 the London University authorities took the novel step of instituting an honours degree in Semitic languages (Hebrew, Aramaic, and Syriac), whereupon the Council of Jews' College decided that all senior students should work for it. I therefore had to give up my English studies and the dreams based upon them, and switched over completely to Semitics. All the lectures were at Jews' College, except for a few on Semitic Epigraphy given at the British Museum. The course meant another three years' hard grind, to which I devoted almost all my time, apart from a few hours' private teaching. A new pupil whom I obtained was the son of a wealthy Jewish bullion broker, an Oxford graduate a little younger than myself, who paid me half-a-guinea a lesson. His family lived in a palatial mansion, the door of which was always opened by a uniformed, statuesque flunkey, who showed me in with impassive demeanour. But unfortunately this source of income soon dried up, for after a few weeks my aristocratic pupil informed me that as he could not otherwise find enough time for horse-riding in Hyde Park he would have to give up his Hebrew studies. This lapse, however, has not prevented him from becoming a worthy leader of a section of London Jewry.

Soon after embarking upon my Semitic course I moved to Kilburn. As I was now one of the senior students I could no longer resist or evade the invitations that reached me to preach in a synagogue now and again, but although I acquitted myself satisfactorily I did not become any more reconciled to entering the ministry. I took great pains in the composing of my sermons and always copied them out on small sheets for use in the pulpit. Above all I made doubly sure to take my manuscript with me, particularly owing to an incident that occurred at the time. A well-known minister at a West End synagogue ascended his pulpit one Sabbath morning to preach, and after thrusting his hands into all his pockets in search of his sermon in vain and realising that he must have left it at home, he descended silently and ignominiously back to his seat with all the eyes of his astonished congregation glued upon him. Moreover, I took a leading part in the affairs of the College Union Society and Literary Society, and when the Union of Jewish Literary Societies was founded in 1902, I was active at its Conferences and elected on its Executive. At a session of the inaugural Conference I read a paper on "The Need for a Jewish Library," at which the chair was taken by that venerable Maecenas, Frederic David Mocatta (1828 - 1905), who bequeathed to the Jewish Historical Society of England the greater part of his library, which formed the substantial nucleus of the Mocatta Library, University College, London.

From time to time, Mrs. Friedlaender, the wife of the Principal, would invite a senior student to lunch, and on one occasion extended the honour to me. In the course of the meal she asked me: " What would you like to drink, Mr. Cohen — hot water or cold ? " I had never been asked such an embarrassing question before in my life. I believe that I replied: " I have no particular preference, but am better used to cold."

VI

I began my travels abroad while still in my student days, for travel then was easy and comparatively cheap. There was no need for passport and visas (unless you wanted to go to Russia or Turkey), and currency restrictions were utterly unknown. My first venture on to the Continent was in the summer of 1902, when, with a fellow-student, I went by boat from the London Docks to Ostend for ten shillings return. Gay and fashionable as this seaside resort then was (at a time when picture-postcards of the Belgian King were freely sold with irreverent doggerel about Leo and Cléo de Merode), I soon tired of it. So I bought a fifteen-day season ticket for 23 francs

UNION OF JEWISH LITERARY SOCIETIES, SUMMER ASSEMBLY, RAMSGATE, 1904
Back Row: Rev. G. S. Belasco, Lucien Wolf, Rabbi Dr. Emil Hirsch, A. M. Hyamson, Israel Abrahams.
Front Row: F. S. Spiers, Miss B. Pool (Mrs. A. Blok), Prof. Sir Israel Gollancz, Israel Cohen.

(about £1), which enabled me to journey about day and night throughout the length and breadth of the country. Thus I saw the charm and beauty of Bruges and Ghent, the cathedrals and art-galleries, the commercial bustle and night-life of Antwerp and Brussels, the Swiss-like scenery along the Meuse from Namur to Dinant, the awe-inspiring Grottoes of Han with their magnificent chambers of stalactite and stalagmite, and finally the quaintly picturesque city of Luxembourg, built in three tiers like a cup, so that one could look down into it from the topmost rim.

In the following summer I toured through the Rhineland, from Cologne to Basle. It was a region not only of beauty but of historic interest, both general and Jewish. There were Jewish communities, large or small, on both sides of the Rhine, some of them, like Cologne, dating back to Roman times, with evidence that Jews had been settled there even before the Germans. I was young enough, as I sailed from Bonn to Bingen, to be thrilled by the panorama on both banks, with the succession of fabled castles and mouldering towers, of melancholy monasteries and lofty spires, surrounded by vistas of vineyards and clusters of hamlets. Our approach to the famous Lorelei, surmounted by a fluttering flag, was heralded by some schoolgirls singing Heine's haunting lines to Schubert's rapturous notes, and as we passed the town of Bacharach I conjured up a vision of the Rabbi immortalised by Heine in his fragmentary story of a former age of intolerance.

Of some twelve cities that I visited in the course of five weeks the largest and most important was Frankfort (on the Main), where I stayed at a modest hotel in the same street in which Goethe was born. I lingered in the room in which he first saw the light and also in his study, and examined many drawings, manuscripts and books illustrative of his life and work. Near by I also visited the house, with its Gothic façade, dating from the sixteenth century, that had been the birthplace of the Rothschilds. On the ground floor there was still a small synagogue — testimony to the piety of the founders of the financial dynasty — and on a verandah upstairs was a booth for celebrating the Feast of Tabernacles. Frankfort was in those days, and until the advent of Hitler, a veritable Jewish metropolis, with many synagogues and Rabbis of rival schools. It had a large public library, in which I found a separate collection of Judaica and Hebraica, and in the basement was a fascinating exhibition of old Hebrew books and manuscripts. From there I went to Heidelberg, where I was as much attracted by the student life as by the picturesque scenes from the mountain cafés, and made an excursion to the neighbouring village of Walldorf, where I saw a statue to its famous son, John Jacob Astor, who had emigrated to America and founded the family fortunes. This jaunt through the Rhineland, however, was only a prelude to my visit to Basle, where I arrived in time to be present at the Sixth Zionist Congress. It was the Congress of August, 1903, the last at which Herzl was alive.

It was the first time that I had seen a gathering of Jews from all parts of the world, and the manifold contrasts of types, of physical and facial appearance, of dress and demeanour, of language and gesture, which it presented, were a source of ceaseless wonderment. I felt in a new world. It was a veritable microcosm of the Diaspora, in which there were delegates and visitors from every clime representing all shades of thought and spheres of culture. The Basle Stadt-Casino swarmed with an animated throng, in which Rabbis rubbed shoulders with free-thinkers, the Socialist with the bourgeois, the Hebraist with the Yiddishist, the American plutocrat with the starveling from a Polish Ghetto, the artist with the journalist, the veteran savant with the student. The most exotic figures were two "mountain Jews" from the Caucasus, in their native garb, with black astrakhan hats and a belt to which was attached a cartridge pouch. About a third of the delegates came from Russia (which then included Poland), while those from Palestine were so few that they were hardly noticed. Many speeches were delivered in Russian, other speeches and all resolutions had to be translated into that language, while Hebrew was spoken but rarely. Most of the speeches were in German, and others were in Yiddish, English, French, or Polish.

The Congress made a deep impression upon me, not only because it was engaged in seeking a solution of the problem of Israel's future, but also because it was the last Congress at which Theodor Herzl

STUDENT YEARS

and Max Nordau were both present, and the outstanding question under discussion was the British Government's offer of an autonomous territory in East Africa. Those two dominated the assembly throughout the sessions — Herzl as leader and chairman and Nordau as speaker and pleader. Such were the violent feelings aroused by the British offer, which many delegates regarded as aiming at something utterly different from the Zionist ideal, that Herzl had often to call for silence by a redoubled rap with his mallet, while his repeated appeal, " *Ich bitte um Ruhe* ! " uttered in his soft yet resonant voice, still echoes in my memory after the passage of years. Nordau was a brilliant orator, whose masterly survey of the position of the Jews in the world was one of the principal features at the opening of every Congress. He spoke from a mere scrap of paper in the hollow of his hand, but it was evident from the orderly sequence of his address and well-phrased sentences, from the marshalling of facts and arguments, punctuated by striking ideas, ironic asides, a touch of humour, and an occasional note of tragedy, that here was a piece of work that had been fashioned in the study. The cumulative effect was overwhelming.

Nordau gave his powerful support to Herzl's proposal for the appointment of a commission of inquiry to investigate the British project, and when a roll-call showed a majority in favour of this proposal there followed a most moving scene. Amid cheers and groans the Russian members of the " Actions Committee " (General Council) trooped off the platform into the middle of the hall, where they were joined by the mass of the Russian delegates, and all marched out into an adjoining hall to give vent to their indignation and sorrow. Herzl followed them and begged them to come back, assuring them of his undying loyalty to Zion; and when I returned to the press table the next morning I found that the Russians were in their places again.

During the Congress I made the acquaintance of many people, most of whom I met at subsequent Congresses (for I attended them all until 1946), and with some of them I became lifelong friends. One day, in the square outside the Congress hall, I was introduced by a friend from London, Dr. Angelo S. Rappoport, to a man of about thirty, tall and spare, with dark eyes and small black, imperial beard, puffing vigorously at a cigarette, whom I had noticed arguing vehemently in a little group. His name was Dr. Chaim Weizmann, and Rappoport and he had been fellow-students in Berne and Geneva. I had previously heard of Dr. Weizmann as one of the so-called "Democratic Fraction," including Martin Buber, who had severely criticised the Zionist leader at the previous Congress on the ground that in his programme he did not lay sufficient emphasis upon the importance of Jewish culture. But at the Sixth Congress Weizmann played a rather quiet part. He made only one speech, devoted very largely to expressing approval of the Sinai Peninsula project[1] (which had to be dropped owing to the Egyptian Government's objection), but he prefaced it with a reference to the East Africa scheme, to which he said that he adopted "a positive attitude." Despite this, however, he voted against the resolution to send a commission of inquiry to investigate the territory, and a few days later allowed himself to be elected on the "Committee for the study of the East Africa expedition." Subsequently he became a strong opponent of the scheme.

It was at this Congress that I again came into brief personal contact with Herzl. The press correspondents were dissatisfied with the arrangements made for their convenience, and decided to send a deputation to Herzl in which I was included. He assured us of his sympathy, as he was a journalist himself, but he asked for our indulgence in view of the circumstances, and he pacified and honoured us by agreeing to be photographed together with the group of journalists.

After the Congress I went to Strassburg (as it was in those days) and Baden-Baden for a brief stay. I then journeyed to Speyer, particularly to see the subterranean Jewish bath in a small garden at the end of the Judengasse, dating from the early thirteenth century, which had been used by women for ritual ablution. From there went to the ancient city of Worms, where Jews are believed to have

[1] This project was also known as the El Arish scheme, El Arish being the northern part of the Sinai Peninsula. The leader of the expedition that investigated the territory was Leopold Kessler (1864 - 1944), an expert mining engineer (who later became Chairman of the Board of Directors of *The Jewish Chronicle*). The opposition of the Egyptian Government was based on the alleged ground that the scheme would require more water from the Nile than it was willing to give.

JOURNALISTS AT THE SIXTH ZIONIST CONGRESS, BASLE, 1903
The Author (in light waistcoat) standing just behind Dr. S. Werner and Dr. Theodor Herzl

first settled in Roman times, and where there was a quaint synagogue originally built early in the eleventh century. Close to the synagogue was a little chapel named after the famous mediæval commentator, Rashi[1], who studied in Worms for some years and, according to unconfirmed legend, also maintained a Talmudical academy there. The last city that I visited was Düsseldorf, where I wished to look at the birth-place of Heine in the Bolker Strasse. The house was then converted to a butcher-shop and there was no sign that one of Germany's greatest lyric poets had his first glimpse of the world there.

I attended the Congress as the special correspondent of *The Jewish World*, with which my connection had gradually become closer. When Herzl died in the following year I received a telegram from the Editor, asking me to let him have a poem on the tragic event. I was unable to sit down to it until midnight, but by four in the morning I had finished a blank-verse ode, which I delivered at the office six hours later. In the same week I attended a mass meeting in memory of the departed leader, at the Great Assembly Hall, Mile End, which was packed from the floor to the upper gallery with about seven thousand people. It was a poignant scene of mourning and distress. There was a look of grief on every face, and there was much sighing and sobbing. There was a feeling that not only was Herzl dead but Zionism was doomed.

Very shortly afterwards, as I was sitting in my room in Oxford Road, I received some unexpected visitors. The entry in my diary for July 23rd, 1904, reads:

Visited this afternoon by Dr. A. S. Rappoport, Dr. Weizmann, and H. Snowman. Over tea Dr. Weizmann spoke on the Zionist crisis: the method of bluff and ostentation — the Viennese tone — must be dropped, and serious work started. Complained of incompetence of Herzl's colleagues on Small Actions Committee (Executive). He was surprised to find Peretz's portrait on my walls and that I read Yiddish.

This brief record of Dr. Weizmann's remarks on that occasion suffices to show the critical attitude that he then maintained towards both Herzl's policy and the Zionist Executive in Vienna.

[1] Formed from the initial letters of Rabbi Shelomoh (Solomon) ben Isaac. He was born at Troyes in 1040 and died there in 1105.

A JEWISH PILGRIMAGE

In the summer of that year I took a brief holiday in Holland, partly to see the attractions of the country, including the art galleries with their unique collections of Rembrandts, Teniers, and other masters, and partly to study Jewish life there and to visit places of historic interest. In Amsterdam I was impressed by the sombre and stately interior of the early eighteenth century synagogue, which was illuminated only by candles in bronze sconces. In the Jodenbreestraat I visited the house where Rembrandt had lived and painted Jewish types. On the Amstel I took a boat to Ouderkerk, where in the old Portuguese Jewish cemetery I saw the grave of Menasseh ben Israel, the great-hearted Rabbi who came to England to plead with Oliver Cromwell for the re-admission of the Jews, who had been expelled by Edward I in 1290. I also visited the Record Office in Amsterdam, where I was shown the register containing the original marriage certificate of Menasseh ben Israel and his signature.

After spending a fortnight in seeing all that I could to satisfy my youthful curiosity, not only in Amsterdam but also in The Hague, Rotterdam, Leyden, and Haarlem, I went to the fashionable seaside resort of Scheveningen. There, without any letter of introduction, I called on Josef Israels, who was universally esteemed as Holland's greatest living painter. Although already eighty at the time, he still worked three hours every morning regularly in his studio at The Hague, and returned in the afternoon to his villa facing the sea-front. He looked a small, withered, and wizened old man, wearing dark glasses, but seemed possessed of an energy that belied his age. He spoke quite tolerable English, so I took the opportunity to ask him whether he thought that there was such a thing as Jewish art. His reply, of which I have preserved a record, was as follows:

No. The term "Jewish Art" was invented by some German journalists, and has been exploited by them. There is a Jewish art publishing house in Berlin which has given strength to the idea and is fond of describing the work of every Jewish artist as Jewish art. But I am not a Jewish artist, nor do I want to be. I am a Dutch artist. Solomon J. Solomon is a good English artist; Liebermann is a German artist; and I believe I am not a bad Dutch artist. But Hermann Struck—him you can call a Jewish artist. I know him well, and his work, especially his studies of Jewish types, may rightly be described as Jewish art.

I asked Israels whether he thought that a Gentile artist could portray a Jewish theme as skilfully as a Jewish artist, to which he replied:

There have been Gentile artists who painted Jewish subjects — for example, Rembrandt, who was very fond of Jews and lived in the Jewish quarter in Amsterdam. He painted Rabbis and synagogue scenes and left a picture, " The Jewish Bride." But only the title is Jewish. The man in the picture, Boaz, is a German. But the woman, I think — if you look well — has a Jewish appearance. Perhaps she was a Dutch Jewess.

Israels then went on to speak of Jewish life in Amsterdam as he knew it before the middle of the nineteenth century, when he had lived in the Ghetto for a couple of years. He said that the scene in the market on Fridays, when the women were busy shopping for the Sabbath, had an atmosphere like Rembrandt's " *Nacht-Wacht.*"

VII

On my return to London I devoted myself to final preparations for my examination, for which I sat, together with three fellow-students, in October, 1904. We all passed and were thus the first to obtain the London B.A. Honours degree in Semitic languages. My fellow-candidates all became Rabbis. One was Dayan H. M. Lazarus, who has served for many years as a distinguished member of the *Beth Din* (Court of the Chief Rabbi) and also acted as Deputy for the Chief Rabbi. I left the College to become a journalist. My decision evoked censorious comment from some members of the College Council, who demanded that I should enter the profession for which I had been trained. But other and more reasonable members argued that it would be wrong to make me act against my convictions and inclinations, and that the knowledge and training I had acquired would ultimately prove serviceable to the Jewish community in other ways, particularly in the press, where it was necessary to watch over Jewish interests.

The discussion about my " defection," however, was quite trifling in comparison with the sensational case of another student, Herman Leonard Pass, who had left Jews' College a little before my time.

A JEWISH PILGRIMAGE

He went to Cambridge, where he graduated in Oriental languages in which he won various scholarships, and assisted Dr. Schechter in arranging the old Hebrew manuscripts which the latter had brought from Cairo. Pass was an adherent of orthodox Judaism and took part regularly in conducting the Sabbath services of the small congregation at Cambridge. He was so punctilious in matters of ritual observance that he complained when a fellow-student, Abraham Wolf (also an *alumnus* of Jews' College, who later became Professor of Logic and Scientific Method in the University of London) simply read the weekly portion of the Law without cantillating it according to the accents (which were not written on the parchment scroll and had therefore to be carefully memorised). He was appointed by the Jewish Religious Education Board in London as lecturer to pupil teachers, and I attended one of his lectures at Toynbee Hall. Suddenly Pass vanished from the Jewish scene, and after a time there appeared, in 1901, a surprising announcement in the press that he had been received into the Church of England. Nobody could explain how this change could have taken place in such a zealous devotee of Jewish orthodoxy. Pass made steady advance in his new faith, became Examining Chaplain to the Bishop of Oxford, and was appointed in 1919 Principal of Chichester Theological College, which he directed with marked success until his death, as a Canon, in 1938.

Chapter Three

ADVENTURES IN JOURNALISM

1905 — 1908

I

I EMBARKED upon the career of a journalist with the hope derived from what I had already done, and also with a sense of temporary security, as my earnings from private lessons sufficed for my essential needs. Soon after I became free to do with my time what I wished, I was easily persuaded by my friend Henry Ospovat, at the end of 1904, to join him on a trip to Paris. He was anxious to visit the Louvre and to study French types, and the sketch-book that he took with him gradually filled with drawings of characters that caught his fancy in cafés and cabarets. But for me the main attraction was the prospect of calling upon Dr. Max Nordau, who was then at the zenith of his fame, for I thought that the publication of an interview in a London paper with an author whose iconoclastic works, *Degeneration* and *Conventional Lies of Civilisation*, had made him an international celebrity would smooth my path in the profession I had chosen.

I had already translated Nordau's pamphlet on Zionism and was desirous also of rendering into English his new play, *Doktor Kohn*, which dealt with the problem of anti-Semitism. So, soon after securing a room in a humble hotel near the Madeleine, I wrote him a note asking for the favour of an interview. The reply came almost by return of post, written with his own hand (for he never employed either secretary or typewriter) in the violet ink of which he was so fond. It said that the play had already been translated, but he would nevertheless be pleased to see me and fixed the time. His friendly response dispelled the timidity that I, a young man of twenty-five, felt at the thought of being alone with the most formidable and trenchant critic of the day. I was encouraged by the friendly manner in which he received me in his study, and pleasantly surprised at the ease with which he spoke English. He sat in a high-backed armchair, and as he leant back the light from the oil-lamp on the writing-table (for electricity had not yet come into general use) played upon his striking face, illuminating the snow-white hair and parted beard, the massive brow, the keen piercing eyes, and the firm lips of the orator. He spoke freely and forcefully, first on various current questions of the Zionist movement, and then on the theme of idealism in literature. He dismissed the rumour that he was willing to accept the leadership of the Zionist Organisation, emphasised the indissoluble connection of the Jewish national idea with Palestine, and insisted with a vigour that seemed strange in one of such unconventional views on contemporary culture that Hebrew must again become the living speech of the Jewish people in the Holy Land. Turning to the question of literature, he deprecated the principle of "art for art's sake" and stressed the cardinal importance of the ethical purpose that should animate all literary creations. He spoke so copiously that there was little need for me to put any but a few leading questions, and the interview, for the most part, took the form of a monologue.

Two or three days after my return to London I wrote down the whole of the interview as well as my memory served me, for I had not dared to take any notes in the great presence, and then sent a typewritten copy — ten pages in all — to Dr. Nordau, with a request that he might be good enough to read it through and make any corrections before I offered it to a paper. By return of post I received an indignant postcard in violet ink, on which he wrote that he had not been aware that I had interviewed him for the press, otherwise he would have declined the honour, but as I had taken the trouble to write out my article his professional conscience forbade him to prevent me from making use of it, and he would therefore correct the typescript and return it. The following day the article came back, with autograph corrections, and with another note, which showed that the original indignation had been succeeded by a feeling of amiability. The interview was much too long for a column article so I divided it into two parts, the first dealing with Zionism and the second with literature. The first was at once accepted by the *Daily Chronicle* and the other just as promptly by the *Pall Mall Gazette*. But I could not call upon international celebrities every day, and had to write on themes suggested by current events or on subjects within my knowledge. Russia was then, as to-day, a country that appealed to general interest, and as some of its famous writers had sought liberty in emigration I wrote an article on " Genius in Exile " (on data culled from George Brandes' *Impressions of Russia*), which was published in the *Star*. Then I did an article on Yiddish, to which there were frequent references in the press and about which there was much misconception. After being rejected by two or three papers it was accepted by the *Manchester Guardian*, whose distinguished editor, C. P. Scott, wrote me a charming personal letter of thanks with his own hand. It was the beginning of a long and friendly association with that paper, which has continued for over forty years. Thus encouraged, I persisted, but far more articles were rejected than accepted. Since I was so familiar with the East End it was only natural that I should seek and find material in that hive of multifarious activity. My visits to Mazin's bookshop suggested a description of that exotic literary emporium, which also found a place in the *Manchester Guardian*. But a more fertile source was the club of Russian Jews, to which I was attracted one night by a red lamp above the open doorway.

On the slanting pane was painted the one word " Volkshaus," and when I entered I found myself in a long, narrow room crowded with excited young men and girls, debating, gesticulating, and smoking. It was the meeting-place of the London branch of the " Bund," the Jewish Socialist party of Russia, Poland, and Lithuania.[1] On the walls were portraits of Karl Marx, Bakunin, and other heroes of Socialism; on some reading stands were papers in Yiddish, Hebrew, Russian, and German; and on a bookstall was a motley assortment of

---

[1] The Bund was founded in Vilna in 1897. It was dissolved in Russia after the First World War, and in Poland it was merged into the Communist party after the Second World War.

A JEWISH PILGRIMAGE

Yiddish and Russian booklets, mostly dealing with Socialism and the revolutionary agitation in Russia, and including Yiddish translations from Marx, Lassalle, and Kropotkin. Most of these publications were printed in London, but I was told that since 1903 Geneva had become the chief printing centre of the Bund outside the Empire of the Tsar. The " Volkshaus " was situated between two synagogues, and as its members were known to be irreligious its windows were often broken by little boys who were incited by their Orthodox parents to throw stones and dirt. Disturbances were also often caused by a band of Anarchists, who attended the lectures given there solely for the purpose of interrupting and creating disorder.

Not only did I describe the animated scenes and curious characters in this " Volkshaus " in an article which Scott published in his paper, but I drew from it for months an abundance of interesting material which I used for contributions to other papers. Most Jewish political refugees from Russia found their way there, and I was able to gather from them some sensational stories. Many of them had assumed false names to outwit the Russian police, and those who arrived here with a beard had it removed the next day. In a Shoreditch garret I had a talk with a strapping young fellow, Mordecai Strick, who had been in the Russian Army. He related to me the ingenious plot by means of which he had effected the escape from the Sebastopol Prison of Feldman, the hero of the famous revolt (in June, 1905) on the ship *Potemkin* on the Black Sea, and he drew for me a sketch of the interior of the jail to show how he had tricked the warders.

Far different was the talk that I had with a ninety-five year old Jewish woman in Stepney, a Mrs. Hart, who formed a link with Nelson. She told me that her father, whose name was Richard Barnett, had been forced into the Navy by a press-gang, fought on board Nelson's *Vanguard* in the Battle of the Nile, and was afterwards bought out by his father. In support of her statements she showed me an interesting log-book that had been kept by her father during the voyage of the *Vanguard*, extending from December 24th, 1797, to January 31st, 1800. This private log-book, which must have been a contravention of the regulations, consisted of eleven faded and worm-eaten sheets of quarto size. It contained a fairly detailed account

ADVENTURES IN JOURNALISM

of the Battle of the Nile, which was illustrated by a sort of plan of the fight and accompanied by a list of the casualties.[1] Richard Barnett, who was probably one of the first Jewish sailors in the English Navy, was born in 1779 and died on June 20th, 1819. He was an uncle of Samuel Phillips, a man of letters, who was a literary critic on *The Times* and a contributor to *Blackwood's Magazine*, and who was held to be of sufficient importance to have his bust displayed in the Crystal Palace.

I enjoyed the freedom, the excitement, and the variety of experiences afforded by free-lance journalism, and gradually extended my connections. I began to do book reviews, was a frequent contributor of paragraphs of Jewish interest to the London Correspondence of the *Manchester Guardian*, and wrote notices about the Yiddish plays at the Pavilion Theatre in Whitechapel (whose manager was always pleased to give me a seat in a box or the stalls). On one occasion, at the performance of a Yiddish opera, *The Spanish Inquisition*, I was allowed to go behind the stage, where I saw the leading lady drinking a glass of stout, the Inquisitor smoking a cigarette, and the Mother Superior flirting with the limelight man. I also wrote a few articles on artists and their art (with the help of my friend Ospovat), which were published. But, although constantly busy, I had repeated disappointments and became hardened to the sight of foolscap envelopes addressed to me in my own writing and containing rejected manuscripts. My efforts seemed to fail to find the recognition or yield the rewards that I thought they deserved, so that I had to eke out my income by translating erudite German articles for the *Jewish Quarterly Review*, doing research work at the British Museum, and acting as invigilator of examinations at the London University. I was anxious to get a position on a newspaper and called on Israel Zangwill, by arrangement, at his chambers in the Temple, to see whether he could help me. After I told him what I had already done in six months he encouragingly remarked that I was getting on well and had only to persevere. Besides, he thought that any introductions

[1] See the *Jewish World*, October 20th, 1905, *Manchester Guardian* (London Correspondence), September 16th, 1905, and *The Jewish Chronicle*, May 6th, 1955. Barnett's real forename was Abraham. He adopted the name of Richard only on joining the Navy and resumed the name of Abraham after leaving it.

to editors that he might give me would not influence them. "The man you should see," he said, "is Lucien Wolf. He certainly has influence in Fleet Street. Did you see his big article in to-day's *Times*, on the leader page?" However, I did not go to see Lucien Wolf. The outcome of my visit to Zangwill was that when, some weeks later, he was asked by the editor of a new journal, called *The New Weekly*, to let him have a couple of articles on "What the Jews have done for England," he recommended me for the commission and I earned eight guineas.

II

Towards the end of July, 1905, I went to Basle again to attend the Seventh Zionist Congress. This time I was to act as the special correspondent not only of the *Jewish World* but also of the *Manchester Guardian*. From that year I represented the *Guardian* at all the following Zionist Congresses until that of 1946 (with the exception of the one in 1907, which was covered by a Jewish member of its regular staff). The Congress of 1905 was both momentous and tumultuous. It was the first from which the lamented founder of the movement was absent, and when, at the opening session, Max Nordau paid a glowing tribute to him in an eloquent memorial address there were many who were unable to restrain their tears, even some members of the Council on the platform covering their faces with a handkerchief.

Since the Congress of 1903 the Zionist world had been sharply divided into two opposing camps over the question of the British Government's offer of a territory in East Africa for an autonomous Jewish settlement. On the one side were the Palestinians or *Zioné Zion* (Zionists of Zion), who were adamant against any Jewish national settlement outside Palestine, on the other were the so-called "Territorialists," who maintained that the true aim of Zionism was to obtain an autonomous settlement in any country and showed no preference for the Holy Land. Now that the Commission of Inquiry had submitted their report on the territory in East Africa and the Congress had to take a decision on the British offer, the controversy had increased in bitterness and the rival camps were at daggers drawn. Even the Territorialists, whose leader was Israel

Zangwill, were split into two sections — one, calling themselves "Political Zionists" and drawn from various countries, and the other consisting of Socialists belonging mainly to the Russo-Jewish Social Democratic Federation.

After the debate in the Congress had lasted one night until half-past two in the morning, the voting on the British offer had to be deferred in order to hear the report of the Credentials Committee on the validity of the election of a large number of delegates from Russia belonging to the Palestinian party, which was contested by the Territorialists. The Committee found that the bulk of the disputed elections were valid and its report was adopted by Congress, whereupon the Socialist section of the Territorialists, seeing that their side would be greatly outvoted, broke out into a storm of protest. Standing on chairs and tables, they shouted defiance at the "præsidium" on the platform, and their demonstration was reinforced by booing from the galleries. Here, where the visitors were packed to the ceiling, a large number of fellow-Socialists redoubled the turbulent protest, instigated by Russian women students of Berne University, who cheered frantically. The latter suddenly showered down a hail of leaflets on the delegates below, and the Socialist group started a revolutionary song. All attempts of the chairman to quell the disturbance were in vain, and when a swarm of demonstrators from the galleries poured into the hall the tumult and disorder became indescribable. The chairman and "præsidium" then left the platform, and pandemonium raged unchecked until four in the morning, when, amid the mingled strains of the Zionist *Song of Hope* and the *Marseillaise*, the delegates gradually dispersed.

When the Congress resumed at midday the galleries were closed to the public and the cards of delegates and press correspondents were rigorously scrutinised. Dr. Nordau, who took the chair, implored the Congress to preserve decorum during the voting on the British offer, and then the resolution formulated by the Executive, which combined a dignified rejection with a re-affirmation of the principles of Zionism, was adopted by an overwhelming majority. But passions were still seething. A dramatic scene followed, in which Zangwill accused Nordau "before the bar of history, of treason to the Jewish people," because (in accordance with Continental procedure) he had submitted the Executive's resolution to the vote before one that Zangwill wanted to put as an amendment. Thereupon the irate Zangwill and most of those delegates who were in favour of the offer withdrew from the Congress, and later in the day they held a meeting of their own at which they created the Jewish Territorial Organisation for the establishment of a Jewish autonomous settlement in any part of the world. The practical outcome of the Congress was the election of a new Executive, who chose David Wolffsohn, of Cologne, an intimate friend of Herzl, as President, and in consequence the headquarters of the movement were transferred from Vienna to Cologne. From then until the outbreak of the war in 1914 the movement was exposed not only to the continued hostility of the anti-Zionists but also to the guerrilla attacks of the Territorialists, whose failure to find another land only aggravated their rancour.

From Basle I went to Vevey, where I saw a colourful open-air pageant, "La Fête des Vignerons," and then to Geneva, where I visited the "Imprimerie Israélite," a name that concealed the identity of the principal printing-centre of the Bund. I was welcomed by two Russian Jews with whom I spoke in Yiddish. They were glad to hear that I was acquainted with the "Volkshaus," gave me a collection of their pamphlets and bulletins dealing with the struggle against Russian tyranny, and promised to send me all future issues of their organ, *Letzte Nachrichten*.

Soon after I returned to London I began to receive not only this Yiddish paper but also a bulletin in German, *Russische Korrespondenz*. The latter, which always reported incidents in the persecution of the Jews in Russia, was edited in Berlin by a Russo-Jewish publicist, Leo Motzkin, a friend of Dr. Weizmann, to whom I had been introduced at the Zionist Congress. These publications usually contained news that did not reach English press correspondents in Russia, and occasionally disclosed secret documents from the Russian Ministry of the Interior. I was thus able to supply *The Times*[1] with a confidential document on "The Censorship in Russia," and other papers with kindred contributions.

[1] September 12th, 1905.

III

Fortune seemed to favour me at last in the autumn of 1905. A Lancashire cotton-manufacturer, Franklin Thomasson, had inherited a very large estate from his father, who stipulated that part of it should be devoted to the advancement of the Liberal cause, and he therefore decided to use £300,000 for the establishment of a new Liberal morning paper, to be called the *Tribune*. As soon as I read this news I wrote a letter to Mr. William Hill, who had been appointed Editor, applying for a position, and gave a detailed account of my qualifications. After waiting for some weeks I was requested in September, 1905, to call for an interview, and found that Hill was sympathetically disposed and inclined to engage me as a member of the editorial staff. He asked me what salary I would expect, and I ventured to suggest four pounds a week. He thought that very reasonable and promised to let me have a definite reply within ten days. Within less time than that I received a letter from him informing me that he was pleased to appoint me as " general writer and reporter " at four guineas a week, to begin from the 1st of January, 1906. I need not describe how happy I felt and with what a light heart I looked forward to continuing as a free-lance only till the end of the year.

About a month before the *Tribune* was due to begin to appear, I had another interview with Mr. Hill, who told me that I would be assistant to Mr. Edward G. Hawke, the Literary Editor (who had previously been on the *Manchester Guardian*). He also said that there was a possibility of sending me as a special correspondent to Warsaw, which was then a hotbed of revolutionary agitation, or even to Constantinople, and asked me to call again in the evening to be introduced to Mr. George H. Perris, who had been appointed Foreign Editor. Perris said that he would like to send me to Warsaw because, with my knowledge of Yiddish, he thought that I would be able to secure information to which another correspondent could not gain access. He then introduced me to a tall, black-bearded man in his room, Dr. David Soskice[1], who was leaving that night for St. Peters-

[1] Father of Sir Frank Soskice, Q.C., M.P., Attorney-General to the Labour Government of 1945 - 1950.

burg to act as special correspondent. Dr. Soskice gave me a letter of introduction to a Bundist named Nadel, in Whitechapel, and said that it would be advisable that I should learn a little Polish. The next day I went to see Nadel, a dentist, who said that he would inform his friends of the Bund in Warsaw that I would be coming and that one of them would call at my hotel. He gave me a card on which he wrote a message in Russian, which I was to present to my visitor. I then saw Perris again, who told me to go ahead with the arrangements for my mission — to study Polish and to obtain a passport. I was making good progress in Polish when I discovered that, although I got a passport (which then consisted of a single sheet of thin paper of foolscap size) without difficulty, it was impossible for me to secure a Russian visa. For the Tsarist Government, although anything but Christian in practice, would not allow anybody but a true Christian to enter their country, and as I did not possess a baptismal certificate my projected journey to Warsaw had to be abandoned.

The *Tribune* made its appearance under the most promising auspices, for there was a Liberal landslide in the General Election of January, 1906, which returned the Liberals to power with an enormous majority over the Conservatives, and it seemed as if a big London Liberal daily was assured of success. The staff included several men of outstanding ability and distinction. The principal leader-writers were Leonard T. Hobhouse, H. N. Brailsford, J. A. Hobson, and J. L. Hammond. The literary editorship was shared with Edward Hawke by Philip Gibbs; William Archer was the chief dramatic critic, and A. Clutton Brock the art critic.

On the eve of the publication of the first number the proprietor gave a reception in the newly equipped building in Bouverie Street, which was attended not only by all members of the staff but also by a large company of politicians, authors, and journalists. In this festive scene the tallest member of the staff, Randal Charlton, about six foot four in height, who had just published a novel, *The Virgin Widow*, stood in front of a buffet, asked the waiter to fill a dozen glasses of champagne in a row, and wagered his colleagues that he would swallow them one after the other. We looked on expectantly. By the time

ADVENTURES IN JOURNALISM

he reached out for the sixth glass he suddenly sank to the floor with a thud. Two strong men immediately lifted him to his feet, escorted him through the throng, helped him down the stairs, and heaved him into a hansom. A volunteer was wanted to accompany him home, and impulsively I responded. Fortunately the cold night air had a sobering effect upon the tipsy giant, and by the time we reached his lodgings he had recovered the use of his legs, but I did not leave him until I had seen him into bed.

My work was primarily book-reviewing, and I had a desk in the same room as my chief. Near me was another desk, which was occupied in the later hours of the evening by an ex-officer of the Guards, Captain Harry Graham, who looked after the social gossip and occasionally wrote dramatic notices (and afterwards became well-known as a prolific writer of humorous verse and amusing plays). Before long I was also asked to help on the reporting side, especially whenever there was an event of Jewish interest, or a meeting of an academic nature, or an international conference that called for a knowledge of French or German.

From the beginning of 1906 the Aliens Act, which had been passed by the Conservative Government just before it went out of power, came into force, and as its principal victims were Russian Jews I volunteered to inquire into its administration. The Act provided for the continued admission of refugees from political or religious persecution, as well as of persons who had at least five pounds in their possession, or had relatives in England who would support them and prevent them from becoming a charge on public funds. I used to go every morning to the London Docks where the immigrant ships arrived and where a special Board met to examine the aliens in order to decide which of them could be admitted. Journalists were not allowed to enter the room where the examination was held, but had to stand about outside and wait for such fragments of information as they could afterwards pick up. The Secretary of the Jews' Temporary Shelter (Mr. A. Mundy), a well-known institution in the East End for befriending Jewish immigrants, was however, permitted, as a matter of grace, to be present at the hearings, and he took me in with him as his assistant. I was thus able not only to make a note of the Board's decision in each case but also to talk to the immigrants and gather from them more particulars than the members of the Board elicited before arriving at their judgment. I was also able to go on to the ship to talk to them. I found that owing partly to faulty interpretation by an official, partly to a misreading of the Act by the Board, and partly to the natural nervousness of the immigrants who omitted to state facts that should have ensured their admission, many of them were rejected and escorted back to the ship, which had to return them to the German or Dutch port from which they had sailed. The fate that then awaited them was to be transported back to Russia, and in the case of men who, owing to ill-treatment, had fled from the Russian Army, it meant that they would be shot.

The *Tribune*, therefore, began to expose the injustices committed by the maladministration of the Act. It published daily names and particulars of immigrants who were entitled by the terms of the Act to admission, but had nevertheless been sent back to what seemed certain death. I collected so much information that Mr. Brailsford, who wrote leaders on the subject, called in his friend Henry Nevinson from the office of the *Daily Chronicle* so that I could pass some of it on to him, and his paper combined with the *Tribune* in arousing public feeling. Gradually the agitation for amending the Act was taken up by all the Liberal papers of the country. It reached a climax when a young Russian Jew, David Rabinowitz, who had deserted from the Russian Army after refusing to fire on his fellow-Jews, and was certainly entitled to asylum in England according to the Act, was sent back to the Continent. As soon as I brought this news to the office, the editor decided to save Rabinowitz. He telegraphed to the *Tribune's* correspondent at Hamburg, Albert Kinross, the novelist, to go at once to Bremen to meet the ship on which Rabinowitz was and to buy him a shipping-ticket for any place to which he wished to go. Within twenty-four hours a wire was received from Kinross, announcing that he was just in time to prevent Rabinowitz from being handed over to the police, and that he had bought him a ticket for Buenos Aires and safely seen him on board the vessel that was going there[1].

[1] Several years later I read a short story based on this incident, by Albert Kinross, which appeared in an American magazine.

Mr. Brailsford promptly sent particulars of this and other cases by messenger to Ramsay MacDonald, who had recently been elected to the House of Commons for the first time, with a view to putting questions to the Home Secretary, Herbert Gladstone. The result of all this agitation was that the Liberal Government, which had opposed the measure for restricting alien immigration when it was proposed by the Conservatives, issued revised regulations to the Immigration Boards to ensure that they exercised clemency in future in favour of all alien immigrants who were refugees from persecution or who satisfied the economic test.

In the spring of 1906 I received at the *Tribune* office a letter with an Austrian post-mark from Lemberg. It was in Yiddish and came from the famous author Sholem Aleichem (né Solomon Rabinowicz), who was known as the Jewish Mark Twain. He wrote that owing to the massacres in his native land of Russia he had to leave and had been giving readings from his works in Rumania and Austria. He was anxious to do the same in England and would be grateful if I would undertake the arrangements and let him know what were the prospects of success. I therefore formed a reception committee, with Joseph Cowen (who was then one of the Zionist leaders in England) as chairman, and organised a dinner in honour of the distinguished visitor at a Jewish restaurant in the East End, at which I proposed his health. Sholem Aleichem gave his first public reading at the South Place Institute, with Israel Zangwill in the chair, and kept his large audience in a constant state of laughter. In the course of our talks he told me of his friendship with Tolstoi, Gorki, Chekhov, and other leading Russian authors of the time, who had suggested to him that relations between Jews and Russians might be improved if the best popular Yiddish writings were translated into Russian. He had acted upon the suggestion, but in vain. He also gave a reading in Manchester, at which the chair was taken by Dr. Weizmann, who was at that time a lecturer on biochemistry at the local University.

After a stay of a couple of months Sholem Aleichem went to Switzerland, where he wrote a play for the celebrated Yiddish actor of America, Jacob P. Adler. He came back to London to read the play to Adler, who was then appearing in the East End, and I was invited with one or two other friends to be present at the reading, which took place in a bedroom at the Three Nuns Hotel in Aldgate. One of those present was Sholem Asch, then a slim and shy young man of twenty-five, who had just arrived in England and was staying at the same hotel. The play, which was called *David ben David*, had as its central figure a young Jewish millionaire, who was fired by the ambition to establish a Jewish State, but after he had aroused frenzied enthusiasm and extravagant hopes his mind became unhinged and he met with a tragic end. We followed the dramatic developments, which were relieved by flashes of humour, with silent and tense expectancy, as Sholem Aleichem read his manuscript with varying inflexion and suitable gestures. Adler fidgeted and nodded his head occasionally, and when the reading was over he made some criticisms, which the author agreed to consider. A little later Sholem Aleichem went to America on a visit, and I kept in touch with him for some years.

IV

In the summer I decided to take my holiday in Galicia, although that part of Austria was not known to be a pleasure resort. As I had been barred by the Russian Government from entering Poland, I wished to get as near to it as possible by going to Cracow, which I could do without difficulty. Upon mentioning this to a friend, the late Elkan N. Adler, a City solicitor and a bibliophile, he gave me an introduction to William M. Voynich[1], an antiquarian bookseller in Shaftesbury Avenue, who could be useful to me. Voynich belonged to the P.P.S. (Polish Socialist Party) and gave me letters of introduction to two leading members, Ignaz Daszynski, a Deputy in the Austrian Parliament, and Alexander Wronski, a distinguished publicist. I first travelled to Berlin, where I stayed a couple of days, and even during that brief halt I met with evidence of anti-Semitism, as, while sitting outside the Café Bauer in Unter den Linden, I was offered by a kerbside vendor a postcard with an anti-Jewish caricature.

On reaching Cracow I first called upon Wronski to obtain an account of the underground activities of his revolutionary organisation

[1] Husband of E. L. Voynich, authoress of the novel, *The Gadfly*.

in Poland. I found a black-bearded man seated at a pedestal desk, and I no sooner presented my letter of introduction than he pulled open the top drawer on either side and grabbed a revolver in each hand. I calmly asked him what he meant, whereupon he smilingly replaced the weapons, closed the drawers, and said that he just wanted to show me how well prepared he was for any surprise attack. He told me that his real name was Dr. Jodko, but in political circles he preferred to be known as Wronski. He described to me in detail the activities of the central fighting organisation of the P.P.S., which was the principal body engaged in the struggle to secure an independent Poland — the training of patriots in the use of arms, the making of bombs, the spiking of cannons, and the construction of barricades. He told me also how they derived a good part of their funds by seizing money of the Russian Government, and emphasised that they felt perfectly justified in doing so, as they, acting for the future Polish State, were at war with Russia. I found Daszynski — a tall, lean, lantern-jawed figure — equally communicative, but less spectacular: he did not preface his discourse by a display of revolvers. He spoke particularly about the part played by the Polish Socialists of Austria in helping their brethren on the other side of the frontier. Twelve years later, as I shall relate in a future chapter, I met Jodko and Daszynski again — in the resurrected State of Poland.

From Cracow I journeyed to another important city in Galicia, Lemberg, which was the centre of activity of the Ukrainian (or Ruthenian) revolutionary party in Russia. Although more numerous than the Poles in Russia, the Ukrainians did not boast of such a large and energetic organisation, but they also had a special fighting corps, manufactured bombs, smuggled arms across the frontier, and carried on subversive propaganda among the Russian soldiery. From both cities I sent long despatches to the *Tribune*, and I took back with me a photograph of a group of the secret police of Warsaw, which it printed.

On returning to London I called at Voynich's shop to convey greetings from his compatriots and to relate my impressions. He told me that a young member of the P.P.S. had recently arrived as a refugee and he had engaged him as an assistant at one pound a week.

He asked me to accompany him down to the basement, where he introduced me to a tall, thin, fair-haired young man, who was dusting books. The name of the refugee was August Zaleski. He then little dreamed that he was destined to become one day Poland's Foreign Minister and Ambassador in Rome.

In the summer of 1906 there also arrived in London a distinguished Jew from Poland, Nahum Sokolow, then in his middle forties. He was a polyglot journalist and author, and famous throughout the Jewish world as editor of the Hebrew daily in Warsaw, *Hatzefirah*. He told me that the reason why he had come was to investigate the history of the emancipation of the Jews in Western Europe in order to help more effectively in the struggle for liberation in Eastern Europe. As the political conditions in the two regions were fundamentally different, I doubted whether such an inquiry, conducted mainly in the British Museum, could be of much use. In any case, Sokolow did not return to Poland to apply its results. The true reason for his leaving Warsaw was that his paper had to close down owing to financial difficulties. In order to find the means for subsistence he contributed a series of articles to *The Jewish Chronicle*, and as he sought connections with the non-Jewish press too I introduced him to the editor of the *Tribune*. I also took him to Voynich, in whose shop he made the acquaintance of Zaleski, and the friendship that sprang up between the future President of the Zionist Organisation and the future Foreign Minister of Poland proved of no little value to the Zionist cause.

Sokolow remained in London only a short time, as in September, 1906, he was appointed General Secretary of the Zionist Organisation and settled in Cologne. He owed his call to the President of the Organisation, David Wolffsohn, who, being a business man, needed as assistant and counsellor a man of wide culture, well-versed in international affairs, a part for which Sokolow was the ideal choice. He had been an admirer of Herzl and an adherent of the Zionist movement from the First Congress, and he brought to its service a wealth of knowledge, boundless energy, and remarkable versatility. I next met him at the Zionist Congress of 1907 in The Hague, where I represented the *Tribune*. This Congress was dominated by the

ADVENTURES IN JOURNALISM

controversy between those known as Political Zionists, who were opposed to any activity being undertaken in Palestine without political guarantees, and the so-called practical Zionists who pressed for work to be begun without any such guarantees. The principal spokesman of the "politicals" was Dr. Alexander Marmorek, a well-known bacteriologist from Paris, while the most persuasive advocate of the "practical" school of thought was Dr. Weizmann. The result of the argumentative battle was the decision to establish an office at Jaffa, under the direction of Dr. Arthur Ruppin, to begin practical work on a small scale.

Ever intent upon exploring new territory I took my holiday that year in Italy, where, in less than a month, I visited ten cities, including Milan, Venice, Florence, Rome, and Genoa. With the help of Baedeker and with the enthusiasm and curiosity of youth, I studied and inspected everything of historic, artistic, and Jewish interest, and made ample notes. My impressions and observations found expression some months later in a dozen travel-sketches, which appeared mostly in the *Jewish World*[1]. They were translated into German by Noemi Baneth (who afterwards became the wife of my friend Henry Snowman) and published in Berlin under the title of *Israel in Italien*. Thus, my first book was printed in Germany.

From the beginning of 1908 I began to hear rumours of the financial difficulties in which the *Tribune* was floundering, and of the futile endeavours of the proprietor to secure help from wealthy Liberals. Unfortunately, it was too high-brow to secure a circulation large enough to attract an adequate income from advertisements, and as the proprietor was unwilling to sink any more money in the concern, and there was nobody prepared to take it over, it came to an end after a meteoric career of little more than two years. At midnight, before the appearance of the last issue of the paper announcing its own death, all the staff, with heavy hearts, trooped down into the basement to hear some words of thanks from Mr. Thomasson for the loyal support that we had given him, and words of regret for the misfortune he had been unable to avert[2]. Some

[1] Most of these travel-sketches are included in my *Travels in Jewry* (Edward Goldston, Ltd., 1952).
[2] The full story of the *Tribune* is told in the novel, *The Street of Adventure*, by Philip Gibbs.

members of the staff, having scented trouble betimes, had already secured positions in other offices, but most had to wait weeks and even months before they found something suitable. The highest appointment that a colleague of mine obtained, although not until after an interval of several years, was that of an Ambassador. For after the establishment of the Soviet Union, Mr. Theodore Rothstein, who had been the Russian expert in the Foreign Department of the *Tribune*, was made Soviet Ambassador in Teheran.

A couple of months later I went up to Manchester in the spring to spend the Passover week with my family. It happened to be the time when Mr. Winston Churchill, then a Liberal, was contesting the North-Western division of that city, which included the Jewish district of Cheetham. It was the famous by-election caused by his elevation to the Cabinet. As I was leaving the synagogue one morning during the festival I met the late Nathan Laski, the head of the local Jewish community (father of Mr. Neville Laski, Q.C., and of the late Professor Harold Laski), who told me that he was going to take the chair at a meeting in the afternoon on behalf of Mr. Churchill and asked me to support him on the platform. I felt flattered by the invitation and readily agreed. It was a large and enthusiastic meeting, and I had the honour of sitting between the Liberal candidate (who was then unmarried) and his mother, Lady Randolph Churchill, still strikingly handsome, who usually accompanied him on his political campaigns. Although there is no Jewish vote in this country nowadays, the position was different nearly fifty years ago. I appealed to the Jewish electors to vote Liberal on the ground that it was the Liberals who had brought about the political emancipation of the Jews in this country and it was the Conservatives who had passed the Alien Immigration Bill. Mr. Churchill was defeated by his Conservative opponent, Mr. W. Joynson-Hicks, but was shortly afterwards elected for Dundee.

V

I had to become a freelance again. Before the *débâcle* I had been offered the editorship of the *Jewish World* by Lucien Wolf, who was at that time the editor of this paper by day and the foreign editor of the *Daily Graphic* by night. After leaving the *Tribune* office about midnight I used to call on him for a chat, and he would ask me to contribute an occasional article to the *Jewish World*. He also used to write for the *Fortnightly Review* under the pseudonym of " Diplomaticus," besides contributing now and again to the *Neue Freie Presse* in Vienna, and it was therefore natural that, after a time, he should wish to be relieved of the editorship of the *Jewish World*. Not knowing what the fates had in store for me, I declined the offer. So now I tramped up the stairs of one newspaper office after another, was received with sympathy as a victim of the Fleet Street tragedy, and was consoled with promises that never materialised. But thanks to the personal relations that I thus established I secured the acceptance of many of the articles with which I bombarded editors. Besides stories and sketches for the Jewish press, many of which also appeared in America and some (in translation) in the Zionist weekly, *Die Welt*, I wrote a succession of articles on topical subjects, of which there seemed no lack. My discovery in the British Museum of Professor Leon Kellner, Herzl's literary executor and a famous English scholar, provided me with interviews on Austrian Jewry and on " The Cult of English in Austria." The visit to London of Dr. Jacques Faitlovitch, who had travelled in Abyssinia, furnished me with articles on the native Jews of that country, the Falashas. Events in connection with the Zionist movement and the futile efforts to find a substitute for Palestine by Israel Zangwill, who expended his energy and sarcasm in public speeches of an hour-and-a-half attacking Zionist policy, always provided interesting " copy." An International Congress for the History of Religions at Oxford, at which Professor Paul Haupt, of the Johns Hopkins University, tried to show that Jesus was of " Aryan " origin, was a windfall, for I represented six papers there and made twenty pounds in a week. But if there were also other weeks in which I earned more than I did at the *Tribune*, there were far more in which I made much less.

At the same time I took part in communal activities, especially in the work of the Union of Jewish Literary Societies, and when I heard that Sholem Aleichem, while celebrating his literary Silver Jubilee in Russia, began to spit blood and was ordered to Nervi, on the Italian

A JEWISH PILGRIMAGE

Riviera, I got the Union to hold a meeting for his benefit at University College, London. I delivered an address on the life and writings of the sick humorist and made an appeal for funds, supplemented by letters to the press. The total amount that I obtained was a little over forty pounds, a trivial tribute to a great writer. I sent him ten pounds each week, until there was nothing more left, and each time I received a letter brimful of gratitude and humour as though the amount were ten times as large.

Of all my journalistic "scoops" in those days the most notable was one in which Bernard Shaw played a part. A well-known Hebrew author, Reuben Brainin, whose acquaintance I had made at a Zionist Congress, came to London at the beginning of 1909 and told me that he would like to meet Shaw. He had already had talks with leading writers on the Continent, such as Gerhart Hauptmann, and he was anxious to meet the one whom he regarded as the most original of English writers. I, therefore, wrote to Shaw for an appointment, hardly expecting even an answer. To my astonishment Shaw replied that he would be glad if Brainin would have tea with him at his flat in the Adelphi, and asked me to come along too as interpreter. Brainin spoke German as more nearly related to English than the tongue of Holy Writ, but Shaw frankly confessed that his knowledge of that language was only elementary and spoke English, so it was my privilege to translate the remarks of each to the other. The conversation ranged over a variety of topics—the Zionist question, the English translation of the Bible, the Jews' intellectual consciousness, the relative business morality of Jew and Englishman, the need of a race of supermen to solve the social problems arising from the vast aggregations of mankind in large cities, and God's need of man to improve the world. Shaw indulged in paradoxes as usual, as when he explained that he was an advocate of Socialism because that alone would bring about social equality, yet he wished to see a breed of supermen. He was glad to hear that Brainin had written an essay on his dramas in a Hebrew journal many years before, and that when a play of his was produced in a Berlin theatre ninety per cent of the audience were Jews.

Throughout the conversation, which lasted fully an hour-and-a-

ADVENTURES IN JOURNALISM

half, both men paid close attention to my interpretation, and when Brainin rose to leave and expressed thanks for an exhilarating afternoon, Shaw asked him to come and see him when he would be in London again. No sooner did I get back to my room than I wrote out a detailed record of their colloquy, under the title of " Superman and Jew," which was published in the *Evening Standard*.[1] It was reproduced shortly afterwards in Germany's leading paper, the *Frankfurter Zeitung*, was copied in several American papers without acknowledgment or payment, and made the round of the world's press. Shaw evinced his satisfaction by sending me a rather large photograph of himself with an autograph inscription on the mount:

> From G. Bernard Shaw: Souvenir of a visit from Herr Reuben Brainin and Mr. Israel Cohen on the 19th Jan., 1909. The portrait was taken in Stockholm in July, 1908.

Forty years later, when Shaw was in his ninety-third year, and the anniversary of that memorable visit was approaching, I wrote to him to inquire whether I could call upon him again. In return I received a smaller photograph showing him standing, and leaning on a stick, in front of the gate of his house, which bore across it in large letters the name: " Shaw's Corner." On the back, in his clear bold writing, was the note:

> Dear Mr. Israel Cohen. — This will replace the Stockholm photograph. But no visits and no talks. I am too old. G. Bernard Shaw, Ayot St. Lawrence, 16th January, 1949.

I thought that I had secured another " scoop " when, by chance, I heard of an Indian prince who had come to London to see the Secretary for India, then John Morley, in order to secure redress for being deprived of what, he claimed, should have been his share of the inheritance left by his father. I found him in a fourth-floor bedroom in an hotel near Victoria, with a young Hindu servant, and he readily told me his story. His name was Khachar Mansur Ala, and his father, the Chief of the Jasdan State in the Province of Gujarat, died in 1904. The Government of India thereupon, instead of dividing the state equally among the sons and grandsons " according to immemorial custom," put the eldest son on the throne and thus,

[1] February 1st, 1909.

while arranging that the others should receive suitable maintenance, deprived them of their "rightful inheritance and status." After some years of futile effort in India to get the matter put right the prince came to London. He showed me a memorial of some eighty pages that he had submitted to the India Office, told me that he had been waiting many weeks to see Mr. Morley, and asked me if I could help him through the press. I therefore wrote an article on the matter and took it to J. L. Garvin, the editor of the *Observer*, who did a great deal of his work in his home, which was then in Greville Place, Kilburn. Garvin paced up and down the room in carpet slippers and velvet jacket while I did my best to induce him to take the article; but he declined it as he was not convinced of the validity of the claim and thought that publication might annoy the India Office. Nor would any other paper accept it.

VI

Of all the friends of my youth the one to whom I was most closely attached and who was the first to pass away was Henry Ospovat. We had known one another from our schooldays in Manchester, and our friendship continued after we were both in London. As he usually lived in Chelsea or Fulham, we were unable to meet as a rule at any time but the week-end, since the distance that separated us could not be traversed by horse-bus in less than an hour. He no sooner left the South Kensington School of Art than he made good progress as a designer of book-plates and illustrator of books. John Lane, who commissioned him to illustrate Shakespeare's *Sonnets* and *Poems*, held him in such high regard, that when Ospovat was ill on one occasion he called on him in his humble lodgings and brought him a bottle of port and fruit. Ospovat was also commissioned by Messrs. Dent to do drawings for Browning's *Men and Women*, painted several portraits in oil, and worked for a time in the designing studio of Messrs. W. H. Smith. But his most original gifts were not revealed until he began to draw caricatures of popular personalities of the day, such as Marie Lloyd, Harry Lauder, and Beerbohm Tree, when even the most exacting critics began to compare him with the leading caricaturists of the time and to refer to him as a genius. Before he had reached the age of thirty he had already given a one-man show of his varied work, which received lavish praise both in the general press and in art journals. He seemed destined for a brilliant career, but was unfortunately stricken down by an incurable malady when only thirty-two.

In the late summer of 1908 I was in Brighton for a few days, when a sudden downpour drove me to a shelter on the promenade. There, to my surprise, I found Ospovat looking more thin and pale than usual. When I asked him how he was, he replied that he had been examined only a few days before by a London specialist, who told him that he had cancer and could live only another few months. I tried to cheer him up by suggesting that the doctor might be mistaken, but he had no doubts that the diagnosis was correct and was resigned to his fate.

About a month later I had a letter from his sister informing me that he was in a nursing-home near Harley Street. I went to see him and found that the specialist was right. He had a cancerous growth in the chest and was in such pain that he had to be given injections of morphine. His condition became rapidly worse until, after a couple of months, the doctor told me that he did not think he would last more than another day or two. I therefore sent a telegram to his father in Manchester. There had been a rift between them even before Ospovat left home owing to the father's fanatical orthodoxy and the son's religious laxity, and the rift was followed by years of total estrangement. I therefore doubted whether the telegram would elicit anything more than an inquiry about the latest bulletin, especially as I sent it off on a Friday afternoon just before the Sabbath began. To my astonishment I received a wire from the father announcing that he would take the midnight train and asking me to meet him at Euston. It was an act of Sabbath violation that in his eyes, in normal circumstances, would have rendered any Jew worthy of perdition. When I espied him on the platform in the early morning mist, he was trudging along sadly without even a handbag. I expressed my surprise that he, so ultra-orthodox, should travel on the Sabbath, whereupon he replied that he had consulted the Rabbi, who decided that as Henry was on the verge of death, he might go to see him while there was still time. "But you have no luggage," I remarked. "How can I carry on the Sabbath?" was the reply in a tone of reproof.

We walked to the nursing-home, and on entering I whispered to Ospovat's father to remain behind the screen which stood between the door of the sick-room and the bed. I then approached my friend, whom I found in a muzzy state owing to the morphia. I asked him how he felt, and he replied that he would be glad when the end came. I then asked him whether he wouldn't like to see his father, to which he replied that he didn't think his father would care to come. "But suppose your father were near here, wouldn't you like to see him?" He nodded his head drowsily. "Then you'll see him in a moment," I said. His father emerged from behind the screen and I withdrew.

Ospovat lingered on for another few weeks until one afternoon I received a wire from his sister asking me to come immediately. I arrived in time to close his eyes. It was on the 2nd of January, 1909. There were many laudatory notices in the press and a general expression of the great loss to English art[1]. An exhibition of his works, for which arrangements had been made before he fell ill, turned out to be a Memorial Exhibition, and in an article in the *Athenæum* devoted to it the writer, referring to one of his drawings, observed: "One feels that Rodin would claim the author of this powerful drawing as a kindred spirit."

---

[1] The best account of Ospovat's life and work is in *The Work of Henry Ospovat: with an appreciation by Oliver Onions*. Illustrated by Seventy Plates. The Saint Catherine Press, London, 1911.

Chapter Four

IN ZIONIST SERVICE

1904 — 1914

I

FROM the time that I settled in North-West London I felt the need of a Zionist society in that part of the metropolis, as the only Zionist forum in London then was in the East End. The Jewish national movement was regarded as the peculiar craze of foreign Jews, and any Jew born in this country who identified himself with it was looked upon as a crank or at least as odd and abnormal. I therefore thought it necessary that steps should be taken to explode this strange delusion.

Shortly after Herzl's death I discussed the position with some friends, and we convened a gathering of sympathisers at the Hampstead studio of the artist Isaac Snowman in October, 1904. The outcome of this was that we held a well-attended public meeting on January 15th, 1905, in the Board Room of the Hampstead Synagogue, at which we established a society called the London Zionist League. We gave it this name to indicate that membership was not to be confined to any particular district, but should cover as large an area as possible. The first president (although not a founder) was Herbert Bentwich, and I was elected honorary secretary. The inaugural meeting of the League took place at St. James's Restaurant (which was afterwards demolished to make way for the Piccadilly Hotel), and subsequent gatherings were usually held at the Hotel Great Central. Before long we had quite an impressive roll of members, of whom one of the most enthusiastic was a Christian lady, Mrs. Kathleen Manning, who later became the wife of Sir

John (later Viscount) Simon,[1] After six months, however, owing to lack of time I resigned the honorary secretaryship, which was taken over by Mr. (now Sir) Leon Simon, but remained a member of the Executive.

At about the same period I gave a lecture at the Jewish Working Men's Club on Jewish history, with Sir Stuart Samuel, M.P. (an elder brother of Viscount Samuel), in the chair, and before I had spoken for many minutes he whispered to me not to mention a word about Zionism. His ultra-cautious attitude was typical of most English-born Jews at the time, a state of affairs that did not change until after the Balfour Declaration, when he became a Zionist himself.

The apathy that then clogged and cramped the movement in England was in no way lessened by the arrival of Ahad Ha-am (Asher Ginzberg, 1856 - 1927), the creator of Cultural or Spiritual Zionism, despite a sort of glamour that clung to his name. He settled in London in 1907 as the representative of the wholesale tea-business of Wissotzki, with which he had been connected in Odessa. There seemed something incongruous at first about this celebrated Hebrew thinker, whose essays were regarded by some of his disciples almost as inspired as sacred writ, journeying to his office in Mincing Lane every morning like thousands of City men; but by the time he came to England he had already concluded the greater part of his literary labours. He occupied a house in the Belsize Park district, which must have impressed him as a strange contrast to the Jewish milieu in which he had previously lived. I found him anything but the aggressive personality that I had expected from his reputation as a militant controversialist. He was a short, mild-mannered, sandy-bearded man of fifty, with spectacles through which he peered at you with a quizzical look and a half-smile, but his most striking feature was a dome-like head. His home became a place of pilgrimage for both followers as well as others who wished to engage in friendly disputations, and he was always eager to make converts.

I used to visit Ahad Ha-am from time to time, and he honoured me once by having lunch with me in my rooms (smoking a cigarette straight after the soup), but I confess that I was never won over to

[1] She died on March 27th, 1955.

IN ZIONIST SERVICE

his particular brand of Zionism. He was an opponent of political Zionism and primarily concerned not with the material plight of Jewry but with the critical condition of Judaism, by which he understood something different from and more comprehensive than the Jewish religion. The cardinal postulate in his system of thought was the supreme need for a spiritual centre in Palestine, but I was at a loss to understand how such a centre could be created and maintained without an economic basis, a social periphery, and political security. When he made his first appearance at a public meeting in the East End of London, he faced a large attentive audience, who, for the most part, were probably attracted more by curiosity than by a genuine desire to understand his doctrine. During his sojourn in England he wrote little apart from letters, thus consoling himself for his exile by engaging in voluminous correspondence with his friends in various lands — Russia, Germany, America and Palestine. But despite his insistence on the priority of a spiritual centre, in 1917 he joined the Political Committee set up by Sokolow and Weizmann, and after the First World War he recognised the achievements of political Zionism by settling in Palestine for the rest of his days.

The purchase of *The Jewish Chronicle* in 1907 by a group of leading Zionists (including Wolffsohn, Leopold Kessler, Kann, Greenberg, Joseph Cowen, and Dr. N. Katzenelsohn of Libau) was an event of cardinal importance in the history of the Anglo-Jewish community and the fortunes of the Zionist movement.[1] The driving spirit in this transaction was Greenberg, and the Jewish Colonial Trust (the Zionist bank) played a helpful part in the consummation of the deal. Hitherto *The Jewish Chronicle* had been a relentless opponent of the Jewish national cause, but from the moment that it came into Zionist ownership, and under the editorial control of Greenberg (who obtained a life contract), it proved a formidable source of support. Its leading articles now expressed complete agreement with the principles and aims of Zionism, it rebutted the objections that it had previously

---

[1] The full story of the purchase of *The Jewish Chronicle* by a group of leading Zionists is related in Chapter IX of *The Jewish Chronicle: 1841 - 1941* (London: The Jewish Chronicle, Ltd., 1949). The first Board of Directors of the new company consisted of Israel Davis (the former proprietor, as Chairman), L. J. Greenberg (Managing Director), Leopold Kessler, J. H. Kann, and J. Cowen.

advanced, and it devoted far more space than before to reporting events of Zionist interest. When I read a paper on "Zionism and Jewish Ideals" in 1909 at a meeting of the London Zionist League, in reply to an attack on the movement that had been delivered a little while before in Birmingham by Laurie Magnus, a well-known author and uncompromising opponent, *The Jewish Chronicle* printed it in full despite its length. My most distinguished auditor on that occasion was Ahad Ha-am, and my address was afterwards published as a pamphlet.

II

When the *Tribune* came to an end I was able to devote more time to Zionist activity and often spoke at meetings in both the West and the East End. I came into frequent contact with Leopold J. Greenberg (whom I first got to know as editor of a monthly, *Young Israel*), who had served as a member of the Zionist Executive from 1905 to 1907 and continued to act as a political adviser to the President, David Wolffsohn. In March, 1908, he sounded me on the question of going out to Constantinople as political representative of the Zionist Organisation, and when Wolffsohn came to London in the following month to address a mass meeting at the Holborn Town Hall he also had a long talk with me on the subject. Wolffsohn, however, considered me much too young to be a match for the wiles and pitfalls of the Ottoman capital, and chose for the post Dr. Victor Jacobson, one of the leading Russian Zionists. In a further interview he held out the prospect of appointing me as assistant to Nahum Sokolow, who was General Secretary at the headquarters in Cologne.

For some years after Herzl's death Zionism in England was almost riven in two owing to the struggle between the "politicals" and the "practicals," which was aggravated by long-simmering personal differences between the local leaders, while Israel Zangwill, from his "I.T.O."[1] emplacement, bombarded both parties alike with his caustic gibes. The climax was reached at the annual conference of the English Zionist Federation early in 1909 at Sheffield, when the

[1] Jewish Territorial Organisation.

election resulted in the return of Dr. Gaster, a "practical," as president, and of Greenberg, a "political," as vice-president, with a majority of only one over Herbert Bentwich, who belonged to the "practicals." All of the latter who were elected on the new Executive declared that they would not serve with the "politicals," and Dr. Weizmann, who was one of their leaders, firmly adhered to this view. When the conference was over and we were taking leave of one another, he, in an access of emotion, and still addicted to Continental custom, kissed me on the cheek and expressed the wish for an early reconciliation. That kiss from the future President of Israel was the only one that I ever received from a man — except for my father. Dr. Weizmann then returned to Manchester (where he had been a lecturer in biochemistry at the University since 1904), and exchanged some letters with me on the solution of the crisis, but as his proposal, that the Federation should be divided into a northern region (with Manchester as centre) and a southern, would have widened the breach, it met with no support.

After a brief and troubled interregnum, during which I kept in touch with Greenberg, another conference was held in Leeds, where a new and homogeneous Executive of "politicals" was elected under the presidency of Dr. Charles Dreyfus, of Manchester, who had held aloof from the party strife. Dreyfus was the head of an important chemical dye-works and the chairman of the Conservative Association of East Manchester, which was represented in Parliament by Arthur James Balfour, and it was he who, in 1906, first introduced Dr. Weizmann to the author of the future Balfour Declaration. I had been elected on the Executive at Sheffield and was re-elected at Leeds. A few weeks later I was invited to act as secretary and agreed to do so on a half-time basis, so as to be able to continue my literary and journalistic work. The office of the Federation at that time consisted of only one room, partitioned into two, in some premises off Chancery Lane, and most of the business was transacted by Greenberg (whose office was close by) and myself over a cup of tea in a Lyons teashop.

While still at the *Tribune* I wanted to undertake to write a book on Jewish life and therefore obtained an introduction from my chief,

Edward Hawke, to Mr. (later Sir) Algernon Methuen, for whose firm he acted as a reader. Methuen told me that he was interested in Jewish conditions in the East End, as he had at one time been a social worker in the district, and asked me to let him see a synopsis. I drafted the synopsis of a book not limited to the East End but covering all the main aspects of Jewish life throughout the world. Within a few days I was given an attractive contract. I set to work to collect the material and wrote the first chapters while I was secretary of the Federation, but, owing to interruptions, was unable to complete the work for some years.

The summer of 1909 was rendered memorable by the visit to London of a Parliamentary Deputation from Turkey for the purpose of studying the British Parliamentary system and entering into relations with British politicians. It was headed by Talaat Bey, who afterwards became Grand Vizier (and was assassinated in Berlin in 1921), and included two Jews, Sassoon Haskell Effendi and Nissim Mazliah Effendi, as well as Dr. Riza Tewfik Bey, who had a reputation in Turkey as a philosopher. They were known to share the anti-Zionist views of the Young Turks in general, who had overthrown Sultan Abdul Hamid, but the Zionist Federation nevertheless gave a luncheon in their honour at the Hotel Great Central in the hope of inspiring them with more friendly feelings. Riza Tewfik told me that he would like to visit the East End, and I therefore conducted him on a tour one Saturday evening through its highways and byways. I took him to a kosher restaurant, then to a Yiddish play, and finally to a boxing match. On our way back to his hotel, which was off the Strand, we discussed Near Eastern politics, and I tried to find out whether there was any means by which the Turkish Government might agree to an autonomous Jewish settlement in Palestine. " I am quite sure that the Government would never agree," he declared, " and even if you gave me five hundred pounds I could not say anything different, not even for five hundred pounds." I wondered whether he could have been induced to change his mind for six hundred.

Soon after this deputation returned to Constantinople I received a letter from Nahum Sokolow, who was on a visit in that city with

Wolffsohn. The Zionist Executive had already founded two French papers there — *Le Jeune Turc*, a daily for the general public, which advocated autonomy for the nations in the Ottoman Empire, and *L'Aurore*, a Zionist weekly. They were represented for a time in the editorial direction of the daily by Vladimir Jabotinsky (1880-1940), but owing to his criticism of a book on Palestine by Jacobus Kann (a member of the Executive) and to his resenting instructions he resigned (in 1910). Sokolow wrote to me that the Executive also wished to create a scholarly weekly review in French entitled *L'Orient*, to which leading writers in Western Europe would be invited to contribute, and he asked me to obtain the collaboration of English publicists who could provide articles on social and economic problems in Turkey. I secured an article from Mr. Brailsford and promises from other writers, but the project was too ambitious for the time and remained stillborn.

The first Zionist Congress that I attended as a delegate was the Ninth, which was held at Hamburg in December, 1909. There were some stormy scenes there, as the " practical " Zionists had come strongly organised for the purpose of ousting Wolffsohn from the leadership and securing the transfer of the headquarters from Cologne to Berlin. This move, which had been planned months ahead, was led by a combination of Russian, Austrian, and German Zionists, supported by a certain number of delegates from England and other countries. The English delegates who joined in this combination were elected by the Order of Ancient Maccabeans, a friendly benefit society that had secured recognition as an independent Zionist body, and their most distinguished member was Dr. Weizmann. The delegates appointed by the English Zionist Federation were all partisans of Wolffsohn. The task of setting up a new Executive of " practicals " was the business of the Standing Committee (*Permanenz Ausschuss*), of which Dr. Weizmann was appointed chairman, but their repeated attempts to form such an Executive that would secure a majority in the Congress failed owing to the unwillingness of most of those nominated to serve. The hall had been hired only for six days expiring at six o'clock on Friday morning, and from Thursday midnight the Standing Committee made their last feverish efforts, but in vain. They gave up at four o'clock, and thereupon the old Executive — Wolffsohn, Kann, and Otto Warburg — were re-elected amid a tumult of cheers and counter-cries. As Sokolow's name had figured among the various nominations put forward by the Standing Committee, it was obvious that he could no longer continue as General Secretary under Wolffsohn, and he therefore resigned.

III

In February, 1910, I received a letter from David Wolffsohn, inviting me to go over to Cologne, with a view to accepting an appointment at the Zionist Central Office. He wrote that he had had repeated requests from the Zionist Federations in English-speaking countries that correspondence with them should be conducted in English, that he had at length decided to comply with these wishes, and that he would like me to establish and take charge of an English Department for the purpose. Having become familiar with the long-winded German communications from the Zionist headquarters, I sympathised with the secretaries in remote British Dominions who were unable to translate them and finally revolted against the monopoly enjoyed by the German tongue in the official correspondence. So I went over to Cologne for an interview with Wolffsohn, and after discussing the proposal with him and Dr. Max Bodenheimer, Chairman of the Board of the Jewish National Fund (which was devoted to the purchase of land in Palestine), I agreed to begin a few weeks later. I returned to London, tendered my resignation of the secretaryship of the English Federation, and made all preparations for my exodus to Germany. My contract was for a period of two years, but it was more than three times as long before I left Germany — in the middle of the First World War — to return to London.

The Central Office in Cologne was housed in a large flat in the Karolingerring, in the residential part of the city. It included the office of the Jewish National Fund as well as the "Jüdischer Verlag," which acted as a publication department. The personnel had undergone some changes, as one or two other officials besides Sokolow had left, and the office was now under the general direction of Mr. Siegfried Hoofien (a kinsman of Jacobus Kann), who later became

IN ZIONIST SERVICE

Managing Director of the Anglo-Palestine Bank, now known as Bank Leumi le-Israel. The editorship of *Die Welt*, the official organ of the Executive, which had previously been in the hands of Sokolow, was placed under the charge of Dr. Jacob Klatzkin (1882 - 1947), but the latter was not happy in the office, as he was already brooding over those problems of philosophy, the exposition of which in critical tomes brought him some fame in later years.

The only room that was available for me was that in which were stored all the personal belongings of Herzl — his books and bookcases, desks, pictures, and busts — and although little space was left in which to work and move about my discomfort was more than compensated by the inspiration of my surroundings. On one occasion I was visited there by Hans Herzl, who was visibly moved as he fingered some of his father's books. I had first made his acquaintance when he was a boy living under the care of Joseph Cowen, and at the latter's request I invited Hans to come to me from time to time for talks on Jewish history and on Jewish questions in general. I found him rather moody, weighed down perhaps by the consciousness of the great name that he bore and which he was unable to live up to. But it was impossible when he was still in the teens to forecast his future mental development, which led him, after the death of a sister at Bordeaux in 1930, to take his life by shooting himself.

My work consisted primarily in conducting the correspondence of the Central Office and of the Jewish National Fund with all English-speaking organisations, which embraced not only the affiliated bodies in England, the United States, Canada, and South Africa but also the individual societies in Australia and New Zealand, Shanghai and Singapore. There was at that time an ardent Zionist even in Nagasaki, but the little Jewish community of which he was the leading member, as well as himself, had passed away before I visited Japan in 1920. I issued a weekly English bulletin, containing all important news and summaries of the leading articles in *Die Welt*, which was circulated very widely; sent occasional reports to the leading English papers; and studied cuttings of Jewish interest supplied by a London agency. I also wrote a thirty-two page pamphlet on *The Zionist Movement*, and edited a book, *Zionist Work in Palestine*, containing articles by leading authorities, which received very friendly notice in a surprisingly large number of papers.

After the Hamburg Congress there was much criticism and discontent fomented by the Opposition in different countries, which Wolffsohn wished to allay on the spot, but owing to the claims of his business he could not travel often or too far. He had indeed been anxious to visit the United States, as he attached great importance to winning the sympathy of American Jewry, and he urged me to make all personal preparations necessary so that I could set out with him at short notice; but unfortunately the suggestion that was conveyed to the American Zionists met with a frigid response, and a black frock-coat which I had had specially made for the ceremonial occasions in prospect was doomed to hang in my wardrobe, forlorn and forgotten. Barred from America, Wolffsohn decided on a visit to England and asked me to accompany him.

He was given a very enthusiastic reception at the public meetings that he addressed, in the spring of 1910, in London, Manchester, Leeds, and Glasgow. Although a business man, concerned solely with the buying and selling of timber, and lacking the academic training enjoyed by many Zionist leaders, he had nevertheless acquired the art of delivering an effective speech, and, during his presidency, he was certainly, after Nordau, the best speaker in the galaxy of Zionist orators. He generally sketched out his speech in advance and usually interpolated one or two apt quotations from the Bible that could be applied to contemporary matters: indeed, he never travelled without a small Hebrew Bible and a pocket set of chess. His voice was somewhat gruff, but he had a lively humour, a dominating figure, and a charming manner, which compelled attention and earned applause.

Wolffsohn's eagerness to speak in Manchester was in large measure due to the part played by Weizmann at the Hamburg Congress in trying to oust him from the presidency, and also to his desire to correct the disparaging portrait of him drawn by his opponent. He knew that Weizmann, in his Yiddish speeches at Zion Hall in Manchester, usually referred to him as " *der Holzhaendler* " (the timber-dealer), and he resented it. He was certainly not ashamed of his business, nor had he any reason to be; on the contrary, he had a right to be proud of being a self-made man, but was without pride. Born in a humble home, the son of a poor Talmudical scholar, he had passed through a youth of struggle and privation and risen entirely by his own efforts to a position of comfort and wealth. And although denied the advantage of a University education he possessed a great deal of Jewish traditional knowledge, which, combined with strength of character and shrewdness of judgment, served him in good stead as a Zionist leader in the days before the First World War.

While we were in Manchester I called on C. P. Scott at his house in Fallowfield and had a chat about the Zionist situation. He evinced a warm sympathy with Jewish national aspirations and was particularly anxious to learn about the currents of feeling in Constantinople. I also went to see Weizmann in his chemical laboratory at the University. We naturally spoke about Wolffsohn's visit, but in the midst of his test-tubes and retorts he displayed a calmness that he seldom showed on the platform.

Besides addressing public meetings and spending some time at the Jewish Colonial Trust, to the establishment and progress of which Wolffsohn had contributed in very substantial measure, he also took part in a conference between representatives of the Zionist Federation and the Order of Ancient Maccabeans. The Federation challenged the recognition of the O.A.M. as an independent body, a status that had been granted by the Zionist Executive, on the ground that it did not represent a special point of view (like the Orthodox Mizrachi or the Socialist Poale Zion), and the resultant rivalry and recrimination had a very disturbing and depressing effect upon the movement in England. The conference, which was held on Sunday, May 8th, 1910, at Kensington Palace Mansions, where Wolffsohn was staying, was intended to bring about a friendly understanding between the two camps, but the discussion, which lasted the whole day, proved abortive, as the O.A.M. delegates would not surrender the right of direct communication with headquarters. On the following day, therefore, Wolffsohn and I, together with his wife, who had accompanied him on the trip, returned to Cologne.

In the summer of 1910 I went to Switzerland for a holiday and stayed for a time at Vevey. One evening I rode into Montreux, and as I was walking along the promenade that bordered the Lake I met Dr. Weizmann taking a lonely stroll. We had a long chat about the Zionist situation, in the course of which he expressed his disappointment at the outcome of the Hamburg Congress and also the hope that a change of régime would be brought about at the next Congress. Before we parted he took me up one of the narrow streets branching from the main road and, stopping in front of a small pension, he pointed to an upper window and said: "That's where I once stayed in my student days for a franc a day."

IV

Wolffsohn lived in a medium-sized villa, furnished with taste and comfort, about five minutes' walk from the Zionist Office. He always arrived at the Office about midday, after having transacted his business affairs, and generally returned in the afternoon. He took a keen interest in all current matters, especially in the conduct of *Die Welt*, and although the political situation did not involve any great activity on his part he was certainly kept busy by the agitation of the Opposition. Articles attacking him appeared in Jewish papers in Berlin, Vienna, Vilna, and Warsaw, and he seldom allowed them to go unanswered in his own organ. Meetings of the Executive were not frequent, nor was there any need that they should be. When the two other members, Warburg from Berlin and Kann from The Hague, came to Cologne, they sometimes preferred to confer in the more picturesque surroundings of Bad Godesberg, where they could sit on the terrace of a restaurant overlooking the Rhine. Occasionally Wolffsohn would go to Slovakia to inspect timber and would take the opportunity of stopping at Budapest, where he tried to obtain the Government's approval of the constitution of the Hungarian Zionist Federation, but his efforts in this direction were in vain.

The Wolffsohns were childless, they were fond of entertaining,

IN ZIONIST SERVICE

and they were charming hosts. Wolffsohn was at his best on a Friday evening, when, after grace had been said with all the traditional melodies, he would love to relate incidents from his store of experiences. He was rather fond of referring to his visit to South Africa, which he had undertaken (a couple of years earlier) in the interests of his health and which had developed into a triumphal tour. At a civic banquet in his honour in Cape Town he was seated next to the Mayor, whose name was Lieberman, and he found it just as hard to make himself understood in English as his neighbour did in German, whereupon, as though by common inspiration, they began to talk to one another in Yiddish and got on splendidly.

It was at Wolffsohn's house that I first met a number of interesting people who all played a notable part in the Zionist world and who have all since passed away. Perhaps the most important was Leo Motzkin (1867 - 1933), who was then engaged on his monumental history of the Russian pogroms and who presided over many Congresses between the two wars. Another was Aaron Aaronsohn, the discoverer of "wild wheat" in Palestine, who organised a secret intelligence service in that country for the British Army in the First World War and disappeared in an aeroplane over the English Channel early in 1919. Dr. Arthur Ruppin (1876 - 1943) came to discuss the work of the office which he had established in Jaffa, and Dr. Ignaz Zollschan (1877 - 1948), who had made a great reputation with his scholarly work on *Das Rassenproblem*, passed through Cologne on his way from Vienna to London to attend a Universal Races Congress.

Wolffsohn was an easy man to work with, for he was always natural and frank, conscious of his limitations, which he made no attempt to conceal, since these were greatly overbalanced by his gifts and qualities. The last service that I rendered him was in connection with the preparation of his opening speech for the Tenth Congress, which was held in Basle in August, 1911. Two months before the event he invited me to take a walk with him one morning, in the course of which he mapped out all the leading points and ideas that he wished to embody in the address. It was evident from the sequence of his suggestions and the facility with which he unfolded them that he had given them careful thought. He asked me to draft the speech in English on the basis of his outline, and when my draft was ready it was translated into German by a colleague. But this German version was then thoroughly revised and carefully amended by himself, for it was to form not only his opening speech at the Congress but also his valedictory address as President.

Wolffsohn went to the Tenth Congress with the fixed determination to resign. The state of his heart had caused him increasing alarm during the past year, and he had no inclination to go on fighting the Opposition at a cost both to his health and to the movement. Had he wanted, he could have probably retained the presidency for another two years, but he thought it wisest to retire after securing a majority control for his friends over the Jewish Colonial Trust and the Jewish National Fund. And so the Congress, in which there had been many stormy passages, came to a peaceful conclusion with a dramatic scene in which Wolffsohn was kissed on both cheeks by all his previous opponents, headed by Dr. Tschlenow and Mr. Ussishkin. Wolffsohn afterwards drily remarked that he might have been spared those osculations.

The new Executive of " practicals," with Professor Warburg as President, immediately had the Central Office transferred to Berlin, and with it I went too.

V

I enjoyed my eighteen months' sojourn in Cologne, which I remember as a city of leafy boulevards and wooded parks, of clangorous tramcars and horse-carriages, of beer-restaurants and wine-restaurants, of cafés and pastry-shops. I was able to combine some journalism, especially as correspondent for the *Morning Post*, with my office work; and at weekends I often went for excursions on the Rhine or into the country. The people then were amiable and care-free, priding themselves on their *Gemütlichkeit*, and contrasting the geniality of the Rhinelander with the severity or hauteur of the Prussian. They were fond of life and especially of holidays, for which Cologne, as a Catholic and Cathedral city, gave them ample opportunity, with its numerous festivals and saints' days. There was a mingling of military and musical elements, for it was a garrison centre with an opera-house and a large concert-hall. I was present at the first performance given there in 1910 of *Der Rosenkavalier*, which was conducted by Richard Strauss himself, and recall the tumultuous and prolonged applause that broke out at the end of the performance, when the composer appeared on the stage, bowing right and left, triumphantly happy. The Gürzenich Hall was dedicated to classical concerts, but it was also the scene of the principal functions in connection with the annual carnival-tide, which extended over three months. The inaugural event took place on " the eleventh of the eleventh (month)," and from then there was a succession of dances and cabarets every few weeks until the grand climax was reached on Shrove Tuesday. The Master of the Revels, who had to combine wit with showmanship, secured the collaboration of playwrights and poets, artists and musicians, for satirical and topical verse had to be written and catchy songs composed.

The city was given up entirely to three days of merry-making. Thousands of visitors flocked into it to join in the festivities, and the streets were thronged with people, most of them in gay costumes or at least with coloured hats, red and yellow predominating. The climax was reached on " Rose Monday " with an imposing spectacular procession of symbolic tableaux on decorated cars, on which rode the Master of the Revels and his colleagues in gaudy uniforms and fools' caps. It was the season when conjugal fidelity was at a discount, and sociologists noted that the month of December always showed the biggest number of illegitimate births in Cologne. The jollity and junketing on the third day ended at midnight with outbursts of song all over the city, in which one could clearly discern the resounding strophe: "*Lieb Vaterland, magst ruhig sein !*"

VI

Berlin forty years ago seemed almost a paradise in comparison with the disastrous change that overtook it after the First World War, not to speak of the catastrophe that engulfed it after the Second. It was perhaps because of the greater measure of tolerance then enjoyed by the Jews and the entire absence of any violent anti-

Semitic agitation that Zionism did not make any greater progress. It was seldom referred to in the leading papers, even though — or perhaps because — some of these were owned and edited by Jews. The Jewish question was, indeed, discussed in political circles and political journals, and it even formed the theme of public lectures by Professor Werner Sombart, who, although critical of Jewish ability, posed as a friend of the Jews and did not betray any symptoms of the Nazi ideologist into which he developed under Hitler. On the other hand, Maximilian Harden, Germany's most redoubtable political writer, being of Jewish origin (his father's name was Witkowski), studiously avoided all references to Jewish matters in his lectures, which always attracted a crowded audience, even to the extent of necessitating the display of a notice announcing: "Sold Out." Berlin offered me the opportunity, which I welcomed, of extending my journalistic activity, and I became the correspondent of the *Glasgow Herald* as well as of the *Globe* (a London evening paper long since defunct), besides contributing occasionally to the *Evening Standard* and other papers. It was there too that I was able to collect the bulk of the material for my book *Jewish Life in Modern Times*, which, although begun before I went to Cologne, was completed during my stay in Berlin.

The transfer of the Zionist headquarters to the German capital gave the movement a vigorous stimulus, although it misled foreign newspaper correspondents into misrepresenting it as a secret instrument of German policy. The fact was that the German Foreign Office was indifferent, as it knew that the Ottoman Government was hostile. There was, indeed, little for the Zionist leaders in those days to do apart from systematic propaganda, pending more favourable times. The new Office was located in a quiet residential street in the West End, off the Kurfürstendamm, and comprised only the Central Office, the "Judischer Verlag," and *Die Welt*, as the office of the Jewish National Fund remained behind in Cologne. But the Berlin Office soon expanded under the new Executive, and additional departments were created for the purpose of correspondence with the Zionist Central Committee in Russia (located in Vilna) and with the Warsaw headquarters of the Zionists in Poland. It was a scene

IN ZIONIST SERVICE

of constant activity, for not only did we have as close neighbours the headquarters of the German Zionist Federation, with its weekly organ, the *Jüdische Rundschau*, appearing cheek by jowl with *Die Welt*, but there were more frequent meetings in the conference room and a much larger stream of visitors both from Germany and abroad than had been possible in Cologne. Moreover, whenever members of the Executive wanted to address a public demonstration, they could do so with the certainty of a more resounding echo than could have been expected in the Rhineland. It was even possible to get an occasional news item about the movement printed in the *Berliner Tageblatt* or the *Vossische Zeitung*, an event that aroused all the more gratification because of the general apathy of German Jewry to the Zionist cause.

The outstanding member of the Executive was Nahum Sokolow (1861 - 1936), who, after leaving Cologne, spent nearly a year in Warsaw, where he revived his Hebrew daily, *Hatzefirah*, and then settled in Berlin. A scholar of multifarious range, embracing both Rabbinic and secular learning, an accomplished polyglot, a prolific writer, a popular speaker, and an entertaining *causeur*, he possessed the presence and the poise of the ideal diplomatist. He took the political affairs of the movement under his charge, but that did not amount to much in those days, since the Young Turks were just as hostile to a large Jewish settlement in Palestine as the old Sultan had been. Thanks to the political calm Sokolow came to England in 1912 for a twofold purpose: to revive the interest of the British Government in the aims of Zionism, which had lapsed since the rejection of the East African project in 1905, and to seek some means of inducing the Tsarist Government to abandon its policy of antagonism. In neither respect did his efforts prove fruitful, as the British Government were then preoccupied with the Balkan problem, and there was no general agreement as to the most suitable personality for a mission to St. Petersburg.

But after returning to Berlin he came back to London again early in 1913 and was received at the Foreign Office, thanks to the friendly mediation of a former British Consul in Warsaw, Captain Arthur Cecil Murray, who had become assistant secretary to Sir Arthur

Nicolson, then Permanent Under-Secretary for Foreign Affairs. He had previously submitted some memoranda and had a long talk with the Earl of Onslow (Sir Arthur's private secretary) and Sir Walter Langley, in the course of which he urged the desirability of Britain taking an interest in Jewish colonisation in Palestine on both humane and political grounds. The representatives of the Foreign Office replied that Great Britain was not entitled to protect anyone in the Ottoman Empire except its own subjects, whereupon Sokolow pointed out — what was new to them — that all the Zionist financial institutions in Palestine (the Jewish National Fund, the Anglo-Palestine Bank, and the Palestine Land Development Company) were registered as English companies. He then informed them that he was leaving shortly for America and asked to be permitted to submit further material on Zionist policy. He was assured that further information "would be read with great interest," and that on his return to England he would be furnished with recommendations to the British representatives in Turkey and Palestine.

Sokolow then went to the United States, where he achieved much success by his speeches and lectures in many cities and infused new vigour into the movement. In Washington he was received by the Secretary of State, William Jennings Bryan, who evinced sympathy for Zionist aspirations, and in New York he secured the formation of a company for economic enterprises in Palestine, the chairman of which was an eminent lawyer, Louis Dembitz Brandeis, who afterwards became a Judge of the United States Supreme Court. From the United States Sokolow went to Canada, where he also met with an enthusiastic response, and then returned to Berlin to take part in the conflict over the language question at Jewish schools in Palestine.

This conflict was the most important issue that engaged the attention of the Zionist Executive in Berlin. It was provoked by a change of policy on the part of the leaders of the German Jewish philanthropic organisation, the "Hilfsverein," who, although at first in favour of Hebrew as the medium of instruction in their schools, gradually sought to displace it by German. This attempt was bravely resisted by most of the teachers, who went on strike, with the result that new schools were opened with Hebrew as the medium.

Matters were brought to a head in connection with the projected Technical Institute at Haifa, the building and equipment of which had been largely financed by Russian and American Jews. The support derived from America was almost entirely due to the personal efforts of Dr. Shmarya Levin (1867 - 1935), a member of the Zionist Executive, who had carried out a propaganda tour in the interests of Hebrew culture, while the interests of the Russian contributors were represented in the Board of Governors of the Technical Institute by Dr. Levin as well as by Dr. Tschlenow, another member of the Zionist Executive, and by Ahad Ha-am. On the other hand, the heads of the " Hilfsverein " also provided a certain amount of money for the Institute, and they were the principal officers of the Board. The controversy raged long and furiously before a compromise favourable to the Hebraists was reached eventually, though the outbreak of war in the following year rendered it quite superfluous.[1] It was not clear at the time why the " Hilfsverein " leaders had suddenly become such zealous champions of German *Kultur* in the Holy Land, but when the First World War broke out it was commonly said that it was due to secret pressure exercised by the German Government in pursuance of their *Drang nach Osten* policy. No other explanation seemed so reasonable and convincing.

The most assiduous combatant in the language conflict was Shmarya Levin, who had formerly been a " Crown Rabbi "[2] in Russia and a member of the Duma. He united in his style of oratory the erudition and fervour of a religious leader with the practical outlook of a politician, and words and ideas gushed from him in a tempestuous and unceasing stream. He addressed meetings in all parts of Europe except Russia, to which he could not return without serious risk ; he always spoke for at least an hour, by which time he was bathed in sweat, for his hands worked in vigorous accompaniment to his speech ;

[1] I wrote a pamphlet on the subject, under the title of *The German Attack on the Hebrew Schools in Palestine* (published by *The Jewish Chronicle*, 1918).

[2] According to a Russian law of 1835 the main functions of the " Crown Rabbi " were to act as registrar of births, marriages, and deaths and to impress upon the Jews observance of the moral laws and obedience to the laws of the State and to the appointed authorities. His office was quite distinct from that of the spiritual Rabbi, who had to have a seminary training and combine Talmudical erudition with unimpeachable piety and ritual conformity.

and when the meeting was over he would be escorted by a band of admirers to a café, where, after some refreshment, he would become engrossed in a game of chess.

VII

Apart from the language question, the main issues with which the Zionist Executive in Berlin were concerned were the continued conflict — though on a diminished scale — between the " practicals " and the " politicals " and the control of the financial institutions. The meetings of the " Actions Committee " were attended by Wolffsohn, who loyally respected the new leadership while criticising it, but he firmly insisted on the management of the Jewish Colonial Trust and the other banks as well as of the National Fund remaining in the hands of himself and his friends. These matters again formed the dominating themes at the Eleventh Congress, which was held in Vienna, in September, 1913. The choice of city was a concession to the Zionists of Austria and to those of Eastern Europe in general, but the motive suggested by Wolffsohn's friends was that Vienna was considered by the Executive to afford a more favourable terrain on which at last to beat him on the question of the banks. In any case the local Jewish community, the largest and most important in Central Europe, provided a worthy meeting-place and a resonant sounding-board for Israel's biennial parliament.

It was my first visit to the Austrian metropolis. I found it possessed of beauty and dignity, of charm and gaiety. It was still the hub of a mighty empire, with its medley of contending nationalities and an atmosphere of good living and sprightly music. In the cafés were whiskered officers in gorgeous uniforms with clinking swords, reading the papers or ogling some pretty woman, and little dreaming that within a few years Vienna was to be reduced to the bankrupt capital of a petty Republic.

The Congress was attended by over five hundred delegates, including a larger number from the United States and Canada than at previous Congresses. Among them was Professor Solomon Schechter, head of the Jewish Theological Seminary in New York, who had recently created a sensation in American Jewry by the announcement of his adherence to the Zionist movement. I was particularly pleased to meet this sage and venerable scholar, as I had been a student of his when he held the Chair in Hebrew at University College some fourteen years before. Another American delegate whom I met for the first time was Mr. Louis Lipsky. He was then assistant-editor of the *American Hebrew* (which was edited by the historian and folklorist, Joseph Jacobs), and our meeting resulted in my becoming the Berlin correspondent of the paper — a function that I was able to discharge even during my subsequent internment in Germany.

The Vienna Congress was distinguished in some respects from all the previous ones. For the first time Nordau, whose brilliant survey of world Jewry had always formed the attractive prelude, had failed to appear, and his absence was in no way mitigated by his written message, conveying a warning against any reckless handling of the financial institutions, which sounded like a veiled reprimand of the Executive. His place was taken by Nahum Sokolow, whose speech was factually satisfactory but inevitably suffered by comparison. For the second time Hebrew played a conspicuous part in the deliberations: a Hebrew address was given by Shmarya Levin with his usual fire and force in the opening session, and in a later session devoted to cultural matters several delegates spoke in that language.

The greatest enthusiasm was aroused by speeches in which Menachem Ussishkin and Dr. Weizmann pleaded for the establishment of a Hebrew University in Jerusalem, partly in the interests of the Jewish spiritual renaissance and partly in the interests of the Jewish students of Central and Eastern Europe, who had already begun to suffer from harsh discrimination — either exclusion or limitation — at various universities. It was announced that a fund for the purpose had already been started with a substantial gift from an anonymous well-wisher. The donor was David Wolffsohn, who was anxious that the benefits of higher education that had been denied to himself should be enjoyed by others. He had been elected President of the Congress and presided with exemplary impartiality, although he had to listen to sharp criticism of his previous régime. The inflexible stand that he made on the question of the financial institutions proved victorious: he and his friends remained in control of the banks and the Jewish National Fund. Little did he dream that it would be his last Congress, for within twelve months he passed away at the age of fifty-seven. Little did all others dream that there would not be another Congress for another eight years. And still less did anybody imagine that it was the last Congress of its kind, at which it was possible for Russian Jewry, the fount of so much inspiration in the past, not only to be represented but to play a dominant part in moulding the future of the Jewish national movement.

VIII

The three years that I spent in Berlin passed on the whole quite pleasantly. Throughout that period I lived in the Bayreuther Strasse, not far from Wittenberg Platz, and within convenient walking distance from the Zionist Office. My life fell into a sort of routine. I was always busily occupied, for in addition to my work at the Office I wrote a news story for the *Glasgow Herald* six evenings a week, and plodded away at my book, *Jewish Life in Modern Times*. I posted my despatch for the paper at the Bahnhof Zoo in time for the night-train for the Hook of Holland, but never sent a telegram as the important events of the day were covered by Reuter. Then I went to a neighbouring restaurant for supper, and afterwards to the Café des Westens, nicknamed " Café Grössenwahn " (Megalomania), in the Kurfürstendamm, where I could browse over English and other foreign newspapers at leisure and chat with some of the interesting habitués who gathered there every night. It was from one of these that I first heard the name of Einstein as a man of extraordinary brilliance, some years before any inkling of his genius reached the general world.

There was, of course, no lack of opportunities for social diversion and intellectual recreation both within the Jewish community and without. There were many Zionist gatherings, of which the most spectacular was the students' *Kommers* (" beer evening "), where, under the spirited command of the chairman, accoutred in a gorgeous uniform and armed with a sword that did duty alternately as gavel and baton, young Israel, wearing blue and white sashes (the Zionist colours) showed that they could drink as copiously and sing as lustily as any corps of pure-blooded and cheek-slashed Teutons.

At least once a year I visited England, stayed with my family, looked up friends, and addressed Zionist meetings in London and the provinces. By the end of 1913 I had finished my book and brought the manuscript over to London, so as to deliver it personally to my publishers.[1] And when I returned to Berlin early in 1914 I looked forward to a period of continued tranquillity, for even the best informed of newspaper correspondents had not the least glimmering of the world crisis that was slowly approaching.

---

[1] When my *Jewish Life in Modern Times* was published by Methuen & Co. in 1914, it met with a very good reception in England and America. In the *Nation* Israel Zangwill described it as "the most compact and comprehensive work of its kind in existence, a treasury of facts and figures which should be in the hands of every student of the Jewish problem." The *Daily News* wrote: "The best attempt of the kind that exists. . . . It is encyclopædic." The *New York Times* wrote: "An admirable piece of work, which almost completely answers any question on the Jewish race of the present day which an intelligent reader could fairly demand from him. It is written in a terse and distinguished style."

Chapter Five

INTERNMENT AND IMPRISONMENT
1914 — 1916

I

WHEN Austria declared war upon Serbia at the end of July, 1914, I discussed the situation with a journalistic colleague who had been living in Berlin for ten years and was regarded as an expert on international affairs, and he agreed with me that the conflict would most likely be localised and that there was little probability of England being dragged in. So, without feeling uneasy about the future, and never dreaming of the possibility of such a thing as the internment of civilians, on the morning after the first Austrian shots were fired across the Serbian frontier I took the train for Schandau, a pleasant health-resort just beyond Dresden, to enjoy a holiday. And I thereby wrought my own undoing, for it was not until twenty-two months later, of which I spent nineteen in an internment camp, and during which I was imprisoned three times, that I was able to set foot on English soil again.

I had not been at Schandau more than a few days before I personally felt the impact of war. When I called at the local post-office for my correspondence I was followed in by a policeman, who wanted to see my passport. I produced the document and satisfied him that I was a harmless holiday-maker and not a Russian spy who was said to be lurking in the neighbourhood. But immediately after England declared war upon Germany I was visited by a big, burly gendarme, armed with rifle, revolver, and sword, who also wanted to see my passport and took possession of it. He told me that he would have to send a report to the Commandant of the nearest garrison

INTERNMENT AND IMPRISONMENT

and asked me to call on him in three days. When I returned his visit I was informed that I would be watched carefully but treated considerately, that I was not to walk beyond the limits of the town, and that when I wished to go back to Berlin the passport would be returned to me. So I remained and recuperated at Schandau until the end of August, when I retrieved the precious document and travelled back to Berlin.

On reaching my lodgings I was told by my landlady that I had to go to the *Polizei Präsidium* (Police Presidency) to obtain a permit of residence. I went, and the unexpected sequel to my application was that I was arrested and taken to an adjoining prison called *Stadtvogtei Gefängnis*. The warder who received me thrust a small bundle of laundry into my hands and conducted me to a corridor on an upper floor, where he unlocked a heavy door, ushered me into a large cell, and locked the door behind me with a resounding clang. There were already two prisoners in the cell, which was for four. They were both Russian Jews, one who had settled in South Africa and had come to Germany on a visit, and the other a medical student who was attending lectures at the Berlin University. They told me that they had been in the jail since the beginning of the war, and when, in answer to their questions, I hazarded the view that the war might last about six months they were stupefied.

The cell was a clean, white-painted room, with a lofty barred window looking down upon a courtyard. There were two tiers of two beds each and a long plain table with four stools. On the wall were four small racks, each containing some eating utensils, a washing-basin, German New Testament and Prayer-Book, and a printed booklet of prison regulations. There was also a sort of chart with designs showing a different position for the mattresses and bolster for each day of the month; and there was a water-tap and sink, with an adjoining lavatory.

At three o'clock all cells were unlocked and unbolted, and all the inmates of the jail trooped out into the courtyard, where we were allowed to stroll about for an hour. There were about a hundred fifty altogether, the majority Englishmen and the rest Russians, Frenchmen, and Belgians. They were mostly between the ages of twenty and forty and had been imprisoned since the beginning of the war. Soon after we returned to our cell the door was again unlocked, and two convicts, under the charge of a warder, brought in a pail of whitish soup for our "supper." It was a glutinous and repulsive concoction, which I emptied into a bucket, but my fellow-prisoners tackled it bravely and gave me some of their bread and cheese to stay my pangs.

We had to be in bed by nine as the electric light was then switched off by the warder in the corridor. My companions soon fell asleep, but I remained awake for hours. The mattress was as hard as the floor, and I kept tossing and turning from side to side incessantly, as my whole body ached. Throughout the night I heard the slow, stealthy tread of the warder in the corridor and had an eerie feeling every time he reached our door, when he stopped, lifted the disc over the peep-hole, and peered into the darkness of our cell.

At half-past six in the morning our door was unlocked again and we got up and washed. Half-an-hour later a couple of Polish convicts brought in a pail of brownish liquid, which they called *kawa* (coffee), and another came with a basket of chunks of brown bread, or *chleb*. Then a warder came round for orders for foodstuffs which we were allowed to get from outside, and I put myself down for some butter and cheese, besides a shilling dinner from a neighbouring restaurant. Soon afterwards we again trooped down into the yard, where I extended my acquaintance with my fellow-prisoners and heard stories of their varied experiences.

The hours dragged on like days and the days like months until the morning arrived when an official from the Prussian War Office paid his periodical visit to listen to personal petitions for release. He could see only about a dozen men each time, but fortunately I secured a good place in the line of applicants outside his room. He was a tall, ascetic-looking individual, with high red collar and glistening brass buttons on his blue tunic. He politely offered me a chair, said that in England all Germans of military age were interned, and asked me what I had to say for myself. I replied that England had no conscription, that if I had remained at Schandau I should have been left at liberty, and that some friends of mine on the staff of the Berlin University could vouch for my character and conduct. The result was that he gave me a permit entitling me to immediate release: he told me to take it straight to the police station in my district and to present myself there every third day. A warder showed me down the stairs into the street, and as I slipped a coin into his expectant palm I drew a deep breath of relief. The following day all who were still in the prison were transferred to the Ruhleben Concentration Camp, a few miles from Berlin.

II

At my local police-station an official stamped my permit on the back with the date and returned it to me with a curt: " Every third day now." My visits to the place became outstanding events in my life during the next couple of months, for my continued liberty depended upon them. Having nothing else of importance to do, I killed time by going occasionally to the American Embassy, in front of which Englishmen used to foregather to pick up news, but after we were warned that the German police might seize some of us for examination I gave up those excursions. I found it safer to visit the Reading Room belonging to the American Church in the Motz Strasse, where I was able to read American papers, particularly literary periodicals.

I felt too restless to attempt any writing and was unable to send any despatches to the newspapers of which I was the correspondent, but as I wished to communicate with my family I obtained a letter of introduction to the Chief Censor, Dr. Matthias Erzberger, a leader of the German Clerical Party, from my Zionist friend, Dr. Franz Oppenheimer (1864 - 1943), a well-known economist. I was readily admitted into the office of Dr. Erzberger, a burly, scholarly-looking man, who gave me the required facilities; but as I left him I little dreamed that he was destined some four years later to sign the pact of surrender on behalf of his country and then to be assassinated by a fanatic as a reward for his courage.

Towards the end of October there was an increasing agitation in the Berlin press for the internment of all Englishmen in Germany as a reprisal for the internment of Germans in England. I therefore prepared for the evil day. I packed all my books, papers, and other belongings in the wooden cases that I had brought from London four-and-a-half years before, and had them transported to the safe asylum of the Rabbinical Seminary, at which my friend, Dr. Ismar Elbogen (1874 - 1943), was a Professor. I retained only my clothes and other personal possessions, which I kept in a suit-case, and patiently awaited the hour of doom.

It came at seven in the morning, on November 6th, 1914. My landlady tapped at my door to inform me that a gentleman wished to see me, and I knew his mission before he spoke. He was a police detective who had come to take me away, but he allowed me time to get ready. He told me that all British subjects between the ages of 17 and 55 throughout the German Empire must be arrested and transported to the Concentration Camp at Ruhleben. He advised me to take a blanket, pillow, and bed-sheet, as well as toilet requisites, and my landlady whimpered as she made a parcel of the bedding. Then, carrying my suit-case, I accompanied my captor to the police-station, while the servant-girl tripped behind us with the bedding. There were a dozen Englishmen already waiting there, with their bags and parcels, and after all our personal particulars had been noted we were driven in taxi-cabs — at our own expense — to the *Stadtvogtei* Prison.

On arriving at the jail we found a long queue of taxi-cabs in front of us, for hundreds of Englishmen had been collected from all parts of Berlin and beyond. We were hustled into single cells, which were locked and bolted; left to our melancholy thoughts for a few hours; and then ordered out again with our baggage. In the street was a long avenue of armed policemen, between whom we had to march four abreast, and as some men found it difficult to keep in step owing to their burdens they were yelled at and abused as "*Englische Schweinehunde!*" We were taken to the Alexander Platz station of the City Railway, and from there conveyed in special trains to the *Auswanderer Bahnhof* (Emigrants' Railway Station). There we lined up again in fours, were bawled at repeatedly by the truculent policemen, and after trudging along on a country road for some distance we came to a big wooden gate, which swung open, and

INTERNMENT AND IMPRISONMENT

above which, on the cross-bar, was the legend: *Trabrennbahn Ruhleben*. It was a trotting-course: my new home for the next nineteen months.

III

I do not propose to narrate here a detailed history of the Ruhleben camp during the period of my internment, as I have already done so in a previous book[1], but as this has long been out of print, and as a new generation has since arisen that has probably never heard of the Camp, I think it desirable to give at least a summary account of its conditions, besides the story of my own personal tribulations.

At the time when I entered the Camp the accommodation consisted of eleven stables, from which the horses had been removed a couple of months before, and each horse-box was furnished with four military beds — two fixed on each other on either side — four chairs and a table. The horse-boxes were assigned to the older men and those who were respectably dressed, and after they were all occupied the rest had to mount the steep narrow staircases to the hay-loft, where they had to arrange themselves as comfortably as they could on a thick layer of straw. We were each provided with a military blanket, a towel, and a pewter bowl, all of which showed signs of previous long usage. There were only twenty tin washing-basins for the 200 men in each barrack, as the stable was called, and there was only one tap, so that the pandemonium in the mornings can easily be imagined. We were marched, always four abreast, to the kitchen three times a day to fetch our meals — coffee *Ersatz* and black bread in the morning, vegetable soup at midday, and cocoa *Ersatz* in the afternoon — but these were all so repulsive that we bought what food we could from the canteen until we began to obtain parcels from England. Throughout the first week there was a constant succession of arrivals in large contingents from all parts of Germany. They comprised all sorts and conditions of Englishmen — old residents in the country, tourists, students, people who had been taking a cure at Wiesbaden or Homburg, and hundreds of merchant seamen and fishermen. There was also a considerable number of coloured men

[1] *The Ruhleben Prison Camp* (Methuen & Co., Ltd.), 1917.

A JEWISH PILGRIMAGE

from Britain's colonies — the West Indies, West Africa, and Aden — who were assigned to a barrack of their own.

At the end of the first week we were all lined up in front of our barracks, and the Commandant ordered all Jews who wanted kosher food to step out. This segregation was apparently prompted by a desire to respect our religious principles, but it entailed periodical pinpricks and even petty persecution for the two hundred odd who responded. We were first removed to the waiting-room of the Emigrants' Railway Station, where there was only a thick layer of straw to lie on, and where the space scarce sufficed for one-fourth of our number. We had to make our beds with our blankets on the straw and also to find room for our luggage, so that after we had all squatted down we were so closely packed that it was almost impossible for anybody to move about without treading upon somebody. Our kosher food was provided by the Soup Kitchen of the Berlin Jewish community and was brought in pails in a motor-car, but the satisfaction that it afforded us at midday on the Sabbath was turned into distress at midnight when we were attacked by an epidemic of diarrhoea. The cause of the trouble was due to the fact that the food had been cooked on Friday and remained in the coppers until Saturday, when it was heated up again and absorbed some of the metal lining. It was a ghastly experience, which at first resulted in a sudden diminution of the zealots for kosher, but after the kitchen authorities had taken the requisite precautions confidence was restored and the deserters returned.

After four harassing days in the crowded, smelly waiting-room we were marched back into the Camp and allotted to Barrack VI, a stable that had the distinction of being nearest to the latrines. We were under the charge of a big, blustering guard, a policeman in civil life, who could not give an order without yelling and abusing us as "*Sau-Juden*" or "*Verdammter Judenpack*." There were a dozen horse-boxes on either side of a stone-floored passage, and each box, about ten foot square, had to be occupied by six men. The boxes were filthy, reeking of dung, and bare of everything except cobwebs. We had to fetch straw from the railway-station to cover the stone floor, and spread over it our military blankets, on which we lay at

IN THE RUHLEBEN PRISON CAMP, 1915
The Author is in the centre of front row

INTERNMENT AND IMPRISONMENT

night side by side, covering ourselves with our own blankets and overcoats

After a couple of weeks we were each given a sack into which we stuffed the straw and also a small sack for a pillow; and six weeks later we were at last furnished with beds, which we had to carry from the railway station. They were grimy, rusty, ramshackle bedsteads, which we had to fix up in three tiers of two each against three walls, leaving just enough room to get to the manger, which was used as a receptacle for tinned foodstuffs until we put up some little cupboards and shelves. We had a floor-board for the centre of the box, and bought a folding-table from the canteen. There was no heating for the first fortnight, and when the steam-pipes were at last installed they functioned only from midday until the early evening. The conditions in the hay-loft, which was overcrowded and insanitary, were much worse, and after the place was condemned by the American Ambassador on one of his visits it was cleared.

We soon became reconciled to our segregation, which was even welcomed by the more observant among us, as they were able to hold religious services undisturbed. There were daily prayers in one orthodox horse-box, while Sabbath services, attended by a larger number, were held in the central passage. On the approach of Passover in 1915 we were provided by the Jewish communal authorities of Berlin with the dietary requisites for the celebration, which were sold in a wooden shed built close to our barrack. This shed was afterwards converted into a small synagogue, which was equipped with the traditional accessories, including an Ark of the Law. The creation of this place of worship led to a serious dispute in our little community, for there was a fundamental difference of opinion over the name by which it should be known. Indeed, so vehement at one stage did the controversy become that it utterly blotted out all interest in the war, and the attempt of the visiting Rabbi to effect a reconciliation only led to resignations from the committee. After his departure I was elected chairman of the congregation, and a warden and an honorary secretary were also chosen. I then decided that we should have no more meetings, with the result that henceforth our congregational life flowed in peace.

But although harmony was restored in our barrack we were subjected to occasional annoyance by some of our fellow-captives solely on account of our being Jews. There was a Camp magazine that printed insipid anti-Semitic jokes until I argued with the editor and convinced him of the folly and injustice of such malicious gibes. There was a little cinema in the Camp at which the film *The Shylock of Cracow* was shown, and when there appeared on the screen the figure of a grey-bearded old Jew gloating over a heap of coins somebody called out " Barrack Six ! " and there was a guffaw of laughter. When a passing agitation arose for a badge or medal to commemorate our captivity, some posters were stuck on our barrack wall, giving as a design " Façade of Barrack VI " and as motto: " *Ich dien* — if released." The sting contained in those last words, that Jews sought their release by volunteering for the German army (for there were indeed some cases in various barracks of German-born sons of British subjects, both Christians and Jews, having so volunteered), was more than I could bear. At a crowded meeting, therefore, attended by men from many barracks, on the morning when those posters appeared, I went on the platform and lashed out against the anti-Semitic coward who skulked behind anonymity, challenging him to step up and vindicate himself. I pointed out that anti-Semitism was cruel enough to the Jew in freedom, who could shun it or shelter himself from it; but in a prison camp, from which there was no escape, it made the Jew drink the cup of bitterness to the dregs. Fortunately the numerous academic element was free from any anti-Jewish prejudice, and I received an attentive and sympathetic hearing when (by request) I read chapters from my *Jewish Life in Modern Times* (the first copies of which reached me at the end of 1914) at meetings of the Historical Circle and the Social Problems Circle.

IV

By the time that all British subjects in Germany were interned at Ruhleben the Camp contained about 4,500, and the accommodation had to be increased by the construction of a dozen wooden barracks,

INTERNMENT AND IMPRISONMENT

which were more habitable than the stables. The administration was divided between the military authorities, whose main business was to prevent us from escaping, and our own barrack captains, whose function was to look after our interests and comfort. The authorities spent a minimum on necessities for our welfare, especially food, and were it not for the parcels that we received from England and from the Red Cross in Switzerland we should have starved. The medical staff seldom consisted of more than one doctor, who was kept much too busy to give anything but perfunctory attention, and it was months before there was any improvement. Our spirits were sustained mainly as a result of our own efforts, by means of the various activities and amenities that we introduced, thanks largely to funds supplied by the British Government. We organised a regular school, at which a multitude of subjects were taught by University men. We had musical and dramatic societies, which provided excellent performances, for many of the men were highly qualified and some even distinguished in their profession. We had numerous artists too, who arranged an exhibition of works done in the Camp. There were athletic societies that fostered all forms of sport, from football and cricket to boxing and golf. We had a well-stocked library, of both serious and light literature (sent over from England); and we also had a literary and debating society, of which I was chairman for several months. I spent much time in the library and devoted a great deal of my leisure to the study of Italian.

From a heterogeneous herd of internees, the Camp gradually developed into an organised community, with most of the facets of a free community, supplemented by its own peculiar features. We had our own habits and customs, our fashions and etiquette, our characters and celebrities, our rumours and excitements. Captivity produced little change in most of us, and after the first copious outpouring of mutual sympathy in the early months our individual foibles and characteristics asserted themselves. Cut off though we were from the rest of the world, we had a variety of interests arising from our daily occupations and diversions, from the antipathy between barracks and captains, and from the antagonism between prisoners and guards; we had our cliques and coteries, our gossip and scandal, our problems and politics; though all these things, vital as they were for the time, and reflected in our Camp magazine, were petty beside the ardent yearning for liberty that made us all kin.

V

We suffered not only from restriction of freedom but also from the manner in which it was exercised. We chafed particularly against the limitation of our correspondence (two nine-lined postcards or one four-paged letter per week) and the strict censorship — first by our captains and then by military officials — to which it was subjected. The consequence was that those who had friends or relatives in Berlin were tempted to circumvent these annoying regulations by getting letters smuggled out of the Camp, and it was because I also once indulged in this practice that I again made the acquaintance of the *Stadtvogtei Gefängnis*. I was one of ten who were discovered to have sent out letters through the medium of a German corporal, and as this was regarded as a heinous offence we were summoned one by one to the office of the Commandant, where a red-faced martinet bawled threats at us that we would be sentenced to solitary confinement in a fortress if we did not confess everything. A " protocol " containing an admission of our iniquity was then drawn up for each of us to sign, and a few hours later we were ordered to pack up our things immediately and get ready to be removed.

The ten letter-smugglers were joined by three men who had slipped out of the Camp for the night and voluntarily returned the following morning; and as, heavily laden, we slowly made our way towards the gate a huge crowd assembled, calling to us to cheer up. We were escorted by five soldiers, helmeted and armed, as though we were dangerous rebels, and marched to the railway-station; and from there we travelled all together in a fourth-class compartment, in which several of us had to stand. We were taken to the *Stadtvogtei*, where the leader of our escort counted us as we passed into the charge-room and finished by announcing to the head-warder: " *Dreizehn Stück* ! " as though we were so many head of cattle. For the third time within seven months I was tramping up the stone steps of the same prison and felt almost like an inveterate criminal.

INTERNMENT AND IMPRISONMENT

For the first two days we had a rather easy time, as our cells were left open until six o'clock, so that we could visit one another and go down into the courtyard whenever we wished. Three of my friends and I had a large cell, which was used as a sort of club, in which card-playing was the chief pastime. We were joined by some Belgians, a Frenchman, and a Russian, who occupied a large cell in the same corridor, and who were glad of the distraction provided by our company. One of the Belgians was a poet, who paced the corridor with solemn mien and excogitated verses on his plight in the style of Baudelaire, which he recited while beating the air in time with the rhythm. Another was a vivacious musician, who belonged to the orchestra of the Berlin Opera House and whose only crime was that he had been out of doors one evening after eight. Two other men were suspected of espionage, and I learned the names of two others who were acting as spies in the Ruhleben Camp. The most conspicuous prisoner was a Boer giant, seven-and-a-half feet tall, whose feet always hung out over his bed. He had been the chief of President Kruger's bodyguard, and had been taken prisoner in the South African War and interned in Ceylon. He afterwards wandered through Austria and Germany as a waiter at country beer-restaurants, where he sold signed photographs of himself until his arrest.

After two days we were all moved into single cells and allowed only one hour's exercise in the courtyard in the morning and another hour in the afternoon. The night-warders, however, allowed us all to gather in the Belgians' large cell, which presented a spectacle reminiscent of a scene in *Die Fledermaus*. As the electric light was switched off at nine candles were used, stuck in empty beer-bottles. Besides the prisoners already mentioned there was a tall young Rumanian, who told us that he was an engineering student and wrongly suspected of espionage; and there was also a German Socialist, who had been betrayed by his wife as an anti-war propagandist, so that she could enjoy the embraces of her Danish lover undisturbed. Four of the men at one end of a long table were gambling at cards, with others looking on, and at the other end one of the Belgians was frying potato pancakes in oil on a spirit stove. The Frenchman delivered a mock-heroic speech with his hand on his heart and danced a *pas seul* with astonishing nimbleness, and beside me sat the Belgian poet, who told me of the outrages committed in his country by the Germans. Suddenly, while we were all eating potato pancakes washed down with steaming coffee, the cell was opened by a grey-bearded warder, who announced that we must break up the party. But when he felt some coins pressed into his palm he left us with a warning that we must be ready to leave at eleven. He then returned with a colleague, and after we had made a collection for their benefit we were given a respite until midnight.

A few days later we were visited by a military officer, who asked each of us the reason why we had smuggled letters out and noted our replies. On another day, when we were in the courtyard we saw a haggard face between the bars of a window on an upper floor, and presently a little crumpled note came flying to our feet. We opened it and found it contained a message in German: " A Serbian begs for a cigarette." We put a couple of cigarettes and a few matches into a match-box, which was wrapped up in paper, and one of us deftly threw it into the lonely Serbian's cell. The look of gratitude on his face was one of the things I shall never forget. Scarcely was the incident over than we heard cries of distress from the first floor and the quick rush of feet along the corridor. We hurried up the stairs to the cell from where the cries had come and found that a Belgian who had been brought in that morning had attempted suicide with a razor. He was stopped in time and removed to the hospital on the top floor.

After we had been in prison a fortnight we were suddenly ordered to pack up and get ready to return to Ruhleben. We actually rejoiced to go back, for despite the interesting time that we had had at *Stadtvogtei* the prospect of a prolonged stay there filled us with aversion. We were escorted by seven policemen armed with revolvers, and when we entered the Camp again we were welcomed heartily by our fellow-captives.

VI

We soon relapsed into the drab monotonous routine of Camp life. The succession of plays and concerts, the studies and sports, provided some distraction, but there was always a craving for something new, something exciting. With the collaboration of a friend I wrote the script for a mock trial, a breach of promise case, which proved a great success, especially because of the unexpected dénouement — the judge offering his hand to the jilted bride. But much more popular was a mock parliamentary by-election in the summer of 1915, which I suggested, and which I organised with the co-operation of some fellow-prisoners after obtaining the permission of the military authorities. The idea was to elect an M.P. for Ruhleben who should represent our interests and voice our grievances in the House of Commons. For eight days our "constituency" seethed with the turmoil of a political campaign. There were three candidates, with their agents, committees, and canvassers — a Conservative, distinguished by his portly figure and monocle; myself, true to my early convictions, as Liberal; and a variety artist representing the cause of Woman Suffrage. At a crowded meeting in the Grand Stand Hall, presided over by our "Mayor," a Councillor of the Manchester Corporation, the Conservative candidate promised a number of improvements in the "Borough," including an electric railway; my programme included old age pensions at forty and a compensation of £1,000 a year for all men interned at Ruhleben; while the Woman Suffrage candidate held out the alluring prospect of bringing the men's mothers, wives, and sweethearts into the Camp. There were committee-rooms and open-air meetings, posters and placards, sandwich-men and hecklers, ribbons and rosettes of varied hue; there were demonstrations and recriminations, scrimmages and disturbances; and there was a traditional polling-day, on which nearly two-thirds of the "burgesses" recorded their votes. The result was declared by the "Mayor" at a tumultuous meeting: the Conservative came at the bottom of the poll, I was second, and the victor was the man who promised to bring women into the Camp. But his victory proved an inescapable nuisance, as he was teased and taunted for months because of the non-fulfilment of his pledge.

The excitement quickly died down, and again we were plunged into the dreary round of our monotonous existence. Had we known how long more, even approximately, we should be kept interned,

A JEWISH PILGRIMAGE

we could have borne our lot more patiently, if not contentedly. We scanned such newspapers as we were allowed to see, or were able illicitly to obtain, with all the perspicacity that we could summon, in order to divine how long more the war would last, but we soon realised that it was a hopeless quest. It was this uncertainty, this utter ignorance of the duration of our continued captivity, that aggravated our ordeal and frayed the nerves of weaker natures. As month followed month without any sign of the approach of our release the number of those who sank into a state of depression and melancholia increased, and some had to be removed to a mental asylum. A few attempted suicide, but they were prevented in time. Some others tried to escape, but very few succeeded.

In an atmosphere that bred mental aberration the moral values of society were also not immune. The friction and irritation engendered by the herding of educated men in stables found an outlet in vigorous language that ranged between the merely vulgar and the unprintably obscene. Coarse and filthy vituperations first came from the lips of the lower stratum of our community, to which they were native, but they gradually percolated through the higher strata, until even the university graduate would utter them unblushingly. Oaths and expletives that were bandied by navvies were ironically repeated by respectable business-men, and repeated so often until they became an integral part of their normal vocabulary; and thus every man selected for release to England was advised by his friends to go into a sort of quarantine before venturing to emerge in the bosom of his family.

VII

A report that an agreement had been concluded between the British and German Governments for the exchange of civilian prisoners who were unfit for military service first reached us in the spring of 1915, but not until the following September was the first batch of men sent back to England under this arrangement. All who applied for release had to be examined by the Camp doctor, who gave priority to those whom he had been treating as out-patients and those who had lain in the Camp hospital or in a Berlin sanatorium. My turn for examination at last arrived in November, when I was one of about two hundred who were lined up on a wet, dreary morning outside the doctor's consulting-room. I had been a frequent visitor of his for months owing to my recurrent attacks of sciatica (due to the cold, damp, and draughty conditions of the barrack), for which his uniform remedy consisted of aspirin tablets, and I reminded him of the fact as he examined me. But he maintained a stolid silence and made some mysterious mark opposite my name. A few days later most of those who had been examined were summoned to the Captains' Office to be photographed for their passports, and then followed weeks and months of weary waiting and suspense. Releases took place only on the sixth of the month, but the number to be exchanged from Ruhleben was determined by the number of Germans sent back from England, and the names of those selected were not made known until the day before their liberation.

I had hoped to escape the rigours of a second winter in Ruhleben, but the months passed slowly, the number of those released grew less each time, and my health became worse. My appeals to the doctor, as the year 1916 advanced, merely procured me fresh supplies of aspirins: the business of release, he said, belonged to his colleague. And as the tablets failed to allay the pain with which I cried out in the night, to the distraction of my " box-mates," I one day plucked up courage and hobbled with a stick to the military office to urge my case. I was told that my name had been put down for release on April 6th. But that day came and went, and I was still in the Camp.

At last, after another two months, I was released, together with fourteen others, at six in the morning on June 6th, 1916. We were accompanied by a military escort in the train from Berlin to the frontier station of Goch. There our luggage, which had already been inspected in the Camp, was again thoroughly searched. We were also personally examined by some officials. We emptied all the contents of our pockets on a bench, and each article was closely scrutinised. Then our pockets were searched, our coat collars and lapels were felt, the lining of our hats was turned inside out, and our ties were undone to see if any of them contained a hidden message, while a few of our party had also to take off shoes and socks. At length we were each given our passports, our German escort withdrew, and we entered the Dutch train that took us to Flushing, from where we sailed for England.

Chapter Six

INTERLUDE
1916 — 1917

I

IT naturally took me some time to adjust myself again to life in London, partly because of the change-over from prolonged internment in an enemy country to unfettered liberty in my native land, and partly because it was over six years since I had left England. The process of adjustment was retarded by the fact that not only was it impossible for months to rid myself of the memories and visions of Ruhleben that clung to me, but also because it took a considerable period to liquidate the associations that I had formed there. My most blissful experience on returning to London was to sleep in an ordinary bed, between clean white sheets, in a room all to myself, and although I kept on dreaming of scenes in the Camp or the jail, and even had an occasional nightmare, it was delightful to wake and find myself in my brother's home in Hampstead. Nor was it only in the night that I was haunted by recollections of my captivity, but in the daytime too, at least during the first few weeks, I could not shake off the uncanny feeling, as I was walking in the street, that I was being followed or shadowed by somebody, and I would turn round to make sure that it was merely a delusion.

This state of mind was doubtless induced by the fact that for several months I talked, wrote, and lectured about nothing but Ruhleben. It may also have been due in some degree to a peculiar incident at Tilbury, where my fellow-prisoners and I were landed. After being questioned in an office by several officials, representing various Government departments, as to my personality and treatment

INTERLUDE

in Germany, I was about to enter a train when I was intercepted by two detectives, who spoke to me very sharply. They wanted to know how I had managed to get out of Germany, as though I had committed a grave offence in doing so, and warned me in rather menacing tones that I had "better be careful." I replied that they could get full information about me from the Foreign Office, whose representative had asked me to come and see him in a few days and let him have a memorandum on the latest conditions at Ruhleben. That was by no means the only occasion when Scotland Yard showed an undeserved interest in me. Several months later, when I was living in Brondesbury, I had a visit one evening from a detective, who said that he was looking for an Army deserter who bore the same name as myself, and although he knew that I was not the man, he had been told by his chief at the Yard that he might as well look me up at the same time. He pulled out a note-book and pencil and inquired what I had been doing since my return. I thought his visit and its purpose somewhat of an intrusion, but as it was war-time I promptly complied and kept him so busy taking notes that after twenty minutes he said that he had enough and left me in peace.

There were two men from Ruhleben — one, P., who returned in the same batch as myself, and the other, E., who had come back some time before — who both had rather peculiar experiences. P. told me his story when we were having dinner together in a West End restaurant. He said that he had never applied for release, but the suggestion had come from one of the German officers in the Camp. He had been sent for one day and asked whether he would like to go to Berlin to see a dentist. As he had never complained about his teeth he was surprised by the question, but, tempted by the prospect of a day out, he replied that he would be very pleased to go. The following morning he was escorted into the city by a corporal, who took him to a flat in the Potsdamer Strasse. It was a large, richly-furnished apartment, without a dentist's plate on the entrance door and without the least evidence that dental operations of any kind were conducted there. He was welcomed in the most friendly manner by a man in civilian dress, who made him feel quite at ease and regaled him with appetising refreshments and a good cigar.

The man asked P. whether he would like to go back to England, and, on receiving a reply in the affirmative, said that he could easily arrange this for him if he would render a little service in return.

P. was enjoined to maintain strict secrecy about his visit, otherwise he would get into trouble, and was brought to the flat again twice by military escort for further explanation and instruction. He was told that he would be required to send from London information of a kind that he could easily obtain and that would be useful to the German War Office, and that he would be supplied with a handkerchief impregnated with a chemical for making invisible ink, which he was to use. He was to pen an innocuous note, as though to a relative, in ordinary ink on the back of a postcard, write his secret message between the lines in the ink made from the handkerchief soaked in water, and forward the card to a certain address in Amsterdam. He would receive a reply, of which the material portion would be rendered visible if the card were dipped in a chemical solution. As soon as P. arrived in London he went to the War Office with the handkerchief and related the story of his release. He was therefore requested to attend there every morning for a fortnight and to write bogus messages (supplied to him) in invisible ink, in the agreed manner. The replies that came back from Amsterdam proved to the satisfaction of the War Office that P.'s story was true. He was thereupon dismissed merely with a formal "Thank you."

E., who was a naturalised Englishman born in Germany, told me his story in Brixton Prison. I had known him in Ruhleben as a man who had previously been in solitary confinement in a Berlin jail for four months under suspicion of being an English spy, and several months after he was in the Camp he succeeded, in company with another man, in escaping to Holland. Some time after I had returned to England I was surprised to receive a letter from him written from the Brixton jail, asking me to come and see him. Our interview took place in a gloomy room, with a table between us, and a warder taking notes at one end of the table. E. told me that after reaching Holland he made his way to Rotterdam, where the British Consul, after keeping him waiting a few days while communicating with the Foreign Office, provided him with a free passage to

INTERLUDE

Tilbury, and that he no sooner landed than he was arrested by a couple of detectives and brought to Brixton. He said that the charge against him was that he had volunteered to travel on a Zeppelin on a visit to London and to point out to the captain some important places to be bombed, and that he was to be put on trial very shortly in a special court. He denied most emphatically that he had ever made such a fantastic proposal and asked me if I would be willing to attend the trial in order to give evidence as to his character. As he was known by his pre-war friends in Ruhleben to be a man of irreproachable probity, and he was the son-in-law of a former Mayor of a provincial city, and as the charge against him seemed to me utterly incredible, I readily agreed to appear as a witness.

Accordingly, a few weeks later I was summoned to the trial, which was held at Westminster Hall under the late Justice Sankey. Owing to a previous case, which lasted until lunch-time, a short adjournment was made and a court official told me that I could eat lunch with him and E. in a restaurant inside the building. After the modest repast we were walking back through a long corridor when E. slackened his pace so as to be a little behind the official, slipped a crumpled note into my hand, and called my attention to a near-by lavatory, which he presumed that I wanted. I hurried into the cubicle, read the note, which suggested something that I should say in evidence (and the nature of which I have long since forgotten), and then dropped it into the pan and pulled the chain vigorously. In my testimony, given at one end of a long table, with Justice Sankey at the other end, I stated merely what I knew of E.'s character, which was not very much, and was then dismissed. Some time later I heard that E. was found guilty of the charge, and that he was sentenced to be imprisoned until the end of the war, when he was to be denaturalised and deported to Germany.

Not until a few years after the war did I learn how the evidence was obtained that led to his arrest. He had indeed written a letter making the alleged proposal and addressed it to the German military censor in the Camp, but the latter had to cope with such vast heaps of correspondence that he often had the assistance of an English prisoner. As chance would have it the letter came into the hands of the Englishman, who intercepted it and handed it over to the Camp Captain. The latter decided that the incriminating document should be conveyed to London without delay, and therefore entrusted it to a seaman who was to be released very shortly, and who concealed it in the inside of a heel of his boot. It was probably because E. owed his departure from Germany to his own ingenious escape and not to the help or consent of the German authorities, and was thus able to disavow any real intention of carrying out his offer, that he was saved from what might have been a capital sentence. Many years later, after the Second World War, I heard from a friend in Ecuador that he had come across E. there as a prosperous dealer in property.

II

My return to liberty confronted me with the task of earning my living again and I therefore lost no time in utilising my experiences to the utmost advantage. I wrote numerous articles on all aspects of the life and conditions in Ruhleben, and they were all published, as there was a widespread interest in what was the only British internment camp in Germany. My contributions appeared in the London morning, evening, and week-end papers, as well as in provincial journals; and in some papers I had more than one article, as I also dealt with such problems as the exchange of civilian prisoners between England and Germany. A whole series of articles was published in the now long defunct political weekly, *The Outlook*, and my first contribution to the *Evening Standard* immediately brought me a telegram from the editor, Mr. Arthur H. Mann, who wanted me to go through his piles of German newspapers to write an account of internal conditions in the enemy country. The publication of my articles brought me a ceaseless stream of letters from persons all over Britain inquiring after their relatives and friends in Ruhleben. The answering of all these missives consumed a great deal of time, which I could ill afford, but I was glad to be able to relieve their writers' anxiety.

There were also many people who sought information from me about conditions in Germany in general. Notable among them were the Rothschilds, who invited me to New Court. It was my first visit to that hoary citadel of international finance, and I was quite taken aback when, as I stepped into the passage leading to the forecourt, a stalwart janitor, looking like a City policeman in mufti, emerged from a gloomy doorway and asked me whom I wanted to see. I was ushered into the board-room, where I was given a friendly welcome by the two brothers Leopold and Alfred, both in the seventies, and greeted formally by their nephew Charles (who was afterwards afflicted by melancholia and committed suicide). Alfred was a victim of rheumatism, which accounted for the stack of variegated cartons with pills, tablets, powders, ointment and liniment, methodically arranged on a side-table as in a chemist's shop. The interrogation was led by Leopold, who, after listening to an account of life in Ruhleben, plied me with questions to find out all that I could tell him about the situation in Germany, especially about food queues and the mood of the people, with a view, I presumed, to divining how long more the war might last. As the interview was coming to an end he asked me if I smoked, and when I answered in the affirmative he pressed a bell, a tall attendant entered, and he whispered something into his ear. On leaving the room a few moments later I was handed a big brown box: it contained a hundred cigars of a superior brand.

On the following day I called on Israel Zangwill at his chambers in the Temple. He was quite grey, although only in the early fifties, and spoke in a very despondent tone about the future of civilisation. We discussed the idea of my going to America to lecture on my experiences as a prisoner of war, and he promised to get me interviewed beforehand by representatives of the Hearst Press if I decided to go. It was while I was still at Ruhleben that the thought of such a lecture tour first occurred to me. I had an interview with Lord Newton, who was an Under-Secretary at the Foreign Office, on the subject, and subsequent correspondence, but eventually dropped the project as I became increasingly involved in different affairs in London.

After furnishing the press with articles for some months I wrote a book about Ruhleben. I worked at it for several hours daily and systematically, while my memory of innumerable details was still fresh, and with the aid of a collection of Camp magazines which

A JEWISH PILGRIMAGE

the military authorities had allowed me to send to England while I was still in the Camp. I finished the manuscript in ten weeks (a record that I have never equalled), and it was published by Methuen & Co. in the spring of 1917. I had every reason to be satisfied with the reception accorded to *The Ruhleben Prison Camp* by the press, for it was the subject of many laudatory reviews.[1]

III

No sooner had I delivered the manuscript of my book to the publishers than I began to make arrangements to lecture on Ruhleben. A West End agent whom I approached thought that the subject would not prove sufficiently attractive, so I organised the first lecture myself. I hired the Hampstead Conservatoire (now the Embassy Theatre) for the purpose, had tickets and posters printed which I distributed myself among shops in Hampstead and Kilburn, inserted an advertisement in many papers, and engaged sandwich-men to parade along Finchley Road, Kilburn High Road, and Oxford Street. I tried to obtain some distinguished public personage to take the chair, in order to make the function more attractive, but my efforts were in vain. I was thereupon advised to ask Horatio Bottomley, who revelled in the limelight, especially as a war orator, and whose roguery had not yet been exposed. I called upon him at the office of *John Bull*, of which he was editor, and he said he would be quite pleased to preside. Then, leaning back in his chair and interlacing his fingers across his stomach, he said: " But, of course, it's a business proposition." I was somewhat taken aback. " How much ? " I asked. " Fifty pounds," snapped Bottomley. " I've never heard of such a thing," I replied and wished him " Good day." Fortuntaely neither he nor any other chairman was needed to ensure the popularity of the lecture, for there was such a queue at the box-office on the eventful night that I could not begin until half-an-hour late. I spoke

[1] The *Times Literary Supplement* wrote: " The work is wonderfully full of facts and touches the life of the camp at many points with the practised hand of the journalist, trained to observe and report." The *Manchester Guardian* called the book " an historical document of value," the *Glasgow Herald* " the most vivid and authoritative account of Ruhleben Camp that has yet appeared," the *Yorkshire Post* " the most moving and the most comprehensive story of Ruhleben that has appeared," while the *Star* stated that it was " worthy to rank as the standard record of life at this famous camp." The American press was equally laudatory.

INTERLUDE

for nearly an hour-and-a-half and showed many lantern-slides made from photographs of scenes in Ruhleben and from drawings in the Camp Magazine. The lecture was generally voted a success, and yielded a satisfactory profit, especially as it led to my repeating the lecture on numerous occasions in the succeeding months.

Among those who attended the lecture was a variety agent, who asked me if I would be willing to give it in an abridged form as part of the programme at a music-hall. He told me that Bottomley, who then posed as a great patriot, was engaged to speak at three music halls, for half-an-hour at each of two houses a night, for a week, but could not appear on Thursday night as he had to see his paper to press. He inquired if I would take Bottomley's place on those three occasions for £12 a night (minus his commission). I readily agreed. It was a novel experience to wait behind the scenery on a music-hall stage until a comedian had finished his patter or some acrobats had concluded their turn before I could begin my discourse, but the audience immediately became serious. The only incongruous note struck was when, at one music-hall, the conductor thought it necessary to provide my lecture with musical accompaniment, and the orchestra had actually played a few bars of some unrecognisable composition while I spoke until I got him to stop their performance.

My lectures took me to all parts of Britain, from Plymouth to Aberdeen, and from Bournemouth to Blackpool. I spoke in Town Halls and theatres, in clubs, hotels, and hospitals, in literary institutes and military camps. Among my manifold experiences two were unusual: at Troon, where I was the guest in the mansion of a Scottish whisky millionaire, I was roused in the morning by a Highland piper who played an air on his bagpipe as he marched up and down the terrace; and in a stately Elizabethan home near Banbury, in accordance with old-time custom, a tin bath was brought into my bedroom by a couple of maids, who filled it with pails of hot water. By the time I had given my last lecture I had delivered it sixty times, and the number of people who queued up after each to question me about relatives and friends at Ruhleben must have amounted to a total of a few thousand.

Meanwhile there was a growing agitation in the press and in

Parliament for an "all for all" exchange of civilian prisoners between England and Germany, so that the men at Ruhleben should not have to endure a third winter there. There were two members of the House of Commons who particularly interested themselves in the matter, Lord Henry Bentinck and Sir Charles Seeley, who put questions with which I supplied them to the Government, and invariably received the reply that the problem was receiving careful and sympathetic consideration. The agitation led to the formation of a Ruhleben Prisoners' Release Committee, of which Sir Thomas D. Pile, Bart. (a former Lord Mayor of Dublin) was the chairman and I acted as secretary. There was a widespread demand for a public demonstration in order to exercise pressure upon the Government, with the result that such a meeting was held in February, 1917, at the Kingsway Hall, with the Bishop of London (Dr. Winnington Ingram) in the chair. The principal speakers were Lord Henry Bentinck and T. P. O'Connor, M.P., who were supported by two former prisoners from Ruhleben, Sir Timothy Eden, Bart. (elder brother of Sir Anthony Eden) and myself. All the speeches were loudly applauded and the resolutions submitted were adopted unanimously, but the meeting failed to achieve its purpose, and after about another fifteen months the Release Committee was dissolved.

As a token of appreciation of the services that I had rendered, a member of the Committee took me as his guest to a public dinner in honour of the famous criminal lawyer, Marshall Hall, and one or two other celebrities. He introduced me to the tea millionaire, Sir Thomas Lipton, whom he informed that I had been in Ruhleben; whereupon Sir Thomas, offering me his brawny hand, said: "*Was* you?" It was convincing proof that a knowledge of English grammar was unnecessary for the making of a fortune.

Chapter Seven

BACK TO ZIONISM

1916 — 1918

I

ALTHOUGH busily occupied with writing and lecturing on Ruhleben during the first twelve months after my return to England, I lost no time in picking up the broken threads in the Zionist world. The English Zionist Federation, which had been in the doldrums for a few years before the war and for some time afterwards, began to be the scene of increasing interest and importance from the summer of 1916, and as I was elected on the Executive I learned of the talks that were taking place about the possibilities that were expected to present themselves in Palestine in the event of an Allied victory. The men who had kept the Federation alive during the most precarious period of its existence had displayed an invincible faith and indefatigable zeal beyond all praise, and but for their dogged determination, despite scanty resources and in the face of scoffing criticism, it is extremely doubtful whether there would have been any organisation to serve as a fulcrum for those who negotiated with the British Government. The most notable of those men were the Rev. J. K. Goldbloom, still vigorous over eighty, and at least six others, who have passed away — Joseph Cowen and Leopold Kessler[1], who both held office as President, Paul Goodman, the author, who served the Zionist cause for over forty years, and M. M. Shire and Phineas Horowitz, who were untiring propagandists. The office of

[1] Leopold Kessler had been appointed by Theodor Herzl as the leader of the expedition sent in 1903 to El Arish and the Sinai Peninsula to investigate the suitability of the region for an autonomous Jewish settlement. He was also a Director of the Jewish Colonial Trust, Anglo-Palestine Bank, Jewish National Fund and *The Jewish Chronicle*.

the Federation was now in Leadenhall Street and much more roomy than the poky little place off Chancery Lane in 1910.

The Executive of the World Zionist Organisation was represented in England at that time at first only by Nahum Sokolow, who arrived before the end of 1914. He stayed at the Regent Palace Hotel, and a suit-case that he kept under his bed was the nucleus of what gradually developed into the London headquarters of the movement. Not having seen him since before the war, I was all the more enthralled when he told me of the initial soundings that were being made in political circles to ascertain the attitude of the British Government to Zionist aspirations, which seemed to be approaching the dawn of their fulfilment. Sokolow had soon been joined by another member of the Executive, Yehiel Tschlenow, a Moscow physician[1], and they, together with Chaim Weizmann, had an exploratory conversation with Mr. Herbert (later Lord) Samuel towards the end of 1914.

At that time Dr. Weizmann was only a member of the *Actions Comité* (General Council) of the Zionist Organisation, but thanks to the introductions that he had received to Arthur James Balfour (from Professor Samuel Alexander) and to Lloyd George and Herbert Samuel (from C. P. Scott, of the *Manchester Guardian*), and also to his appointment in 1916 as Director of the Admiralty Laboratories, which were then under the control of Balfour as First Lord of the Admiralty, he was very advantageously placed to engage in negotiations in Government circles about the aim of Zionism. One evening, shortly after my return to London, I met him at a West End theatre during an interval, and he told me that he and other leading Zionists were trying to formulate a statement of British sympathy with Zionist aspirations that would be acceptable to the Government. He asked me if I would also attempt such a formulation, and I agreed to do so. A couple of days later I took my draft to his house (then in Chelsea), and the door was opened by a slim, stocky young man in khaki, who was a stranger to me. When Dr. Weizmann appeared he told me that the young man was Vladimir Jabotinsky, who had come to England to raise a Jewish legion to join the British troops

[1] Dr. Tschlenow died in London on January 31st, 1918.

in the invasion of Palestine. I was afterwards to hear Jabotinsky address the Executive of the Zionist Federation on this project, which was a source of keen difference among Zionists, and I was at once impressed by his command of English and the vigour with which he spoke.

As I never preserved a copy of the draft that I gave to Dr. Weizmann, I cannot say whether I made any material contribution to the final text that was issued more than a year later. The fact, however, is that scores of drafts were made, co-ordinated, amended, revised, and recast, both in Zionist and Government circles, before the Cabinet agreed upon the terms of the Declaration published on November 2nd, 1917. To the best of my recollection the formula that I submitted eventually formed part of Article 4 of the Palestine Mandate. Several months before the Declaration was issued Dr. Weizmann, whose relations with the Zionist Federation had for some years been rather tenuous, was elected as its President, so that he might be invested with added authority.

Soon after my first talks with Sokolow and Weizmann I had a long conversation with Lucien Wolf (1857 - 1930), who had become Secretary of the Conjoint Foreign Committee (of the Board of Deputies of British Jews and the Anglo-Jewish Association). His connection with the *Daily Graphic*, of which he had been Foreign Editor for many years, had been brought to an end soon after the outbreak of the First World War in consequence of the anti-German feeling then prevalent, although there was not the least ground for imputing to him any pro-Teuton sentiment. He told me of the talks and correspondence that he had conducted with the Zionist leaders on the nature of the representations to be made to the British Government with regard to the status of Jews in Palestine after the expected eviction of the Turks, and made it clear that the principle to which the communal leaders, for whom he spoke, would never assent was that the Jews were a nation. He likewise declared that they were opposed to any demand that Jewish settlements in Palestine should be recognised as possessing a national character in a purely political sense. These views afterwards found expression in a letter in *The Times* of May 24th, 1917, which was signed by the Presidents of the Board of Deputies (D. L. Alexander, K.C.) and of the Anglo-Jewish Association (Claude Montefiore), and which provoked a storm of indignation in the community, followed by the displacement of the President of the Board by Sir Stuart Samuel, who had pro-Zionist sympathies. It was undoubtedly due to the antagonism of a section of Anglo-Jewry that the terms of the Balfour Declaration fell far short of those proposed by the Zionist leaders, but the enthusiasm that its publication aroused throughout the world exceeded all expectations. The vast crowd that swarmed into the London Opera House (now Stoll's Theatre) on December 2nd, 1917, to celebrate the event by a public demonstration was so great that an overflow meeting had to be held at the Kingsway Theatre, at which I was one of the speakers.

I had, indeed, begun to devote myself anew to Zionist affairs both by pen and speech from the summer of 1917, when my activities in connection with Ruhleben began to slacken. I contributed articles on the subject to the press and addressed public meetings in various parts of the country. I also collaborated with an official expert of the Jewish National Fund, Jacob Ettinger, in the writing of memoranda and pamphlets on the acquisition and development of estates in Palestine. Ettinger, who was born in Russia and had been employed by the Jewish Colonisation Association as an agricultural expert in the Jewish farm settlements in Argentina, had come to London to co-operate in the drafting of schemes for the future development of Palestine, but most of his plans were based upon too optimistic an anticipation of the Jewish status in post-war Palestine and consequently possessed only academic interest. As soon as the war was over he went to settle in Jerusalem.

II

Early in 1918 I was invited by the Directors of the Jewish National Fund, whose office had been transferred, soon after the outbreak of war, from Cologne to The Hague, to assist them in raising money for the fulfilment of the important task awaiting them — the acquisition of land in Palestine. There had long been a special committee with an office in the East End for the collection of voluntary contri-

BACK TO ZIONISM

butions, but although they had the co-operation of numerous local committees throughout the country, the total amount received, partly owing to war conditions, was comparatively small. The main reason was that under the Ottoman régime the purchase of land in Palestine was hampered by political and legal difficulties, and there was therefore little inducement to give large donations for an object that seemed incapable of realisation in the early future or on an impressive scale. But now that Ottoman rule was doomed and Britain had promised to facilitate the establishment of a National Home for the Jewish people, and as, moreover, it was generally expected that Jews from many lands would rush to it as soon as the war was over, it became supremely necessary to furnish ample resources for the purchase of land.

I was provided with an office at the Jewish Colonial Trust, in Wallbrook, and from there I wrote letters to a selected number of wealthy Jews who had never before identified themselves with the Zionist cause, but who, I thought, would have now been rendered sympathetically disposed by the Government's Declaration. In each case I asked for a personal interview without plainly stating its purpose, deeming it best to arouse curiosity sufficiently to elicit a favourable response. Before long I was able to call upon several well-known members of the community, and received amounts ranging from £50 to £200, which were much larger than had previously been customary. Among the donors was the eminent artist, Solomon J. Solomon, R.A., who gave me his cheque with the remark that the time had now come to show practically his desire for the realisation of what he had hitherto only prayed for. But I was anxious to obtain much larger sums and therefore decided to write to Sir Alfred Mond (afterwards the first Lord Melchett), who was one of the leading industrialists in the country and a prominent member of the House of Commons (as Liberal representative for Swansea), and who held a position in the Government as First Commissioner of Works. I was prompted to write to him because, although he had never previously associated himself with the Jewish community, he had issued a very notable statement on the publication of the Balfour Declaration, in which he wrote:

> *The establishment in their old land, under the aegis of the British Government, of a home where the Jewish people will be at liberty to develop their national genius and freely to exercise their virtues of industry, thrift, and organisation in their own way marks an epoch in the world's history. . . . The dignity and importance of our whole race will be enhanced by the existence of a national home where those of our people who have been compelled to live under less favourable conditions than we enjoy will be able to establish themselves on the soil of their ancestors.*

This frank recognition of the Jews as a nation and expression of solidarity with them made me very hopeful of a prompt and friendly reply, but three weeks after I had posted my letter I was still without any acknowledgment. I therefore wrote a gentle reminder, but the weeks rolled by and I was still without an answer.

Early in October, 1918, Dr. Weizmann returned from Palestine, where he had spent several months as head of the Zionist Commission authorised by the Government to act as the medium between the British authorities and the Jewish population. The Executive of the Zionist Federation decided to accord him an official welcome at a public dinner in his honour at the Holborn Restaurant, and entrusted me with the organising of the function. I called upon Herbert Samuel and invited him to take the chair, and he readily agreed. When drawing up the list of guests I included Sir Alfred Mond in the hope that he would accept and I would thus have the opportunity of approaching him personally. He accepted, and thereupon I invited him to propose the toast of the chairman, to which he promptly agreed. I clearly remember asking Dr. Weizmann whether I should send an invitation to Dr. Moses Gaster (the retired Chief Rabbi of the Sephardi community), and he replied with an emphatic " No." I was not altogether surprised, although it was at Gaster's house that Weizmann, Sokolow, and other leading Zionists had a memorable meeting on February 7th, 1917, with Herbert Samuel and Sir Mark Sykes, who was a Secretary of the War Cabinet (with a special interest in the Middle East), and some important decisions were taken. For after that meeting Gaster was not invited to any meetings of the Political Committee set up by Weizmann and Sokolow in the Bureau that they opened at Empire House, Piccadilly, as they apparently thought that their deliberations would proceed more smoothly without the presence of that tempestuous personality. They doubtless remembered that Gaster had been a bitter opponent of Herzl during the latter's later years, and although Weizmann had also been an opponent of Herzl, he was unwilling to take the risk of having a bellicose colleague.

The dinner to Dr. Weizmann was a great success, among the speakers being Viscount Bryce and Sir Mark Sykes. When it was over I introduced myself to Sir Alfred Mond and asked him if he could now let me know when I could have the pleasure of calling upon him. He thereupon made an appointment for a couple of days later in his official room in the House of Commons. During the interval I thought over the amount for which I should ask in case Sir Alfred invited such a suggestion. He was generally reputed to be a millionaire, and it was therefore natural that I should expect a larger sum than I had hitherto obtained, but I could not recall any donation to any Jewish cause in this country until then exceeding a few hundred pounds. As I made my way to the House of Commons I wondered whether I should be so bold as to suggest £1,000 or £2,000. Would he feel offended at my asking for so little or annoyed at my expecting so much? Before I could make up my mind I was ushered into Sir Alfred's room and given a friendly welcome.

I soon realised that Sir Alfred liked to talk, so I decided to be a patient and appreciative listener. He spoke about the approaching end of the war, the confused situation in Russia, the future of the Jews in that country and other parts of Eastern Europe, the future of Palestine, and the implications of the Balfour Declaration. Now and again he would rise from his chair, continue talking as he paced up and down the length of the room, turn to me for a sign of corroboration, and then resume his seat. He also spoke about his personal interest in the establishment of a Jewish national home, referred to the anti-Semitic attacks against him in his constituency, and said that if he were not returned at the next election he would devote his time to the Zionist cause. He must have spoken for about fifty minutes, with very few words from myself, when, returning from his repeated walks across the room, and resuming his seat, he said: "Now, tell me: how much do you want?"

I thought it best to play for safety and not to mention any figure, so I replied: "I shouldn't like, Sir Alfred, to suggest any limit to your generosity."

He got up again for another turn up and down the room and then sat down. "I'll tell you what," he said. "I'll give you £5,000 a year for five years. Do you think that would do?"

It was by far the largest sum that I had ever heard of as a gift to any Jewish cause, but although it vastly surpassed my expectations I betrayed no astonishment. "Thank you very much indeed, Sir Alfred," I said. "It will certainly do splendidly."

"Good," he responded. "I think it should make some of our rich Jews sit up and do the right thing."

I thanked Sir Alfred again very heartily, and he asked me to come and see him again. As soon as I was out in the street I took a taxi to the Zionist Bureau to report on my interview. I met Dr. Weizmann and Mr. Israel Sieff as they were coming out and told them the news. "These are *Mashiach's Zeiten* (Messianic times)!" exclaimed Dr. Weizmann.

I cabled the news to the Jewish National Fund, and then called at the offices of *The Times*, Reuters, and the Press Association to hand in a short paragraph. The following morning the news was in all the papers and it went the round of the world's press. It was the beginning of an increasingly active interest in the Zionist cause on the part of Sir Alfred Mond, continued by him as Lord Melchett until his death, and transmitted to his son, the second Lord Melchett, and his daughter, Lady Reading.

My experience with the (first) Marquis of Reading was quite different. He had been a political colleague of Sir Alfred Mond for many years and his only son[1] was married to a daughter of the latter. I therefore hoped that Mond's example would influence him, although I did not expect so magnificent a donation. I called upon Lord Reading with an introduction from Herbert Samuel, who stated in

[1] The present Marquis of Reading, Minister of State.

his note that I wished to speak on a matter relating to the Zionist movement.[1] I was deeply impressed by his appearance and personality: he was a tall, handsome, and distinguished-looking figure, his classically cut features radiating a blend of wisdom and august dignity. He was not as loquacious as Mond (although in public speaking far more eloquent), and much more restrained, smoking a cigarette all the time and watching the smoke as it curled up from his nostrils.

I opened the conversation by stating that I wished to interest his lordship in the Palestine Restoration Fund, which was intended to provide the Zionist Executive with the means for the transport of settlers and for laying the foundations of the Jewish national Home. He asked me whether it was proposed to establish a Jewish State and also what were the relations between the Zionist Organisation and the League of British Jews (an anti-Zionist body that came to an early end). After I replied to these questions he said that he had often thought about the Zionist movement, and while he was in sympathy with certain aspects he took exception to the nationalism that it advocated. He believed that the emphasis of the national aspect would serve as a handle to Anti-Semites, who would reproach Jews with having a " dual nationality." I evinced surprise that he appeared to admit the existence of such a thing, as the expression involved the use of the term " nationality " in the two different senses of citizenship and ethnical nationality, which one could have simultaneously without any conflicting loyalty.

I then reminded Lord Reading that when he was in America he had publicly expressed sympathy with the Zionist cause. He countered by saying that he then spoke as British Ambassador and that he naturally supported the policy of the British Government. I urged that inasmuch as so many prominent British statesmen had already declared their sympathy with the movement, he might likewise do so in a similar capacity. He replied that he was no longer a member of the Government, and that I was speaking to him in his individual

[1] My visit to Lord Reading took place on December 3rd, 1919, thirteen months after my interview with Sir Alfred Mond, but as I called upon them both for practically the same reason it is convenient to relate the two stories one after the other.

capacity. I rejoined that as the realisation of the Zionist scheme in Palestine would be so beneficial to British interests, and as it would also afford considerable relief to the oppressed Jewish communities in the east, there was adequate ground for supporting the movement.

Lord Reading went on to say that he had frequently discussed the matter with Mr. Herbert Samuel, that the difficulty he always found was in regard to the national aspect, and that if he made any statement manifesting sympathy it would have to contain a reservation. Then, lowering his voice, as though he might be overheard, he remarked: " One has to be so careful." I could not help wondering at this distinguished statesman, who had held the high offices of Lord Chief Justice and of British Ambassador to the United States[1], apparently fearing, just because he was a Jew, lest a word or act of his might be seized upon to taunt him with a lack of perfect loyalty to the British Crown. When I asked him if he were prepared to show his sympathy in a material form, he said that he would be quite willing to give a contribution to the Zionist Organisation, provided it were understood that he was not a supporter of the movement. Finally, he said that he would think the matter over carefully and let me have a statement together with his contribution.

Some weeks later I received a modest cheque, with a covering letter that it should be devoted to medical work in Palestine, but there was no statement.

III

The year 1918 was crowded for me with a succession of multifarious activities. I continued working in the morning for the Ruhleben Prisoners' Release Committee until it was dissolved in the middle of that year, and collaborated with Ettinger in the afternoon. I lectured on both Ruhleben and Palestine, and visited at least two dozen cities — from Bournemouth to Leeds, from Grimsby to Plymouth, and from Birmingham to Dublin — in the interests of the Palestine Restoration Fund. I had my first article published in the *Fortnightly Review* (then under the editorship of W. L. Courtney), wrote pamphlets on " Anti-Semitism in Germany " and " The

---

[1] Lord Reading was appointed Viceroy of India in the following year, 1920.

Turkish Persecution of the Jews " for the Ministry of Information, served for a brief period in the Jewish Department of that Ministry, secured donations for the Jewish National Fund, was appointed Director of Publicity of the Zionist Bureau, was sent on an important mission to Poland, and found time for the most momentous event of all — my marriage.

Among my many friends dating from my student days were a doctor and his wife living in Dalston, whom, after my return from Germany, I used to visit from time to time. There, one evening, in the autumn of 1917 I met a vivacious young schoolmistress, named Tessie Jacobs, for whom I felt an instinctive attraction. She possessed all the qualities, physical and intellectual, with which I had endowed the ideal woman of whom I had dreamed in the days of my captivity. In figure and features, in charm of presence, she seemed to me all that was desirable, and her lively temperament and sense of humour captivated me. I soon decided that I would like her to share my life, and fortunately her inclinations coincided with mine. She then knew little or nothing of the causes and interests to which I was devoted, but she was quick to learn and my enthusiasms soon became hers.

We married at the end of July, 1918, at a little synagogue in Camden Town, where she had sung on the choir and taught at the religion classes. In the following year we went to live in Pattison Road, Child's Hill, a locality on the border of Hampstead Heath, which is said to contain secret tunnels used in his escapades by the eighteenth century highwayman, Dick Turpin; and there we have remained to the present day. Our union has been happy and has been blessed with two sons, with whom we have reason to be satisfied, for the elder, David, obtained his London B.Sc. degree with first-class honours in electrical engineering when he was only nineteen, and the younger, Jonathan[1], gained an open classical scholarship at Balliol before he was seventeen, and the careers of both have well fulfilled their early promise. In the first years of our marriage, when my attendance at Zionist meetings at night usually prevented me

[1] Now Lecturer in Logic and Metaphysics at St. Andrews University (Queen's College, Dundee), and author of *The Principles of World Citizenship*.

from getting home until midnight and even later, I often found my wife in a state of anxiety and alarm about what might have happened to me. Now, after thirty-seven years, the tables are turned. I sit at home at night waiting for her to return from meetings, for she is a popular speaker in great demand. But I wait, not with anxiety, but with pleasurable anticipation of the story of her latest oratorical adventure.

IV

Shortly after the issue of the Balfour Declaration the British Government created a Jewish Department in the Ministry of Information for the purpose of favourably influencing Jewish opinion in America, which was still neutral, as well as of gaining the goodwill of the Jews in Central Europe. The fortunes of the Allied Powers had then reached a critical stage, and it was believed that by propaganda astutely conducted a definite improvement could be achieved. The Director of Enemy Propaganda was Lord Northcliffe, under whose energetic and skilful guidance the Government's Zionist policy was abundantly exploited, though, needless to say, the loyalty of the Jewish subjects of the Central Powers remained unaffected. I worked in the Jewish Department, at Crewe House, for a short time. Pamphlets in various languages (especially English, French, German, and Yiddish) recording speeches and articles on Zionism, were published in tens of thousands and distributed both in English-speaking countries and on the Continent; a weekly bulletin (in English and German) of Jewish news, giving special prominence to Zionist matters, was circulated; and brief messages of a kindred character were telegraphed to friendly or neutral centres, whence they were immediately transmitted to Berlin and Vienna, to Sofia and Constantinople. Thus, thanks to this propaganda, nobody in those days was allowed to entertain any doubt that Great Britain would fulfil the Balfour Declaration in accordance with the most liberal interpretation. I had been working at the Jewish Department for little more than a week, when, as I got off a bus in Park Lane one morning, to go to Crewe House, I heard a loud report that sent people scurrying with joyous excitement in all directions. It was 11 o'clock on the eleventh of November, 1918, and the report was a signal that the war was over.

There was now no need for the continued existence of the Jewish Department. Without loss of time I went to see Mr. Sokolow at the Regent Palace Hotel and offered my services for the Zionist Bureau. He appointed me Director of Publicity and Propaganda, and the following day I began my duties in a bright room overlooking Piccadilly. I thus resumed my connection with the Secretariat of the World Zionist Organisation, which continued until a few months after the beginning of the Second World War. Mr. Sokolow went to Paris to prepare for the representations to be made to the Peace Conference, and Dr. Weizmann remained in control of affairs in London.

But interest in Palestine suddenly became momentarily submerged by alarming news from Poland. Reports were arriving from the Continent daily that the Poles were celebrating their newly won independence by organising pogroms against the Jews. The British Government published a warning against a continuance of these excesses, and declared that if the newly formed States in Eastern Europe indulged in bloodshed at the birth of their independence they could not reckon upon the help of the Western Powers in the task of their construction. But despite this admonition further messages arrived of more serious outrages against the Jews in Galicia. It was therefore considered necessary that somebody should go out there immediately to investigate the situation, as the welfare of three million Jews was at stake, and see whether the outrages could be stopped. Although such a mission had never been envisaged as within the competence of the Zionist Organisation, the latter had acquired such prestige that Dr. Weizmann decided to take action. He asked me whether I was willing to go, and I agreed.

Chapter Eight

POGROMS IN POLAND
1918 — 1919

I

OWING to the nature of my projected mission to Poland, and owing also to the difficulties of travel across Europe immediately after the First World War, the consent of the British Foreign Office was necessary. Dr. Weizmann therefore had a talk on the subject with Sir George Clerk, private secretary to Mr. Arthur Balfour, who was Foreign Secretary, and received his approval. I also had an interview myself with Sir George to discuss the scope of my inquiry, and Balfour readily agreed to provide the requisite facilities, which included a request to the French Government to allow me to cross the frontier into Switzerland without delay. In view of the widespread interest that had been aroused by the excesses in Poland, I went to see Mr. H. Wickham Steed, then Editor of *The Times*, and he commissioned me to write some articles on the results of my investigation.

I left London on December 6th, 1918, and reached Cracow on January 1st, 1919. The inordinately long time occupied by the journey was due primarily to the route that I had to travel — first to Paris, and thence to Geneva, Berne, Zurich, and Vienna. It was also partly due to an enforced wait of eight days at Berne for an Austrian visa and a stay of five days in Vienna, as well as to a slight attack of influenza. At the British Legation in Berne I saw the Minister, Lord Acton, who read me the telegraphic message that he had received from the Foreign Office in regard to my mission, and which agreed with the terms of Lord Balfour's letter to Weizmann. In my hotel

POGROMS IN POLAND

I met Mr. August Zaleski, whom I had not seen for over eight years, and who was now head of the Polish Mission in Berne. He told me that the Polish Government would welcome my inquiry, as they were anxious to arrive at a friendly understanding with the Jews, and he kindly provided me with a visa for Poland as well as with letters of introduction to the leading members of the Government, including Marshal Pilsudski, the Chief of State.

I travelled from Zurich to Vienna together with Mr. Philpotts, the British Commercial Attaché in the Austrian capital, who was returning to his post. Our Austrian train showed the damaging effects of war. Many windows had been smashed and were boarded up; the previous plush cushions of our compartment were replaced by a straw mattress; and at night the only light was a dim one in the corridor or none at all. During my stay in Vienna I met some Jewish refugees from Lemberg (as the city of Lwow was still called), where the worst of the pogroms had taken place. They gave me a detailed account of the distressing situation there as well as of the tense relations between Jews and Poles in general; and one of them, as he described some of the incidents of which he had been a personal witness, became quite hysterical. I called at the Polish Legation, where I had a long talk with Dr. Wladislaw Gumplowicz (whose acquaintance I had made in Cracow twelve years before): he gave me his version of the Lemberg pogrom, and, although a Jew himself, tried to make out a good case for the Poles.

From Vienna I journeyed to Cracow in the company of Dr. Emil Schmorak, a lawyer from Lemberg, who had come to Vienna to obtain funds for the relief of the victims of the excesses, and who was returning home. The journey took nearly twenty hours and was a veritable nightmare. All the carriages and corridors of the train were packed; there was no heating or light; and some people even lay outstretched on the roof. When we reached Cracow we went to a dozen hotels in search of rooms, but found them all full of fugitives from East Galicia, Jews and Poles. At last we came to a third-rate hotel, where, by tipping the porter, we got a dirty, shabby room with two untidy beds. We then called on Dr. Osias Thon, the Rabbi of the community, whom I had met at Zionist Congresses.

A JEWISH PILGRIMAGE

He explained to me that there was a Provisional Government of Galicia, called the Polish Liquidation Commission, of which Count Lasocki was the President, and that he had been to see him a few times about the liberation of four leading Zionists[1] from Lemberg who had been seized after the pogrom by the military authorities as hostages "to ensure that the Jews kept the peace." I was in Cracow for a week, during which I had several interviews with Count Lasocki and his principal secretary, as well as with Ignacz Daszynski, the leader of the Polish Socialist Party, two professors of the local University, and a Jewish lawyer, Dr. Zimmerman, who furnished me with considerable documentary material on the outrages in West Galicia[2].

Count Lasocki gave me a friendly welcome, denounced the pogroms, deprecated the seizing of Jewish hostages, and assured me that he had telegraphed to Lemberg more than once that the arrested Zionists should be transferred to Cracow, where they would be set free. He rang up the Director of Police to secure me immediately a room at the relatively superior Hotel Saski. He then introduced me to the Director of the Polish Press Bureau, a grey-haired old man, named Zuk, who took me to the office of the paper *Naprzod* to see its editor, Daszynski. I reminded the latter of our first meeting twelve years before and explained the purpose of my mission, whereupon he launched forth upon an hour's discourse on the Polish situation in general and the Jewish question in particular. Zuk, who had an English wife, invited me to his house for dinner, where I met a Professor Marchlevsky, who also had an English wife. We engaged in a general discussion about the relations between Jews and Poles, and I found it necessary to explain the difference between ethnical nationality and citizenship, maintaining that a Jewish nationalist could at the same time be a good and loyal Polish citizen. The Professor declared that a Jewish nationalist was for him a foreigner and would be treated accordingly, and hence, if a student registered

[1] They were three lawyers, Dr. Leon Reich, Dr. Michael Ringel, and Dr. Alexander Hausmann, and a journalist, Josef Tennenblatt.

[2] A fuller account of my mission to Poland in 1918 — 19 is given in my *Report on the Pogroms in Poland* (Central Office of the Zionist Organisation, London, 1919) and in my *Travels in Jewry* (Edward Goldston, Ltd., 1952).

himself as of Jewish nationality he could not expect equal treatment with a Polish nationalist and was subject to a *numerus clausus* at the Cracow University. I thereupon asked him why the Jews living in East Galicia, where the Poles were fewer than the Ukrainians, should be expected to declare themselves Poles rather than Ukrainians. He replied that he could not answer the question, that it was complicated, and he hoped the Peace Conference would settle it satisfactorily.

I also had a discussion with Professor Wladislav Nathanson, a baptised Jew, who was a natural physicist and had studied at Cambridge under Joseph Thomson. He pleaded the ignorance of Polish peasants in extenuation of their hostility, and said that they were easily egged on to attacks. He argued that Jews had all rights, but I instanced several wrongs. He maintained that assaults upon Jews could be explained by historical conditions, and remarked that Jews were cowards — an accusation that I indignantly rebutted by citing cases of Jewish heroism in the war. Then he tried to hedge by saying that he was not a politician but a scientific student; taunted me with a recent study of the question, which I disproved; and finally admitted that the new Poland, owing to the change of régime, was in a state of anarchy and unable to maintain proper order. I left him rather heated, and realised how anti-Jewish a converted Jew could be.

II

Deputations of Jews from various towns in the vicinity of Cracow came to see me at the hotel, to relate their local grievances and seek redress. In one town a communal leader had been interned without any explanation; in another a Jewish newspaper had been suppressed; and in a third, where the Jews formed the majority of the population, the authorities were gerrymandering the electoral constituencies by adding parts of adjacent rural areas, so as to ensure that the Jews should be in a minority in the town council. In all these cases, and various others, I called on Count Lasocki to make representations and he promised intervention.

I was informed by Dr. Thon that the hostilities against the Jews in Galicia began immediately after the collapse of the Austro-Hungarian Monarchy, while those against the Jews in Congress

Poland followed very soon after. The departure or desertion of the Austrian troops anxious to return home left numerous towns without proper protection. The general state of confusion that arose was taken advantage of by peasants as well as by townsfolk, who were incited by anti-Semitic agitators, to make attacks upon Jewish shops, dwellings, and synagogues. The Polish troops, instead of defending the Jews and their property, either remained passive or participated in the plundering expeditions. The attempts of the Jews to defend themselves were frustrated by the Polish military and civil authorities. As soon as the news of threatened disturbances in neighbouring towns reached the Jews in Cracow, they organised a militia numbering close upon 1,000 for the defence of their brethren, and the Liquidation Commission gave their approval. The Jewish militia were supplied with arms, and detachments were sent to various towns, but only in very few cases, and then only for a very brief period, were they able to render any protection. For the Military Commandant in Cracow objected to the creation of the Jewish militia and ordered that it should be disarmed and dissolved both in Cracow and in the provincial towns to which detachments had already been despatched. Moreover, the local Jewish communities were not allowed to form any self-defence corps, nor were Jews admitted to the town militia, so that they were at the mercy of any armed band that chose to attack them.

There had been an organised onslaught upon the Jews at Chrzanow, about two hours by train from Cracow, only a few weeks before, so I went there to investigate the situation, accompanied by a student. There was still abundant evidence of the outrage. On some houses we saw chalked inscriptions, "Here lives a Pole," "Here lives a Catholic," which were intended to secure immunity for the occupants. We visited some damaged houses and shops, where the windows had been broken and replaced by boards, and iron shutters battered and wrenched away. We went to a restaurant that had been turned into a shambles, and to a confectionery shop from which everything had been plundered and which now contained nothing but débris. The owner of a small shop that had been demolished told me that he had only recently come back after fighting four years in the war: this was his reward. We were conducted around by a Jewish doctor, and when we returned to his house members of the Jewish community council, headed by their president, came in all excited and gave a hysterical account of their experiences during the pogrom. Later, as we made our way to the station in the evening we passed a lighted hall, from which came the stentorian voice of Daszynski preaching liberty — while the Jews went in fear and trembling. We returned to Cracow in a pitch-dark train, and on arriving saw the trams beflagged in honour of Paderewski's visit.

After having been in Cracow for a week I received a telegram from Colonel Wade, head of the Allied Mission, informing me that he would be in Warsaw for some days and would like to see me. I therefore decided to go there at once to meet him. But before doing so I called again at the Polish Liquidation Commission and was told that the four Zionist hostages were at last being transferred to Cracow, where they would be at liberty.

III

I was impressed by the size of Warsaw and its metropolitan appearance, by its long and spacious boulevards and its dignified public buildings; and likewise impressed, though in a different way, by the line of demarcation that distinguished the Jewish quarter, whose inhabitants wore long, black gaberdines, top-boots, and ear-ringlets, from the rest of the tumultuous city. I took a room at the Hotel Bristol, where Paderewski and his wife had a private suite, and on the day of my arrival lunched at the Hotel d'Angleterre, where Napoleon Bonaparte had once stayed.

I received a mass of information, both about the pogroms and the Jewish position in Poland in general, from two Jewish leaders, Yitzchak Gruenbaum and Heschel Farbstein[1], both of whom played a very prominent part in the Zionist movement and were afterwards elected to the Polish Parliament. Gruenbaum in particular traced for me the growth of Anti-Semitism in Poland from Tsarist times and described the internal differences and parties that divided the Jewish community. There were not only all shades of Zionists, but

[1] Died in Jerusalem, 1948.

also *Bundists* (Socialists), *Folkists* (who wanted Jewish autonomy in Poland), and assimilationists. He also gave me a detailed exposition of the grounds upon which the majority of Polish Jewry demanded the rights of a national minority. He maintained that it was unjust that the 300,000 Jews in Warsaw, which then had a total population of 800,000, should contribute more than half of the municipality's revenue, and yet receive practically nothing in return for their own institutions. And he urged that as the Jews formed 15 per cent of the total population, they should have the right to elect a similar percentage of the members of Parliament.

I first met Colonel Wade, who was adorned with red tabs and coloured ribbons, at the home of Farbstein, where several Zionist friends were invited to meet him and discuss the situation. He expressed confidence (in bad German) in the fulfilment of Jewish political demands, and before he left he asked me to call upon him the next morning. In our private talk he was rather less friendly, said that the question of national rights was difficult, and repeated the reproaches of the Poles that the Jews did not identify themselves with their cause. He also harped upon the Polish story that the Jews in Lemberg had helped the Ukrainians in the fight against them, but I was able to prove to his satisfaction that this was quite unfounded.

During my two weeks' stay in Warsaw I made a study of the Jewish quarter and of its social and economic conditions, and attended some large public meetings at which political questions were debated at great length with vitriolic vigour. But of far greater importance were the talks that I had with several official Polish personages. At the War Office I saw the Minister, Colonel Wronchinski, and the Chief of General Staff, Count Szeptycki, two stalwart figures, and asked them to rescind the order for the suppression of the Jewish paper, *Novy Dziennik*, which they promised to do. At the Foreign Office I was received by the Minister, Wassilevsky, an elderly, rather ineffectual man, who assured me that no members of the Government were Anti-Semites and that there had been no pogroms. He then referred me to the head of the Political Section, Dr. Jodko, whom I reminded of our first meeting in 1906 in Cracow. Jodko recalled the occasion and inquired after our mutual friend, the London bookseller, Voynich. He also made a fervid profession of racial tolerance, agreed that Jews should receive compensation for damage sustained, but emphasised that the Government's finances were " not brilliant."

The longest conversation that I had with a political leader was with M. Grabski, the head of the National Democrats (an anti-Liberal party), who was known to be the adviser of Paderewski. He was staying in the same hotel with me, and invited me one night into his room. He was obsessed with the idea that Jews both in Poland and abroad were against the new State, and it took me some time to make him realise that Jewish protests were provoked and justified by Polish hostility, but were not aimed at the State as such. He admitted that he had formerly been an Anti-Semite, but declared that he was no longer one. He proposed that a conference of all Polish parties should meet with leading Jews to come to an understanding on condition that the Jews declared in favour of a Great Poland, including Danzig and Vilna. It was an exhausting discussion, during which the Secretary of the Foreign Ministry nearly fell asleep, and I did not emerge from the room until one in the morning.

I had two talks with Paderewski, the world-celebrated pianist, who, although utterly lacking any experience of political affairs, had felt impelled by a sense of patriotism to try to direct the fortunes of the new-born Republic. In our first conversation he was very friendly. He protested that he was philo-Semitic, and assured me that he would keep the promises that he had given to the Jewish leaders in America, that he would do all in his power to improve the Jewish position in Poland. But he pleaded that he had not been back in the country long and it would take him some time to make a thorough study of the situation. The interview was cut short by his wife coming into the room and pulling his coat-sleeve. After a fortnight, during which Paderewski became the Prime Minister of a Coalition Government and I had the opportunity of acquainting myself more closely with the annoyances and attacks to which the Jews even in Warsaw were subjected, I had another talk with him. This time I found him less conciliatory than before. He sought to justify a military raid that had taken place a few days before in

Nalevki, the Jewish quarter in Warsaw, on the ground that it was necessary to search for weapons in the fight against Bolshevism, although, in fact, no weapons were found in Jewish houses, but soldiers had robbed and assaulted Jews. He also urged that the Government could not issue an appeal to the Poles to preserve the peace without also making a similar appeal to the Jews, otherwise it would be one-sided. He concluded by repeating that he would keep his promise to the Jewish leaders in America, and the interview was again broken off by his wife coming in and tugging him by the sleeve. (After about twelve months Paderewski gave up the harassing task of trying to govern Poland, left the country, and returned to the concert-hall. There are least his wife was unable to pull at his coat-sleeve).

The following morning I went to Palace Belvidere for an interview with Marshal Pilsudski. I was received in a large ante-chamber by a military officer and then passed on to another officer in more magnificent uniform and resplendent top-boots, who ushered me up a flight of stairs and through a series of saloons to a spacious drawing-room with a parquet floor and bright tapestried furniture. Poland's national hero came in with a slow step, coughing, and suffering from a cold. His military attire consisted of black trousers, grey tunic with high collar and white cuffs; and as he bade me be seated I noted the resolute yet furtive look, the drooping moustache, and the close-cropped hair, which picture postcards throughout the country had made familiar. At his suggestion I spoke in German, and began by saying that I had come to study the Jewish situation in Poland owing to the unfavourable impression that had been created by the pogroms.

Pilsudski replied that the excesses had been caused by the sudden collapse of Austrian rule and the absence of authority and by the hatred of Jewish dealers who had profited in the war. When I inquired whether Polish landlords and peasants had not also profited by the war, he said they had done so through dealings with Jews. As for the pogroms, Pilsudski remarked that one could not expect the Government to issue a formal condemnation, as it was understood that they were opposed to violence of any kind. He admitted that the Poles were not philo-Semites, but said that the Jews in the country were very numerous and formed a foreign body whom they would like to get rid of. The Poles were not a wild people, and their present hostility could not continue. As soon as the independence of Poland was declared equal rights had been granted to Jews as in Western democracies, and more could not be expected. He justified the internment of the four Lemberg Zionists as a military measure to calm the incensed Poles, but could not say what proofs there were that Jews had violated neutrality in the fight between Poles and Ukrainians, He agreed in principle that the Government should compensate the victims of pogroms, but the whole question was still under consideration. Before leaving Marshal Pilsudski I asked him for a letter of introduction to General Rozvadovsky, who was in command of the Lemberg district, and he instructed his adjutant to attend to it.

There was no British Minister or Consul yet in Warsaw while I was there, but an official British Mission consisting of Richard Kimens and Rowland Kenney arrived for a preliminary exploration of the scene. At their request I wrote out a report on the situation for transmission to the Foreign Office, and they kindly undertook to forward my first article for *The Times* in their diplomatic " bag."

IV

From Warsaw I returned by night train to Cracow and there met the four "hostages," who had now been liberated. I again travelled by night to Lemberg in a damaged compartment of a crowded train, without light or heat and with little sleep. I found the city deep in snow and noticed that many buildings had been badly punctured and damaged by machine guns and hand-grenades. There were no " droschkies " or trams, so I had to trudge on foot into the town to an hotel, while a Jewish porter carried my handbag. The electric power-station in the district had been put out of action by the Ukrainian bombardment, and at night therefore the only light in the hotel was provided by candles stuck in beer-bottles.

My Zionist friends, who were gathered in the house of their president, were delighted to see me and gave me a warm welcome as their first visitor from Western Europe after nearly four-and-a-half years. They listened intently and with hushed breath as I related my experiences since I had arrived in Poland, but, despite their sufferings in recent weeks, or perhaps because of them, they were much more anxious to hear about the Balfour Declaration and the prospects of its implementation. Having satisfied their hunger for news from London, Paris, and Warsaw, I sought information about the local pogrom, and was given a detailed account, which can only be summarised here[1].

The pogrom was political in origin and military in character. The Jews of Lemberg, anticipating an armed struggle between the Poles and the Ukrainians for possession of the city, determined upon a policy of neutrality. After the Ukrainians seized the city on November 1st, 1918, the Jews organised a militia for the protection of their lives and property, and its neutrality was officially recognised by Poles and Ukrainians. But many of the Polish soldiers who tried to drive out the Ukrainians raided Jewish homes for the purpose of robbery, and when they were repelled by a Jewish patrol, the Ukrainians announced that they, with the help of the Jewish militia, had thrust Polish forces back. The Jewish Defence Committee published a correction of this announcement, but it was ignored by the Poles, who obtained possession of the city on November 22nd and disarmed and imprisoned the Jewish militia. A Jewish deputation then appealed to the Chief of the Polish General Staff, but he replied that his forces were engaged on "a punitive expedition," which could not be dropped. A military cordon was drawn round the Jewish quarter, machine-guns were posted in each street, and systematic looting began of shops and houses. All who resisted were brutally assaulted or shot, and many women and girls were outraged. The orgy of plunder and vandalism continued for two days, culminating in the destruction by fire of some fifty many-storied houses and a large synagogue with historic contents. The casualties amounted to 73 persons killed and over 250 injured, and the damage was estimated at about £5,000,000. The sequel to the outrage was that the General who was in command of the troops was recalled and put into a lunatic asylum.

Some friends took me on a tour through the Jewish quarter to

---

[1] A fuller account is given in Chapter V of my *Travels in Jewry*.

POGROMS IN POLAND

see the devastation that had been committed. We passed through streets where whole blocks of houses had been burnt out: on the front of some of them was a round charred patch showing that each house had been set on fire separately. Besides the synagogue that had been entirely destroyed, attempts had been made to set fire to two others. In the Rabbi's robing-room of one of these were cases of benzine still lying on the floor, and the interior of the other presented a scene of desolation, with charred fragments of prayer-books and Pentateuchs scattered here and there.

I was given a collection of documentary material relating to the outrage, which had been carefully compiled during several weeks. The Galician Zionist Executive had elected the four "hostages" as their delegates to a Zionist Conference that was shortly to take place in London, and asked me to secure permission for them to travel. I therefore called at Potocki Palace to see Colonel Wade (who had come to discuss the question of an armistice with Ukrainian delegates), and he agreed to make out a certificate that would procure the necessary permit from the military authorities. We discussed the Jewish problem for a couple of hours, during which we could hear the booming of cannons a few miles away.

After four days in the dismal, bombarded city, and having completed all that I could do, I drove through a blizzard to the station, to return to Cracow. But as there was no through connection I had to stop at Jaroslau and stayed at a little Jewish hotel, where the sitting-room was converted for me into a bedroom. The following day I continued my journey, in a damaged and draughty compartment, in which I froze, and reached Cracow late at night. I spent one more day in this ancient capital of Poland to pay final visits to my friends and the Polish Liquidation Commission, and secured more detailed reports of pogroms and other anti-Jewish excesses that had been committed in 130 towns and villages in November and December, 1918, and January, 1919. At last my mission was over, and after dining in the evening at the Hotel Saski with the four released hostages and discussing what steps should be taken in Paris and London to secure peace and justice for the Jews in Poland I left early on the following morning for Vienna.

V

Owing to the Polish-Czech war that had broken out over the possession of Teschen there was no direct train to Vienna, and I had therefore to travel to Oswiecim and change there. Little did I dream while I was in that town that it was destined to acquire such macabre notoriety in the Second World War under its better known name of Auschwitz. I looked up the secretary of the Jewish community, who told me that there had been two local attempts at pogroms, the first having been warded off by the Jewish militia from Cracow, while the second resulted in some of the hooligans being injured. He conducted me to the Jewish cemetery, where many graves had been violated and tombstones damaged. On returning to the station an official wanted to subject me to a " body search " in a cubicle, but I protested that as I was on an official mission, with the approval of the British Government, I should be exempt. He therefore dispensed with the search, gave me a stamped disk, and allowed me to go on to the platform.

From Oswiecim I travelled to Kandrzin (in German territory), and after changing there again and spending the night in changing at three further stations, with intervals between and in an Arctic frost, I was at last in the train that brought me to Vienna thirty hours after leaving Cracow. I stayed in Vienna a couple of days, during which I reported to the Jewish National Council on the results of my investigations and gave interviews to the press. I was also brought into contact with Professor Dnystriansky, a member of the Ukrainian National Council, who gave me an exposition of his Council's demands; and then taken to Parliament House to hear a representative of the German Bohemians hold forth on their territorial proposals. They all thought that as I was going to Paris, where the Peace Conference was taking place, I would surely as a lover of justice propagate and support their views.

When I reached Berne, on February 8th, 1919, I found that August Zaleski was very eager to have my impressions, but on hearing my account of what I had learned and what were my conclusions he was deeply disappointed. I emphasised that although weeks had elapsed since the excesses his Government had not yet published a condemnation of the people responsible and until this was done public opinion in the Western world would not be satisfied. On the day after my return *The Times* of February 8th containing my article on " The Pogroms in Poland " arrived, and Zaleski spoke to me about it in a tone of serious perturbation. He said that it would do Poland a great deal of harm, whereupon I replied that the article showed that the Poles had done the Jews a great deal of harm, and he surely could not expect that I should suppress the truth.

The first International Socialist Conference since the First World War was then taking place in Berne, and I attended some of the sessions. The main topic of discussion was the attitude to be adopted to Bolshevism, upon which I heard some trenchant speeches by the Swedish statesman, Branting, the German revolutionary Kurt Eisner, the British delegates Ramsay MacDonald and Arthur Henderson, and others. Eisner, who was shot dead a couple of weeks later in Munich by a political reactionary when he was on his way to open his dissident assembly, struck me as a mild-mannered person with his pale face, unkempt beard, and gentle looks. Among those attending the Conference was Mr. H. N. Brailsford, who told me that he was going to Poland as a member of a British Economic Mission, and at his request I gave him a letter of introduction to the Jewish leaders in Warsaw.

VI

I was back in Paris by the middle of February and was glad to meet my wife there. It was her first visit to the French capital, but we were unable to do much sight-seeing together, as I had to spend much time in reporting on my mission to Nahum Sokolow and other Jewish leaders who had assembled in connection with the Peace Conference. They were concerned not only with the question of Palestine but also with that of national rights for the Jews in various lands of Central and Eastern Europe. Delegates from these countries were holding daily conferences for the purpose of formulating demands that would not only secure civil and political equality for those Jews who were not yet emancipated, but that would also safeguard the rights of those who might be transferred from the jurisdiction of one State to that of another. There were also delegations from the Jewish representative organisations of England, France, and the United States, and there was much heated discussion between them and the delegates from Eastern Europe as to the propriety and expediency of the term "national" in relation to the proposals for Jews to be submitted to the Peace Conference.

The outcome of these deliberations was that the Peace dictators required that Poland and about ten other States should sign Peace Treaties that embodied special clauses safeguarding the rights of racial, religious, and linguistic minorities amounting to a total of 25 million, of whom the Jews formed one-fifth. Another product of these discussions was that the delegates from Central and Eastern Europe created a permanent organisation, under the name of Committee of Jewish Delegations, with its seat in Paris, to watch over the interests of the Jews in those regions. The "Minorities Treaties," as they were called, were regarded at the time as one of the outstanding and most beneficial achievements of the Peace of Versailles, but unfortunately the hopes reposed in them were doomed for the most part to be frustrated, and consequently the Committee of Delegations and other Jewish representative bodies were kept constantly busy until the next World War broke out twenty years later.

Chapter Nine

PROTESTS AND POLEMICS
1919 — 1920

I

ON returning to London I thought that I had finished with the question of the pogroms in Poland, and should be able to devote myself anew entirely to matters connected with the Jewish national home. But I was soon disillusioned, for reports about fresh excesses continued to flow into the Zionist Bureau and called for action. They came from various sources — from the Zionist offices in Vienna and Copenhagen, to which they were brought by couriers from Cracow and Warsaw, and from Jewish delegates who travelled from Poland to Paris. Brief messages from Reuter also appeared in both the English and the Continental press, as well as in the American papers. It was obvious that the Polish Government, even if it had endeavoured to do so, had quite failed to prevent the continuance of the attacks. The Zionist Executive, in response to telegraphic appeals, made approaches to the Foreign Office and also provided some friends in the House of Commons with material for questions. Finally, they decided to hold a public demonstration at the Queen's Hall, at which I should deliver a full report on my mission and a resolution condemning the outrages should be adopted, so that public attention should be focussed upon the happenings in Poland and its Government be prodded into action.

It was considered desirable that the chair at a meeting of such a character should be taken by a person eminent in the political world. I therefore approached (the first) Lord Reading, and, as he declined,

A JEWISH PILGRIMAGE

went to Lord Buckmaster, but he likewise refused. Both of them seemed to have scruples about associating themselves with public criticisms of a State that was in the initial stage of establishing itself. I therefore called on Lord Parmoor, a Conservative Churchman (father of the late Sir Stafford Cripps), and upon my explaining the situation to him he readily agreed to preside, as he was entirely free from the inhibitions that restrained his fellow-Peers. But while Lord Reading and Lord Buckmaster were apathetic or cautious, some Polish Jews were strongly opposed to the demonstration and tried to persuade the Zionist Executive to abandon it. The painter, Leopold Pilichowsky, who was President of the Union of Polish Jews and a friend of mine, was particularly perturbed. He feared that the Warsaw Cabinet would be seriously annoyed and that Polish feeling against the Jews might become even more embittered. But the Zionist leaders were unmoved and resolved to go ahead with the arrangements.

The demonstration at the Queen's Hall took place on April 9th, 1919, and was attended by over 3,000 people. Lord Parmoor made a dignified and impressive chairman, and my speech was followed with close attention. After I had spoken the following resolution (which had naturally been approved by the chairman) was proposed by Mr. Hermann Landau, O.B.E., President of the Jews' Temporary Shelter, and seconded by Mr. J. D. Kiley, M.P. for Whitechapel :—

> That this public meeting, after hearing the Report of Mr. Israel Cohen, expresses its profound condemnation of the pogroms committed against the Jews in Poland and Galicia, and calls upon the British Government to insist upon the creation of constitutional safeguards for the free and peaceful development of the Jewish people in the Polish Republic; and that a copy of this resolution be forwarded to the Prime Minister, the Foreign Secretary, and the Secretariat of the Peace Conference.

Before the chairman submitted the resolution to the vote, Mr. Pilichowsky requested and was given permission to speak, but he was interrupted by members of the audience, who resented his attempt to whitewash the Polish authorities. Thereupon Lord Parmoor put the resolution and declared it to have been adopted unanimously.

The sequel to this demonstration was a leading article in the *Morning Post* two days later, which was significantly headed "Apocryphal Pogroms." It was a flagrant attack upon my veracity and integrity, and maintained that my account of "the alleged pogroms" did not "bear the test of even a cursory examination." I was particularly chagrined by the following passage, in which my internment in Germany was linked up with my report on Poland in terms that seemed to contain a malicious innuendo :—

> Mr. Cohen is himself a martyr; but not to the Poles. He was, we understand, a prisoner at Ruhleben until 1917, when he was so fortunate as to obtain his release. But so far from cherishing any resentment against the Germans his speech might almost have been calculated to help them.

I interpreted this passage to mean that I owed my release from Ruhleben to an act of favouritism on the part of the Germans, and that in return I wanted — as was put rhetorically at the end of the leader — "to discredit Poland and to help Germany." As this was not only entirely untrue but also, in my opinion, a calumny, I discussed the matter with a legal friend, and, on his advice, consulted an eminent expert on the question whether there was adequate ground for suing the *Morning Post* for libel. The expert advised me against taking action, and I therefore contented myself with sending the editor a long letter refuting the criticisms in the leader and concluding with the sentence : "I have not the least hesitation in stigmatising these allegations as utterly unfounded, untrue, and pernicious." My letter was published in full.

A couple of months later, in anticipation of a visit of the Polish Premier, Paderewski, to Oxford University, to receive an honorary degree, the *Morning Post* published another leading article to vindicate Poland. It discredited the reports of the pogroms, which it attributed to malicious propaganda, accused me of having helped to organise the campaign, referred again to my internment in Ruhleben, and again alleged that I felt no resentment against Germany. I replied in a long letter (occupying a whole column), in which I rebutted the attempt to belittle the pogroms, and refuted the reproach — with its obvious insinuation — that I had no grievance against Germany by referring to the evidence contained in my book, *The Ruhleben Prison Camp*, in a review of which the *Morning Post* (March 9th, 1917) had written :—

> Mr. Cohen's popularity was due to his staunch attitude at all times as one of the Stock-Engländer (out-and-out Englishmen), his courage in cases of German bullying, and his indefatigable efforts to improve the conditions of existence at Ruhleben.

The *Morning Post* replied to my letter in a further leader in the same issue (June 18th, 1919) also occupying a whole column, and entitled " The Plot against Poland," in which previous arguments were rehashed, and I was pityingly described as " the innocent victim of an unscrupulous propaganda." Why this Tory organ should have served as an assiduous and pliable mouthpiece of the Polish Government I never discovered. It may have assumed this role because *The Times*, which had published my report from Warsaw and also a further article, adopted a critical attitude to Poland. When I returned to London I found that *The Times*, while not questioning the extent and gravity of the outrages, was unwilling to publish another article on the subject, as originally arranged. Instead of this, I was asked to write an article describing the position and the grievances of the Jews in Poland and explaining the proposals that the representatives of the latter were submitting to the Peace Conference for the solution of their problems. The article was published on May 22nd, and the same issue contained a long leader on it, acknowledging the grievances of the Jews and pleading for their just treatment by Poland, while at the same time advising the Jews not to make any impracticable demands.

These polemics and discussions in the press, however, were but a feeble echo of the continued atrocities in the resurrected Republic. In Pinsk fifty-six Jews had been shot dead early in April under the pretext that they were Bolsheviks, and in Vilna a fortnight later eighty were shot with a similar excuse, while there were repeated reports of assaults and lootings. Public protests were made in many leading cities in Europe and America to bring pressure to bear upon the Polish Government to suppress the evil. The leaders of the Anglo-Jewish community, lay and ecclesiastical, after much deliberation, decided to proclaim June 26th a Day of Mourning and Protest, on which all Jews throughout the country should give expression to their sorrow and indignation. At the Queen's Hall there was a solemn service, at which the Chief Rabbi, Dr. J. H. Hertz, delivered an impressive address to a crowded audience, while in the East End there was a mass meeting at the People's Palace, at which I was one of the speakers. There was another huge gathering at the neighbouring Great Assembly Hall, and after these demonstrations were over a procession of Jews, estimated at 100,000, marched solemnly and silently through the City and the West End to Hyde Park, where further speeches of protest were made.

I was unable to take part in the procession as I had to hurry to King's Cross, where my wife was waiting to accompany me to Leeds. There, as indeed in almost all the provincial communities, the Day of Mourning and Protest was observed with every mark of solemnity. All Jewish shops, offices, and factories were closed, thousands of non-Jewish employees joined with their Jewish fellow-workers in their manifestations of grief, and the local press published special articles. A vast concourse, numbering over 4,000, had assembled in the Town Hall, over which Sir Michael Sadler, Vice-Chancellor of Leeds University, presided. It was by far the largest gathering that I had ever addressed, and the account that I gave of my visit to Poland and of the barbarities committed there was followed with the keenest interest and in tense silence, broken only by an occasional cry of " Shame! "

At the end of the meeting I was approached by the artist, Jacob Kramer, who said that he would like to draw a sketch of me as a souvenir of the occasion. He assured me that it would not take more than half-an-hour if I came round to him in the morning. So I went to his small and humble studio, sat as directed, and, within the promised time, the artist, by a swift succession of skilful strokes, made a large drawing of my head, which I had framed and am glad to possess to this day. From Leeds my wife and I travelled up the next day to Newcastle, where I addressed another meeting of public protest.

But despite all the demonstrations and declarations in England

and many other countries in Europe, as well as the more imposing manifestations of indignation in America, the excesses in Poland continued and its Government seemed helpless to stop them. Nor was there any improvement as a result of special Inquiry Commissions despatched from America and England. In the summer of 1919 a Commission sent by President Wilson, and headed by Henry Morgenthau (a former American Ambassador to Turkey), made a tour of inquiry and collected a mass of evidence; and four months later a British Government Commission, headed by Sir Stuart Samuel, made a similar investigation and amassed further material. But it was all in vain. The Polish Government refrained from conducting an inquiry of its own and punishing those guilty of the outrages, so that the afflictions of the Jews continued until their tormentors grew tired.

II

There was another momentous question that aroused world-wide interest at the time and provoked a bitter controversy in which I took part. It was the relations between Jews and Bolshevism. It was generally admitted that a number of Bolshevik leaders in the early years of the Russian Revolution were Jews, but their proportion was exaggerated not only by rabid Anti-Semites but also by superficial commentators on international affairs, who could not possibly substantiate their extravagant assertions. It was an irresistible temptation to identify most of the Jews in Russia with Bolshevism (although they were the gravest sufferers by it), and consequently to taunt Jews in other countries too with this state of affairs. Such was the psychological climate in both political and press circles in the closing months of 1919, when a vigorous and even virulent correspondence broke out in the columns of *The Times*.

It was started by the publication in that paper of an unusually long and very remarkable letter sent by a British officer in South Russia to his wife.[1] This was printed in large type under the title of " The Horrors of Bolshevism," which did not in any way exaggerate its contents, and it was rendered additionally attractive and sensational by being furnished with such cross-heads (which were quite unusual

[1] *The Times*, November 14th, 1919.

in such a staid organ) as " Unprintable photographs " and " Outrages on Women." All sorts of ghoulish and sadistic atrocities, including wholesale rape and " women with their breasts cut off to the bone," were attributed to the Bolsheviks. But the appalling feature of this letter was the prominence assigned to Jews, who were represented as little less than arch-fiends. It stated that " 80 to 90 per cent of the Commissaires are Jews," that " in towns captured by Bolsheviks the only unviolated sacred buildings are the synagogues, while churches are used for anything, from movie-shows to slaughter-houses," and the writer asked: " If a Commissary steeped in murder, with torture and rape, with mutilation, happens to be a Jew, as most of them are, should he receive exceptional treatment ? " The management of *The Times* was apparently so bent upon securing the widest possible publicity for this letter, that it had it reprinted as an eight-page pamphlet, which was sold at a penny, with a reduction on large orders.

The letter had a very depressing effect upon the Anglo-Jewish community, and it was obviously necessary that some step should be taken to counteract it. I, therefore, wrote a reply to *The Times* to disprove the oft-repeated allegation that in Russia Jews and Bolshevists were interchangeable.[1] I pointed out that the leader of the Menshevists was a Jew and that there were as many Jewish leaders among the anti-Bolshevists as there were Jewish Commissaires among the Bolshevists; that the only attempt on the life of Lenin had been made by a Jewish girl, Dora Kaplan; that there were cases of synagogues having been defiled; that Jewish communal organisations had been suppressed and their buildings requisitioned; that the Zionist movement was denounced as " counter-revolutionary " and as " an instrument of Entente Imperialism," that Zionist societies had been suppressed in many cities, Zionist funds confiscated, and Hebrew newspapers proscribed.

The following day *The Times* published (in larger type than that accorded to my letter) a letter signed " Philojudaeus," who evinced his philo-Judaism by asserting that " the evidence that Jews play a principal part in the Bolshevist conspiracy all over the world is too

[1] *The Times*, November 21st, 1919.

strong to be ignored," though he agreed that "much of it is but *prima facie* evidence, and may admit of refutation." He added:

> If Mr. Cohen can refute it, he will be doing a great service to his people and to humanity, for unless it is answered I fear that when Bolshevism fails, thousands of innocent Jews will be massacred on the pretext that they abet Lenin or sympathise with his crimes.

I thereupon wrote a longer letter than my previous one to *The Times*,[1] in which I pointed out that the Bolshevik leaders of Jewish birth were not in any way connected with the Jewish community, had never taken part in Jewish public life or represented Jewish ideals, and that it was therefore unjust to saddle the Jewish people with the iniquities of a handful of its renegade sons. I also referred to the facts that in the Jewish communities in Russia there were several political parties but no Bolshevist party, that some leaders of Russian Jewry had been victims of Bolshevist terrorism, and there had been regular pogroms of Jews by Bolshevist troops.

The following day *The Times* published a letter (again in large type) signed "Janus," who, after referring to my two letters, gave a list of "28 conspicuous Bolshevists, most of them Commissaires," whom he described as "either full-blooded Jews or of Jewish extraction." I examined the list very carefully, and, with the help of friends who had a special knowledge of prominent personalities in the Russian Revolution, I discovered that as many as ten were either non-Jews, or anti-Bolshevists, or dead Bolshevists. I therefore sent in another letter setting forth this information, which was promptly published. But in the same issue[2] containing my third letter, appeared a fresh indictment in a letter nearly a column long, in large type (the type uniformly used for the attacks), on the editorial page. The lerter was signed "Verax," and from its contents, fluent style, and all the attendant circumstances I strongly suspected that it had been written by an influential and even authoritative member of the editorial staff. "Verax" expressed the view that the Jews regarded themselves as "the Chosen People destined, one day, to be the rulers and law-givers of mankind," and that they thought no price too high

[1] November 25th, 1919.
[2] November 27th, 1919.

for revenge upon Russia for her oppression of them. He contrasted the Law of Moses, which he misrepresented as equivalent to the *lex talionis*, with " the Law of Christ with its doctrine of forgiveness." He argued that the Jews had worked and plotted against Russia for centuries, that " throughout Russia and indeed, throughout Central Europe, including Hungary and what remains of Austria, Bolshevism and Jewry are regarded as practically synonymous." He concluded by declaring that " the only sound policy " for the Jews was " for their representative leaders to dissociate themselves whole-heartedly and publicly from Bolshevism and all its works," and to help to overthrow it, otherwise the collapse of Bolshevism would be followed by a massacre of Jews.

The pontifical contribution of " Verax " provoked a rejoinder from the Chief Rabbi, Dr. Hertz[1], who reproved *The Times* for publishing a virulent attack upon " the Jew, his sacred Scriptures, and his religious faith." I also replied to him in my fourth and longest letter,[2] in which I disposed in detail of both " Verax's " theological and political argumentation, and stated that it was not for the Jews but for the Allied and Associated Powers to deal with the Bolshevik regime.

On the same day when my first letter appeared in *The Times* I was surprised to receive the following letter from its proprietor, Lord Northcliffe :—

THE TIMES,
21st November, 1919

Dear Mr. Cohen,

I was very pleased to see your letter in The Times. The matter is one of the utmost importance. We do not want any anti-Jewish feeling in this country.

I did not say to Mr. Falk[3] that I wished Mr. Paul Dukes[4] to see an Anglo-Jewish leader of Zionist sympathies. What I said was that Mr. Dukes had made a statement to me as to the probability of great massacres of Jews in Russia, which I thought ought to be made known to some leader of English Jewry. He certainly gave me the impression

[1] November 29th, 1919.
[2] December 1st, 1919.
[3] Mr. Bernard B. Falk, formerly editor of the *Weekly Dispatch*, etc.
[4] Now Sir Paul Dukes, who was a British secret agent in Russia during the First World War.

that many of the so-called commissaires are Jews, though he also said that Jews had suffered at the hands of Bolsheviks. What I wish to try to do is:—
(1) To stop any chance of anti-Jewish feeling in Great Britain.
(2) To let Jewish leaders here know Mr. Dukes' views. He was with me for several days and I found him accurate and straightforward.

Yours faithfully,
Northcliffe.

I replied to Lord Northcliffe, assuring him that the Jewish community of this country would be deeply indebted to him if he would use the powerful influence of his papers to prevent the dissemination of misunderstanding and informed him that I would be happy to arrange an interview between Mr. Dukes and Lord Rothschild, who was the Acting President of the Board of Deputies of British Jews in the absence of the President, Sir Stuart Samuel, who was then on his mission in Poland. The interview took place in the Office of the Zionist Organisation, in Great Russell Street, on November 26th, and I was the only other person present. Mr. Dukes repeated the statement contained in Lord Northcliffe's letter and also stressed the necessity of a public denunciation of Bolshevism by Anglo-Jewish leaders, as urged in the anonymous letters in *The Times*.

After the interview I wrote to Lord Northcliffe that it had taken place and added the following:—

In your letter of the 21st inst. you emphasised your wish to stop any chance of anti-Jewish feeling in Great Britain. I very greatly regret to have to point out that this wish is likely to be frustrated by some of the anonymous letters on the subject of Bolshevism that have recently appeared in the columns of The Times. *I refer particularly to the long letter from a British officer, which has been reprinted in pamphlet form, and to the letters of " Philojudaeus," " Janus," and " Verax." I am afraid that the pamphlet is likely to cause considerable harm as it magnifies the part taken by the Jews in the Bolshevist movement and tries to condone or explain away the pogroms committed by Denikin's troops. Would it not be possible to withdraw this pamphlet from circulation, or at least to delete the objectionable passages in any new edition that may be necessary?*

I should like to call your particular attention to the baseless and unjust attack upon the Jewish people contained in the letter of "Verax" published in yesterday's Times. The letter has aroused considerable indignation throughout the Jewish community. I feel sure that I only need call your attention to this matter to ensure the prevention of any similar attacks in the future.

To this letter I received the following reply from Lord Northcliffe:

THE TIMES,
November 30th, 1919.

Dear Mr. Cohen,

I do not at all agree with you that an ostrich-like policy of ignoring the fact that a considerable number of the chief Bolsheviks are Jews is likely to do good — nor have my newspapers ever magnified the part taken by Jews in the Bolshevik movement.

I know Jews very well. My oldest and most intimate friend is a Jew, but I also know public opinion well. Here in Great Britain there is practically no anti-Semite feeling. There are, of course, jokes about Jews as there are jokes about Scotsmen. But if leading English Jews do not, in an important manifesto, widely circulated here, in Russia, Germany, Poland, Austria, and the United States, express the detestation they privately utter of the horrors perpetrated by renegade and other Jews in Russia, I am convinced that we may get something like Anti-Semitism here.

I hope you will not mind my frank speaking. I know exactly what the Jewish brain means to our national progress and success, and I do not want this country to be made so unattractive that it will not remain here.

Yours faithfully,
Northcliffe.

To this letter I replied as follows:—

2nd December, 1919.

Dear Lord Northcliffe,

I am much obliged to you for your letter of the 30th ulto. I am certainly not in favour of ignoring the participation of Jews in the Bolshevik movement, but I should like to emphasise that the Jews in Great Britain are not responsible for their actions. The Jewish Board of Deputies has already passed a resolution dissociating itself from the Bolsheviks, and a letter in a similar sense, signed by ten prominent Jews, appeared in the Morning Post a few months ago. I have no right to say what the leaders of English Jewry may think about your *idea of the circulation of a manifesto, but the increased danger to which the Jews in Bolshevik Russia would thereby be exposed ought not to be overlooked. If there is no misrepresentation of the matter in this country there need be no fear of anti-Semitism.*

Yours faithfully,
Israel Cohen.

Therewith the correspondence concluded. No international Jewish manifesto denouncing Bolshevism was published. There was no collapse of Bolshevism, but there were, unfortunately, Jewish massacres on an extensive scale. The avalanche of slaughter that swept across the Ukraine from the end of 1918 to the end of 1920, and across White Russia from the middle of 1920 to the middle of 1921, resulted in the extermination of over 100,000 Jews. The outrages were committed for the most part by troops of the Ukrainian Government in consequence of their defeat by the Bolsheviks. They were ostensibly acts of reprisal against the Jewish population for sympathising with Communism, of which they were falsely accused; but numerous excesses were also committed by Soviet regiments and by the " White " troops of General Denikin, as well as by Polish forces of occupation in White Russia — these mutually warring forces being all agreed upon one thing only, that the Jews should be killed.

After the lapse of thirty-six years it might seem to be of no account to recall the time when the Jews in the Soviet Union were all stigmatised by the Western world as Bolsheviks and saddled with the misdeeds of their Government. On the contrary, it is of supreme importance to recall that phase of history, for we recently reached a stage in the evolution of the Soviet Union when its Jews were suspected and accused by their Government of holding the very reverse sentiments — of harbouring sympathies with the Western world. And whereas the wholesale indictment of Russian Jewry a generation ago was responsible for widespread Anti-Semitism, the Soviet Government's recent distrust of its Jewish subjects influenced it and its satellites towards a policy of Anti-Semitism. In short, no matter what the views and feelings of Russian Jewry may be, they seem doomed, with ineluctable recurrence, to be the victims of a fickle fate.

Chapter Ten

THE ZIONIST HEADQUARTERS

1919 — 1920

I

THE Zionist Bureau that had been maintained at Empire House, Piccadilly, at the time when the Balfour Declaration was issued and for over a year later was transferred in the spring of 1919 to Great Russell Street. The inevitable increase of activities necessitated by the new era that had begun required more spacious premises, and these were provided by three contiguous four-storied houses, numbering 75 to 77, in the sedate and august neighbourhood of the British Museum. Originally built as private residences for eighteenth century gentry, they were hardly suitable as the headquarters of an international organisation, but they were adapted to its purposes as skilfully as architects and carpenters could contrive. The most important part of the Central Office of the Zionist Organisation, as it was henceforth called, was situated in the corner house, No. 77, and it was in the sombre rooms on the first floor occupied by Chaim Weizmann and Nahum Sokolow, and in the large austere-looking Conference Room, that constant deliberations took place which, after years of fluctuating hopes and countless heart-aches, eventually led to the establishment of the Jewish State. It was there that I spent most of the days of over twenty years of my life, and also part of my nights, for periodical meetings of the General Council would often begin at a late hour of the evening and continue until the small hours of the morning.

Soon after the Office was opened there began an influx of Zionists from the Continent, most of them with the title of "Doctor"[1], who believed that their services would be useful and even necessary in the new administration that was being set up. They came from Berlin and Vienna, from Prague and Vilna, from Salonika and Constantinople. Some were members of the Executive elected at the last Congress, in 1913, who thought that after the war they had a right to resume their functions until the next Congress would be held. Others had occupied leading positions in their various countries and were now prepared to make their homes in London. Consequently there quickly grew up an elaborate administrative apparatus, with numerous departments and sub-departments, which spread to all the rooms on all four floors of the three houses. But after trying to fit themselves into some suitable niche, and finding that they were redundant or that they could not adjust themselves to the new milieu, most of them left, voluntarily or otherwise, within a couple of years or less, and either returned to their former homes or went to Palestine.

One of the leading members of the old Executive was Dr. Victor Jacobson (1869 — 1934), who had a long Zionist history. Although originating from the Crimea, he looked more like a typical French politician or journalist, with his dapper figure, short spruce greyish beard, and pince-nez. He had been a Russian member of the General Council for many years and had acted as manager of the Zionist bank at Beyrut as well as of its offshoot in Constantinople. In the Ottoman capital his work had been more of a political and diplomatic than of a financial character, as he had to try to influence local Government circles to adopt a less hostile attitude to Zionism. At the London Office he was in general charge of the administration, but after a couple of years he went to Berlin, where he became one of the directors of the "Jüdischer Verlag" (the Zionist publishing house). Four years later he was appointed by the Zionist Executive as their political representative in Paris and also at the League of Nations in Geneva.

Another member of the old Executive who came to London at the time was Dr. Shmarya Levin, one of the most rapid and brilliant speakers on the Zionist platform. In his student days in Berlin he

[1] The degree of Ph.D., the usual mark of a graduate of a Continental University.

THE ZIONIST HEADQUARTERS

had belonged to the same Zionist society as Jacobson and Leo Motzkin[1], and after a career in Russia as a Rabbi and as a deputy in the Duma, he left his native country for ever and became one of Zionism's most assiduous and popular propagandists in various parts of the world. He did not cultivate the classic cadence and measured style of oratory of a Nordau, for he was of too impulsive and ebullient a nature. Words came pouring from him in torrents, lava-like, sweeping everything before them with an irresistible rush, so that only the most nimble minds could follow and savour the gems of wit and wisdom from his rich storehouse of Jewish lore. Not for him was the studied pose or the carefully calculated declamation. He spoke as his soul prompted him, carried away by his own passion, and almost down to the end he presented the spectacle of a dynamo of inexhaustible energy.

During the whole of the First World War Levin was in the United States, where he was tireless in his advocacy of the cause, and he also carried out a speaking tour across Canada. At the London Office he took charge of a short-lived Education Department, but he spent more time outside the Office, travelling about to all cities, from Brighton to Glasgow. Unfortunately his speeches were seldom or never reported, as he did not speak in English, and he was annoyed when he read in the Anglo-Jewish press an account of a speech by a less important English fellow-speaker, simply followed by the line: " Dr. Shmarya Levin spoke in Yiddish."

The first treasurer of the Executive was Boris Goldberg, who had been a Zionist leader in Vilna for many years and also a member of the General Council. He was a wealthy merchant and a lover of Hebrew culture. Burly, black-bearded, and pleasant in manner, he radiated with the kindness of human nature through his gleaming spectacles. He kept open house in Hampstead, where his handsome wife dispensed gracious hospitality to all who cared to come, especially on a Friday evening, when their home became " Liberty Hall." In addition to the finances of the Organisation, he also had

---

[1] Leo Motzkin (1867 — 1933) played a very prominent part in the Zionist movement as chairman of the General Council and of Congresses, and was for many years chairman of the Committee of Jewish Delegations, whose headquarters were in Paris.

charge of a Trade and Industry Department, but after a time he realised that this Department could get on well without him, and so he went to settle in Palestine. Shortly afterwards the sole official of the Department followed him there, and the Department was closed.

II

Of the many people of varied importance who took part in the affairs of the Zionist Office in the first years of its existence and left after a brief spell, never to return, the most distinguished was Dr. Max Nordau. He was also the saddest, for he came to London from five years' exile in Madrid, whither he had had to flee from his beloved Paris at the outbreak of the First World War as an Austrian subject, although he had been anything but pro-German. Once a writer of international renown, whose every utterance had commanded respectful and even deferential attention, he had now come back to a changed world, in which he was little known outside the Zionist community, and in this community too there had been a fundamental change. The new leaders, Weizmann and Sokolow, had formerly been the protagonists of "practical" Zionism, whom he, as the political Zionist *par excellence*, had previously flayed with pen and tongue; now they had become the spokesmen of political Zionism, and he had to content himself with the part of the candid critic. Moreover he was now a man of seventy and still a refugee, for the French Government would not yet allow him to return to his home. He was given the cordial and courteous welcome befitting one who had once shared with Herzl in the leadership of the movement, and was assigned a large room on the first floor of the Zionist Office; but when Sokolow came back from the Peace Conference in Paris and wished to occupy that room by virtue of his position, Nordau, who had no official status, was allotted a smaller room on the ground floor. He was deeply chagrined by this transfer, which he considered a personal affront, although it was necessitated by the limitations and deficiencies of an old house that was never designed as a political headquarters.

Shortly after his arrival Nordau was welcomed at a public

THE ZIONIST HEADQUARTERS

reception in his honour, held at the Prince's Galleries, Piccadilly, by the English Zionist Federation, which was attended by a very large and enthusiastic gathering. Dr. Weizmann, who presided, paid a glowing tribute to the services rendered by the patriarchal-looking veteran and presented him with an illuminated album, in which he was acclaimed as "a sage, revered, and well-tried counsellor." There followed a few other speakers, of whom I was one, after which Nordau gave an impressive address, in which he contrasted the tragic situation of the Jews in Eastern Europe with the promising prospects afforded by the projected National Home in Palestine. The reception was outwardly a social success, but Nordau left it much disgruntled, as was revealed many years later in his biography written by his widow and his daughter. For in a letter that he wrote at the time to his wife in Paris he complained that at the function there was "no meal" but only refreshments; and he commented sarcastically:—

The tickets were sold at ten shillings and sixpence. First I said the ten shillings were for the food and the sixpence for my eloquence. Later I judged that the sixpence were for food and the ten shillings for the lecture.

Nordau was invited to all meetings of the Executive, which were frequent and animated, and soon showed himself a severe critic. He was ruthless in his analysis of the interpretation of the Balfour Declaration as it had become commonly accepted, and pressed Weizmann and Sokolow to secure from the Government a broader interpretation, or the assurance of a generous fulfillment, which they felt sure they could not obtain. He demanded a vast and immediate immigration of Jews into Palestine, regardless of the fact that there were no funds for the purpose and that the country was still under military administration. One day I had to accompany him to a fashionable photographer who wanted his picture for the press, and on our journey in a taxi, both there and back, he argued all the time, vehemently and dogmatically, in favour of a wholesale influx into Palestine. "We must have hundreds of thousands of Jews there at once," he said. "Many may die on the road, but only by getting tremendous numbers into the country at once shall we be able to make it our own." How these hundreds of thousands were to be transported, fed, and housed were problems that he declared could be easily solved by the " iron will " of the Jewish people.

Having been deprived of his savings by the French Government, Nordau was without appreciable means during his nine months' stay in London. Joseph Cowen therefore was asked by the Zionist Executive to suggest to him that he should accept a salaried position in the movement, but his pride revolted at the idea and he spurned it indignantly. He covered his moderate expenditure (he lived in a modest boarding-house near the Office) by writing for the Jewish press. I was requested to invite him to contribute an article to *Haolam*, for which I afterwards brought him a cheque for ten pounds, but he hesitated to accept it until I assured him that the paper made it a principle to pay all its contributors.

Nordau's dominant characteristic was his dogmatism. He always felt so sure of his ground that his judgments took on the form of something absolute, infallible, and invincible. But there were two occasions in London (at least within my knowledge) when he had to admit that he was mistaken. A few days after his arrival I met him in the morning in Great Russell Street, just opposite the British Museum, walking in the direction of Gower Street. After the preliminary greeting I ascertained that he thought he was going to the Zionist Office, and when I pointed out that he was going in the wrong direction he stoutly maintained that I must be mistaken. I replied that I was on my way then to my official duties at the Office, and as I went there every day I wasn't likely to forget my bearings. He then agreed to retrace his footsteps, and as he caught sight of the Office he good-humouredly admitted that he was in the wrong. Some time later I arranged with Nordau to take him out to dinner one evening and said that I would call for him in his room at six o'clock. A previous appointment made me a few minutes late, and when I reached his room I found that he had gone. On making inquiries I was told that he had asked somebody where I lived and had probably gone to my house. I therefore immediately rushed home, and soon after I got there Nordau arrived. He at first said that he was positive that I had told him I would take him home to dinner, but when I explained to him that I could not possibly have done so as my wife was in bed with our newly-born son he admitted that he must be mistaken. So I gave him a drink and some fruit, and after he had delivered his judgment on some pictures on the wall, he left and I accompanied him to the nearest bus-stop. The next day I took him to lunch at the National Liberal Club, where his venerable appearance attracted much attention.

Nordau's persistent efforts to secure permission to return to Paris met at last with success in September, 1920, thanks to the intervention of the Greek statesman, Venizelos, who had the greatest admiration for him and whose acquaintance he had renewed in London. As the French Government, treating him as an enemy alien, had confiscated all his property, Nordau came back to a home of poverty, from which books and pieces of furniture had to be sold to pay tradesmen's bills. He therefore decided that he would go to the United States on a lecturing tour in the hope of retrieving his fortune, but the plan had to be abandoned owing to the breakdown of his health. When I passed through Paris in April, 1921, on my return from the Far East, I climbed up to his modest fifth-floor flat to greet him, but was told by his wife that he was not in a condition to receive me. But at the farther end of a gloomy lobby I caught a glimpse of the bowed figure of one who had once been an intellectual titan of international fame pass slowly from one room into another. And so he passed from my sight for ever.

After nearly two years of stoical suffering, Nordau died on January 22nd, 1923. There was mourning throughout the Jewish world, and eloquent tributes were offered by the press, platform, and pulpit to the greatness of the man who had been a valiant and illustrious champion of his people.

III

Shortly after the Office was established there began a steady trickle of visitors from the United States, both Zionists and non-Zionists, and occasionally non-Jews too, especially journalists. For the most part they were birds of passage, although in some cases they stayed on in London for weeks and even months. They were all critical at first of the cramped accommodation at the Office, which they had preconceived as an imposing building of mammoth proportions, worthy of a world-wide organisation, but they were favourably impressed by the efficiency of the work carried on inside it as well as by the devotion of the workers and the small rewards meted out to them.

One of the first and the most eminent of our visitors from across the Atlantic was Justice Louis D. Brandeis, of the United States Supreme Court of Justice, who stayed in London for a couple of days on his way to Palestine and again on his return. He was accompanied by Jacob de Haas, whom he called his "teacher in Zionism." I had known de Haas very well twenty years earlier, when he was assistant-editor of the London *Jewish World*, to which I was a regular contributor, and before Herzl suggested to him to go to America to propagate the Zionist cause. He introduced me to Brandeis, who made a complimentary reference to my *Jewish Life in Modern Times*, which he said he had read.

Brandeis was a tall, distinguished-looking figure, lean and ascetic, rather serious in mien, restrained in manner, and laconic in expression. He was the very antithesis of most leading Zionists on the Continent and also of many in America. As a judge he was more accustomed to listen than to speak, and when he spoke it was in slow and measured terms, the very reverse of the torrential eloquence that was customary on Zionist platforms. That was why, when he addressed a public meeting at the Clerkenwell Town Hall, his speech was disappointing. It was astonishingly brief, and the only point in it that I still remember was that he looked upon everybody who did not do his utmost for the Zionist cause as a " slacker."

In the same year I made the acquaintance of Felix Frankfurter and Benjamin V. Cohen. Frankfurter, who was then Professor of Law at Harvard University and now adorns the bench of the United States Supreme Court of Justice, was a member of the American section of the Zionist delegation to the Peace Conference in Paris. It was he who obtained from Emir Feisal, the head of the Arab Delegation (afterwards the first King of Iraq), that historic letter, in which he wrote: " Our deputation here in Paris is fully acquainted

THE ZIONIST HEADQUARTERS

with the proposals submitted yesterday by the Zionist Organisation to the Peace Conference, and we regard them as moderate and proper." It was, however, in connection with the Jewish question in Poland that I came into close touch with Professor Frankfurter. The Zionist Executive at that time were seriously concerned with that question, as I have already related in previous chapters, and at one of their meetings (after my return from Poland) devoted to this formidable problem Frankfurter was present by special invitation to give advice, and I was impressed by the keenness and intelligence with which he grappled with a complicated subject that was quite new to him.

Benjamin Cohen, who has figured so prominently in the American Delegation to the United Nations, also came to London originally on his way to the Peace Conference. But after almost all his fellow-Americans had returned home, he remained in London and occupied a front-room on the second floor of the Zionist Office. It was commonly said (by those who resented the critical attitude of some American Zionists to the London Office) that his only function was to send Brandeis confidential reports on what was happening at the Office. A more friendly view was that he was co-operating with others in the laborious and rather contentious task of drafting the articles of the Palestine Mandate. Such, at any rate, is the account given in his Autobiography by Dr. Weizmann, who pays a tribute to his drafting skill. The final text of the Mandate was not agreed upon until the spring of 1922, but Benjamin Cohen had returned to America before the spring of 1921, for when I got back to London at that time from my journeyings in the Far East I entered into occupation of his room.

IV

From the very beginning the Zionist cause enjoyed the support of many Christian friends, who were influenced either by their study of the Bible and their belief in the prophecies about the restoration of Israel, or by their sympathy with the sufferings of Jewry and their desire to see them ended through the recovery of national independence. Most of them evinced their interest by writing letters to the

Zionist Office for literature, while others gave expression to their friendship in a more active form. There were three in particular who were often seen in the Zionist Office in its early days, each a distinctive personality.

The Rev. William Hechler was a survival from the time of Herzl. He had been Chaplain to the British Embassy in Vienna in the closing years of the nineteenth century and had rendered the founder of the Zionist movement valuable services by introducing him to the Grand Duke of Baden, who secured for Herzl an audience with the German Kaiser, and Herzl showed his appreciation by immortalising him in his romance *Altneuland* as the Rev. William Hopkins. But although Hechler's efforts in the field of diplomacy led eventually only to a mirage, the Zionist Executive, fifteen years after the death of Herzl, felt that a debt of gratitude was due to him and granted him a small pension, for which he called at the Office every month. Hechler was a sincere believer in the Biblical prophecies and carried his proofs of them in the huge pocket of his big black cloak, which he seemed to wear in summer as in winter. He was a burly bearded priest, rendered more bulky still by his long flowing robe, from which he would produce a well-thumbed Bible with marked passages and a sort of scroll with an elaborate calculation based upon Daniel, pointing to the date of deliverance.

Professor Patrick Geddes was quite a different type. His services were invoked in the very early days of the National Home, in connection with proposals for the structural expansion of the Hebrew University, and for a year or two his bearded and bespectacled figure was very familiar at No. 77. He was constantly producing plans, charts, and blue-prints for the extension and beautification of the University in accordance with suggestions from the London Executive, and his plans were later reduced in scale as a result of decisions of the Jerusalem Executive, until poor Geddes felt frustrated and realised that the time for the execution of his grandiose scheme must be deferred until funds would be more plentiful.

In contrast to Hechler and Geddes was the political negotiator, James A. Malcolm. He was a British Armenian, who had been in close contact with Sir Mark Sykes during the war, in connection with

THE ZIONIST HEADQUARTERS

the organisation of the Armenian effort. Sykes, who was in charge of the Middle Eastern Department of the Foreign Office and assistant-secretary of the Imperial War Cabinet, had spoken to Malcolm of his anxiety about the lack of pro-Allied feeling among American Jews, whereupon Malcolm offered to bring him into touch with some leading Zionists in England who might be able to exert some influence through their American friends. Accordingly Malcolm introduced Weizmann and Sokolow to Sir Mark Sykes, who had Lord Milner's authority for his negotiations with them, and from that moment the efforts to obtain from the British Government an official expression of sympathy with Zionist aspirations took a new and decisive turn for the better, and eventually led to the Balfour Declaration. I saw Malcolm in the Office from time to time and learned to appreciate the value of the service that he had rendered.[1] I therefore understood his profound disappointment when he found that Weizmann in his Autobiography, *Trial and Error*, had not even mentioned his name. Weizmann subsequently acknowledged the omission, but Malcolm was hardly consoled, as the acknowledgment could not be embodied in the book, and, owing to Weizmann's failing health after its publication, a revised edition was out of question.

It was from James Malcolm that I obtained a letter of introduction to Sidney Webb, whom I wished to see in the interests of the Hebrew University. In addition to my work as Director of Publicity and Propaganda, which included the editing of a weekly paper, *The Zionist Bulletin*, I had continued calling upon wealthy members of the Jewish community to obtain donations for the Palestine Restoration Fund. But as the needs of the University were urgent and made a specialised appeal, it was thought that an attempt should be made to secure a grant from an educational trust created by the multi-millionaire, Sir Ernest Cassel, of which Sidney Webb was a trustee. I therefore went to see Webb on a Sunday afternoon, January 11th, 1920, at his house in Grosvenor Road, Westminster Embankment. I found him and his wife Beatrice — for they received me together — rather cool and apathetic. I did my best to explain the important

[1] He died in 1952.

part that the Hebrew University was destined to play, not only as the prime spiritual factor in the development of the new Judaea and as the place of learning to which Jewish students barred from the inhospitable Universities of Central and Eastern Europe would soon be flocking, but as a future beacon of light throughout the Middle East. Sidney Webb listened impassive and sphinx-like, and Beatrice looked on in cool dignity, while the frigid atmosphere was scarce tempered by the tea of which I was invited to partake. In the few words that the famous Fabian deigned to utter — at times his eyes seemed half-closed — he said that he did not think that the terms of the Cassel Trust would permit of a grant to an institution in a foreign country, but he would nevertheless see what he could do. However, by the time that I left the Webbs I gave up all illusion that I could expect anything, nor were my expectations belied. But, when, ten years later, Sidney Webb, as Lord Passfield, Secretary of State for the Colonies, issued his White Paper, which threatened to whittle down the Balfour Declaration and the Palestine Mandate and breathed such a spirit of hostility that Dr. Weizmann felt obliged to resign his position as President of the Jewish Agency, I recalled the chilly afternoon that I spent in the house of the Webbs in Grosvenor Road.

V

On April 24th, 1920, the Supreme Council of the Peace Conference met at San Remo and resolved that the Balfour Declaration should be incorporated in the Treaty of Peace with Turkey and that the Mandate for Palestine should be allotted to Great Britain. The way was thus cleared for the replacement of military rule in Palestine by a civil administration, and also for the first practical steps to be taken for the establishment of the Jewish National Home. Early in May Weizmann and Sokolow were back in London. While they were still in Paris a report reached the Office that Weizmann intended coming back separately. This news caused great consternation as it seemed to confirm previous rumours that some coolness had arisen between the two leaders. A telegram in strong terms was therefore despatched to Weizmann, informing him of the official welcome that the heads of the English Zionist Federation intended giving him and

THE ZIONIST HEADQUARTERS

Sokolow on their arrival at Victoria Station, and pointing out that it would create a very unfavourable impression if they came back separately. The message had the desired effect. The two leaders arrived together and were accorded an enthusiastic ovation both at Victoria and also in Great Russell Street.

The Executive lost no time in deciding that among the urgent measures to be taken was the despatch of emissaries to North and South America and other parts of the world to expound the implications of the Balfour Declaration and to raise the funds that were necessary. They invited me to undertake a mission for this purpose to Australasia and the Middle and Far East, which would occupy the best part of a year, and after obtaining my wife's assent I agreed.

In order to facilitate my journey and to make an effective impression upon the leaders of the Jewish communities that I was to visit, it was considered essential that I should carry credentials from the British Government as well as from the Zionist leaders and other eminent Jews. I was therefore furnished with a general letter of introduction from the Foreign Office bearing my photograph and signature, with a number of letters from Lord Milner, Colonial Secretary, to the Governors of British Dominions, as well as with messages from Chaim Weizmann, Nahum Sokolow, Herbert Samuel, Sir Alfred Mond, Lord (Robert) Cecil, Lord Rothschild, and Max Nordau. It was arranged that the cost of the journey should be borne jointly by the Zionist Organisation and the Jewish National Fund, and that the money I raised should be shared correspondingly between them. To ensure the success of my mission it was thought advisable that I should visit Palestine for a month before sailing to Australia, so that I should obtain the requisite information and inspiration. But just before I was about to leave London alarming news came from Budapest of attacks upon Jews by the " Awakening Magyars," whereupon Sokolow urged me to go there *en route* to investigate the situation and draw up a report, even though this diversion would mean curtailing the length of my stay in Palestine. The Executive gave me a complimentary luncheon at the Holborn Restaurant on May 14th, 1920, at which Sokolow, who was in the

A JEWISH PILGRIMAGE

chair, made a felicitous speech. He wished me every success and predicted that whatever else might be the outcome of my mission it would give birth to a new book. The following day I set out on my long journey.

Chapter Eleven

MISSION TO AUSTRALASIA
1920

I

THE mission that I undertook in 1920 was, quite apart from all personal considerations and material results, a unique event, for it was the first time in Jewish history that the emissary of a great organisation accomplished such an extensive and peculiar journey for the Jewish national cause, and likewise the first time that several of the communities included in the itinerary were ever addressed upon that subject. During the eleven months that I was away from England I crossed the Continent for my first pilgrimage to Jerusalem, visited most of the Jewish communities between the Red Sea and the Yellow Sea and between the Antipodes and Manchuria, travelled from Shanghai to Singapore and from Java to India, and revisited Palestine before returning to Europe. Altogether I sailed in twenty ships, my voyages varying from twelve hours to twenty-four days, and the whole extent of my journey on land and water was at least 30,000 miles. In those days ample time was required for long journeys, for aeroplanes did not yet venture beyond short distances.

As I formed a mission of one, I had to act in manifold capacities — as organiser and speaker, as propagandist and fund collector, as reporter and correspondent, as diplomatist and occasionally even preacher. I met with a cordial reception wherever I set foot, and likewise with a hospitality that was always flattering and sometimes even embarrassing. There was everywhere a keen desire to learn of the progress already made in Palestine, of the prospects in store for the early future, and also of the history of the chain of events that

A JEWISH PILGRIMAGE

led to the Balfour Declaration. The warmest interest was shown by those Jews who originated from Eastern Europe, especially Russia. I found them in all the cities of Australia and New Zealand, in China and Japan, above all in the great commercial centre of Manchuria — Harbin, and in smaller numbers in the other lands of the East through which I passed. I have already written a full description of these journeyings of more than thirty years ago[1], but as the book has long been out of print I need no excuse for giving a summary of it here.

II

My first place of call was The Hague, where I saw the directors of the Jewish National Fund in order to learn of its activities up-to-date and of the plans they had in mind for their share of the funds that I was expected to raise. From there I went to Vienna to prepare for my journey to Budapest, but when I informed Chief Rabbi Dr. Chajes and the Zionist leader, Robert Stricker, of my intention they earnestly advised me not to go, as they thought it would be too risky. They said that I could find out much more in Vienna about the terrors in Hungary than I could in Budapest, where people were afraid to speak; but a friend who had recently fled from there assured me that for one with a British passport it was quite safe. As there was a censorship of letters beyond the frontier I was advised not to write to anybody about my forthcoming visit. So a Viennese Zionist telegraphed to a cousin in Budapest that he would arrive on a certain day on business, and that a room at an hotel should be reserved for him; and in due course I presented myself to the cousin and claimed the room.

While in the train to Budapest I carefully studied the British Government's White Paper on the " Alleged Existence of ' White Terror ' in Hungary." That White Paper might have been more justly called " Whitewash." A Jewish fellow-passenger, who had often been in Budapest recently, told me in half-an-hour more than

---

[1] *The Journal of a Jewish Traveller*, John Lane, The Bodley Head, 1925.
The *Times Literary Supplement* wrote: " Mr. Cohen possesses several special qualifications for carrying out and describing the enterprise which is the subject of this book."
The *Manchester Guardian* called it " entertaining and delightful . . . valuable and unusual."

the authors of the Government report had learned in six months; and during my stay in the city I collected such a mass of material about the organised persecution of the Jews that I was astonished that any doubts were still felt about its reality. There were no acts of violence there by day. It was at night that the outrages were committed, when little groups of " Awakening Magyars," armed with iron staves covered with leather, or officers of various terrorist groups, sallied forth, bravely attacked an unsuspecting Jew from behind, and belaboured him until he was senseless. No wonder that the Allied Missions stationed in Budapest knew so little of the " White Terror," and that the British Minister, with whom I had a talk at the Legation, thought that there was some exaggeration.

But wherever Jews dwelt in the provinces terror was rampant day and night. They were dragged out of their homes, abused, flogged, robbed, tortured, and driven or deported to some other town or to Budapest itself. They were compelled to sign fictitious confessions of penal offences, and if they refused at first they were beaten until they submitted. The tortures inflicted read like a chapter from the Inquisition. In the Komarom fortress men had to drink blood from their own wounds; some were buried neck-deep in the earth ; and others had to hold a mouse in their mouth or to eat the hair pulled off their chin.

I spent many hours among the fugitives and " deportees " who were interned in a Jewish school, under the supervision of the police, until their fate was decided. Those who originated from Poland or Galicia were transported to their native land; but there were many scores of Jews born in Hungary who were also evicted from their homes. Old and young, men and women, they were all huddled away in the middle of the night from towns and villages where they had lived useful and peaceful lives for decades. In one of the schoolrooms I came across a father who was teaching his young son a page of the Talmud, and who calmly informed me that he had resumed at the passage where they had left off " at home." Such was the spirit that no terror could daunt.

The main instigators of the terror were officers who were no longer wanted for the army and who found their livelihood by plundering Jews. The excuse offered for their conduct was that they were taking reprisals upon the Jews because some of them had helped in the short-lived Communist régime of Bela Kun. But the Jewish community was in no way responsible for the actions of the Jewish Communists, who, in fact, were freethinkers and disclaimed any connection with Jewry or Judaism. The Government took no steps to suppress the terror and, indeed, denied that there was any. But what was much more remarkable — the leading Jews in the country made no protests. They were proud Magyars who feared that the escutcheon of their native land would be sullied if they gave expression to any grievances; and besides, they dismissed the victims of the outrages as aliens who should go. In such circumstances, what help could an outside Jewish body afford?

Before leaving Budapest I addressed a meeting of the local Zionist association on the Zionist situation in German. The members were quickly and secretly called together by word of mouth, for the association was illegal, and its constitution had not received official approval. The meeting was held in an out-of-the-way building, behind closed doors; the chairman uttered a warning against any applause that would betray our presence; and when the meeting was over the audience dribbled out in twos and threes at intervals, so as not to attract attention.

I returned to Vienna by steamer on the Danube, and after writing and despatching my report to London took the train to Trieste, where I boarded a ship for Alexandria.

III

Among my fellow-passengers were a score of young Jews, mostly men, but also some girls, who travelled steerage. They were sturdy and muscular, most of them with tanned faces, and all with straight backs. They had come from Poland and Galicia, from Czechoslovakia and Holland, and they were going to Palestine. Several had been students, but all had undergone some training as farm-labourers, for they were going to work on the land as *Halutzim* (pioneers). They all had interesting stories to tell of the obstacles they had overcome to

MISSION TO AUSTRALASIA

get away from their homes — of the opposition of their parents, and of the tantalising difficulties with passports and visas. Some of them had to climb over the Carpathians to avoid the frontier guards, others had been imprisoned by the Czechs for a few weeks. Now they were all happy and enthusiastic, discussing throughout the day their plans for the future, and when night came down upon the sea, and the steerage was steeped in darkness, they gathered round and sang Hebrew songs with a lusty refrain. At first they were songs of oppression and exile, of the poverty and pathos of the Ghetto, but soon they burst forth into a robust and lilting chorus, proclaiming the redemption of the Land of Israel and heralding the dawn of a brighter era.

I parted from them at Alexandria, where I was awaited by the leaders of the Jewish community. I was welcomed by Baron Felix de Menasce, and an "At Home" in my honour was given by the president, M. Tuby, at whose house I delivered an address on the Jewish situation and the Zionist outlook. I was informed that over £5,000 had already been subscribed for the Palestine Restoration Fund, and it was expected that my appeal would give a fillip to the collection as many were present who had never attended a Zionist gathering in their lives. After a couple of days I went to Cairo, where I lost little time in going to see the Pyramids and the Sphinx, and had the uncomfortable experience of riding the last part of the way on a camel. The heat was too oppressive for any communal function, but one evening I attended the performance of a Yiddish play in aid of the Restoration Fund.

IV

I travelled to the Holy Land through the Sinai Desert in a train from Kantara that snorted its way past Rafa and Gaza, and I felt some relief when I changed at Lydda into another train, despite its discomfort, for the completion of my pilgrimage to Jerusalem. Never shall I forget my first impression of the Holy City, with its ineffable charm, its radiant pinkish-brown colouring, its picturesque grouping and its melancholy desolation. I had an excellent guide in Professor Patrick Geddes, who, after first conducting me to the site of the Hebrew University on Mount Scopus and explaining his plans for that institution, took me for a two hours' walk round the walls of Jerusalem, through all sorts of curious byways and alleys, while all the time unfolding his ideas for beautifying the city.

I had only two weeks at my disposal for seeing the country and gathering information, so that I was kept fully occupied (especially as I lost a few days through the gastric trouble that often attacks a newcomer to the Land of Israel). But thanks to the help and advice that I received I was able to form a good impression of Palestine as it then was under the military authorities, and also of the plans for the development of the Jewish national home as soon as the Civil Administration would begin a few weeks later. From Jerusalem I went by car (as one of four passengers) to Jaffa, and on to Tel-Aviv, then merely an infant townlet with a few thousand inhabitants, whose most important building was a higher-grade school. Anxious to see something of the early settlements, or "colonies" as they were called, and to begin with Petach Tikvah, which could not be reached then by railway, I again went by car, but when we got within about a mile of the place we floundered in such a sea of soft, yielding sand that my companion and I had to leave the machine and continue on foot. The elderly colonist to whom we had an introduction sent a couple of Arab farmhands to help the chauffeur to bring the car along, and meanwhile I heard of the tribulations that Petach Tikvah had suffered under the Turks during the war. On our return journey we struck out along a good hard road, but after a time we found ourselves in a narrow path overhung with low brambles, the road became bumpy, we ran into a flock of sheep, and were followed by a scared jackal.

The following day I went to Rishon le-Zion, strolled through its famous wine-cellars, and was enraptured by its beautiful avenue of palms. I was told that G. K. Chesterton had been there a few weeks before, and that after he had been given an account of the settlement and asked if he would like any further information, he replied that he was "not interested in collecting facts." Half-an-

MISSION TO AUSTRALASIA

hour's drive in a trap brought me to Ness-Zionah, from where I reached the picturesque approach to the plantations of Rehovoth.

Having learned something of the growth, the management, and the activities of the Judaean settlements I took the train to Haifa, whose principal attraction in those days consisted of its proximity to Mount Carmel, from whose wooded slopes I had a fascinating view of the Mediterranean. The Fortress of Acre had been turned into a prison where Jabotinsky, who had been sentenced by a court-martial to fifteen years' imprisonment for organising a self-defence corps against the Arabs, was confined. I was allowed to visit him, found him naturally depressed, and assured him that the Zionist leaders were doing their utmost to get his sentence quashed (in which they succeeded a few weeks later).

One afternoon Professor Geddes, an architect, and myself set out in a motor-car from Haifa to Tiberias, but the machine broke down after we had passed Kfar Kana and it was already dark. The chauffeur told us that it would take some time to repair the damage, so we started walking in the hope that he would soon overtake us, and the Professor kept up our spirits by singing Scottish songs, but we had walked fully two hours before the car caught up with us. On reaching Tiberias late at night we felt almost bathed in heat, for the surface of the Lake is 700 feet below the level of the sea. The next day we strolled through the old Jewish quarter, visited the co-operative settlements of Kinnereth and Dagania, and then returned to Haifa, from where I travelled back to Jerusalem.

Before leaving the Holy City I went one Sabbath evening to the Western Wall, that grim solid remnant of the ancient Temple. I had conceived this hallowed ruin as standing in a large open space reminiscent of the courts of the Temple, but found that it formed just one side of a narrow blind alley. The approach was through a zigzag of byways, crooked and cobbled, which were infested with old bleareyed beggars squatting on the ground against the walls and whining for alms with outstretched hands. In front of the Wall stood a group of men with devout mien, wrapt in prayer, as so many countless generations had done before when belief in the restoration of Israel to his land had seemed a Utopian fancy. Throughout the centuries the venerated ruin, whose surface had been smoothed by the kisses of countless pietists, had been a symbol of national endurance and impregnable faith. Now the symbol was to be crowned at last by joyous fulfilment.

V

I set sail from Port Said on July 1st for Fremantle, and was on board long enough to sort out the medley of impressions that I carried away, and to map out the addresses that I was to give. Soon after we emerged from the Red Sea we encountered a violent monsoon, which kept me in my cabin for a couple of days while the ship rocked and tossed, groaned and writhed; but we weathered it without mishap and felt consoled when we put in at Colombo, where we enjoyed the enchanting scenery for many hours. Two days before we reached Fremantle a cable was brought to me conveying greetings from the Rabbi of Perth. He was Rev. D. I. Freedman, who had left Jews' College only a few months after I had entered it, and he headed a small deputation that welcomed me when I stepped on shore.

An elaborate programme had been arranged for the four days that I spent in Perth — meetings and receptions, luncheons and lectures, calls and collections. The first function was in the Zionist Hall, where I was greeted with the strains of Hebrew song by young boys and girls decked out in the Zionist blue and white and waving little Zionist banners. The same evening there was a public meeting in the Town Hall, attended by both Jews and Gentiles. I spoke of the place that Palestine had always held in Jewish memories and aspirations, how all attempts to secure its restoration to the Jewish people had failed, how it had been delivered by the forces of the Power that had issued the Balfour Declaration, and how the realisation of the promise that it contained depended now upon the financial support that must be given by Jews throughout the world. The following day, at a reception given to me by the Municipal Council, I dwelt upon the part played by the Australian troops in the redemption of Palestine, and emphasised the importance to Australia of that land coming under British control, as that should ensure the uninterrupted connection between the mother country and the Commonwealth.

My first appeal for money was made in the synagogue, where the attendance was surprisingly large. Rabbi Freedman allowed me to occupy his pulpit, and from there I gave an address in which I asked: of what worth were all the prayers for the restoration of Zion that had been offered up in that shrine, if they found no outlet in the material sacrifice necessary for that end ? I called for a first donation of £1,000, and although I noted some looks of astonishment I repeated my request, and in order to overcome any reluctance I suggested that the amount could be paid in five instalments, one-fifth down and the rest within four years. After a pause an elderly man rose and said that he would be pleased to give £1,000 if five other persons would give a similar sum. I thanked him for his offer, and asked him to withdraw his condition. He promptly assented, whereupon there broke forth such thunderous applause as had never before been heard in that sacred edifice. The second response was for £500, and after that, for over an hour came an almost uninterrupted succession of calls until a total was reached of £8,000. The next two days the Rabbi and I called upon all members of the community who had been absent from the synagogue, and raised the total to £10,000 payable in four years. It was an excellent achievement for a community of only 2,000 souls. When the result was telegraphed to Melbourne and Sydney, *pour encourager les autres*, the reply came back: " Was there not a naught too many ? "

The Governor, whom I visited, showed great interest in my mission, and expressed pleasant surprise at the success of my initial appeal. The Premier likewise evinced his friendly sympathy and entertained me to lunch in Parliament House, at which the Speaker, the President of the Council, the leader of the Opposition, and the Rabbi were also present. When I left Perth at the conclusion of my visit there was a crowd of people on the platform, who gave me messages for relatives and friends in the various cities that I was to visit.

On reaching Kalgoorlie the following day I found that the little Jewish community, who knew that I would have a wait there for nearly an hour, had arranged a reception for me in the station refreshment room, where there was a festively decked table. I was told that the Jewish population had formerly numbered over a hundred, but it had dwindled owing to the decline of gold mining. In response to my appeal it was readily agreed to organise a collection and forward the money to Perth; and after we had drunk a toast to " The Jewish National Home " I took my seat in the long Trans-Continental train, in which I spent the next two days and a half crossing the Great Australian Desert. It was not an unpleasant journey, for the train was furnished with comforts and conveniences: dining-car and sleeping-berth, lounge-car, with cosy arm-chairs and writing-desks, a drawing-room with a piano, and even a shower-bath. For hundreds of miles we saw nothing but low saltbush and bluebush; every few hours we stopped at a primitive station for the pumping of water; and at one place we saw some copper-coloured aborigines who gave a display of javelin throwing for pennies.

On arriving in Adelaide I was welcomed by the President of the Jewish Congregation, the minister, and all the committee. The Jews of Adelaide boasted of a fine record, for among the pioneers of South Australia had been Jacob Montefiore, a cousin of Sir Moses Montefiore; Jews had acted as Mayors of the city for an aggregate of thirteen years; and the Hon. V. C. Solomon had been Premier at the end of the last century. Owing to the brevity of my stay I addressed only one meeting, but the financial response was satisfactory. Before my departure I called upon the Governor, Sir Archibald Weigall, who was interested to learn that a predecessor of his, Colonel Gawler, the second Governor of South Australia, occupied a notable place in the history of British schemes for the restoration of Jews to Palestine.

I found on reaching Melbourne that the example set by the Perth community had made a profound impression and that there was a general desire to emulate it. The Zionist sentiment prevailing among its 6,000 Jews was probably due to the fact that a large proportion of them had arrived as poor immigrants from Eastern Europe and attained a high degree of prosperity, but at the same time they gave repeated evidence of their British patriotism, for there was not a single meeting at which I appeared that did not begin and end with

MISSION TO AUSTRALASIA

the National Anthem. My most active supporter was a native of Cracow who had arrived in Melbourne about twenty-five years earlier with only a few shillings, and had gradually built up his fortune as a rubber merchant and his fame as a generous philanthropist. The most successful meeting was presided over by General Sir John Monash (1865 — 1931), who had distinguished himself in the First World War as the brilliant Commander-in-Chief of the Australian Forces. Although he had not previously identified himself with Zionism, yet, since his return from the battlefield he had begun to take an active and keen interest in Jewish affairs, and he readily put aside an important engagement for the sake of the meeting. Indeed, he told me with pride that a famous kinsman of his had once been interested in the Jewish colonisation of Palestine, and when I asked him whom he meant he replied: "The historian of our people, Graetz." The name of Monash proved such an attraction that the hall was packed and many people had to be turned away. The financial response was gratifying, as by the end of the meeting the total contributed by Melbourne Jewry was over £20,000, an amount that was further increased by visits to Geelong and Ballarat.

Another distinguished Jew whom I met was the Hon. Justice Isaacs (1855 — 1948), a member of the Commonwealth Supreme Court, who was afterwards appointed Chief Justice, and, as Sir Isaac Isaacs, became famous as the first Australian-born Governor-General of the Commonwealth. He was the son of an immigrant tailor from Russia, began life as a school-teacher, and then devoted himself to law. He was a dour-visaged sexagenarian of medium height, with small grey moustache, and fresh complexion. The aspect of Zionism about which he was most concerned was the question of Jewish nationality, as he could not understand nationality apart from a state or territory from which it was derived. I replied that his definition was faulty, and that he confused nationality with citizenship. He told me that he was making a serious study of Hebrew grammar, which he had neglected since boyhood, and wished to know something about the adaptability of Hebrew to the needs of modern speech.

Among the novel experiences that fell to my lot in Melbourne was to occupy the pulpit in two synagogues. My addresses served a practical as well as a moral purpose, for they were delivered during the Sabbath morning service to congregations that included many people who had not attended the public meetings, and they resulted in further additions to the Fund. Apparently I acquitted myself of the preacher's rôle with some meed of satisfaction, as a deputation from another synagogue called upon me and offered me the vacant position of minister at an attractive salary. I declined with thanks.

Before leaving Melbourne I had a brief interview with the Commonwealth Premier, W. M. Hughes, whom I had previously heard speaking in the Federal Parliament. When I presented my letter of introduction from Sir Alfred Mond, " Billy " Hughes said that Mond had been very helpful to him in England and asked if he could be of any assistance to me. I thanked him for the offer, but told him that I was leaving for Sydney the next day. He thereupon remarked that he hoped I had not come to recruit emigrants for Palestine, as Australia could not spare any.

The Jews in Sydney impressed me as the most English of the Jewish communities in the Antipodes, and, although then only 8,000 in number, they had attained high distinction in both the commercial and the political worlds. The two Montefiore brothers, Jacob and Joseph, cousins of the illustrious Sir Moses, who came to Sydney in the early part of the nineteenth century, gave a powerful impetus to the economic progress of New South Wales. In the seventies Sir Saul Samuels represented the Government in the Upper House, served as Vice-President of the Executive Council, and was afterwards Agent-General in London. Other Jews who rose to fame were judges and members of the Legislative Assembly; and at one time both the Speaker and the Deputy-Speaker were Jews, namely, John J. Cohen and Daniel Levy. This rare coincidence proved rather awkward on one occasion, as, owing to the desire of both the Speaker and his Deputy to attend the synagogue on the Day of Atonement, the Legislative Assembly had to adjourn for twenty-four hours.

With such a record, the local Zionist leaders did not anticipate the same ready response to my appeal that I had received in Perth and Melbourne, and they therefore arranged that I should speak at

MISSION TO AUSTRALASIA

various functions and obtain some press publicity before addressing the principal meeting. So I began at a conversazione at the Hotel Australia, spoke at a luncheon of the Millions Club, gave a lecture at the University of Sydney and a sermon at the Great Synagogue. Then came the principal meeting, at which the Governor, Sir Walter Davidson, took the chair, and which attracted a crowded and representative gathering. But unfortunately my speech was frequently interrupted by the inopportune applause of an ex-soldier, whose nerves had suffered in the war, and whose excessive zeal could not be restrained for fear of something worse. The financial result, although headed by £1,000, was not as satisfactory as I had hoped, and it was found necessary to augment it by my addressing some more meetings and making many private calls in the company of the president of the Zionist Society. On the latter occasions I always met with a patient and courteous hearing, but I was surprised in some cases to come across a curious fear that the eventual development of a Jewish State might involve the disfranchisement of the Jews in the Australian Commonwealth — a bogy that I had no difficulty in exploding.

VI

After the strenuous round of meetings and visits in Australia it was a relief to get on board the great Pacific liner that was to take me to New Zealand on its way to Vancouver. I was able to admire the beauty of Sydney's harbour as the ship slowly moved away, and a few days later beheld the almost equally beautiful harbour of Auckland. As there were only 2,000 Jews[1] in the whole of the Dominion (of whom a fourth were in Auckland), and the pulse of Jewish life was reported to beat there even more feebly than in Australia, my expectations were but modestly attuned; but in the end New Zealand proved the most successful chapter in the whole of my tour.

I was welcomed on landing by the Nathans, whose family had been settled in Auckland from the very day on which the British

[1] The Jewish population of New Zealand is now estimated at about 4,200.

flag had been planted there; and I learned that the first two Mayors (as well as later ones) had been Jews. The enthusiasm displayed by the little community when I addressed them in the synagogue was indeed heart-warming, and the list of donations was headed by three sums of £1,000 each. The local press described the event the following morning as "the most enthusiastic meeting held in the eighty years' history of the Jewish community of Auckland." The Christian community cordially associated themselves with their Jewish fellow-citizens. I was given a civic reception in the Town Hall, and the Mayor presided at a public meeting, at which I was supported in a rousing speech by an officer who had been the first New Zealand soldier, in General Allenby's campaign of liberation, to set foot on Palestinian soil. Nor was it only money that I obtained but also a very fruitful idea, for at an "At Home" given by Mrs. David Nathan, she told me of her keen interest in the Plunket nursing system, which flourished throughout the Dominion. She suggested that the Jewish women in New Zealand might be encouraged to raise special funds for introducing this system into Palestine, and the result of my putting her into communication with the founders of the Women's International Zionist Organisation in London was that they adopted Plunket nursing as the first item of their social welfare work in Palestine.

Midway between Auckland and Wellington I stayed at Rotorua for a week as the guest of a Jewish hotel-proprietor, to take the famous baths for rheumatism. It is a modern town laid out by the Government as a pleasant health-resort in the heart of Maori-land, a region unparalleled for its array of weird wonders. You can see geysers and thermal springs, boiling fountains and bubbling pools, menacing craters and hot fissured soil, set amid placid lakes and frowning mountains. The neighbouring Maori village of Whakarewarewa was full of surprising novelties — hot springs in which the women washed their clothes, and hot mud-pools, one of which formed jumping frogs that disappeared, while another repeatedly created models of lilies which melted away. The week at Rotorua soon sped, for it had a cosmopolitan interest provided by settlers who had come from a variety of distant lands. But the strangest

IN A MAORI VILLAGE NEAR ROTORUA, N.Z., 1920
The Author (on the left) is seen with Maori Guide and a local Clergyman.

MISSION TO AUSTRALASIA

inhabitant was a little Polish Jew, who had a drapery store. He told me that he had fled from Warsaw thirty years before to join the pioneers at Rishon le-Zion, but after two years' hard toil his strength gave out, so he sailed to Australia and thence to New Zealand.

When I arrived in Wellington I found that the city tramcars had been covered for the past fortnight with posters advertising the Zionist demonstration that was to take place, with the support of the Prime Minister and the Acting Governor-General, at the Town Hall. And when the representative of the *Wellington Evening Post* came to interview me, I discovered we had been school-fellows together at the Manchester Grammar School. I therefore felt sure of a cordial reception and adequate publicity. My campaign was opened at a private meeting in the house of the President of the Congregation, Michael Myers, a prominent solicitor, who was afterwards knighted on his appointment as Chief Justice of the Dominion, and it was followed by a public meeting for the Jewish community. The mass demonstration in the Town Hall, over which the Mayor presided, was the largest gathering that I addressed in the whole of my tour, for there were close upon 3,000 people there. It was rendered particularly noteworthy by the participation of the Acting Governor-General, Sir Robert Stout, and of the Prime Minister, W. F. Massey, both of whom spoke in glowing terms of the Jewish people and the restoration of Zion. Mr. Massey also paid a tribute to the Jew who had once been Prime Minister of New Zealand, Sir Julius Vogel (1873).

As in North Island so also in South Island there were only two organised Jewish communities, in Christchurch and Dunedin, but their combined numbers were equal to only one-half of the Wellington congregation. In those remote and sparse communities Judaism naturally had a struggle for existence: there were difficulties of conformity with traditional rites, and mixed marriages were almost inevitable, although these were probably not more frequent in South than in North Island. Owing to the brevity of my stay in Christchurch I was able to address only a private meeting of the congregation, but I was interviewed by both local papers, one of which published

A JEWISH PILGRIMAGE

a sympathetic leader. It was with a sense of relief that I reached Dunedin, for it marked the southernmost terminus of my wanderings. The Mayor presided at the public meeting in the Burns Hall (sacred to the memory of the Scottish national poet, for the people of Dunedin have preserved both the Scottish loyalty and Scottish accent of its founders), and there was a crowded platform of the leading notabilities of the city. The financial response was in every way satisfactory, donations being received even from Jews who had long withdrawn from the community.

On returning to Wellington I was tempted to undertake a visit to a Jewish family at Masterton, nearly seventy miles distant, but as the day chosen was a Sunday, when trains were also allowed to rest, I was taken by motor-car, accompanied by a nephew of David Wolffsohn, Herzl's successor. It turned out to be the most perilous journey that I have ever made in my life. The road rose slowly ever higher and higher and then tapered away into the narrow ledge of a mountain, with frequent and sudden bends. It was the famous Rimutaka Gorge. On our left were heavy clouds hovering over a black yawning abyss, and on our right grim rocks sundered here and there by gaps through which the howling wind blew with such tempestuous fury that I thought we should be lifted up and hurled below. It was a sickening ordeal, lasting an hour-and-a-half, which left me shaken and exhausted, so I resolved not to return by road, but to wait until I could go back by train. Fortunately the people whom I had come to see made me most welcome. The Jewish New Year was to begin in the evening, and they asked me to stay until after the festival. The head of the family was a wealthy octogenarian, who lived in a fine large house built mostly of timber, and nearby were the homes of his three married sons. Their name was Castleberg, a most fitting cognomen for that mountainous district. After I had shown them my letters of introduction from the eminent people in London, they held a private family council and told me that they would contribute a thousand guineas. The journey had proved worth while. When I was back again in Wellington, I was at last able to count up the results of my month's activities in New Zealand, and found that the total came to over £20,000.

VIII

I returned to Sydney for another few days, during which a leading Jewish bookmaker took me into Tattersall's Club to obtain contributions and within fifteen minutes I collected £100. One evening I dined with the Speaker of the Legislative Assembly, Sir Daniel Levy, in his official apartments; and on the last day he presided at my final address, at the conclusion of which he presented me, in the name of the Sydney Zionists, with a handsome little gold watch, whose face showed the hours by Hebrew letters.

From Sydney I travelled north to Newcastle, where I was met by a Jewish deputation headed by the Mayor, and after a brief stay and a single meeting I went on to Brisbane, where the Minister of Education welcomed me in the name of the State authorities. The Brisbane community bore a certain resemblance to that of Perth by virtue of the large number of Russian Jews, many of whom had travelled through Siberia to Shanghai, whence they had sailed southward. I also came across many Gentiles who were fervent believers in the British-Israelite theory. The few days that I spent there were crowded with a variety of functions, public and private, which yielded a substantial addition to the Palestine Fund.

My mission to Australia was now over and had realised nearly £60,000 from a community of 18,000 souls[1]. But I had other lands to conquer, and when I stood on the deck of the Japanese liner that was to take me to Hongkong there was a happy throng of newly made friends on the wharf, who waved repeatedly and sang *Hatikvah* with fervour and gusto until I was borne away to sea.

---

[1] The Jewish population of Australia is now estimated at about 55,000.

Chapter Twelve

TRAVELS IN ASIA

1920 — 1921

I

THE voyage from Brisbane to Hongkong took eighteen days, but it was anything but tedious. During the first part it was smooth, sultry, and somnolent, but it was pleasantly diversified by a colourful panorama embracing the mainland on the one side and picturesque isles with exotic foliage on the other. Our first stopping place was Thursday Island, the home of the pearl-fishing industry, where we stayed a few hours; and after we crossed the Equator there stretched before us the quaintly shaped island of Celebes. The first port in the Philippines where we made a brief halt was Zamboanga, a paradisical spot, with avenues of luxuriant palms traversed by curious little carriages that were curtained to keep out the heat. I espied a fruit-shop which bore a Jewish name, and on entering found that the owner had come from Syria, from where he and his wife had fled on the outbreak of the First War, owing to the oppression by the Turkish Generalissimo. He asked me whether it was really true that England had given the Land of Israel back to the Jews, and when I replied that it was under British rule, and Jews could return to rebuild it, but that it was not yet theirs, he said, with an air of resignation: " So we must still wait for the Messiah."

As we were approaching Manila I learned that we were to remain there a whole day, so I conceived the plan of calling a meeting of the local Jewish community — if I could find one. I studied the Manila Directory in the ship's library and wrote out the names and addresses of several persons whom I thought to be Jews, and as soon as we landed I took a car to the office of the first on my list. He was a lawyer, who also sported the title of Colonel, and after I told him of my mission and my desire to address a meeting of the Manila Jews he looked at me with an air of astonishment as though I proposed undertaking some extraordinary exploit. But when I showed him my letters of introduction from Lord Milner, Lord Rotshchild, Herbert Samuel, and the other eminent people, he handled them with reverence and was visibly impressed. He was willing to help me by giving me the names and addresses of some other Jews whom I could call on, and if a sufficient number responded favourably he would hire a hall, at which the meeting could take place in the evening. But he warned me not to be optimistic, as, although there were a few hundred Jews in Manila, all immigrants from various countries, they had not yet combined to form an organisation or build a synagogue.[1] Only those who still had a flickering Jewish consciousness met together on the two most solemn days of the Jewish calendar — New Year and the Day of Atonement — for public worship, after which they hibernated for another twelve months.

The result of my feverish efforts during the day and of further consultation with the Colonel was that the meeting duly took place. It was the most unconventional and least lucrative gathering in the whole of my tour. The hall had a capacity for a few hundred, but our total attendance was six Jews and a Christian reporter, who had been specially invited to record the memorable function. After I had spoken and appealed for donations, I had the utmost difficulty to extract a satisfactory response. It was therefore agreed that the Colonel should collect as much as he could and send it on to the Zionist Office in London. Nearly a year later I received a cheque for a few hundred dollars.

II

On reaching Hongkong, in the middle of November, I felt transported to a totally different world, where Jewish life was materially rich but spiritually poor, although it was sustained by a

[1] A synagogue was built a few years after my visit.

strong sense of communal solidarity and loyalty to tradition. From my hotel I was driven in a rickshaw to the Jewish Recreation Club, which was furnished with all the comforts and amenities of a social or political club in the West End of London. It was situated in the more elevated part of the city, from where the harbour below was as resplendent as a Swiss lake, encircled with wooded hills, jewelled with green islets, and dappled with ships, junks, and a swarm of curious sea-craft. As I sipped my tea and chatted with the president, I learned something of the romance attaching to the community, for its origin was due to the spirit of commercial enterprise of the Sassoons.

The founder of their fame and fortune was David Sassoon (the scion of a stock that came from mediaeval Spain), who was born in Bagdad in 1792 and removed forty years later to Bombay, where he established the firm of David Sassoon and Company. He was blessed with eight sons (besides four daughters), and it was upon their energetic co-operation that he built up the prosperous business of bankers and merchants throughout the East. After he had opened a branch in Calcutta, he sent out his son Elias to create branches in China and Japan, and upon his death Elias left the firm, founded the rival house of Elias David Sassoon and Company, and established branches in all the cities where there were offices of the parent company. The managers and clerks for all these business centres were Jews brought out from India and Bagdad, who thus formed the pioneers and parents of the new community. They worshipped in synagogues built by their employers, who were famous for their piety and benevolence, and observed and perpetuated the Sephardic ritual and customs of their native land. But what impressed me as peculiar was that the present generation had preserved the Arabic speech of their fathers, which they often used in conversation with one another. When the Sassoon houses were first established, I was told, their books and correspondence were conducted in Judaeo-Arabic written in Hebrew characters, but now everything was carried on in English.

After tea we adjourned to the adjoining synagogue, which had been built by Sir Jacob Sassoon, a son of the aforementioned Elias. It was a handsome structure, surmounted in front by two pagoda-like turrets, while the interior had the amplitude of space and scantiness of seating accommodation that I found characteristic of synagogues in the East. Prayers were read by a layman, for the community, which numbered only a hundred souls, had neither Rabbi nor any other religious functionary. I was then shown an interesting parchment scroll of the Law that had formerly belonged to the Jewish congregation of Nanking, which was now defunct. It was some inches longer than the scroll customary in Western communities, its caligraphy had several peculiarities, and, like all scrolls of the Law in the East, it was kept in a cylindrical case of chased metal to preserve it from the prevalent humidity.

Besides the employees of the Sassoon houses and their families, Hongkong Jewry comprised several other persons, mostly merchants or brokers, some of whom had come from Europe or America. They had played their full part in the development of the colony, and some had displayed a benevolence that had benefited their non-Jewish neighbours even more than their own co-religionists. Sir Ellis Kadoorie, the owner of the two leading hotels in the colony, had presented a school for the Chinese and another for the Hindus, besides the Helena May Institute as a home for English girls; and a previous philanthropist, the Hon. E. R. Belilios, had founded a school for English girls. It was in the Helena May Institute that I addressed a public meeting, after having spoken to my fellow-Jews in their club. The Governor, Sir Reginald Stubbs, who presided, not only commended my appeal to the audience, but, unlike other Colonial officials who took the chair at my meetings, contributed something himself.

The Jews of Hongkong, although their nearest Jewish neighbours lived in Shanghai, which was then separated by a voyage of three days, and in Singapore, two days farther still, did not live an altogether isolated life. For these were then regarded as short distances in the Far East, and there was such a regular interchange of visits between the members of these communities that they were almost as familiar with one another as the Jews of Manchester with those of Liverpool, and consequently I benefited by the advance information I was thus able to gather.

III

In Shanghai the dominating element was also Sephardic, derived like Hongkong Jewry from India and Iraq, for the first Jew to set foot there, about 1850, was likewise Elias David Sassoon; but there were also many Jews from Western Europe and America. They formed the organised congregation, with synagogues, school, and benevolent society, comprising about 500 souls, most of them engaged in commerce. But since the end of the First World War there had grown up a community of Russian Jews, estimated at about 1,000 in all, who had fled or drifted here and found a living for the most part as small tradesfolk or artisans. I passed my Sabbath eve and Sabbath morn in the very odour of sanctity. I attended the evening service in a synagogue over the school, where there was a fair attendance, and was invited home by Mr. Sassoon J. Solomon, a pious scholar, who had a remarkable library of Hebrew lore, and who spent his days on the books of the Sassoons and his nights on the books of the Cabbala. The Sabbath "loaves" were like large, flat, blistered pancakes, though tasting unmistakably like bread, and I afterwards came across loaves of this shape in Singapore, Rangoon, and Calcutta. Most of the dishes were of the Bagdad or Levantine school of cookery, and there were varied Oriental fruits, such as the pawpaw and the pumelo.

I inquired of Mr. Solomon about the Jews of Kai-Feng-Fu, who were believed to date from the twelfth century and he told me that he had taken an active part in investigating their conditions and in bringing eight to Shanghai.[1] There were only two of them left: they were employed by Jewish firms, but they were too thoroughly assimilated, mentally and physically, to be able to understand anything of the Jewish faith, and it was only a question of time before these last two survivals of the ancient colony would become extinct.

When I attended the synagogue in the morning, at which the service began at seven o'clock, I found some rickshaws waiting outside. I was told that the moot question whether the use of these vehicles was permissible on the Sabbath would have to be solved by the new

[1] The first Jewish settlements in China are believed to have taken place in the third century, if not earlier.

Rabbi who was then expected. For there were some orthodox Jews who, living at a distance from the synagogue, were carried to it in a rickshaw, the Chinese doorkeeper paying the fare, whilst after the return journey it was paid by their domestic. They therefore suffered a twinge of conscience, from which they were anxious to be relieved.

My first appeal was made in the house of the president of the local Zionist Association, Mr. Edward I. Ezra, a veritable magnate. He invited all members of the community to a reception by means of an advertisement in the press and nearly 500 came. His house was of palatial proportions and baronial magnificence, situated in extensive and beautiful grounds, which contained summer-houses, a boating-lake, bowling-green, and tennis lawn. The reception was in a large, ornate ball-room, where the proceedings were opened by a jazz band, to which a great number danced, but the pressure of the throng soon forced a migration into an adjoining chamber, where refreshments were served on a lavish scale. When the merriment was at its height Mr. Ezra advanced to the orchestral dais, the music stopped, and he introduced me in complimentary terms. In replying I contrasted the gaiety before me with the widespread distress in Eastern Europe, which a Jewish Palestine was designed and destined to alleviate. I also announced that Mr. Ezra had promised the first donation — £1,000.

As I moved about among the guests I met many men of marked diversity of origin, type, and activity. There were prosperous Bagdadi merchants and brokers, Russian Jews who controlled the local cotton market, American Jews who had businesses with ramifications from New York to Tientsin, a Hungarian Jewish doctor who had been in Siberia, an Italian Jew who had fought in Tripoli, and a French Jew who was a member of the French Municipal Council. I also met a young Russian Jew who was in the service of the Chinese Government, and another from Nagasaki, who told me that there were only four Jews left in that city, that the synagogue had been closed for months, and that the scrolls of the Law were to be transferred to Shanghai. As for Mr. Ezra himself, he owned the three leading hotels of the city and one in Peking, a daily newspaper, and a large block of office buildings which bore his name. He asked me if I would be willing to accept an appointment in connection with his business, but I declined.

A few days later there was a public meeting in one of Mr. Ezra's hotels. It was well attended and honoured by the presence of the British Consul-General and a Judge of the United States Supreme Court, both of whom supported my appeal. There was at first a shyness to subscribe on the spot and a preference was expressed for private canvassing, but I insisted upon the method that had proved successful in the Antipodes, with the result that there was a good response, including three further donations of £1,000 each. But as many were absent, I had to spend much time and energy on the following days in visiting offices and counting-houses, accompanied by the editor of the local Zionist monthly *Israel's Messenger*, Mr. N. E. B. Ezra, who was by far the most zealous and militant Zionist in the whole of the Far East.[1]

IV

The voyage to Kobe was rough and cold, but fortunately brief, for on the third day we reached the entrance to the Inland Sea. The famed beauty of this Sea was veiled by a grey sky and the melancholy of winter, and my first glimpse of the city was of gaunt factory-chimneys seen through a deluge of rain. There was no organised Jewish community in Kobe, although there were about 200 Jews there. Half of them were from England, America, and Bagdad, having businesses of their own or representing foreign firms: the other half were fugitives from Russia, waiting either to return there or to cross the Pacific to America. It was in the house of the head of the Russian colony that I felt most at home: the languages spoken were English, Yiddish, and Russian, and the dishes and drinks were all reminiscent of the Ghetto.

It was impossible to convene a meeting at short notice in such a community, so I decided to go first to Yokohama for a few days in order that a meeting could be arranged for my return. But before

[1] In consequence of the flight of Jews from Central Europe from 1933, owing to Nazi persecution, the number of Jews in Shanghai increased to over 20,000, but after the late war it gradually dwindled to less than 300.

leaving I called upon a number of Jews in their offices, in the hope of obtaining donations, but the response was feeble and fitful. Each man gave me the names and addresses of two others, while imploring me not to betray the source of my information, and thus the list slowly improved. Two men brought home to me the tragedy of the isolation of the little Jewish colony. One was married to a Japanese wife, but he pretended to bear no relationship to his slant-eyed Eurasian son, who remained mute throughout the conversation. The other man was the offspring of an English Jew and a Japanese mother: he had a Jewish name but Japanese features, and his views were suspiciously anti-Semitic. But there were only a few cases of such Judeo-Japanese marriages, the social ostracism that they involved serving as a deterrent.

In Yokohama the Jewish community was rather larger than that of Kobe. Less than half consisted of the resident element, commercial folk hailing from England and America, from the Levant and Bagdad, while the larger part comprised refugees from Russia. The poorer among the latter had been looked after by the Joint Distribution Committee of America, which had opened a Jewish Immigrants' Hostel, and this Hostel included a small synagogue in which I addressed a public meeting. In order to convene it I wrote a letter to the Chief of Police for permission, asked the British Consul to support my application with a note, and published an announcement in the two local English papers. I was then summoned by the Chief of Police for an interview, in which, with the aid of an interpreter, I had laboriously to explain to him the meaning of the Zionist movement and the purpose of my mission; and after I had satisfied him that they had nothing to do with Bolshevism he granted his permission. The attendance was only moderate: it included two police officials (to make sure that I didn't preach any subversive doctrine), two Japanese journalists who understood little of my English and nothing of my Yiddish, and a number of Russian refugees who were staying at the Hostel. Nevertheless, I raised a couple of hundred pounds, which was afterwards supplemented by personal calls.

At the end of the meeting I was approached by a Christian missionary, the Rev. O. St. M. Forester, and his wife, who told me that they were keenly interested in the purpose of my visit. Mr. Forester showed me a greenstone signet ring with the Hebrew inscription, *Shaalu shelom Yerushalayim* ("Seek ye the peace of Jerusalem"), and told me that it had belonged to his wife's grandfather, the first Anglican Bishop in Jerusalem, Michael Solomon Alexander. Bishop Alexander was born of pious Jewish parents in Posen at the end of the eighteenth century, emigrated to England as a young man, became the Rabbi of the Jewish congregation at Plymouth, and a few years later both he and his wife were converted to Christianity. He was afterwards ordained Bishop of the United Church of England and Ireland at Jerusalem, and spent the last four years of his life in that city. Mr. Forester also boasted of a link with Jewry, for he was the nephew of the two charming sisters, Lady Bradford and Lady Chesterfield, to whom Disraeli addressed love-letters after the death of his wife.

The press reports of the meeting aroused considerable interest, especially as they were somewhat imaginative. They stated that " an agreement was reached to establish a kingdom for the Jews," and a Kobe paper facetiously commented that it was not stated " which of the gentlemen present was to wear the crown." It was perhaps to unravel this secret that many journalists called at the hotel to see me, but as they all spoke English badly and I spoke Japanese not at all they left none the wiser. The police continued their interest in me: they sent an official to find out how much money I had collected and the names of the contributors. He affected surprise on learning what was the total, which he entered into a note-book, and showed his disappointment when I told him that I had already sent the list of subscribers to London.

Accompanied by a native guide from Yokohama I went to Tokyo, to call upon the British Ambassador, Sir Charles Eliot. We discussed the question of the possible emigration of Russian Jews from Yokohama to Palestine, and Sir Charles showed a keen interest in my travels and future plans. My guide told me that the papers said that I must be a cousin of the King of England, since I was going to make a kingdom in Palestine; but when we approached the Imperial Palace and he noticed my prompt obedience to the sentry who forbade me to use my camera, he probably doubted whether I possessed any royal blood.

My most notable experience was in the old capital, Kyoto, where the eye could feast upon far more scenes of beauty than in the larger cities. Its ornate shrines were encircled by landscape gardens and cloistral groves, in which there were curiously gnarled trees and tall stone lanterns. I went there in response to a letter from an Englishwoman, who wrote to me that she had been interested in Zionism since Herzl's time and was anxious to hear about its latest progress. She was an old lady named the Hon. Mrs. E. A. Gordon, whom I found in her hotel, lying on a couch, crippled with neuritis, yet mentally alert. She had lived in China and Japan for several years, knew the languages of both countries, and tried to prove her strange theory that the Japanese were part of the Lost Ten Tribes by advancing various data respecting names and customs, which seemed to me easily explicable on the ground of accidental similarity.[1] She had been a Lady-in-Waiting to Queen Victoria, and told me that the latter had believed in the British-Israel theory and insisted that the firstborn son of the then Duke of York (now the Duke of Windsor) should be named David, because it was he who was destined to lead the Jews back to Palestine.

A few months later, when I was in Jerusalem (April 1st, 1921), the High Commissioner (Sir Herbert Samuel, as he then was) informed me that he had just received from Mrs. Gordon a cheque for £500, to be used for various purposes according to his discretion; and when I was in London a couple of months later still, Mr. L. J. Greenberg, the editor of the *Jewish Chronicle*, revealed to me the interesting fact that the £2,000 which had enabled the Zionist Organisation in 1903 to send a commission of investigation to the territory in East Africa offered by the British Government for a Jewish settlement had been given by the self-same Mrs. Gordon.

On my return to Kobe I addressed a meeting in the little synagogue, which was fitted up in a room on the upper floor of a private dwelling. The shrine was furnished plainly and adorned with Zionist flags, and besides the small gathering of Jews there were two police officials in

[1] For details see *The Journal of a Jewish Traveller*, pp. 151 - 152.

A JEWISH PILGRIMAGE

mufti. After I had spoken the leader of the community made a fervid appeal in Russian, and a satisfactory response followed. My mission in Japan being now over, the next place in my itinerary was Harbin, so I took the night train for Shimonoseki, where I boarded a ship for Fusan.

V

After a rough voyage of twelve hours under sombre skies I landed at Fusan, on December 19th, 1920, and another twelve hours in a comfortable train brought me to Seoul. Here I spent a day strolling about, gazing at the white-garbed Koreans with their comical little top-hats (protecting their top-knots) and the numerous Japanese police-stations (to keep watch over the Koreans); and after another twenty-four hours in the train, through snow-covered country dotted with miserable mud-houses, I reached the dismal station of Mukden. I had been given the name and address of an American Jew, Mr. Herskowitz, living in the old Manchurian capital, by a Zionist in Kobe, and succeeded in tracing him. He told me that there were altogether only eight Jews in the city — three from America, one from England, and the others from Russia. They were all engaged in the fur trade and intended leaving again after some years. Though few in number they represented three or four different points of view on the Zionist question: the most pugnacious was a Bundist[1], who scoffingly spoke of Palestine as a chimera and was quite positive that Jews in the Diaspora would find their salvation only in Socialism. Mr. Herskowitz warned me of the Arctic cold that I should find in Harbin, and I therefore gladly agreed to exchange my winter over-coat for a heavier fur-lined coat and my trilby for a round one of fur, which I could exchange back again on my return.

From Mukden I had to travel over another twenty hours before arriving at my destination, but the journey was fairly tolerable in the sleeping-car, although the only refreshment obtainable consisted of glasses of weak, milkless tea supplied by the Russian conductor from the steaming samovar in his cosy cubicle. Harbin was the very

[1] The Bund was the Jewish Socialist organisation founded in Vilna in 1897: it was fundamentally opposed to Zionism.

coldest city that I had ever struck. The streets were thickly covered with ice, so that goloshes were necessary: whenever I stepped from the centrally-heated hotel into the open air, little icicles formed on my moustache: and when I came back into the warmth my frosted glasses became dim with vapour. It was a Russian city on Chinese territory and was administered by the Chinese Eastern Railway Company, with the joint blessings of the Russian and Chinese Governments. It was the junction of the Siberian and the Chinese Railways, and as its territory enjoyed neutrality it had acquired cosmopolitan popularity. The population was largely Russian, including some 10,000 Jews, for the laws of the Tsar confining his Jewish subjects to the Pale of Settlement did not apply here. Half of the Jews had settled in Harbin before the First World War, the other half had been attracted as to a city of refuge, having come from all parts of the Russian Empire, though many were fugitives from the terrors of war, Bolshevism, and famine. There were two large synagogues and some small ones, a secular school and a religious one, an orphanage and a home for the aged needy.

The vigorous Jewish consciousness of the community manifested itself in a struggle of parties, in which the Right, Centre, Left and Extreme Left, were always engaged. There were ceaseless public discussions, especially on a Saturday night, between the rival adherents of Zionism pure and simple, Zionism without Orthodoxy and Orthodoxy without Zionism, Zionism with Socialism and Socialism without Zionism, Hebraism in Manchuria, and Yiddishism in Palestine. The speeches at these discussions had to be delivered in Russian (though many of the speakers would have preferred Hebrew or Yiddish), as the Chinese police representatives who were always present wished to be sure that nothing subversive was said; but whether they understood some of the hair-splitting utterances on Palestinian Territorialism or on the complexities of Diaspora psychology, I rather doubted, even though they smiled occasionally.

I soon realised that there were not scores but hundreds of Jews in Harbin who were eager to go to Palestine, and many of them indulged in the fond dream that I would facilitate their journey. The manager of my hotel and the head-waiter were the first to bespeak my services, and they were followed by a number of released prisoners of war, men who had fought and bled in the armies of their native country, Austria or Hungary, and saw no early prospect of repatriation. Jewish national sentiment was kept alive by a Zionist weekly in Russian, which was edited by a former lawyer in Petrograd, who had secured an important position as a Commissary with a confidential mission to some place near the Siberian frontier so that he could easily escape into liberty. There was therefore no need for me to gain converts: my task was confined to spreading information and obtaining donations from a relatively small group who had succeeded in becoming or remaining wealthy despite the economic typhoon that had swept away the fortunes of so many.

The meetings that I addressed, both public and private, were marked by great enthusiasm. At some I spoke partly in Hebrew and partly in Yiddish, and at others in German, according as the circumstances required. At one gathering, a police official demanded that I should speak in Russian, so that he could follow, whereupon the chairman told him that special permission had been obtained for me through the good offices of the British Consul to use any language that I chose. The official retorted that he knew nothing about this, so the chairman suggested that he could ring up his superior on the telephone and find out. The conscientious functionary promptly agreed and elbowed his way through the throng to seek a telephone. Thereupon I resumed my speech and was just concluding when he returned with a grin. On another occasion the electric lights suddenly went out in the middle of my address, but I continued unperturbed in the darkness, in which nothing could be seen but the glow of cigarettes, and after some minutes the lights came on again.

My final meeting was in the large hall of the Commercial Club, and as it had accommodation for only 700 admission was by tickets, which were all soon snapped up. The function was announced for eight o'clock, I was advised to be there at half-past eight, I arrived at a quarter to nine (as I thought that I knew local habits), but had to wait until nine before the chairman appeared and a bell signalled for the people to take their seats. After I had spoken the chairman declared an interval, the audience swarmed into the restaurant for refreshment, and glasses of tea with lemon were brought to the platform. Then the bell rang again as in a theatre, the audience trooped back to their seats, and there were more speeches to enforce my appeal. The result was that my week's labours yielded £10,000. By the time the committee had rescued me from a little crowd who wanted further information it was nearly midnight, but not too late to retire to a private dining-room, where a substantial repast was spread and toasts were drunk to the continued success of my tour.

VI

I left Harbin for Tientsin, but without knowing whether there was a Jewish community there. I sent a telegram to a Jew whose address had been given to me in Yokohama, and was surprised on arriving at half-past six in the morning, when it was still dark, to be welcomed by a deputation of four. They took me to an hotel, and told me that they had fixed up a meeting for the afternoon and there was a Jewish community of about 300. Tientsin was an up-to-date city, with broad thoroughfares, electric tramcars, modern houses, and large public buildings. It was as cosmopolitan as Shanghai, but smaller. The meeting took place in the Gordon Hall, which was built as a memorial to General Gordon. Most of the people present were Russian Jews, but there were also many from Iraq and America. I was introduced by one chairman in Russian and by his co-chairman in English, and I spoke partly in English and partly in German. The British Consul-General was not only present but supported my appeal by a speech and by giving a donation himself.

In the evening I had dinner in the home of my Russian chairman, where I met a curious instance of the Jew without a fatherland. He was born in Constantinople of a father born in Galicia, he had a German name but had never been in any German-speaking country, he had spent his childhood in Egypt and afterwards settled in China. At the time of his birth Galicia was part of Austria, and he was therefore technically an Austrian subject. Galicia had now become part of Poland, but the ill-treatment of the Jews in that country had embittered him too much that he should think of increasing their number. He wanted to become a Jew politically and nationally, with a Jewish passport. He was deeply disappointed when I told him that this was not yet possible.

In the train that took me to Peking I had an experience that illustrated the ubiquity of the Jew. The only other passenger in my compartment, who seemed to be an Italian or Frenchman, turned out to be a Russian Jewish mining engineer, who had an appointment with one of my generous supporters from Harbin. And I even found a solitary Jew, named Regine, resident in Peking. He had also come from Russia, yet was the first to publish and edit an English paper, *The Peking Post*, which had only a brief career. He had nevertheless perpetuated his name in the ancient city by presenting the Central Park with the Regine Fountain.

It is impossible here to attempt to give an adequate impression of the awe-inspiring sights of the Chinese capital, of the colossal wall with cavernous gateways enclosing the Tartar City, of the stupendous red-painted arches beside which the Arc de Triomphe is a mere goalpost, of the Summer Palace with its villas, pagodas, and marble boat, and, above all, of that shrine of majestic and monumental proportions, the Temple of Heaven. I tried to do justice to them when my memories were fresher.[1] But I went to Peking not only to gaze at its wealth of wondrous spectacles but also to see the British Minister, Sir Beilby Alston, in order to invoke his good offices in regard to three important matters with which I had been entrusted by my friends in Harbin. The most urgent was to obtain the release of the chairman of the Harbin Zionist Association, a doctor who was being detained by the Chinese at Urga; the second was to free Zionist meetings from police restrictions; and the third was to render it possible for Jewish prisoners of war who were being repatriated from Vladivostok and wished to go to Palestine, to disembark at Port Said, so that they could travel by train to Jerusalem. Sir Beilby promised to make immediate representations to the Chinese Government in regard to the first two matters, and to cable to London about the third. Subsequently I learned that his intervention on behalf of

[1] In *The Journal of a Jewish Traveller*.

the doctor had been immediately successful, and there were rejoicings in the Harbin community when the long-absent leader came home.[1]

VII

After completing my mission in the northern half of the Far East I travelled south to Singapore, with brief halts at Shanghai and Hongkong and enjoyable détours to Canton and Macao. In Singapore the heat made it necessary to have a cold douche twice a day, and the bed in my airy hotel looked like a big snow-white cage, closed in on all sides and overhead by a mosquito-curtain beneath which one had to dive quickly and dexterously. Jews first began to settle there, in the wake of the pioneering Sassoons, in 1840, and at the time of my visit, in January, 1921, there were about 600, of whom the great majority had originated from Bagdad and India, with later additions from Germany and Russia. The street in which the first settlers met in a house for worship acquired and has retained to this day the name of Synagogue Street. Forty years later there was built the first Jewish house of prayer, facing west like all the synagogues in the East, wherein the Bagdad ritual was observed. The grey-bearded *Hazan* (precentor), in fez and white gaberdine, showed me with pride the Ark of the Law containing twenty-four large scrolls, all in conical cases of beaten silver from Bagdad; but I doubted whether most members of the congregation saw any of them except on the two or three most solemn days of the year. Spiritual life was stagnant as there was no Rabbi of the modern type. The only religious functionary was the *Hazan*, who, although he had been in the British colony for many years, could not speak a word of English. He also acted as teacher of Hebrew and religion to a few dozen children in a small school (Talmud Torah), but how much they learned it was difficult to say as their instructor spoke only Arabic.

There was another and larger synagogue in a better part of the city, built at the beginning of the century by Sir Menasseh Meyer for the convenience of himself and his family as he had had a difference with the devotees of the older shrine. Born in Bagdad, he had

[1] Since the end of the Second World War the number of Jews in China has shrunk to less than 700.

settled in Singapore in the early period of its development and prospered to such a degree that he was reputed to be the richest Jew in the Far East, but despite his enormous wealth he remained devoutly attached to orthodox tradition. He had created an imposing patriarchal domain, where he lived with his sons and daughters, his sons-in-law and daughter-in-law, besides three adopted orphans; and he ensured the ritual fitness of his food by having his own kine, cattle, and poultry in adjacent outhouses and yards, with a qualified slaughterer (*Shochet*) for killing and an orthodox chef for cooking. When I first saw him in the covered porch leading to the main entrance of his mansion, he was wearing a black scull-cap on his grey head, seated in an arm-chair, with a book of Hebrew lore on a little table before him. He told me that he had been to Palestine the previous year with his daughter, and maintained there a house of Talmudic study (*Beth Hamidrash*) and a small synagogue for Bagdad Jews, so I felt sure that I would find in him a generous supporter of my cause. Early the following morning, being the Sabbath, he sent a Jewish manservant with rickshaws driven by Chinese coolies to take me to his synagogue, and after the service I had breakfast with him at a long, richly laden table over which he presided with sedate dignity.

It was only natural that the communal meeting that I addressed should take place in Sir Menasseh's palatial home. The whole of the adult Jewish population came in response to a general invitation published in the local papers and were regaled before the speeches with an appetising tea. There were present even two or three prominent members, who, owing to the heavy slump in their tin and rubber properties, had expressed a preference for the restoration of Zion by the gratuitous agency of the Messiah. Close attention was shown by all alike to my address, and then everybody's eyes were fixed upon our host who was expected to lead off in the financial response. And so, when I announced that he was giving 25,000 dollars (Mexican), about £3,000, and added that this was the largest individual gift that I had hitherto received in the whole of my tour the applause was enthusiastic beyond measure. It was more than the total I obtained from the rest of the community.

VIII

I felt transported to an even warmer climate as I sailed through the equatorial waters to Batavia, but I had not been in Java long before I realised that the tropical atmosphere in the physical world was counterbalanced by a marked frigidity on the spiritual plane. I was met on arrival, on February 6th, 1921, by four young Dutch Jews (three of them in Government service) who lost no time in taking me round to some people in the suburb of Weltevreden, as my tour through the country had to be limited to five days. A rich Austrian Jew upon whom we called, and whom we found (owing to the heat) in pyjamas and sandals, expressed his scepticism about the advisability of bringing the Jews back again to Palestine and argued that they should become absorbed among the nations — a view that I found to be prevalent among the bulk of the Jews in Java. The heat after noon was altogether too oppressive to allow any roving about, but in the cool of the evening I spoke to a small gathering, which included some Christians.

My friends then took me to a club for dinner, and as we sat on the terrace at a table with a red-shaded light, amid the whirring of invisible insects overhead, I heard something about the conditions of Jewish life in what was then a peaceful Dutch colony. There were several hundred Jews — perhaps as many as 2,000 — scattered about from Batavia to Sourabaya, but most of them concealed or denied their Jewish origin. Dutch Jews had been living there for a very long period and there were many holding Government positions; but there was no Jewish communal life, mixed marriages were frequent, and the only form of association consisted of a few struggling Zionist societies. There was not a single synagogue, although on the High Festivals religious worship was held in a private house or public hall in the three or four largest centres.

From Batavia I went to Bandoeng, where there was only a single Jewish household, consisting of a Sephardi and his wife who had come from Bagdad. They were a pious couple, genuinely pleased to welcome one who brought greetings from the Holy Land, and pointed with pride to a picture on the wall, which was an old-fashioned oleograph of the Tomb of Rachel and the Tower of David. It was still dark when I rose the following morning to catch the train for Sourabaya. There was no railway traffic at night, so that, owing to the long distances between the principal towns, journeys had often to be begun before daybreak, but the resultant discomfort was forgotten in the sequence of picturesque views — an endless expanse of luscious vegetation, miles of coco-nut palms, vast rice-fields, and dense forests. After an all-day journey I arrived in Sourabaya, tired and travel-stained, but in less than an hour found myself at a festive table in the leading hotel, in the company of two dozen selected guests. I was introduced by a former settler from the Palestinian village of Zichron Jacob, and my appeal met with a modest response. The following day I was taken round by a young Russian Jew in his motor-car to other members of the community, to swell the list. One of them was married to a native of Maderoe; although ostracised by his fellow-Jews, he readily contributed. There were a few other Jews in the city who had native wives and were made to feel like social outcasts.

Early the next day I travelled on to Semarang, where I addressed a meeting in the Masonic Hall. After the speeches I was approached by an elderly Russian Jew, who told me that he had been a cantor at Kharkoff, from where he had fled to Siberia and joined an operatic company at Irkutsk, with which he had toured from place to place. He took me to the local open-air theatre, where the company were performing the opera *Thaïs* in Russian, and in the foyer I met the manager, a burly individual and his wife, who were both eager to go to Palestine and to take their troupe there. The wife, a native of Odessa, boasted that she had known Abraham Goldfaden, the " Father " of the Yiddish stage, and in the course of our conversation about the Holy Land she asked: " Are they building already ? "

" Building what ? " I asked.

" The *Beth Hamikdash* (Temple)," she replied with emphasis.

By the time I was back again in Batavia I had raised nearly a thousand pounds in five days, and what was lacking to that amount was given by some Dutch diamond-merchants, who were returning on the same boat with me to Singapore.

IX

After a brief rest I was on board another ship bound for Rangoon. We anchored for a few hours at Penang, during which I called on the oldest Jewish resident, Mr. Ezekiel Menasseh, a little grey-haired man, who had left Bagdad thirty years before. He was studying a Rabbinical commentary on the Book of Daniel, and called my attention to a passage in the last chapter, on the basis of which the author calculated that the restoration of Palestine was to take place between 1920 and 1922. This discovery stimulated his generosity, and after lunch his son drove me back to my ship.

At Rangoon I was the guest of a rich member of the community, Mr. Meyer Meyer, whose palatial residence was surrounded by extensive gardens and had an adjoining farmyard for the needs of the household. There were about 500 Jews altogether, most of whom had originated from Bagdad, and they were consequently trilingual, speaking Arabic among themselves, Burmese with the natives, and English with Europeans. They had an endowed synagogue, which was maintained from the rents of adjacent shops, so that membership was free, but that did not make religious worship more popular. It was a large edifice, which was quite full when I gave my address there, but the obtaining of donations was left for personal visits, on which I was accompanied by the president. There were several contributors who had not heard me, and who, indeed, never entered the synagogue except on the Day of Atonement. One was a merchant born in London, who was married to a Burmese woman, and the other, also a native of London, had a Japanese wife. A curious discovery that I made was that there was a little coterie of Anglo-Jewish bookmakers in the city, who travelled regularly between London and Rangoon. We called upon one, whom we found in the native garb of a gaudy skirt, which he preferred to pyjamas, and he gave us both a friendly welcome and a cheque. Another interesting person whom I met was a Pittsburg Jew, who owned a sugar plantation in the Solomon Islands.

At the end of my stay I stepped into a sampan to be rowed back to the ship, which was half-a-mile away, but soon regretted my

A JEWISH PILGRIMAGE

choice of transport, as the frail boat was at the mercy of the furious onrushing tide. But the dexterous boatman, plying his single oar, and standing all the time, brought me safely through treacherous currents to the ship's ladder, up which I clambered with a great sigh of relief and an unspoken prayer of thanks.

X

I heaved another sigh of relief when I landed at Calcutta on March 1st, 1921, as I had reached the last stage of my long itinerary. The history of the Jewish community went back to the end of the eighteenth century. There were about 2,000 souls, originating mostly from Iraq and Southern Arabia, while those from Europe numbered hardly more than a hundred. Like their brethren in Rangoon, the Jews in Calcutta were also trilingual, speaking Arabic with one another, Hindustani with the natives, and English with Europeans. They had three synagogues, two of which were actually cheek by jowl, a circumstance due to an old personal feud that still prevented efficient communal organisation.

It was in the largest and finest synagogue, the "Magen David," that I spoke to a goodly sized gathering, but although I emphasised that this was the first appeal to the Jews of India to participate in the fulfilment of an ancient national ideal, for which prayers were offered up daily, the response fell short of my expectations. Several persons contributed 101 rupees and some £101, and when I inquired about the reason for the final digit I was told that it represented the unity of the Godhead and was intended to bring luck. The senior Minister of the synagogue, who presided, the Rev. E. M. D. Cohen, gave 1,352 rupees, an amount produced by multiplying the numerical value of the Hebrew Tetragrammaton, 26, by the number of weeks in the year. The inadequate result necessitated a round of personal calls, on which I was accompanied by the Rev. Mr. Cohen or by my host, Mr. Ezekiel Gubbay, a wealthy bachelor. Mr. Cohen was a portly, distinguished figure, with a venerable white beard, who wore a suit of tussore silk and huge sun-helmet. Having married at the age of seventeen, he had realised the Psalmist's ideal of "a fruitful vine" and " olive plants." and dinner at his family table resembled a communal banquet.

The richest member of the community was Mr. (later Sir) David Ezra, who was in mourning at the time for his mother. I went to his mansion for prayers one afternoon and found there several men in Bagdadi costume, while through the open doorway of an adjoining apartment came a raucous chorus from an animated aviary — a score of parrots, parrakeets, and other birds, trying to drown the Hebrew supplications. After prayers a flask of rose-water was passed round, and as each person shook it he uttered a benediction, whereupon small cups of black coffee were served. In the large garden at the back I was invited by Lady Ezra to stay for tea. There were some strange pets disporting themselves there — monkeys chained to the ground, and storks and peacocks strutting about, whilst a staff of barefooted servants were looking after them. Lady Ezra evinced a warm interest in my mission and presided at a second meeting which I addressed, partly to augment the financial response and partly to found a Zionist society, which I presented with a Zionist flag. The total result of my week's endeavours was to raise only half a lakh — 50,000 rupees — but although I thought this a scanty tribute I was congratulated upon it by many sympathisers.

I then took the train to Agra, where my eyes feasted on the majestic splendour and towering beauty of the Taj Mahal; travelled all night to Delhi, where I gazed at the memorials and monuments of the historic city, and at last reached my final destination — the city of Bombay. Here I was welcomed by the largest and most enthusiastic crowd that had ever assembled in any station throughout my tour, representing all sections of the Jewish community. First, the president of the Zionist Association, Mr. D. Shellim, greeted me in laudatory phrases and placed a large garland of flowers round my neck, then a little girl tendered me a big bouquet, and before I could recover from these unwonted marks of honour the president of the Bene Israel Society, Dr. E. Moses, bestowed another garland round my neck and also offered me a bouquet. Encumbered with this mass of blooms, I made my way with difficulty through the jubilant throng, who grouped closely round me whilst a photographer took a picture of the scene.

A few hours later there was a gathering at the Masonic Hall, where Mr. Shellim addressed me repeatedly as "Dear Brother," and, after my speech, placed a garland of silver thread round my neck. Then glasses of champagne were served among the elders, who, all standing, drank my health amid joyous acclaim. Two days later there was a public meeting at the Jacob Sassoon Free School, which was attended not only by men, women, and children, but also by at least a dozen infants in arms, but owing to the din I insisted upon the removal of the babies, and after I had given my discourse there was a satisfactory response. In order to explain the aims of Zionism to the general public I arranged a meeting at the Sir Cowasji Jehangir Hall, at which I was fortunate to have as chairman Professor Patrick Geddes, who was Director of the Department of Sociology at Bombay University. Despite the very short notice there was a goodly audience, including Moslems and Parsees as well as Jews, and the chairman set an example in starting off the list of contributions.

In Bombay I felt even more keenly than in Calcutta the lack of proper communal organisation. Not only was there a gulf between the Bagdadi Jews and the Bene Israel, the former looking down upon the latter as people of an impure and inferior stock, but the Bagdadi section seemed to be without a head. Gone were the days when the Sassoons, who had given a powerful impetus to the commercial development of the city, were content to live on the scene of their financial achievements. Their businesses were in the hands of trusted directors, who also had the stewardship of the communal benefactions left by the pious founders, but the paternal solicitude of the former generation was lacking. The most distinguished resident Jew was Sir Sassoon David, a merchant prince and former Mayor, but despite his reputed wealth he lent no ear to my plea. All that he gave me was a curious little document, which he had devised as chairman of the electric tramway company — a tram ticket specially printed for the use of Jews only on Sabbaths and festivals, which could be bought by the observant in advance, so as to avoid the handling of money prohibited on the sacred days.

WELCOME WITH GARLANDS AT BOMBAY, 1921

The greater and older part of the Jewish population consisted of the Bene Israel, whose history could not be traced back further than the middle of the eighteenth century, although their traditions and customs pointed to a much more ancient origin. Indeed, they claimed that they were descended from the survivors of a band of Jews who fled from persecution in Palestine in the second century. Their military record was brilliant, many of them having served faithfully in British Indian regiments for very long periods and fought heroically in various wars. I came into close contact with them at a social gathering that they held in my honour, at which I was garlanded again, and also at a public meeting, at which I found it necessary to allay their fears that the "colour bar" exercised against them by other Jews in India would be continued in the Land of Israel.

I was taken one day to a school compound, where there was a group of Jewish refugees, some from Anatolia and others from Persia, all dirty, dusty, and bedraggled, waiting to be sent to Palestine. They were being looked after by Mr. Shellim, who invited me to have tea at his home, which was close by. He introduced me to a lady as his "Memsah'b Number One," and smilingly said that his "Memsah'b Number Two" was in the other room. His first wife was a Bagdadi Jewess; his second, whom I did not see, an Englishwoman converted to Judaism. It was the only case of a Jew openly living with two legally wedded wives that I came across in the whole of my tour. An even more notable experience was my meeting two Jewish carpet-dealers from Meshed, who told me the tragic story of the persecution of their brethren in that Persian city. Owing to some Jews having killed a dog on a holy day of the Shiites some eighty years before, many Jews were killed on that day and the whole community had been forced to adopt Islam and live as Moslems ever since. The two merchants showed me their passports, in which they were entered with Moslem names and described as of Moslem faith. They spoke Hebrew fluently, and one of them, at my request and in my presence, wrote out a brief statement in Biblical Hebrew.

It was with no small feeling of relief that I boarded the ship for Port Said, for after nine months of incessant travel over such vast distances and in such varied climes — apart from speaking and raising a total of over £100,000 — I was not a little tired. But I could not escape being garlanded twice more, so that I should carry some souvenirs away with me. Nor had I delivered my last speech, for a day before we reached Suez, at the suggestion of Professor Geddes, I gave an address after dinner to my fellow-passengers on the subject of my mission, and answered the questions of many Indian Government officials who were returning home. I could not help recalling that we were probably not far from the very spot where the Children of Israel crossed over in their flight from the land of bondage to the Land of Promise.

I went to Palestine again for a brief visit, partly to report to the Zionist Executive on the results and the lessons of my mission, and partly to see what progress had been made. I noticed that, under the Civil Administration, Hebrew had now become a living tongue to a greater extent than before; that groups of bronzed and brawny young Jews were in many parts of the country, engaged in various kinds of labour; and that the schools were hives of happy activity. But I also heard many complaints of the lack of progress in other spheres uttered by those who had expected that the advent of a Jewish High Commissioner would bring about a rapid transformation, and apprehensions were expressed about the spreading agitation among the Arabs.

A fortnight later I sailed from Alexandria to Brindisi, and on April 18th, 1921, arrived in Rome. There my wife was awaiting me, and we had much to tell one another. As it was the first time she was in Italy we visited various cities — Florence and Venice, Padua and Verona — before journeying to The Hague, where I gave a verbal report to the Directors of the Jewish National Fund. And on May 8th we were home again.

Chapter Thirteen

POLITICS AND PERSONALITIES
1921 — 1923

I

THE aftermath of my mission to Australasia and the Far East lasted for quite a considerable time. No sooner had I returned to the Zionist Office than I wrote letters to all the societies and local leaders with whom I had come into contact, to thank them for their help and hospitality; and as many of the donations were to be paid in four annual instalments, regular correspondence had to be maintained with those responsible for remitting them. Nor was my connection with the host of friends whom I had made conserved and fostered solely through the post. There was hardly a month in which one or two of them did not arrive in London, and as I not only welcomed them at the Office but also entertained them in my home, my wife had to share in my official duties. The more important of these visitors also expected to be introduced to Dr. Weizmann and to be honoured by some minutes' conversation, so that they could write to their families and friends of their thrilling experience; and those who were denied this privilege, either because the Zionist leader had some more important engagement, or because he was out of London, or simply because he did not want to be bothered, made no secret of their disappointment.

But I had other things to do besides looking after the contributions to the Palestine Restoration Fund and welcoming some of their oversea donors. Although the term " Public Relations Officer " had not yet come into vogue, and was indeed unknown in the nomenclature of the departments of the Zionist Office, it was the customary functions of such an official that I had to discharge. I had to answer the inquiries of Press representatives about what was happening in Palestine, about the relations between Jews and Arabs, and about the relations between the British Government and the Zionist Organisation. I had to supply factual material to politicians and lecturers, and to reply to attacks or misrepresentations in the press. I also had occasionally to write articles which were published under other persons' names.

Soon after my return from the Far East I was invited by Dr. Weizmann to his room and introduced to Samuel Untermyer, a famous and wealthy lawyer from New York and a somewhat domineering character, who had just been elected President of the Keren Hayesod in the United States — the Palestine Foundation Fund, which was to finance the establishment of the Jewish National Home (apart from the purchase of land, which was the task of the Jewish National Fund). It happened that at that time an article attacking the Zionist movement and disparaging the prospects in Palestine, written by Henry Morgenthau[1], a former American Ambassador in Turkey, appeared in a leading American monthly, *World's Work*. Untermyer was very anxious to reply to the article, especially as it would form an auspicious inauguration of his presidency of the Keren Hayesod, but he was incapable of writing it. Dr. Weizmann therefore asked me if I would undertake it. I readily agreed. " It must be ready in a couple of days," said Untermyer with some emphasis, " as I have to get back to the States." Two days later I called at the Ritz Hotel, where he was staying, and handed him in the foyer a typed article of over 5,000 words. He glanced through it standing, and complained that some quoted passages were not indented and in single spacing. It was his only comment upon my work, which appeared under his name in the *Forum Magazine* for September, 1921.

Some of the visitors that I received did not seek information but wanted jobs or else money with which to finance a project that they

[1] Not to be confused with his son, Henry Morgenthau, Junior, United States Secretary of the Treasury from 1934 to 1945, who has rendered very valuable services in raising funds for Israel.

would describe in alluring terms. Among the earliest were two British ex-Army officers, who asked for a couple of thousand pounds to enable them to go to Palestine to make a film at a time when nobody had yet undertaken such a thing in that country. They were crestfallen when I told them that the Executive did not think that the Jewish National Home had yet made sufficient progress to be filmed. A Polish Christian unctuously proposed that he should be engaged to undertake Zionist propaganda in Poland. He thought that the idea was very novel since all other propagandists in Poland were Jews. I told him that there were already so many Christians in that country whose conduct had convinced Jews of the necessity of Zionism that a paid Christian propagandist would be an expensive and superfluous luxury.

But I also had a visitor once who did not want any money but actually made me a financial offer. He was a wealthy Jew, the head of a big business in the city, who said he had been reading in *The Jewish Chronicle* my articles on the Jews in China, and that, as I was familiar with that region, I was just the man for him. Would I go out for his firm to China just for twelve months, for which he would pay me a salary of £1,000 besides £1,000 for expenses ? He assured me that the work would be quite easy, as I would only have to carry a small case of samples, and he would supply me with a list of the firms that I would have to call on. I told him that the offer did not attract me in the least, as I had returned from the Far East only recently, and in any case I must talk to my wife about it. She agreed with me that the offer was out of the question, and when I rang him up a few days later and told him of my decision he was quite annoyed.

II

The Zionist Congress that was held in September, 1921, was the first since 1913, and in consequence of the revolutionary changes that had taken place in the interval, it was much larger, more imposing, and more animated than any that had preceded it. The meeting-place was Carlsbad, which had been chosen because of the liberal and congenial atmosphere that then existed there, and also because it was conveniently situated for the Jews in Eastern Europe. Far more countries were represented than ever before, but there were significant differences. There were no Jews from Russia, for Zionism was forbidden there; and, on the other hand, Palestine had sent a larger delegation than on all previous occasions. At the opening session the British Ambassador in Prague, Sir George Clerk (who had arranged the official facilities for my mission to Poland) was present to convey a message of good wishes from his Government and to repeat the terms of the Balfour Declaration, which were received with thunderous and prolonged applause. The deliberations were rendered all the more difficult by the attendance of about 500 delegates, most of whom (especially if they had travelled thousands of miles) were anxious to speak, and by the limited time within which the business had to be completed. But by transferring the discussion of all technical problems and business details, as well as the drafting of all resolutions, to a number of committees consisting of representatives of all parties and of the principal delegations, the Congress completed its stupendous labours in a fortnight. Its concluding act was the election of an Executive of thirteen, headed by Dr. Weizmann as President of the Organisation and Nahum Sokolow as President of the Executive. Six of the members (including Menahem Ussishkin, 1863 — 1941), were to constitute the Executive in Jerusalem and to take charge of Jewish affairs in Palestine. The other seven formed the Executive in London, and they were supplemented by three members of a Financial and Economic Committee.[1]

Shortly after this Congress I was appointed General Secretary, which meant not that I ceased to act as Director of Publicity and Propaganda, but that I had to assume many duties and responsibilities in addition to my previous ones. I had been allowed to attend meetings of the Executive even before, but now it was my business to convene them, to prepare the agenda, to keep the minutes, and to see that all resolutions were carried out. Sokolow usually presided, but in his absence abroad (for he usually spent some months of the year on propaganda tours on the Continent, in America, or in South Africa) the chair would be taken either by Weizmann or another member. I had to write down a fairly full record of the proceedings,

[1] This Committee was discontinued from 1927.

POLITICS AND PERSONALITIES

and as all members insisted on seeing a copy of the draft minutes before they were pasted into a book of foolscap size in case they had any alterations or additions to make, the minutes had always to be typed twice.

There were frequent meetings of the Executive in the closing months of 1921 and the first half of 1922, as the text of the Palestine Mandate was to be ratified in July, 1922, by the League of Nations, and the Colonial Office intended issuing a Statement of Policy before then to which it wished to receive the Executive's formal assent. The situation during that period was full of anxiety and excitement, of rumours and reports, of intrigues and alarms, of interviews with members of the Government and consultations with all sorts of people. An Arab Delegation from Palestine had come to London for the purpose of urging the Government to rescind the Balfour Declaration, and they made an impression in both political and press circles, thanks partly, perhaps, to the venerable appearance of their grey-bearded leader, Musa Kazim Pasha, in his Oriental robes and turban. Another member of the Delegation was Shibly Jamal, a fluent English speaker, who addressed meetings in clubs and elsewhere on the Arab grievances, and I was kept busy following on his tracks for the purpose of correcting his misrepresentations and exploding the anti-Zionist legends that were current. The Harmsworth and Beaverbrook press gave their vigorous support to the Arab Delegation. They conducted an "Anti-Waste" campaign based on the fiction that Palestine was costing the British tax-payer millions a year, and they whipped it up by coupling Palestine with Mesopotamia, from which they clamoured that the Government should clear out "bag and baggage."

Throughout the whole of this nerve-racking and disquieting period the author of the Balfour Declaration remained serene and unmoved, resolved that no jot or tittle of the Declaration should be given up and that the text of the Palestine Mandate — the fruit of three years' careful deliberation and discussion — should be ratified by the Council of the League. His annoyance over the *Daily Mail* opposition prompted him to remark: "I hear this creature Northcliffe is attacking us." He was somewhat puzzled by the conflicting attitude adopted by various leading English Jews and said to Weizmann: "There are two men who are riddles to me. Why isn't Claude Montefiore[1] a Zionist and why is Mond a Zionist?"

III

The Statement of Policy that was submitted to the Executive for an assurance that they would conduct their activities in conformity with it produced a shock. It bluntly dismissed the idea that Palestine was to become "as Jewish as England is English",[2] it emphasised that the Balfour Declaration did not "contemplate that Palestine as a whole should be converted into a Jewish National Home, but that such a Home should be founded *in* Palestine," and it definitely stipulated that immigration must be regulated in accordance with the economic absorptive capacity of the country. The purport of this Statement was a drastic abridgement of the aspirations which it had been believed the Jewish people would be allowed to achieve. The authorship of the document, which came to be known as the Churchill White Paper (as Sir Winston Churchill was then Colonial Secretary) was commonly attributed to the High Commissioner in Palestine, Sir Herbert Samuel, and as the latter had come to London for consultations at the Colonial Office an effort was made by a member of the Executive to induce him to omit or tone down some of the more objectionable passages. The effort was in vain.

The Executive were deeply alarmed by a report that Sir Herbert Samuel had advised the omission of Article 4 of the Mandate with a view to reconciling the Arabs.[3] They felt that the omission of

[1] Anglo-Jewish theologian and scholar (1858 — 1938), founder of the Liberal Synagogue movement in England and an active opponent of Zionism.

[2] The expression used by Dr. Weizmann in reply to a question put to him by Mr. Lansing, the American representative, at the meeting of the Peace Conference on February 27th, 1919.

[3] Article 4 was as follows:—

An appropriate Jewish agency shall be recognised as a public body for the purpose of advising and co-operating with the Administration of Palestine in such economic, social and other matters as may affect the establishment of the Jewish national home and the interests of the Jewish population in Palestine, and, subject always to the control of the Administration, to assist and take part in the development of the country.

The Zionist Organisation, so long as its organisation and constitution are in the opinion of the Mandatory appropriate, shall be recognised as such agency. It shall take steps in consultation with His Britannic Majesty's Government to secure the co-operation of all Jews who are willing to assist in the establishment of the Jewish national home.

so vital an article would be tantamount to its evisceration, and they seriously thought of resigning in a body if it were insisted upon. But on inquiry they were told by Sir Herbert that he had not proposed the deletion of Article 4 nor did he think that the Government would propose it. On the other hand, he thought that if the Zionist Executive were in favour of its deletion, they would weaken the attacks against them; but if they were of opinion that they would thereby lose more than they would gain they could decide accordingly. The Executive refused to give the matter a second thought. For them the inclusion of Article 4 was a fundamental element in the Mandate and absolutely indispensable, and, although far from satisfied with the document as a whole, they heaved a sigh of relief when the Mandate was at last ratified by the Council of the League in London. The Council met on July 24th, 1922, at St. James's Palace, and I was among the small group who were privileged to be present on the historic occasion. The British Government was represented by Lord Balfour, who spoke with his usual fluency and cogency, tinged with a certain degree of parental emotion.

Article 4 soon began to play a very important part in the deliberations of the Executive and in the discussions of all other Zionist bodies. Dr. Weizmann interpreted the last sentence of the Article to mean that the Zionist Organisation was not sufficient by itself to act as " an appropriate Jewish agency . . . for the purpose of advising and co-operating with the Administration of Palestine." He thought that it was necessary to set up a new body consisting of one or two members of the Executive together with some leading Jews who were not members of the Zionist Organisation, and that this new body should be designated the " Jewish Agency " and be distinct from the Zionist Organisation. This view was strongly contested by some members of the Executive, especially by Jabotinsky and Dr. Max Soloweitschik (who had formerly been Minister for Jewish Affairs in the Lithuanian Government), who maintained that the Zionist Organisation alone was entitled and qualified to act as the Jewish Agency, and that there was absolutely no need to create a new body consisting either of some members of the Executive alone or in conjunction with some non-Zionists. Jabotinsky was particularly vehement in his opposition: he repeatedly and emphatically stressed that all members of the Executive were equally responsible and that they had no need of non-Zionist partners. Indeed, he stigmatised Weizmann's conception as that of "a régime of notables," upon which he poured vials of scorn and wrath. This hostile attitude provoked Weizmann to such a state of indignation that he began to threaten that he would resign unless his proposal were accepted.

IV

The discussion about the Jewish Agency, which began in London in the early summer of 1922, was continued at Carlsbad, in August, at the *Jahreskonferenz*, a gathering composed of all members of the Executive and of the General Council ("Actions Committee") as well as of representatives of all Zionist Federations. But so far from the gulf in the Executive being bridged, it became wider. There was a very painful scene at one meeting, at which Jabotinsky's contemptuous denunciation of the project had such a crushing effect upon Weizmann as he sat at the head of the table that he blenched and seemed to slump in his chair. He got up and walked with bowed head out of the room, bringing the meeting to a sudden end. Had I not been present at the scene and somebody had described it to me, I would have suspected him of drawing upon his imagination. I was at a loss to understand how Jabotinsky — a short, spare, stocky individual with an unprepossessing face — could, by means of his rasping, histrionic tirade, have exercised so oppressive an influence over the President of the Zionist Organisation as though he had mesmerised him. It was a scene that I never saw repeated. When the discussions were resumed in London the heated recriminations between Jabotinsky and Weizmann began to tell upon the latter's nerves. Dr. Montague David Eder, who shared the President's views and also his confidence, proposed that Weizmann be given six months' leave on account of his health; and Weizmann, on repeating his threat to resign, made it clear that he was prompted less by the state of his health than by the obstruction by which he was faced.

The situation was bedevilled by attacks that were made upon

Jabotinsky on account of his having signed an agreement with Slavinsky, an agent of the notorious General Petlura, who had organised pogroms in Southern Russia in 1919 - 1921. The agreement had been signed in Carlsbad in September, 1921, ten days before the opening of the Congress, and its object was to authorise the formation of a Jewish self-defence corps which should be independent of the Ukrainian Army. Jabotinsky was attacked on the ground that he had made a pact with the confidant of one whose hands were stained with Jewish blood, but he defended himself on the plea that he had shown all the relevant documents to a conference of the Russian Ukrainian Zionist Federation (held in Carlsbad) and that they, by 12 votes to 6, had signified their approval of his action. He afterwards maintained that this was a local matter, about which the Executive had no right to be consulted, and that he had acted only in his private capacity; and under the moderating influence of Sokolow, at a meeting of the Executive in December, 1922, a resolution was adopted exculpating Jabotinsky, which was to be read at an impending meeting of the General Council.

But when this body assembled in Berlin, on January 14th, 1923, the Labour members, who had their own quarrel with Jabotinsky because of his attacks upon their Socialism, secured the appointment of a special committee to investigate the facts relating to his negotiations with Petlura. A letter was accordingly delivered to him in the evening requesting his appearance before the special committee on the following morning, to submit to cross-examination. He replied by immediately sending a letter to the chairman of the committee, announcing his resignation from the Executive, his secession from the Organisation, and his refusal to appear. He also addressed a letter to the chairman of the General Council, declaring that the rejection of his proposals signified a surrender of Zionist principles, a statement that was vigorously repudiated by the Council.

The departure of Jabotinsky resulted only in a temporary improvement of the atmosphere at meetings of the Executive, as an interview with the President published in a Yiddish daily, *The Jewish Times*, in February, 1923, caused serious annoyance to its members. In this interview Weizmann was reported to have said that he was responsible for all departments of the London Office and that he often had no colleagues with whom to consult. When taken to task, he defended himself on the plea that he had not intended any reflection upon them, but merely meant that some members of the Executive were often away on propaganda journeys; that he had not seen a proof of the interview before publication; and that he had not said at least seven-eighths of what was attributed to him. The incident was closed by Weizmann declaring that he was willing to publish a correction and also to show the statement to his colleagues before it was printed. It was not the only occasion when Weizmann caused himself serious embarrassment by his readiness to talk to journalists without insisting upon the report of his remarks being submitted to him before publication.

Even after this breeze had blown over the atmosphere was anything but calm, partly owing to the difficulty of meeting the Executive's budget. Cuts in expenditure were imperative, and among the measures adopted was the drastic reduction of the Propaganda Department that had been under Jabotinsky's direction. Among the officials dismissed was a carroty-haired young man from the Ukraine, named Michael Postan, who used to produce a Yiddish news bulletin. He thereupon joined the Jewish Correspondence Bureau (afterwards renamed the Jewish Telegraphic Agency), began to attend the London School of Economics, made such progress that he received an appointment there as a lecturer, married Eileen Power, Professor of Economic History at Cambridge University, and when she died succeeded to her Chair and married into the British nobility.

V

But even the economies effected did not produce a state of harmony, as they were insufficient. Weizmann therefore proposed that the Congress to take place in the summer of 1923 should be held in the United States as he thought that this would result in a powerful impetus being given to the movement in that country and Canada, and that consequently increased funds would flow from there into the coffers of the Executive. But this bold suggestion, the execution of which might have made history, was dismissed after little con-

POLITICS AND PERSONALITIES

sideration, as it was realised that the journey would have been much too costly for the majority of the delegates from Europe and the Executive could not possibly subsidise them. Carlsbad had proved so satisfactory for both the Congress in 1921 and the Conference in 1922 that it was decided to have the Congress there again in 1923. But when the arrangements were being discussed Weizmann was still in such a mood of discontent that he declared that he did not wish to deliver the inaugural address or even to figure at all in the opening session, and that he would leave it to Sokolow to open the Congress. The date fixed for beginning the Congress was August 6th, 1923, but until a month before then it was still doubtful what Weizmann would eventually decide. Finally he agreed to discharge his constitutional function as President.

It was not only the affairs in London with which he was occupied: he was also concerned with the affairs in Palestine. After the departure from there of Dr. Eder there was no English-born representative to conduct conversations and negotiations with the High Commissioner and his high officials. Weizmann, therefore, proposed to Lieutenant-Colonel Frederick H. Kisch (1888 - 1943) to accept an appointment as Political Officer of the Executive in Jerusalem, so that he could take charge of all relations with the Government. Kisch had had a distinguished career in the British Army and had also been attached to the British Delegation at the Peace Conference, but as he had never taken part in Jewish public life there was at first some diffidence on the part of other members of the Executive to appoint him. But Kisch, by his charm of manner and patent sincerity, apart from his professional credentials, soon won the sympathies of the Executive in London, and when he arrived in Jerusalem at the end of November, 1922, in the company of the President, he also met with the unanimous approval of the Executive there. Mr. Ussishkin was at that time chairman of the Jerusalem Executive and little suspected that at the next Congress, nine months later, he was to be displaced by Kisch.[1]

Two particular incidents at that Congress, in 1923, stand out among other memories — one humorous and the other serious. In

[1] In the Second World War Brigadier Kisch was Chief Engineer of the Eighth Army and was killed in action in Tunisia in April, 1943.

the course of his verbal report on the work of the Immigration Department of the Palestine Zionist Executive, Dr. Eder, who spoke in German (of which he was hardly a master), wished to say that they had provided the immigrants with barracks and mattresses. But instead of saying " *Matratzen* " he used the word " *Maitressen*," whereupon there was a burst of laughter from the delegates. The other incident was the omission of Ussishkin from the new Executive.

Although Dr. Weizmann had been a friend of Ussishkin for a quarter of a century and had fought with him against both Herzl and Wolffsohn, he came to the conclusion that, owing to his persistent criticism, his domineering manner, and his ignorance of English, he was not suitable as chairman of the Executive in Jerusalem; and as he wished Kisch to occupy that position, he knew that Ussishkin would be unwilling to serve under him. He therefore determined that the name of his old comrade should not be included in the list of the new Executive to be submitted at the close of the Congress for election. I happened to be standing quite close to Ussishkin on the platform when the names were read out by the chairman of the Standing Committee. As each name was announced, it was received by the delegates and visitors with thunderous applause; and when the list was completed, without the name of Ussishkin being mentioned, I glanced at his face. He looked deathly pale, his lips were tightly clenched, but he did not move a muscle. He took his public discomfiture stoically, but he gradually regained his influence and popularity, for he became chairman of the Board of Directors of the Jewish National Fund, and in that position, which he held until his death eighteen years later, he rendered very valuable services, which bore fruit in the remarkable growth of the Fund and the expansion of land in Jewish possession. Time is a great healer, and in the course of the years Weizmann and Ussishkin became completely reconciled.

---

[1] In his autobiography *Trial and Error* (p. 405), Weizmann writes: " The very painful debate with Ussishkin ended in his resignation from the Executive." There was no " resignation," as Ussishkin, like all his colleagues, held office until a new Executive had to be elected. In his Memoirs, *Call Back Yesterday*, Mr. Hugh Dalton quotes Lord Balfour's saying that " in politics there is no friendship at the top."

Chapter Fourteen

SOME SPECIAL MISSIONS

1922 — 1924

I

FROM time to time I had to interrupt my work in London in order to go to the Continent on some special missions. Between the spring of 1922 and that of 1924 there were three such occasions, one of which took me to Paris and the others to Hungary and Rumania.

Early in April, 1922, the Zionist Executive received a cable from Mr. Louis Lipsky, the American Zionist leader, stating that Adolph S. Ochs, the controlling owner of the *New York Times*, who had just been to Palestine, was in Paris, on his way home, and urging the desirability of securing an interview with him on his impressions of the country before he sailed from Europe. The importance of this advice consisted in the fact that the *New York Times* had shown no sympathy with the Zionist movement, and in the fear that if Mr. Ochs did not express himself on his visit to Palestine until he reached New York, there was a risk that he might give utterance in his paper to views that would do serious harm to the movement in America. The Executive agreed that it would be very useful to obtain from him a statement while his impressions of Jewish work in Palestine were still fresh and before he reached the critical atmosphere of his editorial office, and asked me to go over to Paris to see the great man.

I found that Mr. Ochs and his wife were staying at the Hotel de Crillon, and on explaining the purpose of my visit was given a very friendly reception. Mr. Ochs was rather a burly man, in the middle sixties, a little under medium height, slow in speech and masterful in manner. There was also present a tall American in the fifties, whom he introduced to me as Mr. Grasty, a journalist, who was going out to the Near East, including Palestine, to write some articles for the *New York Times*. We had a long and interesting talk lasting nearly two and a half hours, in the course of which Mr. Ochs spoke about what he had seen in Palestine freely and, on the whole, favourably. He said that his stay in the country had been too brief to speak authoritatively about its manifold aspects, but what he had seen of Jewish colonisation and of the men and women directing it and participating in it was most gratifying. I was glad to hear him say that " one must stand in awe and admiration of the enthusiasts who had thrown in their lot with the country, who had shown such courage and determination, and were doing such excellent work for its revival." He regarded them as belonging to a fine type, who would add distinction to any country, and what had already been accomplished exceeded his anticipations. In order to prevent my carrying away an erroneous impression, Mr. Ochs added that his opposition to Jewish nationalism was as strong as before, but he realised his responsibility as the owner of a great newspaper, and in this capacity he would not do anything to thwart the continuance of the work that he had seen, but on the contrary would do what he could to further it.

After the conversation had gone on for nearly an hour Mr. Ochs left the room for a moment or two, whereupon Mr. Grasty asked me rather shyly: "What is this Balfour Declaration you have been talking about ?" I was taken aback for a moment by this confession of ignorance, but was glad that I had the opportunity of dispelling it.

At the end of my visit I asked Mr. Ochs whether he would consent to my committing some of his impressions to writing. He at first demurred, but then said that if I thought a published interview would be of service to the cause he would have no objection. I therefore handed in at his hotel the following morning an account of that portion of the interview which I thought would be of the greatest service, and enclosed with it a note stating that I would call in the afternoon for its return. In the meantime Judge Bernard Rosenblatt, an American member of the Zionist Executive, arrived in Paris, and he accompanied me on my second visit. Mr. Ochs was quite satisfied with my account and made only one or two verbal alterations. He was pleased to meet Judge Rosenblatt and to hear that the latter was going to Palestine, and said that he would be glad to receive from him any article that he might send for publication. He told us that he had received a visit that morning from Lord Northcliffe, who discussed with him the conditions in Palestine and said that he was still a Zionist! Even Mr. Ochs smiled. We might have been favoured with further revelations had not our visit been cut short by the sudden entrance of an American insurance company magnate.

I at once returned to London and distributed copies of the interview to the office of the *New York Times*, to the Press Association of America, and to the English press. I also wrote to Mr. Lipsky, suggesting that the Executive of the Zionist Organisation of America should address a letter of thanks to Mr. Ochs.

That was not the only contribution to the American press on Palestine that I was able to furnish at that time. Mr. J. Ramsay MacDonald had just come back from a visit to the Holy Land, and as I received a request from Mr. Meyer Weisgal, editor of the New York weekly, *The New Palestine*, to obtain a number of articles for him from eminent English politicians for a special issue, I wrote to Mr. MacDonald for the purpose. I received a prompt reply that he would be glad to let me have an article on "Impressions of Palestine," and a few days later came the manuscript. It was written in the bold clear hand of the future Prime Minister, who apparently at that time could not afford to have his MSS. typed. In acknowledging it, Mr. Weisgal wrote to me: "We will send Mr. MacDonald 20 dollars or perhaps 25 dollars to make the figure round and more respectable."

II

Among the various internal problems with which the Zionist Executive were concerned was the anomalous position of the Zionist Federation in Hungary. Although this body had been in existence since the days of Herzl, it had never been legalised, and although its activities were tolerated they were restricted, and it was even liable to prosecution. Repeated efforts had been made by the Federation to secure official approval of its "statutes," as its constitution was called, and they had been reinforced by personal representations made before the First World War by the Zionist leader, David Wolffsohn. But all these endeavours had proved in vain, without any plausible explanation being offered by the Hungarian Government for their unwavering hostility.

After the ratification of the Palestine Mandate by the League of Nations, it occurred to me that there could no longer be any valid objection on the part of Hungary since she was herself a member of the League. I therefore drew up a reasoned memorandum for submission to the Hungarian Government, in which this point was stressed, and urged that the statutes of the Federation should be legalised, so that the Jews of Hungary could co-operate in the efforts for the establishment of the Jewish National Home as freely as those of all other states belonging to the League. The memorandum, together with a covering letter, was signed by Nahum Sokolow, President of the Executive; and immediately after the Congress of 1923, in Carlsbad, towards the end of August, I went to Budapest to present the document to the Government. On arriving there I first called at the British Legation, where I saw the Chargé d'Affaires, Mr. John Balfour,[1] whom I had known from our internment at Ruhleben. He was good enough to arrange an interview for me with the Acting Premier and to introduce me to him personally. The Acting Premier, after reading through the memorandum, said it would be best if I were to see the Minister of the Interior, M. Rakovski, and the Minister for Public Worship, Count von Klebelsberg. I therefore called upon these two Cabinet Ministers at the Praesidium of the Ministry the following day, discussed the question with them, and was assured that they would give it careful consideration.

In the course of conversation with the local Zionist leaders I was told that the main reason why the Hungarian authorities refused to legalise their body was because they were advised to do so by the heads of the Jewish community. The Orthodox section were anti-

[1] Now Sir John Balfour, formerly British Ambassador in Madrid.

Zionists because they looked upon Zionism as a violation of the traditional belief in the Messiah, and the Liberal or assimilated section were opposed because they boasted of their Magyar spirit and looked upon Zionism as nothing less than treason. I therefore decided to call upon the leaders of the two sections in order to argue the matter out with them, but found that they were away on holiday.

The only prominent Jew whom I was able to see at the time was the politician, Wilhelm Vazsonyi (1868 - 1926), who had been a member of Parliament and had been appointed by King Carl in 1917 as Minister of Justice. He was the first Jew in Hungary to hold that position, but resigned it before the Revolution of 1918. He was subsequently elected a member of the National Assembly, in which he figured as a leader of the "Legitimists," who agitated for the restoration of the Habsburgs to the throne. He was a swarthy, thick-set individual, a synthesis of Magyar and Jew, who was far more keenly interested in Hungarian politics than in Jewish affairs, and showed himself quite apathetic on the Zionist question. A couple of years later he launched a campaign against the Government in connection with a forged currency scandal, whereupon an attack was made upon his life by a political opponent, but with no fatal consequence.

III

From Budapest I went to Temesvar (or Timisoara as the Rumanians called it), to convey greetings from the Zionist Executive to the annual conference of the Transylvanian Zionist Federation and to deliver an address. I arrived late at night and was met at the station by the secretary, who told me that the president had kindly offered to act as my host as he thought that I might not be comfortable at an hotel. I found the president a genial, chubby physician in the fifties, who had lost his wife in the previous year. We went on talking for some time after supper until nearly two o'clock, when I said that I was tired after the long journey and would be glad if he would kindly show me to my room. He replied with a smile that he was unable to let me have a bedroom to myself, but I could share his own large double-bed. I was taken aback by this unusual invitation, but

A JEWISH PILGRIMAGE

as I could not expect him to find me a room at an hotel at that hour of the night, and he was to be my chairman at the public conference in the morning, I had no alternative but to conceal my embarrassment and face the ordeal. The bed was certainly wide, but as my companion was rather restless it was hours before I fell asleep. It was a form of hospitality that I had never enjoyed before and certainly did not enjoy on that occasion either.

On the following day, soon after the conference was over, I took the train to Bucharest. It was my first visit to the Rumanian capital, prompted by an invitation to address a meeting on the achievements of the Carlsbad Congress, and I welcomed it because I was anxious to make inquiries about the discrimination against Jews at the universities. Jew-baiting had long been a popular sport in Rumania and one of the commonest forms that it took was attacks upon Jewish students. Although Rumania was pledged by her Peace treaty to accord full civil rights to her Jewish subjects, the university authorities limited their admission to the seats of learning to a very small percentage. Many Jewish candidates were "ploughed" in the entrance examinations, although they were known to be much cleverer than many of the Christians who passed; and even those who were admitted had often literally to fight for the right to attend lectures, as their entrance to the building was barred by groups of anti-Semitic students resolved to beat them up. The authorities, who enforced a *numerus clausus* against the Jews, took no effective measures to prevent the violence, which was a logical consequence of their own policy, and hence the number of Jews at the Rumanian universities was relatively small. They had to be fortunate and tough as well as clever.

The evil effects of this academic hooliganism were vividly brought home to me when I visited the home of a leading Jewish doctor. I found him very distressed as his only son, who had been a student at the university, had recently committed suicide. The young man had been battered and bruised by his fellow-students so often that he was at last driven by despair to take his life. I heard of other Jewish students who regularly took a small knobbed stick in the leather portfolio containing their books, so as to use it to defend themselves. After discussing this scandal with some Jewish friends I decided to interview the Minister of Education, M. Angelescu, and obtained an introduction to him through the British Legation.

On being ushered into the Minister's room I was surprised to find a group of men standing around his desk, although he was engaged in conversation only with one. I was given to understand that the others were waiting their turn, and that there was no objection to their overhearing what was being discussed. But when I approached M. Angelescu and handed him my letter of introduction he waved his audience to the other side of the room so that we could talk with at least a semblance of privacy. He was quite affable in manner and assured me that he was pleased and honoured to meet a representative of the Anglo-Jewish community desirous of obtaining information. He emphatically denied that there was a *numerus clausus* in force at the universities and that Jewish students were liable to physical attacks, and as he stubbornly and smilingly maintained that pretence he cut the ground from beneath my feet. I had therefore to content myself with impressing upon him the concern that was felt by Jews in Western countries for the treatment of Jewish students in Rumania, and was bowed out of the Ministerial presence with exaggerated politeness.

IV

On returning to Budapest (early in September) I again called upon Mr. John Balfour at the British Legation, and he arranged a further appointment for me with Rakovski, the Minister of the Interior. But after waiting for the latter a couple of hours, during part of which I was given a seat in the gallery of the House of Parliament and watched the proceedings, I was asked to call again two days later; and when I did so I was received by a secretary, who told me that the Minister was still studying the position of the Zionist Federation and would reply to me through the Hungarian Legation in London.

I took advantage of this stay in Budapest also to inquire into the position of Jews at the universities, which I found to be even worse in one respect than in Rumania. For in Hungary, in gross violation of the Peace Treaty, there was actually a law imposing a *numerus*

A JEWISH PILGRIMAGE

clausus (to a percentage roughly corresponding to the Jewish ratio of the population), and its existence could therefore not be denied, whereas in Rumania the numerical limitation was applied without any pretence of legal sanction. But acts of violence at the universities had not yet taken place, although they broke out later.

I also went to see the famous Oriental library that had been left by the celebrated Semitic scholar, Professor Ignaz Goldziher. The library, which consisted of about 6,000 volumes, contained many rare works in Arabic and Hebrew, Turkish and Persian, on all branches of exotic lore, which Goldziher had collected in the course of forty years from all the regions of the Near and Middle East. Some of them had been presented to him by their learned authors and contained an inscription of homage and often of gratitude, for not a single Orientalist but considered it a duty and honour to send him a first copy. Many of the books were rare, and those that came from Moslem scholars were probably the only copies on the Continent. And Goldziher had enriched most of them with his own notes and glosses, written on the fly-leaves and the margin, or on slips of paper, which formed a mine of suggestions for those who would delve into them.

Soon after Goldziher's death in 1921 the question of the future of his library began to be talked about. Both his widow and only son, Professor Karl Goldziher, refused to listen to any suggestions for its disposal, as it enshrined for them affectionate memories, from which they did not wish to be parted. The Hungarian Government was anxious to have it presented to the State as a testimony of patriotism, as though the loyalty of the family would remain suspect without such a sacrifice; nor did the proposal that it should be acquired for the State by a group of wealthy Jews in Budapest meet with more favour. Next came a representative from the Japanese Government who wanted it for the Tokyo University, then an emissary from the Sorbonne, followed by some wealthy inquirers from America. But the importance of the collection had not escaped the notice of the Zionist Executive, who saw in it a desirable addition to the Hebrew University Library in Jerusalem, and they therefore asked me to make a preliminary inspection.

SOME SPECIAL MISSIONS

I was received by the little gentle, grey-haired widow with mixed feelings, for while she considered it an honour that her husband's collection should find its final resting-place in the Holy City she was loth to see the room in which it was stored stripped of its cherished treasures. The Goldzihers' home was in a dreary and dismal street, and consisted of a sombre flat that I reached after mounting a dim, circular flight of stone steps. The room containing the library was lined with books that covered the walls from floor to ceiling, while hundreds of works were stacked on shelves in an adjoining passage. In the centre of the room stood an oak table, at which the savant had written, or discussed obscure texts with other scholars, or lectured to students who came from distant lands; while the little space on the walls not covered by books was occupied by the photographs of learned friends who had produced them — Mommsen and Noeldeke, Wellhausen and Budde, Browne in Persian dress, and Snouck-Hurgronje, who had penetrated to Mecca.

I thanked the old lady for the privilege of inspecting the library and said that I hoped to come again to talk to her about it. " But not too soon," she said pleadingly.

V

After receiving my report the Zionist Executive invited Professor Aron Freimann, Director of the Hebrew collection at the Frankfort City Library, and an acknowledged authority on Hebraica, to pay a visit to the Goldziher Library for the purpose of valuing it. The result of his report was that they decided to offer £2,000 for it and sent me to Budapest again in January, 1924, to conclude the transaction. They informed the Foreign Office of my mission and requested that instructions might be given to the British Legation in Budapest to render me whatever help might be necessary.

I found Mrs. Goldziher and her son at first just as loth to part with the collection as they had been some months earlier, but the inadequate pension on which she lived, combined with the thought that the library must be disposed of sooner or later and that no more worthy home could be found for it than the Hebrew University in the Land of Israel, helped to overcome their weakening resistance.

But their consent to the sale was only the first of a series of hurdles that had to be surmounted.

It was equally essential that the Hungarian Government should allow the library to be exported. I therefore called at the British Legation, where I saw Mr. Balfour and the Minister, Mr. Thomas Hohler, and asked them to intervene to obtain the export permit, and within a couple of days I was informed that this would be granted, provided that other conditions were fulfilled. The next step was to get the assent of the Director of the Hungarian National Museum, who had a right of embargo upon any cultural treasures leaving the country. This obstacle was easily overcome with the co-operation of Professor Adolf Strauss, a septuagenarian savant, who had formerly been the teacher of the Director of the Museum, Dr. Pasteina. He took me to see the latter in his office, and Dr. Pasteina readily agreed on condition that he was furnished with five copies of the catalogue and that certain dues (based upon the estimated value of the library) were paid to the foreign currency control office and to a so-called " Horthy Fund," which was said to be devoted to "charitable objects." At my last interview with Dr. Pasteina he told me that the National Museum had not received any copies of a number of British learned reviews and scientific journals from the outbreak of the War in 1914 until 1920, and he asked me if I would do what I could through the medium of the Zionist Organisation, on my return to London, to procure the missing numbers for him gratis. I afterwards succeeded in this effort to a much greater extent than I had anticipated, thanks to the generous response of various learned societies and institutes.

While attending to the sequence of formalities necessary for the export of the Goldziher Library I had to have several interviews with the lawyer of the Goldziher family in connection with the purchase money. It was clearly inadvisable that this should be transmitted to a bank in Budapest, as, owing to the depreciation of the pengo that had already taken place, there was no certainty that its value might not fall further still. It was therefore arranged that the sum of £2,000 should be paid in to a bank in Zurich, and as Mrs. Goldziher did not intend to use more than the interest and she wanted to pay occasional visits to a relative in Vienna it was further arranged that the Zurich bank should remit a quarterly cheque to a bank in Vienna, which would pay it to her wherever she wished. At last, after all these official, fiscal, and financial formalities had been concluded, I arranged with a shipping agency for the transport of the books.

Twenty-two large wooden cases were needed, and after each was packed, nailed down, and bound with cord, a Hungarian official affixed a red seal and an official from the British Legation added a British seal. The cases were ranged in two rows, between which the frail widow slowly passed, touching each in turn as though to retain contact with her husband's possessions until the last possible moment. And as they were borne out of the dwelling she stood with clasped hands and followed them with tearful eyes.

In the course of the two weeks occupied by all these activities, I also resumed my efforts to secure the legalisation of the Zionist Federation. I had a further interview with the Minister of the Interior, but although he was acidly polite, he held out no hope that the Government would relent. I pointed out that Budapest had the honour of being the birthplace of the founder of the Zionist movement, but he remained unimpressed.[1] The day after this abortive interview was the Sabbath, so I went to the service at the beautiful and imposing synagogue in the Tabak Gasse, which Theodor Herzl had attended in his boyhood and where he was first called up to the Law as " a son of the commandment."[2]

---

[1] The Hungarian Zionist Federation was eventually legalised in 1927.
[2] The Jewish ceremony of confirmation.

Chapter Fifteen

JOURNEYINGS IN EUROPE
1924 — 1928

I

I HAD to do a great deal of travelling on the Continent in the interests of the Zionist movement between the two wars. Apart from the missions I have already described, and attending ten Congresses in seven different cities besides occasional meetings of the General Council in Berlin (before the advent of Hitler), I visited all the countries in Europe with the exception of Soviet Russia and Scandinavia. I would probably not have been admitted to the former, whose three million Jews had been cut off from all contact with the rest of Jewry and forbidden to engage in Zionism, which was branded as a " counter-revolutionary movement " and an " agency of British Imperialism "; while in Norway, Sweden and Denmark, owing to the scanty Jewish population, the Zionists, however zealous, were comparatively few in number. My most frequent journeys took place between the winter of 1924 and the spring of 1928. From the middle of December, 1924, to the middle of April, 1925, I visited thirty cities in sixteen countries in sixteen weeks; from the end of December, 1926, to the end of February, 1927, I made a tour of fifteen cities in ten countries in eight weeks; and from the middle of February to the beginning of April, 1928, I was in eleven cities in seven countries in six-and-a-half weeks. Much of this travelling had to be done during the night hours, otherwise it would have been impossible to cover such great distances in such short spaces of time; and in order to be sure of a reservation in a sleeping-car, I no sooner arrived in a place than I planned the time of my departure.

JOURNEYINGS IN EUROPE

The reasons for these tours were twofold — to maintain close personal relations with the principal Zionist workers on the Continent, and to obtain contributions to the Executive's Political Fund. The cities selected, therefore, were mainly centres of considerable Jewish population, such as Warsaw and Vilna, Vienna and Budapest, Prague and Belgrade, Bucharest and Salonika, as well as several smaller communities, some of which I visited on each tour and most of them twice.[1] I held conferences everywhere with the executive of the local Zionist Federation and addressed public meetings, in order to secure a satisfactory response to my appeals, and in many cases I received generous donations from ardent supporters, who gave me their active co-operation. But I did not confine myself solely to Zionist affairs. I made it my business to inquire closely into various aspects of each community and collected a considerable amount of information relating particularly to its religious, political, and economic conditions. Much of this information has been embodied in the revised edition of my *Jewish Life in Modern Times* and in my *Contemporary Jewry*, and many of my experiences, impressions, and adventures have been related in my *Travels in Jewry*.

II

These journeys were undertaken within the first decade after the First World War, when it was already possible to perceive that the glowing hopes aroused by the various Peace Treaties were doomed to disillusion, if not actually to extinction. Poland, Hungary, and Rumania, soon showed that they were not going to worry about the guaranteed rights of the minorities, so far as the Jews were concerned; Lithuania, after a brief flush of philo-Judaism, which even permitted Yiddish speeches in her infant Parliament, gradually began to follow the example of her neightours; and hardly any other State, with the exception of Czechoslovakia, manifested the slightest regard for its obligations to its Jewish subjects. The result of this policy of discrimination and repression was not merely discontent and in many

[1] Other cities that I visited in the course of my three tours, which are not mentioned in this Chapter, were Paris, Antwerp, Cologne, Berlin, Kovno (Kaunas), Cracow, Bialystok, Czenstochau, Lwow, Mährisch-Ostrau, Novisad (Yugoslavia), Strasbourg, Basle, Zurich, Milan, Trieste, Constantinople and Smyrna.

cases material distress but also an intensification of Jewish consciousness, which found expression in the organised fostering of Jewish culture and a widespread yearning to settle in Palestine.

In the greater part of Eastern Europe, whose Jewry had for centuries formed a citadel of religious tradition and a model of piety, Zionism was a much more vital and active force than in any other part of the world — except the land in which it was being realised. It penetrated deeply into all manifestations and ramifications of Jewish life. In Poland, Lithuania, and Latvia, and to a less extent in Rumania (though almost to an equal degree in Bessarabia, then part of Rumania) every Jew belonged to some party or other: he was either a Zionist, an Agudist[1], a Folkist[2], a Bundist[3], or an assimilationist. There was a ceaseless struggle between all these parties, which often embraced conflicting groups (the Zionists themselves being split at least into four[4],) each striving for the supremacy of its own principles and for a decisive and dominating influence in Jewish affairs.

The activity of the Zionist was not confined, as in Western Europe or America, merely to membership of a society, in which he heard speeches or lectures, and to the support of Zionist funds. It took the form of a constant striving for the recognition of the Jewish nationality and all its implications, not only for the establishment of the Jewish National Home but also for the acknowldgement of the rights of the Jews as a national minority in the lands of which they were citizens. The Zionists not only took up a determined stand within the Jewish community for the purpose of ensuring the maintenance of schools on a Jewish national basis, with Hebrew as the medium of instruction, and also the appointment of Rabbis who were Zionists, but carried the fight into the general community and sought election to municipal councils and to Parliament on a purely Zionist platform. Their efforts were crowned with success both within the Jewish community and without. There were Zionist members of Parliament

[1] Member of the " Agudas Israel " (League of Israel), an ultra-orthodox organisation formerly opposed to Zionism.

[2] Adherent of the theory that Jewish national autonomy should be secured in Europe.

[3] Member of the Jewish Socialist organisation fundamentally opposed to Zionism.

[4] General Zionists, Labour (Socialist), Mizrachi (orthodox), and Revisionists (advocates of a Jewish State).

in Poland, Lithuania, Latvia, Czechoslovakia, and Rumania, and there were also Zionist senators in Poland and Rumania.

In establishing and supporting schools with Hebrew as the medium of instruction, the Zionists were opposed by *Bundists*, *Folkists*, and Socialists, who maintained that Yiddish was the only legitimate language of the Jewish people. But throughout Eastern Europe (and particularly in Poland and Lithuania) I found that the Hebrew schools far outnumbered those conducted in Yiddish. Apart from these two languages, however, the Jews had, of course, to familiarise themselves with the speech of the country, and in some cases this was by no means easy. In Lithuania the vernacular in Tsarist times had been spoken only by the Christian population in the villages, while all the rest of the population knew only Russian; but after it became an independent republic the Jews had to learn Lithuanian, for which they had no liking, as most of them were bent upon going to Palestine. Similarly in Latvia they were expected to learn Lettish, and in Bukowina and Transylvania, which had been annexed by Rumania, they had to change over from German or Hungarian to Rumanian. Despite this tangle of tongues, however, the utmost stress was laid upon a Jewish national education, the natural result of which was that the younger generation were conscious and intelligent Zionists before they left school, and Youth organisations flourished. These organisations belonged to different parties, and many of them, known as *Halutz* (Pioneer) unions, were devoted to training the young Jew intellectually, morally, and technically for settlement in Palestine. For the Jews of Eastern Europe supplied the majority of the picked workers who went out to build up the Jewish homeland.

In Central Europe and the Balkans also Zionism was a potent force (except in Hungary, where it encountered the vigorous opposition of the leaders of the community), but nowhere in these regions did it play so dominant a part in Jewish life as in Poland. There were Hebrew schools in Bulgaria and in certain provinces of Rumania and Czechoslovakia, but none in Yugoslavia and Greece. On the other hand, religious conformity in Central Europe and the Balkans was undoubtedly much weaker than in Poland and Lithuania. In Hungary Jews had been baptised by the thousand in the hope of escaping oppression and discrimination.[1] In Bulgaria and Rumania there was widespread neglect of the Sabbath, and the synagogues in these countries as well as in Athens usually presented a deserted appearance except on the most solemn days of the Jewish calendar — New Year and the Day of Atonement.

Such then, in brief, were the main characteristics of the communities with which I became increasingly familiar within the first decade after the First World War. Having already described in some detail my experiences in most of them, I shall confine myself here to giving some account only of those about which I have not previously written, besides relating some events in the former not previously recorded.

III

In the early 'twenties, owing to the rupture of diplomatic relations between Lithuania and Poland (due to the latter's seizure of Vilna) and the complete cessation of intercourse and communication between the two countries,[2] it was necessary, in order to travel from Warsaw to Kovno (at the beginning of 1925) to make a roundabout journey through Danzig, Koenigsberg, and Eydtkühnen — a loss of several days. In the Free City of Danzig I was pleasantly impressed by its quaint and picturesque character, by the patrician houses of the Hanseatic days with lofty ornamental gables and balconied windows, and by curious large stone balls on either side of the steps leading up to many an old house.

I arrived in Riga on January 8th, 1925, early in the morning and was met by three leading Zionists in fur coats and fur hats, who accompanied me to the Hotel de Rome, where I found letters from my wife awaiting me. This ancient Hanseatic city, containing many buildings in Gothic style, had a Jewish community of 30,000, pulsating with a complex of interests and activities, and there and in the city of Libau I spent a busy and nerve-racking week with meetings, conferences, speeches, and social visits. I found my fellow-Zionists quick-tempered and good-humoured, lavish in their hospitality and

[1] From 1919 to 1924 over 11,200 Jews in Hungary were baptised.
[2] I have written at length about these countries in *Travels in Jewry*.

oblivious of punctuality. I was invited by one of them to his house for the Sabbath evening and asked to be there at nine. Knowing the local habits I arrived at 9.15, hungry, but was kept waiting until 10 before the laggard company of thirteen sat down at a long table covered with appetising *delicatessen*. There was much drinking of vodka, one member of the company challenging the rest to follow his example in swallowing a glass at one gulp. After an interval we were served with cutlets, followed by pudding. Then the secretary began singing *Zemiroth* (table hymns) in an emotional strain, waving his hand as he ejaculated an occasional " *Ai-yai, ai-yai* ! " This was the prelude to the singing of a popular Yiddish folksong *Avremmele Melammed hot zwelf Techter* (" Avremmele the Hebrew teacher has twelve daughters "), about a Ghetto character notorious for his helplessness and chronic misfortune and unable to provide so many dowries; it had a catchy refrain in which all joined lustily.

One of the liveliest men at the table was Dr. Julius Brutzkus, a native of Courland, who had been arrested in Moscow in 1920 for attending a Zionist Conference and kept in prison for several months. Another high-spirited guest was Hellman, a former student at the Rabbinical seminary at Slobodka (near Kovno), who had turned Socialist. He gave a realistic rendering of a *Musar* (moralising) discourse in the traditional style, as delivered by the Rabbi in the *Yeshivah*[1] in the twilight, dwelling upon the forlorn plight of Israel among the nations. He compared Israel to fish because there was no society for the prevention of cruelty to fish, whereas there were societies for the prevention of cruelty to animals. And in support of this analogy he adduced the Biblical saying: " *And Israel shall multiply like fish in the sea*," which, he argued, was intended to mean that they were to be without protection. We sat at the table for over a couple of hours listening to humorous parodies of sacred themes and joining in sentimental Yiddish folksongs, after which Hellman and the secretary danced a Chassidic[2] dance while the rest clapped hands in unison.

[1] Talmudic seminary.
[2] The Chassidim are a sect founded in the 18th century, and originally prevalent in Russia, Poland, and Hungary, who believe that intimate communion with God can be attained only by ecstasy in prayer.

A JEWISH PILGRIMAGE

The following evening Dr. Brutzkus and I addressed a crowded public meeting in the Schwarz-Häupter Saal, a large dignified hall, whose walls were adorned with the oil portraits of Emperors and Barons and with emblems of the Teutonic Knights. There was an enthusiastic audience of over a thousand, and hundreds had to be sent away — sufficient evidence of the longing to quit Latvia for Palestine. After the meeting the entire committee and many friends betook themselves to a private room in a popular restaurant, where the consumption of refreshments was punctuated by *schnapps* drinking competitions and two members indulged in a Chassidic step-dance. We were a merry company and did not break up until two in the morning. But the serious purpose of my mission was by no means shirked, and conviviality served to stimulate generosity. My help was also invoked by the editor of a Jewish weekly in Russian, with only a small circulation, who complained that the majority of the Zionists gave their support to a Yiddish paper.

From Riga I took the night train to Libau, a journey of nine hours. It had once been a great transit centre for the exodus of Jews from Russia, but the harbour had become idle owing to a recent American law severely restricting immigration. My cicerone was Dr. Mordecai Nurock, a member of the Latvian Parliament,[1] who told me that the Jewish population was only about 1,200, but there was no harmony in the community: both Agudists and Bundists assailed the Zionists. There was a packed meeting in the evening, and many people had to be turned away by the police. It was eleven o'clock when we reached the house of Rabbi Nurock (a brother of Dr. Nurock) for refreshment, but midnight struck before tea and potato pancakes were forthcoming, and I did not get to bed until two.

The following morning (or rather, later that morning) Dr. Brutzkus took me to the shop of a Jewish dealer who sold amber ornaments, and told me of the long connection of Jews with this trade. Jews at Polanga (on the coast of Lithuania) had been engaged for 400 years in the quarrying of amber and the manufacture of amber articles, and the occupation had descended from father to son. Some Jews had moved to Koenigsberg and Memel, where they continued in the

---

[1] Now a member of the Knesset in Israel.

trade. (The German for "amber" was "Bernstein," and hence the adoption of this name by some Jews, with its alternatives: Bronstein and Braunstein). A Jewish manufacturer of amber wares, who employed twenty people, was anxious to settle in Palestine and transfer his entire business.

I returned to Riga by night train. Later in the day I had a visit at my hotel from a young Zionist who had arrived from Russia only two days before and told me of the persecution of the movement by the Bolshevik régime. He had a big black mop and delicate features and looked half-starved. He had brought information written on thin strips of paper enclosed in cigarettes, and described his last evening in Moscow, where he had lain hidden in a cellar with comrades who wept at his leaving. As a Lithuanian he had been allowed to quit Russia, although on a previous occasion he was sent back from the frontier. Another young Zionist from Russia who joined us later told me that he had come over illegally with some others. For the last 70 versts they had travelled on foot, mostly at night, conducted from village to village by local peasants, whom they paid. They had tramped for three days and had to wade knee-deep through ditches. On the frontier they had been arrested by the Lettish gendarmerie and then brought under escort to Riga gaol, from which they had been released through the intervention of a Jewish M.P. They had been provided with Nansen passports, but some of them had already sent theirs back to their comrades in Russia. Even after being in Riga a couple of days they still had a fear that they were being followed and when walking in the street repeatedly turned round.

IV

I left Riga shortly before midnight for Estonia. My experiences in that little republic are described in the following extracts from my Diary:—

Friday, January 16th, 1925. — *Arrived Dorpat 6.20 a.m. Welcomed by old Jacobson, white-bearded, astrakhan hat, and students in University caps. Coffee and rolls. Drove to Hotel Petersbourg. Midday, Jacobson and I began paying visits. Dinner in widow's flat. Dorpat old Jewish community, 1,000 souls, mostly in trade. Old* synagogue. About 150 Jewish students, some from Reval and Riga, mostly studying economics and commercial subjects. Few going in for medicine as Estonians preferred Christian doctors. Cases of Jewish medical and legal graduates gone into business owing to poor prospects in professions.

Saturday, January 17th. — At midday Jacobson took me to University, ancient building; visited interior, large hall, white wooden gallery. Some professors lectured in Russian, others in German. Dinner in widow's flat. Students come for meals; one told me that after completing his studies he looked forward to going to Palestine — a girl student ditto. After Sabbath Jacobson and I resumed visits. Later at Jewish Club, had frugal supper, addressed meeting, interval for donations, then concluded address. At 1 a.m. entered room where Zionist students (Hasmonea Society) stood respectfully round long table on which was arrayed long row of bottles of beer. Young chairman welcomed me, all drank my health in beer, and I replied. Two songs in Hebrew sung with gusto, resounding refrain. All elated; my visit historic event. Asked to sign my name in book, which was then locked away. Drove to hotel, packed, retired 2 a.m. Awakened 5 a.m., drove to station, coffee and rolls. Old Jacobson came to see me off, also students who had stayed at Club all night, slept on billiard tables. Left 6.35 a.m.

Sunday, January 18th. — *Arrived Reval 10.30 a.m. Met by delegation, drove to Hotel Goldener Loewe, then to offices of Zionist Organisation. Gave address, discussion, donation list.*

Monday, January 19th. — *Visited Parliament House. Left for Danzig en route for Vilna and Warsaw.*

V

I was always charmed by Prague because of its blend of the mediaeval with the modern, its wealth of historic memories, its handsome and venerable buildings, its quaint narrow straggling by-ways, and its warm-hearted people. Its Jewish community was not only the oldest in Bohemia, dating back to the beginning of the tenth century, but also one of the oldest and most interesting in Europe. For a time it was the capital of European Jewry in Talmudic scholarship and spiritual leadership, and its annals were rich in stories of heroism and persecution. It was here that the Cabbalist, the " *Hohe* " Rabbi Loew, of whom there is a tall grim statue, held powerful sway and, as tradition will have it, created a *Golem*.[1] The most striking features of the old Ghetto were the *Rathaus* (Town Hall), surmounted by a clock with Hebrew letters that marked the hours, the Museum full of rare ritual objects and artistic treasures, and the thirteenth century synagogue, the *Altneuschul*, in Gothic style, which one entered by descending a few steps. In the interior of this mediaeval shrine (when I was last there before the last war) there still hung above the cantor's dais in the centre the gold-embroidered flag presented to the Jews of Prague by the Emperor Ferdinand for bravely defending the Karl Bridge against the Swedes in the Thirty Years' War.

The religious fervour of the past had largely evaporated, but Prague was still a citadel of cultural activity and a hub of literary and artistic creativity. It was here that Martin Buber first delivered his discourses " On Judaism," and that such writers as Franz Werfel, Franz Kafka, Max Brod, and others gave birth to their novels and plays. And here too Zionism flourished, so that my visits were not only intellectually rewarding but also materially fruitful.

VI

Budapest lay, so to speak, on the crossroads of my journeyings on the Continent, so that I was there several times, and on each occasion I renewed my efforts to secure the legalisation of the Zionist Federation. I was always received by members of the Hungarian Government courteously but made no apparent progress. On February 16th, 1925, I attended a conference of leaders of the Jewish community convened in his room by Count von Klebelsberg, the Minister for Public Worship, for the purpose of discussing the question. Among those present were Joseph Veszi, the influential editor of the *Pester Lloyd* and a former Member of Parliament, who represented the assimilationist section, and Dr. Adolf Frankl, who was the head of the orthodox congregation. Veszi was spruce, with a grey moustache; Frankl was white-bearded, with a glistening silk-hat in front of him, and every time that he addressed Klebelsberg, who presided, he rose slightly, bowed, and said " *Excellenz*." After I had seen this performance two

[1] A Frankenstein monster.

or three times, I had some difficulty in suppressing a smile; but I was brought back to a serious mood when I realised that the united opposition by which I was faced was bound to triumph. The conference was abortive.

When I was in Budapest again six weeks later I had an interview with the Prime Minister, Count Bethlen, who stated that the Government had no objection to the activities of the Zionist Federation, but that they could not be legalised as long as the official heads of the Jewish community were opposed. After my return to London I received a letter from him, in which he wrote that he had had a conversation with the leaders of the community on the subject, and as they were " against the approbation of the organic statutes of the Zionist Federation " he thought it his duty to ask me " not to insist any more on this question." But the local Zionist leaders persisted in their efforts until the Government at last yielded in September 1927; and when I was in Budapest again in March, 1928, I called on the Foreign Minister, Louis Walko, and conveyed the thanks of the Zionist Executive to his Government for its act of legalisation.

VII

In Yugoslavia there was a Jewish population of 80,000, of which Hitler afterwards exterminated three-fourths. It was dispersed in about a hundred communities, of which the two largest were those in Belgrade and Zagreb. These two cities presented a marked contrast, not only because Belgrade was Serbian and Zagreb Croatian, but also because the former, although the capital, looked uncouth and undeveloped. The most striking building in the principal street of Belgrade was called the " Akademie," but the only part of it that deserved this title was an upper floor, where lectures were given, while the ground floor consisted of a popular café.

The Jews enjoyed not only all liberties and the privilege of imposing a tax for their communal purposes (similar to the privilege then customary in several other Jewish communities in Central Europe), but also received a grant from the Government for their ecclesiastical officials and their Rabbinical Seminary. The Chief Rabbi, Dr. Alkalay, who had visited England and the United States during the

First World War in the interest of Serbian propaganda, was held in the highest esteem. He told me that he had been invited to take part in the marriage ceremony of the King and Queen and had been presented by them with autographed photographs.

Zagreb, which I reached first from Budapest, was a more modern city, for it had long been under Austrian rule and still retained evidences of Austrian culture. It was spaciously laid out, with fine boulevards, while in the morning the market swarmed with peasants in picturesque costumes, wearing white stockings with red ribbons tied in a bow, and all carrying on their heads baskets with vegetables. The Jews spoke Croatian and had a Zionist paper in that language, but they also understood German, in which I addressed them. The Zionist society in Zagreb was larger and more active than any of the other seventy societies that were dotted all over the country, and the Federation to which they were affiliated was promoting the establishment with its own funds of a settlement in Palestine.

In Belgrade there were two Sephardi synagogues, both of which I attended on Sabbath morning. The more recent one was large and ornate, but few worshippers were present when I was there after seven, and decorum was absent. At the smaller and older one, situated in the Jewish quarter, there was a goodly congregation at eight, including many women in the gallery. This better attendance may have been due to the fact that two boys, twins, were celebrating their *Bar-Mitzvah*[1] that morning. They were dressed exactly alike, with a green sprig in their button-hole, and as they walked in the procession headed by the *Haham*[2] and the cantor, carrying in their hands a small scroll of the Law, women in the gallery dropped bonbons in paper on to the floor, making a resounding clatter, and all the little boys rushed to pick them up. Each of the twins cantillated a portion of the Law, and during the final procession there was again a shower of sweets, which the youngsters snapped up. The twins then went to the *Haham* for his blessing and received kisses from their relatives and friends.

The Jews in Belgrade also had two clubs, both well conducted.

---

[1] Confirmation at the age of thirteen.
[2] Sephardi Rabbi.

The larger was for merchants, lawyers, and members of other professions, and the smaller for tradespeople, clerks, and other employees. It was at the former, which had all the usual amenities of a club, that I delivered an address and began my local campaign.

On the night before I was to leave Belgrade for Salonika I suddenly learned, in the course of conversation with the President of the Zionist Federation, that, owing to restrictions on the export of currency, I would not be permitted to take away the money that I had collected. He advised me to call upon the British Minister, late though it was, and ask him if he would be good enough to transmit the money for me to the British Consulate in Salonika. The Minister (Sir Alban Young) was surprised at my visit, but, on my explaining the situation, he kindly agreed to my request, and when I reached Salonika[1] the next day the money was returned to me at the Consulate.

VII

I found Athens a city of regal dignity, spaciously planned, the gleaming white buildings of the University and the National Museum looking radiant under the deep-blue sky, and all dominated by the Acropolis and its ruined temples on the periphery. In front of the palaces of the President of the Republic (in March, 1925) and of the Minister-President there were picturesque soldiers — evzones — in round red caps, short blue tunics with silver buttons, white flannel tights with black garters, and big poms-poms on the toes of their shoes. The police, under British command, were smartly dressed in dark-green uniforms, peaked hats, and leggings. A former palace of the King was occupied by refugees from Asia Minor, many of whom were also housed in quarters beneath the seats of the vast marble Stadium.

There was a Jewish community of about 2,000, which had been in existence for some fifty years, though some of its members were descended from Jews who had settled there in the early part of the nineteenth century. Later infiltrations speaking Espagnol (Judaeo-Spanish) had come from Salonika, Smyrna, and Adrianople, and

[1] An account of my visit to Salonika is given in *Travels in Jewry*.

JOURNEYINGS IN EUROPE

there were also some from Canea in Crete (which accounted for certain families named Canetti), Janina, and Volos. There were two synagogues, one for the rich and the other for the poor, and as strife had broken out between them the venerable Chief Rabbi of Jerusalem, Jacob Meir, came to restore peace and appointed a neutral person as president of the community. The democratic synagogue was on the first floor of a building, of which the ground floor was occupied by a school attended by about a hundred children who were taught Greek, Hebrew and French. It was there that I addressed a meeting (in French). I was informed that a movement had started in favour of settling in Palestine, and a wealthy stockbroker told me that he was planning to transfer his fortune there.

There was no Jewish question in Athens — at least then. Jews were assimilated more or less like their brethren in Western Europe. They regarded Greece as an excellent country from both the physical and the economic point of view, and they were anxious that their fellow-Jews in Salonika (who had lived for centuries under Turkish rule and had a different way of life) should learn Greek and adapt themselves to the requirements of the country. The Government was friendly, and although a local paper was trying to foment Anti-Semitism by printing libellous attacks upon Jews the local population for the most part ignored it. A good impression had been created by the invitation sent to the Rector of the Athens University to attend the inauguration of the Hebrew University in Jerusalem by Lord Balfour.

While I was in Athens in the spring of 1925 Sir Alfred Mond (later the first Lord Melchett) happened to be staying there with his wife and daughter on their return from Palestine, and I had a talk with him on his impressions of the country. I revisited Athens early in 1927, but there was no appreciable change in the Jewish situation.[1]

IX

In Bulgaria I was struck by the paradoxical circumstance that

[1] The total number of Jews in Greece is now about 6,000, half of whom live in Athens. Before the last war Salonika had 56,000 Jews, but now, in consequence of the Nazi deportations and extermination, it has only a tiny community of 1,200.

A JEWISH PILGRIMAGE

although the Jews seemed to be physiognomically more assimilated than those in many other countries, their Zionism was of a more robust and almost militant character. Their assimilation was due to the fact that they had been living in the country even longer than the Bulgars themselves, for they had a continuous history since the fourth century. In the fourteenth century there was a beautiful Jewess of Tirnova named Sarah, who (after being converted to Christianity and renamed Theodora) became the third wife of Czar Ivan Alexander, and she had such a reputation for exceptional intelligence and energy in the political sphere that her name has survived in Bulgarian folk-songs. Despite this romantic memory, however, the Jews were subject to recurring persecution, with the result that their national consciousness was kept keenly alive, and they fostered the Zionist idea even before the days of Herzl. I found that not only was Hebrew taught as a living language in all Jewish schools, but it was also used as a medium of instruction in many subjects. Moreover, the right of taxation, which the Jewish communities exercised for religious and cultural purposes, was also used for levying an annual tax for the *Keren Hayesod* (Palestine Foundation Fund).

I went to Plovdiv (formerly Philippopolis) first, because it was there that the Executive of the Zionist Federation had their office. It seemed to me a frowsy, even ugly city; in some streets there were half-finished houses cheek-by-jowl with others of two or three stories; and the air was made hideous by the savage cawing of a covey of black rooks flying rather low. There were a couple of synagogues, one of which had a *Beth Hamidrash* (House of Study) adjacent, and on entering the latter I found a group of old men gossiping and others poring over some Hebrew tomes. A young man brought in a tray with little cups of Turkish coffee, of which I was offered one, and as I sipped the beverage I chatted with some of the venerable company.

In Sofia I heard a great deal about the anti-Jewish campaign that was waged from 1924 to 1926 after the fall of the Peasant Government. This was followed by the reactionary régime of Tzankoff, under whose protection a military officers' organisation conducted a political and economic boycott, accompanied by physical assaults. They declared the Jews to be " enemies of the Fatherland," demanded they should go to Palestine, and appealed to Bulgarians to boycott Jewish shops. In the main promenade, from the Palace to the Parliament building, there was a military club which displayed on its walls the notice: "Jews and dogs not allowed to walk in this street." At the same time a Macedonian Revolutionary Committee extorted large sums from individual Jews and communities. The result was that hundreds of Jews were leaving for Palestine, taking all their capital with them. One of them said to me: " We Jews are heavily taxed and exposed to extortion, so we all want to go to Palestine. Our youth are learning Hebrew, training as farmers, and anxious to get away. Some day there will be another war here. Why should we have to fight one another for the *Goyim* (Gentiles) —for the Bulgars, the Serbs, and the rest, especially as none of these wars is decisive ? "[1]

I had an interview with M. Minkoff, the Secretary-General of the Ministry of Foreign Affairs (on March 14th, 1925), for the purpose of obtaining permission for the transmission of Zionist funds (as all export of money was prohibited). He complained to me that the Jews made too much noise about the Macedonians' " action ": he said that they should have explained that the " action " was due to the helplessness of the Government, which had been reduced to a small army; that non-Jews too had been victimised; and that the Jews did not contribute to the funds for the relief of Bulgarian refugees. But my Zionist friends denied that Bulgarians had also been robbed by the Macedonians or that Jews had not given money to help the refugees.

The pride of Sofia Jewry was its large and beautiful synagogue. It was one of the finest in Europe and certainly more handsome than any in England. It was Byzantine in style and colouring and had taken four years to build (from 1905 to 1909), and in the vestibule there was a tablet recording the fact that King Ferdinand was present at the opening. From the lofty, gilded, dome-shaped ceiling hung

[1] Since the establishment of Israel about 40,000 Jews from Bulgaria have gone there, leaving only a remnant of about 7,000.

A JEWISH PILGRIMAGE

a huge candelabrum, and there was a similar dome-like adornment over the Ark of the Law, in front of which stood an array of artistically wrought *Menorahs* (seven-branched candelabra). Owing to the size of the edifice it was impossible to worship in it in the Balkan winter, when a smaller adjoining building was quite adequate, but even on a Sabbath morning the service was over by half-past nine, and it was not unusual for many of the worshippers then to hurry off to their business. The Sabbath was largely neglected. I was told that about ninety per cent of all the shops of the Jews throughout Bulgaria were open on that day, a condition due partly to the general economic competition and partly to the numerous Christian feast-days and saints' days, of which there were some every month, when Jewish business-places had also to be closed.

Throughout my wanderings in Europe, nowhere was I greeted by so large a deputation as at the station of Rustchuk. There were about two hundred people, men and women, old and young. Headed by their Zionist leaders walking on either side of me they marched through the street to the *Beth Ha-am* (People's House), where a welcome was delivered, followed by the distribution of cloying sweets, with glasses of water. The principal function was an evening meeting in the hall of the "Bnei Brith" (a fraternal association), where I spoke in French. Here I heard the same story that I had been told in Plovdiv and Sofia of Jews planning to settle in Palestine. I was in Rustchuk again early in 1927, when there was an exceptional winter of snow and frost. The ice-covered pavements were so glassy that I had to get a pair of goloshes, and even then I had to be supported by a couple of friends more accustomed to the trials of the local climate, to prevent me from falling as I made my way to the wind-swept pier, from where a cockleshell of a puffing steamboat took me across a swirling river to Giurgiu in Rumania.

X.

My first visit to Rumania in 1923 prepared me for the conditions that I found when I was there again in 1925, 1927, and 1928. Each successive visit deepened my impression of the harassing plight of the Jewish population. Although assured of all rights by the

Minorities' Treaty, they suffered countless wrongs. Official chicanery, economic discrimination, exclusion from Universities, violent assaults in streets and trains — they were subject to a whole gamut of persecution, from pinpricks to pogroms. No matter what political party was in power, the Government was always anti-Semitic, however much it might protest that the Jews " enjoyed all rights and liberties." When I went to call upon Dr. William Filderman in Bucharest,[1] the head of the Union of Rumanian Jews, I found a soldier in front of his house, to ward off any attack. He gave me a long recital of Jewish woes and of the efforts to get them suppressed, but was opposed to any appeal being made to the League of Nations, as that would bring upon their heads the charge of treason without any prospect of betterment.

The worst and most frequent of evils were the violent assaults by Christian students upon their Jewish fellow-students, connived at or condoned by the Government, which actually supplied the Christian unions with funds and granted them free railway passes for conferences that were usually the prelude to an orgy of riot and outrage. I still saw abundant evidence of this hooliganism and vandalism in Cluj and Oradea Mare (in March, 1928), where synagogues had been devastated and desecrated, scrolls of the Torah rent in shreds, and the windows of scores of Jewish shops shattered, while the military and police kept aloof for hours. I also went to Jassy, whose University had the questionable honour of having on its staff Professor Cuza, a proved plagiarist, who had poisoned with anti-Semitic venom the minds of successive generations of students, one of whom, Codreanu, afterwards founded the terrorist organisation of the " Iron Guard."

I next went to Chisinau, better known by its Russian name, Kishinev, which had secured a tragic place in Jewish history as the scene of barbarous pogroms in 1903 and 1905. I found the city buried under snow, which usually covers it three months in the year, and had the novel experience of being driven in a sledge by a Yiddish-speaking jarvey. I was agreeably surprised by the spaciousness of the city and

[1] Detailed accounts of my visits to Bucharest, Cluj, Oradea Mare and Timisoara (Temesvar), as well as to Czernowitz and Sadagora, are given in *Travels in Jewry*.

its fine broad thoroughfares. The Jews preferred to live under the Rumanian régime rather than under the Soviet Government, even though they were not altogether free from the risk of attacks, as was shown shortly before my arrival. A horde of anti-Semitic students had come from Jassy for the purpose of giving a demonstration of their culture in the Jewish quarter, but the Jews advanced boldly to meet them; and the hooligans would have been in a sorry plight if the gendarmes and the police had not hurried to protect them. The memory of the pogroms was still fresh in the minds of the Jewish community. I was driven to the cemetery to see the graves of the victims, who are laid to rest within a special enclosure, at the entrance to which is a monumental memorial tablet in Hebrew giving the story of the massacres in poignant words.

Finally, I was in Timisoara again. After my first experience in that city I took care not to accept hospitality in a private house except for a meal, but stayed at an hotel. It was a modest establishment but had a scholarly night-porter, for when I returned at a late hour I found him poring in a dimly-lit office over a large Hebrew volume. I asked him what he was studying, to which he replied in a matter-of-fact tone: " The Talmud." He had once attended a Rabbinical seminary and still retained a love for the studies of his youth. Timisoara also retains other memories for me. A wealthy Jewish merchant approached me confidentially and asked me if I could secure him an appointment as Honorary Consul or Vice-Consul for the United States. Another man, who was introduced to me by some Zionist friends at a café, after hearing of my travels across the length and breadth of Europe, said that he would like to have my British passport and asked me how much I wanted for it. His blunt inquiry revealed a feeling of envy of one who was a citizen of a land of liberty and justice.

Chapter Sixteen

CONGRESSES AND CRISES
1925 — 1931

I

A CONGRESS was not only a landmark in Zionist history but the most important event in the current affairs of world Jewry. Between the two wars it assembled every two years and was attended not only by a few hundred delegates, but also by hundreds of visitors and journalists, from all parts of the globe, the total attendance amounting sometimes to a couple of thousand and more. It was held primarily to afford the leaders and the Executive an opportunity of delivering reports on their labours, to furnish the delegates with the opportunity of discussing those reports, and to frame decisions and hammer out policies for the immediate future. In the course of its evolution, the Congress had developed its own machinery and forms of parliamentary procedure, designed to cope with the multiplicity of questions that had to be disposed of within about a fortnight. The difficulty of compressing its deliberations within so short a space of time, and of satisfying delegates, some of whom travelled thousands of miles to make a speech, was such as to tax the ingenuity of anybody but the experienced *Präsidium* that had the conduct of the proceedings. Much of the business was transacted in a number of committees, which dealt with politics, Palestine immigration, agricultural settlement, trade and industry, finance, health, education, and other questions. These committees, which were composed of delegates of the various parties in proportions corresponding to the composition of the entire Congress, formulated the resolutions that were submitted to plenary sessions of the Congress.

There was also a Standing Committee (called *Permanenz Ausschuss*), formed on the same basis as the others, whose function was to act as the steering organ in the often difficult and occasionally critical course of the debates, and above all to prepare a list of nominations for the new Executive and the General Council that would be assured adoption. So voluminous and multifarious was the business that had to be completed within the limited time available that night sessions were an invariable feature. The debates were reported in the *Kongress Zeitung* that appeared daily, and some months later a complete stenographic record was published.

The Congress was the occasion for numerous other meetings and conferences of all kinds. The members of the London and Jerusalem Executives (with their American colleagues) met frequently; the General Council assembled both before and after the Congress; and as soon as this was over there was (from 1929) a gathering of the Council of the Jewish Agency, followed by one of its Administrative Committee. The delegations from different countries held private meetings to formulate their attitude on particular questions, and the parties likewise conferred to decide on points of policy. Moreover, all the important institutions and organisations of the movement, such as the Jewish National Fund, the Jewish Colonial Trust, and the Board of Governors of the Hebrew University also held meetings; and various associations, like those of Hebrew-speaking societies, Hebrew authors, Jewish doctors, gymnastic societies, students, and other bodies, also took advantage of the opportunity.

The plenary session of a Congress could always be relied upon to provide ample material for observation and reflection. One could study the differences in the demeanour and expression of the hundreds of delegates, and in their speech, temperament, and mentality. One could note how the varied parties reacted to the speeches from the tribune or to the interruptions that might punctuate the speeches. One could marvel how the chairman could control this mixed assembly or secure silence after one section of it had been roused to a storm of indignation by another. One could wonder how it was possible for the delegates to grasp the subtle shades of distinction between the competing amendments to an involved multi-paragraphed resolution amid all the hubbub that invariably accompanied the voting on the proposals of the various sub-committees. And one could admire the endurance and the enthusiasm of both delegates and visitors when a crisis arose and a night sitting was necessary, and they remained bravely in their places, with unwavering wakefulness and unflagging attention, until the break of day.

Not only were there addresses to listen to and arguments to follow, but there was also a great deal of literature to consume. There were the voluminous reports of the Executive, the supplementary reports of institutions, the leaflets and manifestoes circulated by different bodies and associations, the daily *Kongress Zeitung*, memoranda of the rival parties on crucial issues, stencilled resolutions of the sub-committees, complimentary copies of all sorts of Jewish papers in all sorts of languages, and moving appeals of all kinds of distressed institutions in Central and Eastern Europe. At the end of each session the accumulation of papers left behind by many a harassed delegate was cleared away, but by the time the next session began there was a fresh crop of printed matter, which was scanned, or fingered, or tossed about, until a few hours later it became mere litter. And as though to counterbalance these ephemeral writings there was always, in some adjoining hall, an attractive emporium of works of modern Jewish literature, as well as of pictures by Jewish artists, which afforded a vivid reflection of the revival and expansion of Jewish national culture.

In short, all the multifarious phases and facets of the movement — political and economic, organisational and financial, social and cultural — were embraced within the ample orbit of the Congress. It was a vast clearing-house for the exchange of thoughts and ideas on Jewish problems, for the testing of plans and the examining of schemes; it enabled Jews from the remotest lands of the dispersion to get to know and understand one another, and to learn of the quality of their brethren from the Land of Israel; it deepened and strengthened the feeling of national solidarity; and it furnished a wealth of information, impressions, and inspiration, that had a stimulating and fructifying influence for many a long day thereafter.

My own work in connection with a Congress began months before it opened, for I had to compile and edit, and in part to write, the comprehensive report of the Executive. This task necessitated the despatch of letters to all the heads of the departments in London and Jerusalem, to all the secretaries of affiliated institutions, and to the secretaries of over forty constituent federations in all parts of the world, inviting them to send me a concise account of their respective activities for inclusion in the report. At least two if not more reminders had to be addressed to all these officials in order to ensure that their contributions were received in good time, for many of them were in Hebrew or German, some in French or Yiddish, and all had to be translated into English and prepared for the printers. But although I began the job early enough, as I thought, it was seldom that the printed report, which usually extended to 400 pages, was ready more than a few days before the opening session. And at the Congress itself I had to act as one of the secretaries, often to interpret the speech of an important delegate from German into English or *vice versa*, to issue a daily press bulletin in English, and to attend meetings of the Executive; while I also found time to act as correspondent for the *Manchester Guardian* and occasionally for other papers too. By the time the whole fatiguing proceedings, which kept me busy at all hours of the day and many of the nights, were over, I was quite ready to go off for a holiday with my wife, who usually arrived on the scene at the concluding session.

II

There was generally something distinctive about each Congress — either a new development in policy, or a radical change in the Executive, or something extraordinary in its external circumstances. It was the last feature that unpleasantly characterised the Congress of 1925. It was held in Vienna, which was chosen primarily in the interests of the Jews of Central and Eastern Europe, among whom there had been a considerable increase of Zionist sentiment. Before deciding in favour of that city, the Zionist Executive exchanged several letters and telegrams with the heads of the Austrian Zionist Federation, as the *Hakenkreuzler* movement, under the leadership of Hitler's "spiritual" comrades, had become increasingly troublesome

CONGRESSES AND CRISES

in Vienna, and it was feared that there might be disturbances during the Congress and even in the Congress building itself. The local Zionist leaders consulted their Government and also the Police-President of the city, and were given promises that every precaution would be taken to ensure that the assembly would take place without incident or risk.

The authorities were prompted by a twofold motive in welcoming the event. The first was purely material and economic: they looked forward to the visit of a few thousand Jews from other countries who would bring their valuable currencies to a city now largely dependent for its solvency upon the tourist traffic. The other motive was political: they wanted to give proof to the outside world that law and order prevailed in their capital and that they were in complete control of it. Had they declined to be responsible for safety, or had they left it an open question, the Congress would not have taken place; and then the city would have been all the poorer and the correspondents of foreign newspapers would have cabled their obvious comments, with the result that the prestige of the Government would have sunk.

But after the preparations had already begun and the large "Konzerthaus" had been hired, the *Hakenkreuzler* threatened that they would prevent the Congress from being held. There were further anxious discussions in Government departments and at the *Polizei-Präsidium*. The authorities remained firm. They would protect the Congress and the delegates from any possible danger and assured the Zionist representatives that there was nothing to fear. They realised that the Jew-baiters were bent upon violence and took concerted measures to avert a possible attack. On the eve of the Congress they not only strengthened the police, but also mobilised the army. Seven thousand troops were employed to form a cordon round the district (including the Ring) containing the Congress building and the numerous hotels at which delegates and visitors were staying. Had the invasion of an enemy been expected, it would hardly have been possible to organise more elaborate and effective counter-measures. But despite this, some friends of mine in taxis on the way to their hotels were attacked, though they suffered only slight injury. Suddenly, only a few hours before the opening session, when I was in the office of the organising secretary, there was a rumour that a bomb had been placed in the basement, and panic spread. Everybody was immediately ordered out of the building, all committees had to suspend their meetings, all offices had to be cleared; and then the military and the police made a thorough search and declared that they had found nothing. But the authorities did not relax their vigilance a moment. There was a military guard in and around the building during all the time of the Congress, both day and night; soldiers ate and slept in a large room in the basement. There were also troops who bivouacked in the streets, with their guns ready in case of a surprise assault. But there was no need to fire a single shot.

Fortunately nothing happened. The Congress was able to follow its traditional course without any interruption (except from delegates themselves) and without any alarm. And Leo Motzkin, who was President of the Congress, was able to indulge his love for an all-night session by protracting the concluding part of the proceedings until six o'clock in the morning, when we returned to our hotels in broad daylight.

III

There were two main themes discussed at the Congress of 1925 — the slow progress in the development of the Jewish National Home and the need of obtaining the co-operation of non-Zionists. Both of these questions implied that the funds at the disposal of the Zionist Organisation for the stupendous task with which it had to cope were utterly inadequate; and it was therefore necessary that they should be augmented as much and as speedily as possible. That was why there was much rejoicing when, at a hastily summoned meeting of the Executive in London, in the spring of 1926, Dr. Weizmann, beaming with a look of triumph, announced that he had just had a talk with the millionaire Bernhard Baron, who promised him the sum of £1,000,000. Baron, who was a Russian Jew by origin, had risen from poverty and obscurity to fame and fortune through his invention of some ingenious mechanism for the manufacture of cigarettes and was the chairman of the firm of Carreras, Limited. It was perhaps but natural that he should have felt honoured by the approach made to him by the Zionist leader, and he must have been very strongly moved to have offered a gift of such magnificence. Dr. Weizmann told us that the prospective donor stipulated that the matter should be kept strictly secret until he would present a cheque for the amount at a public dinner to be held in his honour. Meanwhile he invited the members of the Executive to draw up proposals for the main purposes to which the money should be devoted, so that he could submit a well-considered and impressive scheme to the princely benefactor. He had already suggested to Mr. Baron that the public dinner should be held at a leading hotel in the West End, with Lord Balfour in the chair, and the millionaire readily agreed. The latter even hinted that he might give a further substantial sum at some later date.

The next few weeks were occupied in discussing alternative plans for the allocation of the expected fortune and in making preparations for the historic occasion. The organising of the dinner and the publicity involved were entrusted to me. I engaged the largest banqueting hall at the Hotel Cecil, discussed with the manager the details of a luxurious menu, and had an imposing invitation card printed. I then drew up a list of a few hundred guests, both Jews and Gentiles, including many distinguished personages who were either supporters of the Zionist cause or potential friends, and had all the addressed envelopes in readiness. I also prepared a biography of Mr. Baron and had four dozen copper-plate blocks of his photograph made for distribution to the press.

But on the very afternoon when I intended issuing the invitations Mr. Baron's secretary rang up Dr. Weizmann's private secretary, inquired whether the invitations had already gone out, and, on being told that they had not, said that it was Mr. Baron's wish that they should not go out. As soon as Dr. Weizmann returned to the office and was informed of this strange development, he hurried off to see Mr. Baron to find out whether he wanted only a temporary postponement. Within less than an hour he was back, looking pale and grave. He told us that Mr. Baron wished the whole affair to be cancelled, as he had changed his mind. In short, he had decided not to give the million pounds or any amount like it. It took us some time to recover from the tremendous shock. We were particularly sorry for Dr. Weizmann, who had felt unusually elated by his financial *coup*, and who was now obliged to break the discomfiting news to Lord Balfour.

Dr. Weizmann tried to elicit from Mr. Baron why he had changed his mind, but the latter would not vouchsafe even the least inkling of the motive or person that had influenced him. The millionaire tried to mollify the Zionist leader a little later by giving him a cheque for £100,000 for undertakings in Palestine, but it was done without any publicity. There were various rumours afloat at the time as to who was responsible for his change of mind, and suspicion was directed towards one or two well-known anti-Zionists, particularly Claude Montefiore.[1] I was therefore relieved when Rabbi Dr. Joel Blau[2], the white-haired senior Minister of the Reform Synagogue in Upper Berkeley Street, called on me one day, on his own initiative, to assure me that Montefiore had absolutely nothing to do with the matter. I readily accepted his assurance, as I felt certain that that noble-minded scholar could not have done anything so mean. The mystery was never cleared up. Baron left a great part of his fortune in the form of a trust fund, of which various amounts were distributed annually to a large number of Jewish and non-Jewish charitable institutions until it was entirely used up at the end of ten years.

IV

The other question with which the Congress of 1925 had been largely occupied — the extension of the Jewish Agency by securing the co-operation of representative non-Zionists — had already been approved in principle by a majority of the Congress in 1923; and the subsequent prolonged negotiations about details between Dr. Weizmann, the outstanding and indefatigable advocate of the idea, and Louis Marshall, the distinguished lawyer and recognised leader of American Jewry, formed the subject of the most bitter controversy at all following Zionist assemblies, until an agreed plan was at last

[1] Died in 1938.
[2] Died in 1927.

CONFERENCE FOR ENLARGEMENT OF THE JEWISH AGENCY, LONDON, 1929

From left to right: Leonard Stein, H. Sacher, Lr. M. D. Eder,★ M. Naamani, Dr. A. Ruppin,★ O. Wassermann,★ Israel Cohen, C. Q. Henriques,★ Dr. Weizmann, N. Sokolow,★ Louis Marshall,★ Dr. L. K. Frankel,★ Dr. M. B. Hexter, Dr. G. Halpern.

★ *Deceased*

adopted in 1929. Before this consummation was reached, however, there were interminable discussions in the Zionist Executive (which met over a hundred times between the Congresses of 1927 and 1929) and in the General Council; there were repeated visits by Weizmann to the United States for conferences; and Louis Marshall came to London and presided by courtesy (though contrary to the constitution) at a meeting of the Executive.

The most relentless antagonist of the extension of the Jewish Agency was Vladimir Jabotinsky, who had founded his Revisionist Party in 1925, and who was opposed to anybody but avowed Jewish nationalists having anything to do with the political work for the development of the Jewish National Home. But the discussions were hampered and protracted not so much by the hostility of Jabotinsky, Dr. Stephen Wise, and other opponents, as by the difficulty of securing agreement with the Americans in regard to the articles of the constitution of the enlarged Agency. For the Zionist Executive consisted of members who were divided between London, Jerusalem, and New York; and after harmony had been reached between them on certain minutiae in dispute, the endorsement had to be obtained of the General Council, in which there was also a divergence of views. No wonder that Weizmann's patience was constantly frayed and his temper provoked as he had to listen to rancorous speeches that seemed to him either showy rhetoric or attacks sharpened with a personal barb. He never failed to reply with a stinging rejoinder, which he usually closed with his favourite French slogan: *C'est à prendre ou à laisser*, after which he left the conference room for the others to reflect on what sounded to them like an ultimatum.

Dr. Weizmann was also annoyed because his principal colleague, Nahum Sokolow, failed to display the same enthusiasm for the enlargement of the Agency as he did. Sokolow did not by any means oppose it, but he never waxed lyrical over it. He maintained an air of detachment, as though not quite sure whether the project would go through or not. Indeed, at a meeting of the General Council, at which there was a great deal of argument about having proxies (in the interests particularly of American members unable to attend a meeting in Europe), he even poked fun at this suggestion

A JEWISH PILGRIMAGE

and aroused general hilarity. It was this attitude of his that probably accounted for the fact that during a meeting of the General Council in July, 1928, in Berlin, a sub-committee that was entrusted with the nomination of honorary officers for the enlarged Agency left his name out. When Sokolow heard of this he was incensed and regarded it as a slur upon his dignity. He immediately retired to his hotel and sulked as though he had been subjected to the most serious humiliation. But after the enlarged Agency was finally constituted Sokolow frequently presided at meetings of its Executive with the same urbanity that marked his chairmanship at sittings of the Zionist Executive. Indeed, the time came when the two Executives seemed to have become more or less synonymous.

The actual inauguration of the enlarged Agency took place immediately after the Sixteenth Zionist Congress, in Zurich, in the summer of 1929. Although the Congress began on July 28th and the opening session of the Agency was fixed for August 11th, so as to allow the Zionists ample time to complete their deliberations in comfort, the Congress did not end, after an all-night session, until 8.30 in the morning of August 11th, and the Agency proceedings were due to begin at three in the afternoon. I was not the only one who was thoroughly fagged out and unable to snatch more than a few hours' sleep between the two assemblies. I remember that my lunch that day consisted mainly of milk-chocolate, which I munched in the street as I hurried to the birth of the extended Agency.

There was an air of festivity in the large Concert Hall in which the historic function was enacted, and the place was crammed with over 2,000 people representing all the leading Jewish communities of the world. The platform presented a galaxy of celebrities, for side by side with the Zionist leaders and the American leader, Louis Marshall, there sat Viscount (then Sir Herbert) Samuel, the famous scientist, Albert Einstein, the leader of British industry, Lord Melchett, the distinguished French statesman, Leon Blum, and the celebrated novelist, Sholem Asch. As there was a considerable contingent of English-speaking delegates and visitors, especially from America, there was a demand for the translation of German and Hebrew speeches into English, and likewise a request for the translation of English speeches into German, so that I was kept busy. I had acquired much practice in quickly writing down the English version of what was spoken in German (by using a shorthand of my own), and was equally adept in rendering English into German. When the epoch-making session was over and I joined some American delegates for tea in the garden of the Hotel Bauer au Lac, facing a picturesque part of the Lake of Zürich, I was surrounded by many people who had never attended an international Congress before and admired my fluency as an interpreter. They wanted to know "how the thing was done." I assured them that it was quite simple if you only knew the languages.

By the time that the Agency proceedings, which lasted four days, were over, I was quite worn out, so early on the following day my wife and I took the train to Genoa and went on to Rapallo for a holiday. For the first few days I hardly looked at a newspaper, but when I opened the *Neue Zürcher Zeitung* one morning I read a few lines about Arab riots having broken out in Palestine. The next day the report was longer, and the following day longer still and more disturbing. We therefore decided to leave Rapallo and go to Montreux in order that we might be nearer to London in case my presence there was needed. After another couple of days the despatches about the riots had become so alarming that I decided not to wait for a message from the office but to return home at once. We took the night train to Paris and hurried to London. We arrived in time to be present at the great Protest Demonstration at the Royal Albert Hall, on Sunday afternoon, September 1st. Lord Melchett presided over an audience of about 10,000 people, and he and the other principal speakers, Dr. Weizmann, the Chief Rabbi (Dr. J. H. Hertz), and Colonel Josiah Wedgwood, M.P., united in condemning the Arab atrocities and deploring the breakdown of government in Palestine.

V

The Arabs had massacred 130 Jews and wounded over 300 others. That was their reply to the establishment of the new Jewish Agency, one of whose main founders, Louis Marshall, died in Zurich in the hour of his triumph. Dr. Weizmann hastened back at once to London on receiving a telegram from the Colonial Office with the tragic news from Palestine, and saw Sir John Shuckburgh[1], the Permanent Under-Secretary of State for the Colonies, who had been largely responsible for policy in Palestine. "Have I bungled it?" asked Shuckburgh. "Somebody has bungled it for you," replied Weizmann. "You haven't understood that Palestine is a problem *sui generis* and that officials trained in Sierra Leone are not suitable for Palestine. It's necessary they should have a special training."

Then began a period of two years of storm and stress, of turmoil and travail, with a succession of official investigations and voluminous reports, of political conferences, tantalising negotiations, and protest meetings throughout the world. The Labour Government of Ramsay MacDonald despatched a Commission of Enquiry headed by Sir Walter Shaw, to Palestine, whose task was "limited to the immediate emergency and would not extend to questions of major policy." The Commission sat in Jerusalem as a public Court of Inquiry, with power to summon witnesses, to take evidence on oath, and to hear counsel on behalf of the Government, the Jewish Agency, and the Arabs. The Agency responded to the gravity of the issues at stake by engaging eminent members of the English bar to protect its interests — Sir Frank Boyd Merriman, K.C., M.P. (now Lord Merriman, President of the Probate, Divorce, and Admiralty Division of the High Court), assisted by Mr. Seymour (now Mr. Justice) Karminski, Lord Erleigh (now Marquess of Reading), K.C., and other advocates. It soon became evident that the Commission was not limiting its enquiry to the terms of reference, and consequently the surviving members of the War Cabinet that was responsible for the Balfour Declaration — Lord Balfour, Lloyd George, and General Smuts — published a letter in *The Times*,[2] in which they called attention to this trespass and urged that the Commission must be supplemented by "an authoritative Commission" to hold "a searching enquiry into the major questions of policy and administration." When the Agency's counsel returned to London at the

[1] Died in 1953.
[2] December 20th, 1929.

CONGRESSES AND CRISES

beginning of 1930 they attended a meeting of the Executive at the Zionist Office to deliver a report upon the proceedings in Jerusalem. Seldom had I heard such a crushing indictment of the methods of the Palestine Government as when I listened to Lord Merriman's eloquent and scathing exposure of the manoeuvres adopted by the Commission to conceal the Government's failings and shortcomings. Nor was I surprised, for in his closing speech at the Enquiry Lord Merriman had complained of the antagonistic attitude adopted by the Government counsel towards the Jewish witnesses in contrast to the leniency shown in the cross-examination of the Arab witnesses.

When the Report of the Shaw Commission was published on March 31st, 1930, it caused profound disappointment in Zionist circles, as the Commission had gone beyond their terms of reference in recommending that the whole land question should be authoritatively investigated, since they found that displacement of Arabs from the land was one of the causes of the disorders, and that a new definition of British policy should be issued. The feeling of disappointment was increased when the Government sent out Sir John Hope Simpson to investigate questions of immigration, land settlement, and development, as he had no special knowledge of the basic problems underlying the Palestine Mandate or of Palestine itself. While Simpson was engaged on his task Weizmann was making every effort to persuade Ramsay MacDonald and the Colonial Secretary, Lord Passfield (Sidney Webb), to effect changes in the Administration of Palestine, the heads of which were notoriously anti-Zionist. Lord Passfield at first thought of inviting General Smuts to go to Palestine to overhaul the Administration and make changes among the higher officials, and Lloyd George urged the Prime Minister to cable to Smuts to this effect, but although MacDonald promised that he would do so nothing came of the idea. Weizmann was in frequent consultation with Lord Melchett, who was Chairman of the Council of the Jewish Agency, and from May, 1930, the advice and co-operation of the (first) Marquess of Reading were also invoked. At one stage Reading and Pinhas Rutenberg (chairman of the *Vaad Leumi* or Jewish National Council and the moving spirit of the Palestine Electric Corporation) were negotiating with Passfield, without previous consultation with the Executive, although the latter were informed subsequently.

Dr. Weizmann's habit of conducting political conversations and negotiations without previous discussion with the Executive aroused much dissatisfaction, especially as they thought that he was not as communicative to them as they maintained he should be. They were also disquieted by rumours that the Government intended introducing a Legislative Council in Palestine and by the adverse effect that the political situation had produced upon the prospects of raising funds for Palestine. All these grounds for discontent found vigorous expression at a meeting of the Zionist General Council in Berlin in August, at which Weizmann provided his critics with further and more serious reason for complaint. In the course of a speech that he delivered on August 28th, 1930, dealing with the evolution of Zionist policy, he said:

> *It is not correct to say that the Basle Programme promised us a Jewish State, nor that the Balfour Declaration promised us a Jewish State. In 1919 I spoke of ' Palestine as Jewish as England is English' because I believed it then. Now I don't believe it. We were promised only a Jewish National Home in Palestine. But such as it is, with its limitations, it attracts the best elements in Jewry. I consider it was unwise and detrimental for others to make other statements.*

This utterance provoked indignant dissent from several members and was something of a shock to others. It was used as a rod with which to beat the Zionist leader until the following Congress and later. Not until twelve years later, under the compelling influence of the war, did Weizmann publicly advocate a Jewish State[1], but he had to suffer much for his Berlin indiscretion.

VI

As soon as the meeting was over I went to Wiesbaden, where I had arranged to meet my wife for a holiday and to take the baths for my recurring rheumatism. On the very first morning, as I was looking at a bookseller's window, I met my old friend, Dr. Oscar Levy, whom I had not seen for several years. I had first made his

---

[1] In a signed article " Palestine's Role in the Solution of the Jewish Problem," in *Foreign Affairs* (New York), January, 1942.

CONGRESSES AND CRISES

acquaintance early in the century in the Reading Room of the British Museum, of which he was a regular habitué. He then lived in a flat in Museum Street, and, although he had qualified as a physician in Germany, where he was born, and subsequently obtained English degrees, he seldom spent more than an hour each day on his medical practice, as he had ample private means. In those early days he was a handsome, intellectual-looking man, always immaculately dressed, with a monocle, top-hat, and spats. He devoted his life to the dissemination of a knowledge of Nietzsche's philosophy, of which he was an indefatigable apologist and interpreter. He financed and edited the monumental, authorised English translation of Nietzsche's works in eighteen volumes, and wrote several books and countless articles on various aspects of his teachings. Although he had lived in England for many years, Oscar Levy did not become naturalised here, and therefore returned to Germany shortly after the outbreak of the First World War. He came to see me one evening while I was in the Ruhleben Camp, but it was a very brief interview at the gate, secured by bribing the sentry. After the war was over he was allowed to return to England for a short time, but was ordered to leave by the Home Secretary, Mr. Joynson-Hicks. He thereupon settled with his wife in Wiesbaden, where he bought a large house divided into flats, the rents of which provided them with a sufficient income.

We were both very pleased to meet again after so many years, and spent almost every evening, together with my wife, at a café, in animated talk about all sorts of things. It was during this stay in Wiesbaden that a General Election took place in Germany, in which the Nazis for the first time were returned in considerable numbers. "There's going to be serious trouble," said Levy, "and I'm going to clear out." Shortly afterwards he went to live in Monte Carlo, where he remained until the outbreak of the Second World War, when he was permitted to return to England.[1]

VII

The publication of the Hope-Simpson Report and simultaneously of the Passfield White Paper on October 21st, 1930, intensified the

[1] He died at Oxford, at the age of eighty, in 1946.

feeling of disquiet in the Zionist world. The Report gave a much lower estimate of the cultivable area of Palestine than had previously been accepted, and implied that Jewish colonisation had resulted in the displacement of a large number of Arab peasants. Even more alarming was the White Paper, which foreshadowed fresh restrictions in regard to immigration, threatened the Jews with an embargo on further purchases of land, and commented upon their work in unfriendly and disparaging terms. This document was regarded by the Agency Executive (as well as by Jews throughout the world, and indeed by leading English statesmen and jurists[1]) as a flagrant infringement of the Mandate and a violation of the whole spirit of the Balfour Declaration and of the statements made by successive Governments in the preceding twelve years. Dr. Weizmann immediately resigned his office as President of the Zionist Organisation and of the Jewish Agency as a mark of protest, and informed the Government to that effect. His resignation was followed by that of Lord Melchett from the chairmanship of the Jewish Agency Council, and by that of Mr. Felix Warburg (of New York) from the chairmanship of its Administrative Committee.

The world-wide storm of indignation seriously upset the Government, who were particularly anxious that Weizmann should do everything in his power to calm public feeling in America. They soon realised, however, that it was necessary to rectify Lord Passfield's blunder, and therefore early in November they set up a committee of Cabinet Ministers to discuss the situation with representatives of the Zionist Organisation and the Jewish Agency.[2] Consequently, for the next three months there were repeated discussions and conferences until the Government agreed to publish a statement that was tantamount to a reversal of the Passfield White Paper. Despite Dr. Weizmann's resignation he was requested by the Zionist General Council, which was at that time in session in London, to carry on the duties of

[1] They included Lloyd George, Stanley Baldwin, Sir Austen Chamberlain, L. S. Amery, Sir Herbert Samuel, Lord Hailsham, and Lord (then Sir John) Simon.
[2] Mr. Kingsley Martin, in his biographical memoir of Harold Laski, rather overrates the part, valuable as it was, played by Professor Laski in these negotiations when he writes (p. 209): " It was, however, mainly as a result of Harold's activities that the Prime Minister was induced to invite the Jewish Agency to send representatives to a special Cabinet Commission on policy in Palestine."

his office until the next Congress, and he became the directing spirit in the fight that resulted in the Government's retreat. In addition to the Jewish representatives who took part in the official conferences, Dr. Weizmann was in frequent touch with Lord Reading, who told him that the Government were angry with Passfield and " anxious to get out of the mess he had made." Reading (for whom Harold Laski, Dr. H. Lauterpacht, and Dr. J. Stoyanovsky worked out a brief) was willing to intervene if there were a deadlock or at the final settlement, and also to get together some leading Indian Moslems (including the Aga Khan), to give Dr. Weizmann the opportunity of talking to them. His view was that if the Government formulated an interpretation of the Mandate to which the Jewish Agency objected, then the Council of the League of Nations could demand an interpretation from the Permanent Court at The Hague.

Dr. Weizmann was tireless in his efforts to secure from the Cabinet Committee a document that would explain away the objectionable passages in the White Paper in terms that would reaffirm the Government's obligation to abide by the provisions of the Mandate. He was anxious that one or two leading American representatives of the Jewish Agency, particularly Professor (now Justice) Felix Frankfurter, should come over to London to participate in the negotiations. But the Americans contented themselves with offering comments and suggestions by cable and appointed Harold Laski to act as their observer and spokesman. As immediate replies were wanted on some points Laski telephoned to Frankfurter, who consulted Justice Louis Brandeis, and Weizmann telephoned to Felix Warburg in New York. Weizmann also went over to Paris to consult Baron Edmond de Rothschild and Leon Blum. He was increasingly harassed by the criticisms that came from various quarters, and resented both the absence of the Americans and the interference of Rutenberg. He was also annoyed by the requests of members of the Executive to see every letter addressed to him from the Foreign Office. The cumulative effect of all this irritation was that in the first half of December he told the Executive on three occasions that he would have nothing more to do with the negotiations. But he nevertheless came back.

At last, by February 11th, 1931, the Government's explanatory statement, to which the Agency Executive had given their assent and which was to be in the form of a letter from the Prime Minister to Dr. Weizmann, was ready. But unfortunately on that day, in reply to a question in the House of Commons, Ramsay MacDonald said that the statement would be published, but not as a White Paper, as this might give it a status " which it is not desirable it should have." As soon as they heard of this Weizmann and all his fellow-negotiators were most indignant, as they felt that the whole value of the document, over which they had laboured and struggled for three months, would now be nullified. Weizmann decided to ring up the Prime Minister immediately, but as the Executive were meeting in the evening, long after office hours, and the only telephone from which a call could be made was that in my room, they all adjourned there for the purpose. Connection with No. 10 Downing Street was soon obtained, and then the Zionist leader, sitting at my desk, spoke as follows:—

Mr. Prime Minister, we are all very much troubled at what was said in the House this afternoon. I think it makes the position very awkward. We want it to be made clear that the letter to me containing the authoritative interpretation of the White Paper shall be the basis of the law of Palestine. Unfortunately Lord Passfield still imagines that nothing has happened or changed since the publication of the White Paper. He is causing trouble all the time.

If a question is put to you in the House to-morrow, then you can put the matter right. If you will consult the Lord Advocate,[1] *to whom I have spoken this evening, he will advise you as to the formula to be used. We have to deal with excited and anxious people, and it is undesirable that there should be any misunderstanding.*

I don't want anything controversial at our meeting to-morrow, as, until now, everything has gone on quite amicably. I beg you, Mr. Prime Minister, to take the earliest opportunity of putting the matter right by saying that the law of Palestine will be the interpretation of the White Paper as in the letter to me. We are dealing with an Administration in which we have no confidence, and in which I think you cannot have any confidence yourself.

The result of this intervention was that on the following day Ramsay MacDonald announced in the House that his letter to Dr.

[1] Mr. Craigie Aitchison.

CONGRESSES AND CRISES

Weizmann containing the statement would be published, laid before the League of Nations, and embodied in official instructions to the High Commissioner. The Letter thus had official status, though it was not technically a "White Paper." On February 13th it was published in Hansard, and the next day it appeared in the general press. At the same time Dr. Weizmann heard from Mr. Malcolm MacDonald, who acted as secretary to the Cabinet Committee, that his father admitted to him that he was sorry that he had given such a reply in the House on the 11th, as he afterwards felt that it was wrong. Mr. Malcolm MacDonald was then a friend of Zionism, but eight years later he was the author of a White Paper, which completely put Lord Passfield's into the shade.

VIII

When the Executive, in March, 1931, began to consider the choice of a city in which the next Congress was to be held, they received an invitation from the Italian Government to meet in Abbazia. An official from the Italian Embassy in London called at the Zionist Office to press the invitation, but the Executive decided not to accept it, as they feared that some delegates might publicly make reflections upon the Fascist régime, which would cause a political incident. Mr. Sokolow, therefore, called at the Embassy and explained that Abbazia was unsuitable owing to the lack of a large hall of adequate capacity with a sufficient number of adjoining committee-rooms. The Executive eventually decided in favour of Basle, where so many previous gatherings had been held. The Congress met early in July, in the vast Mustermesse, with 250 delegates, besides over a hundred journalists and about two thousand visitors from all parts of the world. As Dr. Weizmann had resigned the presidency of the Zionist Organisation in the previous October, the proceedings were opened with a speech by Sokolow, president of the Executive.

Dr. Weizmann delivered his report on the political situation the following day. His speech was a very long one, and owing to the strain on his voice and the oppressive heat he had to break off for ten minutes in the middle. He gave a very comprehensive review of the development of Zionism and of events connected with Palestine from the time of the First World War, for the purpose of vindicating his policy and showing that no other course was possible. He denied that he had abandoned the ideals of the founder of political Zionism, and maintained that the Balfour Declaration of 1917 was more far-reaching than the Basle Programme of 1897. The wrong that had been committed by the Passfield White Paper had been righted by the Prime Minister's Letter, but he did not consider that a political "victory," merely a restoration of the *status quo*.

The Congress, which lasted over two weeks, was characterised by two main features — vehement criticism of the policy of the Mandatory Government and an attempt to formulate the ultimate aim of Zionism. They followed inevitably upon the political developments since the riots of 1929 and the discussions that had been going on within the movement since the last Congress. The general dissatisfaction of the Jewish people with the manner in which the British Government had failed to discharge its obligations under the Mandate was reflected in the composition of the assembly. It was significant that the Revisionists, Jabotinsky's party — the most scarifying in their attacks upon British policy — had fifty delegates, in contrast to only seventeen in 1929; and their views were shared on most of the important issues by the majority of the General Zionists and of the Mizrachi (Orthodox) party, as well as by the Radicals, who together constituted the majority of the delegates.

Although Dr. Weizmann, in his political address, had announced that it was his valedictory speech, it was possible that a majority could have been obtained in favour of his re-election, despite the criticism to which his policy was subjected by many speakers, had it not been for an incident after the Congress had begun. This was an interview with a Jewish press representative, in which he was reported to have said that he had no sympathy with or understanding of the demand for a Jewish majority in Palestine, and that a majority was not required for the development of a Jewish civilisation or culture. The explanation given by Weizmann that he had been misunderstood failed to remedy the impression produced by the interview, and as the delegates recalled that he had made somewhat similar observations at the meeting of the General Council in Berlin in the preceding August, the desire of the majority for the termination of his presidency hardened into a determined resolve. The motion of the Political Committee, expressing regret at the interview and characterising his reply as inadequate, was adopted by 126 to 103, and thus was brought to an end a period of fourteen years of distinguished leadership.[1] In the chapter entitled "Demission," in his autobiography, *Trial and Error*, Weizmann makes no mention whatever of the indiscreet interview, but attributes his fall from office to Congress "passing a resolution of non-confidence" in his policy. His inevitable successor as President both of the Zionist Organisation and of the Jewish Agency was Nahum Sokolow, who thus attained the height of his ambition.

IX

In the summer of 1931 I published under the title of A *Ghetto Gallery*[2] a collection of stories and sketches of Jewish life, which I had written at various periods, ranging from 1898 to 1915 (the latest having been written in the Ruhleben Camp). I was somewhat diffident about the reception of the book, as it contained so many of my earliest literary efforts, and was therefore agreeably surprised by the favourable notices in various papers. The *Times Literary Supplement*[3] was particularly complimentary, for it said:

> It is perhaps easy for a Jew to write dignified prose, accustomed as he is from babyhood to the cadences of some of the greatest literature in the world; easy, too, perhaps for him to touch heights of tragedy in telling of the sufferings of his people, since every Jew is obsessed with racial tragedies. But Mr. Cohen has also the gift of comedy and irony of a quality peculiarly Jewish.... The stories have an economy and subtlety rather suggestive of Tchekov.... Mr. Cohen can compel both tears and laughter, and can draw with equal skill a full-length portrait and a background.

---

[1] This account of the reasons that led to Dr. Weizmann's temporary loss of the Presidency is based upon the author's dispatches in the *Manchester Guardian* of July 8th and 20th, 1931, the accuracy of which was never challenged. The interview was given to a representative of The Jewish Telegraphic Agency. (See also *Fifty Years of Zionism*, by Oskar K. Rabinowicz, page 99).
[2] Edward Goldston, Ltd.
[3] November 5th, 1931.

A JEWISH PILGRIMAGE

The *Bookman* wrote:

> Mr. Cohen has rendered a real service to future historians by recounting the story of so many characteristic figures of Russian Jews in the East End of London.

and the *Observer* was equally appreciative.

Chapter Seventeen

A TRANSATLANTIC TOUR

1931

I

FOR the next four years, from 1931 to 1935, the Zionist Executive in London consisted of a triumvirate — Nahum Sokolow, Professor Selig Brodetsky, and Mr. Berl Locker. Professor Brodetsky (1888 - 1954), who, together with Sokolow, now took charge of the Political Department, had been first elected on the Executive in 1928, and despite his exacting duties at the Leeds University he devoted himself with unremitting zeal and energy to the cares and responsibilities of his Zionist office. He seemed to be constantly travelling to and fro between Leeds and London, and he often went to various cities on the Continent to address public meetings, besides occasionally to Jerusalem to attend joint meetings with the Palestine Executive. I had first made his acquaintance soon after he became Senior Wrangler in 1908, when he came to seek my advice in connection with the formation of a students' Zionist Society, and we remained in friendly contact ever after. As for Mr. Locker, who represented the Labour Party, I had known him since the beginning of 1919, when we met at the International Socialist Conference in Berne. Although a native of Galicia he spoke English with remarkable force and fluency, and he enjoyed popularity because he usually drove his points home with the aid of Yiddish anecdotes.

Soon after assuming office, the new Executive asked me to undertake a tour across Canada, partly to enlighten the Jewish community upon the situation resulting from the recent Congress, and partly to raise funds for their current budget. As there were some outstanding financial differences with the Zionist Organisation of America, I first went to New York. I left Southampton, to which I was accompanied by my wife, on the *Olympic* on October 1st, 1931, and returned to England early the following January.

On landing in New York I was welcomed by my old friend, Jacob de Haas, whom I had known from my student days, and with whom I had a long talk about the latest developments in the Zionist world in America. My stay in New York was rather brief, but long enough for me to be deeply impressed by the magnitude of the Jewish community, the multitude of its institutions, and the multifariousness of its activities and interests. I made a point of visiting Carnegie Hall, to attend a service of the Free Synagogue, where I heard a sermon by its Rabbi, Dr. Stephen Wise. I had often listened to his remarkable oratory at Zionist gatherings, and it was therefore a novel experience to hear him as a preacher. He was a tall, powerfully built, and distinguished-looking man, with the typical face of an actor, and a stentorian, resonant voice, and he ranked high among American orators. On the same day I attended a Zionist conference, at which I conveyed the greetings of the London Executive.

II

It is strange that although the history of the Jews in Canada goes back to nearly the middle of the eighteenth century, the overwhelming majority of those dispersed and domiciled within its vast territory cannot point to any record earlier than the beginning of the present century. The first settlers were not victims of persecution in quest of an asylum, but rather soldiers of fortune or traders of enterprise. The pioneer was a romantic figure who came cantering along on horseback, in military uniform, with the conquering army under the British General, Sir Frederick Haldimand, when it entered the ancient city of Montreal in 1760. His name was Aaron Hart, a London Jew, who settled at Three Rivers, and who in time attained such wealth and social esteem that he enjoyed the honour of acting as host to both the Duke of Kent, the father of Queen Victoria, and the first Papal Envoy who visited Canada. He and the little handful of Jews who settled in Montreal at the same time — one of them, Jacob Franks, a Hudson's Bay trader, and another, Henry Joseph, the owner of a large fleet of canoes and a founder of Canada's merchant marine — were quite unlike the hosts of scared fugitives from Russian and Rumanian oppression, who came flocking there more than a hundred years later. But although the Jews were not granted full civil rights by Parliament until 1832, they nevertheless acquired their emancipation a quarter-of-a-century earlier than their brethren in England.

The boon of political equality, however, failed to attract any appreciable influx of Jews during the nineteenth century. The great tide of Jewish immigration that began to surge across the Atlantic in consequence of the Russian pogroms (in the early 'eighties) swept mainly into the United States: a mere rivulet trickled into Canada, and the first steps were then taken to establish Jews as farmers in the Prairie Provinces. But so small was the entire Jewish population at the end of the century, even though numerous communities had already been established, extending from Halifax to Victoria, that it scarcely exceeded 16,000 altogether. At the time of my visit the total Jewish population was 155,000[1], and of that number 125,000 had entered as immigrants since the beginning of the present century. They were distributed very unevenly, the great majority being settled in the provinces of Quebec and Ontario; but whilst there were 65,000 in Montreal, 40,000 in Toronto, and 18,000 in Winnipeg, the rest were scattered among nearly five hundred different centres, ranging from proud and famous cities like Ottawa and Vancouver to the obscurest of isolated villages in the prairies.

III

The Montreal community consisted largely of immigrants who had already been domiciled for thirty or forty years and of their native-born children, with the Russian and Polish elements rather conspicuous. In many respects it partook of the character of the Jewish communities in the United States, whose proximity exercised an irresistable influence upon the developments in Canadian Jewry, though the latter had a closer resemblance to English Jewry in the formal orthodoxy of its religious life. The city was rich in synagogues, large and small, as well as in institutions and organisations of all kinds —

[1] The Jewish population has since increased to 230,000, of which Montreal has 92,000, and Toronto 74,500, while the number in Winnipeg has also increased.

religious and secular, cultural and philanthropic. The institution that impressed me most was the Young Men's Hebrew Association, built and planned on the imposing lines of an American Y.M.C.A. (with the generous aid of the late Sir Mortimer Davis, the founder of the Imperial Tobacco Company), where 4,000 members were able to move about easily in a veritable hive of animated and multifarious activity. Equally notable, though of much more modest proportions, was the Baron de Hirsch Institute, erected in the interests of the welfare of the immigrants, for whom Montreal has always been the principal port of entry; and at the other end of the social scale was the Montefiore Club, which had all the usual amenities beloved of the upper middle class, and whose very existence was necessitated by the social aloofness of the Christian community. The Club was named after the great humanitarian, Sir Moses Montefiore, who showed his appreciation of the fact by contributing a cheque for ten pounds, which was displayed in a frame in one of the rooms.

Montreal is a bi-racial city, in which the English are in the minority as compared with the French; and the Jews, in establishing themselves for the most part in and near the English-speaking districts, thus manifested their preference, whilst their settlement in the midst of a racial minority had (according to a friend with a psychological turn of mind) dispelled the diffidence they might otherwise have felt. They were represented in all sorts of occupations and professions: they had their lawyers and doctors, their architects and builders (some of whom had planned the Dominion Square Building, one of the largest and most gigantic office-buildings in Canada), their industrialists and men of big business, their petty shopkeepers and artisans, their pedlars and newspaper-vendors. Montreal had always been looked upon as the metropolis of Canadian Jewry, especially in matters relating to political questions and the general representation of Jewish interests, but, owing to the vast distances separating it from other communities, it was unable to exercise any effective leadership, and hence the large Jewish centres in other provinces, such as Toronto and Winnipeg, had perforce developed a certain degree of independence. In times of crisis, however, the need for holding counsel together was felt and delegates from all parts of the Dominion assembled for deliberation under the auspices of the Canadian Jewish Congress. There were also periodical conferences of the Zionist Organisation, which has scores of branches extending from coast to coast.

I spent nearly three weeks in Montreal, in the course of which I delivered twelve addresses to all sorts of Zionist and general Jewish bodies, including one on the radio. The last was a talk on " The Political Situation in Palestine " at a meeting of the Canadian Institute of International Affairs, which was held at the house of the late Sir Arthur Currie, Principal of the McGill University. At that time there were 500 Jews among the 2,000 students at the University, and I was told that the authorities did not want any more. The latter maintained that McGill was a private endowment and that a disproportionate number of Jewish students prevented financial supporters from sending their own sons to the University, as they did not wish them to associate with Jews. It was the *numerus clausus* problem of the Eastern European Universities all over again.

IV

Toronto differed from Montreal mainly because it was a younger community, whose members, largely recruited from Russia, Poland, and Rumania, still presented many of the distinguishing characteristics of their native lands, and some of whom still betrayed a peculiar clannishness. There were many synagogues founded by immigrants from the same country, and even from the same town, whose name they bore; and it struck me as particularly curious to find a synagogue which was called " Congregation of the Men of England " (*Anshé England*), not because its members were natives of Great Britain but because they had sojourned there in their westward migration. The Jewish quarter, with its congeries of streets of Jewish dwellings, shops, schools, houses of prayer, clubs, factories, and scores of institutions of all kinds, might have been transplanted from Manchester, whilst its communal life was even more comprehensive and varied. There were certain streets devoted to particular professions, such as those occupied by doctors and dentists, or by dealers in secondhand clothes and old iron. There was even a miniature " Petticoat Lane." Spadina

Avenue was a veritable *Judengasse*, with its synagogues and kosher restaurants, its Yiddish theatre, Workers' Clubs, offices of societies, and well-stocked bookshops, and a stroll through that broad and bustling thoroughfare afforded an insight into the conflicting currents of thought that agitated the local community. The owner of the biggest bookshop, whose popularity seemed an obstacle to prosperity (since so many people read his papers for nothing) was a storehouse of information, especially about Jewish scholars and writers who had passed through the city; and a visit to one of the restaurants, which specialised in different classes of clientele — divided according to professions and *Weltanschauung* — enabled one to meet all sorts of characters.

I was particularly impressed by the predominance of Yiddish, which seemed to be spoken to a greater extent than in Montreal; though the latter, like Toronto, had its Yiddish daily as well as its English weekly. There was a great deal of Jewish activity of a purely secular character, but traditional orthodoxy also had a stronghold there, as I found one Sabbath afternoon, when I sauntered into the *Beth Hamidrash* (house of study) of one of the synagogues and came upon half-a-dozen greybeards poring diligently over the pages of the Talmud. The only features that distinguished it from a similar " house of study " in Warsaw or Vilna were its spaciousness and cleanliness, and, above all, the coat-hangers from which depended the overcoats of the elderly scholars. In the vestry-room there was a plentiful array of coat-hangers for further students — mute testimony to their regard for decency of dress. There was also pointed out to me in another part of the Ghetto the house of a Chassidic Rabbi, in convenient proximity to his little bethel, which were both generously maintained by his faithful followers. But whilst there was an intensity of devotion to things of the Jewish spirit, to the ideals of sacred study and social welfare, there was also a manifold display of industry in the mundane interests of the population at large. Some of the tallest buildings in the city, which was then said to have more sky-scrapers than all the other cities of Canada combined, had been erected by Jewish contractors; and here too were the headquarters of a multiple Jewish tailor, whose familiar and attractive sign was to be seen on scores of popular shops throughout the Dominion.

I addressed several public meetings in Toronto and also gave a talk on the radio. I made my headquarters there for nearly three weeks, as it was a convenient centre from which to visit other places in Ontario — Hamilton, St. Catharines, London, Windsor, Kingston and Ottawa, in all of which I spoke. From St. Catharines I went to see the stupendous spectacle of the Niagara Falls, and quickly retreated after receiving a splashing. From Windsor I was taken by a friend one afternoon by train through a tunnel to Detroit, and after a drive through this dreary city, where I saw a large dump of derelict motorcars, I was brought back to Windsor, to attend a public dinner. There I had the pleasure of meeting the Jewish Mayor, David Croll, who had started life as a newsboy and became a popular lawyer (and later advanced to the position of a Cabinet Minister). In Ottawa I called on Dr. Skelton, Assistant Secretary for External Affairs, with whom I discussed the situation in Palestine, and also on the Governor-General, the Earl of Bessborough, who told me that he had taken a keen interest in that country ever since he had met Baron Edmond de Rothschild, in Paris, who was famous for his munificent support of the Jewish agricultural settlements.

While in Toronto I was a frequent visitor at the office of Mr. Meyer Weisgal, editor of a bright weekly, *The Jewish Standard*. He told me that he had a great difficulty in making it pay and had already secured from his bank manager an overdraft, which he could not increase. He was therefore obliged to find some way of raising the wind, and as Lord (Bertrand) Russell was then on a lecturing tour in the United States, the idea occurred to him to invite him to speak in Toronto. He would engage the largest theatre and felt sure that he would easily pack it on a Sunday evening if only he could suggest an attractive subject on which Russell should speak. He was prepared to offer him 500 dollars, but could not ask him to speak on " The Philosophy of Mathematics " or " The Mathematics of Philosophy." Could I help him by suggesting a catchy title ? I thought for a moment and suggested " The Sins of Civilisation." " Excellent! " exclaimed Weisgal. He telegraphed to Russell, naming the fee and the subject. Russell promptly wired back his acceptance, and (as I learned later when I returned to Toronto from the West) the lecture was delivered in a crowded theatre, and Weisgal not only paid off his overdraft but had a substantial balance to his credit.

V

As I travelled from city to city across the seemingly endless territory from the Gulf of St. Lawrence to the Pacific Ocean, visiting dozens of Jewish communities, great and small, that presented such an agreeable blend of material welfare and traditional loyalty, the thought that occurred to me then and has recurred ever and again since — was that it was a pity that the Jews of Eastern Europe had awakened so late to the suitability of this Dominion as a land of refuge and had availed themselves of its hospitality, while it lasted, in such scanty measure. The openings for immigration had become so few and were guarded so rigorously, that it was sad to think that had there been sufficient foresight among the leaders of Jewry and the requisite capacity for organisation, the millions of Jews then suffering under the scourge of a degenerate civilisation in so many countries of Europe could have been transplanted to a congenial clime (even though parts of it were so bitterly cold in winter), where they would have enjoyed peace, liberty, and security under the British flag, and have been saved from Hitler's clutches. The farther West I journeyed the more recent were the communities, and consequently external assimilation, except in the younger generation, had made much less progress than in the Eastern provinces.

When I arrived in Winnipeg (on November 20th, 1931) I found the city covered with a thick blanket of snow. I was immediately interviewed by the *Manitoba Free Press* (an experience that I had in all other cities), and later went to the office for a chat with its famous editor, the late Mr. J.W. Dafoe, whom I had previously met when he spoke at the Royal Institute of International Affairs in London. I was then taken to "The Pit," as the great Grain Exchange was locally known, and as I entered my ears were assailed by a deafening din and I beheld a scene of pandemonium as crowds of brokers, jobbers, and clerks were rushing here and there and bawling at the top of their voices.

A TRANSATLANTIC TOUR

The Jewish community in Winnipeg was founded only at the beginning of the 'eighties by a band of fugitives from Russian pogroms, who originally intended going on the land, but, for lack of experience, remained in the town. A busy programme had been arranged for my six days' stay, as, besides speaking at several Jewish meetings and banquets, I also gave an address to a joint luncheon meeting of the Canadian Men's and Women's Clubs (which was broadcast) and another at the Women's Press Club. Of all the scores of gatherings that I addressed throughout the country, one of the most successful and enthusiastic was in Winnipeg. It consisted entirely of Jewish women — some three hundred in all — who attended a "Give or Get" luncheon for the benefit of Palestine, which meant that they each gave or got from others a uniform contribution (the amount being ten dollars). And one of the strangest surprises that I had was when I came into the hall of the Zionist building one Sunday morning and found over a dozen stalwart young fellows being smartly drilled by a leader with the authoritarian energy of a sergeant-major in wartime. "What are you drilling for?" I asked. The reply was pregnant with reproach for my ignorance: "To be able to defend our National Home in Palestine, of course."

VI

Most of the communities between Winnipeg and Vancouver came into existence as the building of the Canadian Pacific Railway made progress, and many of the early settlers, deferentially referred to as "old timers," found employment on it. Although separated by long railway journeys, these communities, such as Calgary, Regina, and Edmonton, felt pretty near to one another and were in regular communication with each other. Their communal life revolved for the most part around the synagogue and the school, but they also held frequent meetings for social and cultural purposes. Most of the Jews living in these Western cities had attained positions of comfort after a struggle of several years, and some of them loved to speak of their early ordeals and to contrast with them their relative prosperity. One of them related how he had arrived in London from Rumania thirty years earlier and slaved hard as a waiter in a

A JEWISH PILGRIMAGE

Whitechapel restaurant for six months until he had scraped together enough for his ticket to Canada; now he was the owner of a thriving business and a beautiful home, and the father of college-bred girls (with tinted finger-nails) who listened wonderingly as though he were telling a fairy-tale.

Memories of their native land, and even of their native town, were often preserved for the settlers in these prairie cities through the Hebrew *Melammed*[1] whom they imported from "home" to impart instruction in the sacred tongue and religious lore to their children. Some of these Hebrew teachers no sooner acquired a knowledge of English than they were fired by the ambition to improve their status, and at least three successful lawyers whom I came across and who were well spoken of by the local judges, had originally been pedagogues. The teacher at Calgary recalled that he had met me ten years before at Harbin: he, like a few other Russian Jews, had entered Canada by crossing the Pacific and landing at Vancouver, and he felt happier in the snows of Alberta than in those of Manchuria. It was at Calgary, too, that I heard the wonderful performance of a recently arrived cantor from the Ukraine, whose powerful lungs made the rafters of the synagogue re-echo with his resounding roulades. But although all these communities had set up their little temples and prayed for the restoration of Zion, they also worked for it and contributed to it. A group of Jews in Saskatoon had even gone further: with their savings they had bought some land in Palestine, which they had happily retained while so many of their friends had lost heavily on American stocks, and they were looking forward to undertaking shortly their final wandering across the earth to settle there. One of them told me that he had roughed it farming near Lipton for several years. He had originally lived in a tent, from which, when there was a blizzard, he could not emerge for several days. Then he built himself a wooden house. His face was hardened, his hands were gnarled, his body toughened.

Pleasant memories of Vancouver have clung to me, partly because it was such an agreeable relief, after a continuous journey of a day-and-a-half from Edmonton, to pass from the bleak and blinding

[1] Teacher.

A TRANSATLANTIC TOUR

snows of the Western prairies, through the wild and awe-inspiring panorama of the Rockies, to so genial a climate; partly because this city, with its Chinese, Japanese, and Hindu colonies, brought me into immediate contact again with the Orient; partly because from the lofty room of my hotel I beheld such golden glorious sunsets over the Pacific; and partly because in the large synagogue I saw a crowded and enthusiastic congregation applauding the performance by children in costume of a Yiddish play dealing with the heroic struggle of the Maccabees against the Syrian invaders. By far the greater part of the community consisted of Russian and Rumanian Jews who had arrived as penniless immigrants some twenty-five or thirty years before, and who had mostly attained a position of comfortable independence, occupying fine large houses in beautiful suburbs, where they had probably forgotten the squalor and distress of their youth in their native town, and whence many of them went in quest of a holiday to the sun—swept strand of Los Angeles. Long before almost any of them had settled there a Jew, David Oppenheimer, had so distinguished himself by his services in the development of the city that he was elected Mayor for three successive terms, until the year 1891, and his fellow-citizens showed their grateful appreciation by erecting a monument to him in Stanley Park.

Much smaller and feebler was the Jewish community in Victoria, although it was the oldest in Canada and, indeed, on the Pacific Coast. Its earliest members had been attracted by the discovery of gold in British Columbia in the 'fifties, among them being the father of David Belasco, the famous playwright, whilst another, Lumby Franklin, became the third Mayor of the city in 1866. Owing largely to their isolation, the Jews in Victoria seemed to evince a somewhat anaemic Jewish spirit, though happily there were exceptions, the most notable being a septuagenarian, who had fought in the Russo-Turkish War and had been in Victoria over forty years. It was a city which, thanks to its beautiful situation and mild climate, was regarded by both Jews and Gentiles in the West as an ideal paradise in which to spend their days of retirement, and hence developed a certain aloofness from matters that deeply agitated the Jews on the mainland.

Besides addressing a gathering in the synagogue I spoke at a luncheon of the Canadian Club, and then sailed from Victoria, on the calmest of seas, to Seattle in response to a telegram from the Rabbi of that city, urgently inviting me to visit his community. I addressed a large public meeting, attended a banquet, was driven through wide steep roads to various Jewish institutions, and then took the nightboat back to Vancouver. From there I set out on my eastward journey through the formidable and overwhelming grandeur of the Rockies.

VII

Unfortunately time did not permit me to make a détour to visit any of the numerous Jewish farm-settlements, but when I was in Regina I heard a vivid account of them from Mr. Louis Rosenberg, then the Western Administrator of the Jewish Colonisation Association. He had to preside at a gathering at which I spoke one evening, and, having been at the colony named Hirsch (after Baron de Hirsch, the millionaire founder of the Jewish Colonisation Association), he travelled back post-haste, a journey of twelve hours, including an hour by sleigh and two hours by horse-carriage. He told me that one out of every eight Jewish families in Western Canada worked and lived on farms, and in Saskatchewan one out of every five families. Over three thousand Jewish men, women, and children in the provinces lived miles away from stores, theatres, and the amenities of city life. The first Jewish settlement was founded in 1882, near Moosomin, by a group of fugitives from the Russian pogroms; then followed Hirsch in Saskatchewan ten years later, and others at various intervals. Homestead lands offered by the Government had proved an attraction to the many Russian Jews who arrived in 1905 and 1906, and there had also been an influx of Jewish homesteaders through the Dakotas in the United States into Western Saskatchewan and Alberta. In Western Canada the Jews were working over 150,000 acres of land valued (then) at 3,000,000 dollars, and they raised enough cattle, poultry, and dairy produce to satisfy the requirements of all the Jews living in the West. In the Eastern provinces — Quebec and Ontario — the Jewish settlements were fewer and the farms were smaller.

A TRANSATLANTIC TOUR

VIII

Despite their dispersion among the vast spaces of the Dominion, the Jews had maintained a vigorous national consciousness, which manifested itself, apart from other ways, in their adherence to Zionism and in a veritable cult of Yiddish. There was a chain of Zionist societies from Nova Scotia to British Columbia, which not only displayed a zealous interest in the development of the Jewish National Home but vied with one another in their generous support of its advancement. The enthusiasm for Yiddish struck me as strange and somewhat abnormal. That those who had come from Eastern Europe should continue after twenty or thirty years to talk the language with one another occasionally and to read Yiddish newspapers was perhaps only natural. But there was an ardent attachment to it that was fostered as though from a sense of nostalgia. Never shall I forget a motor-car journey from Toronto, along the wonderful, brilliantly-lit road skirting the Lake of Ontario, to Hamilton, during which my friend who drove and a fellow-journalist who was with us tried to outdo one another in their rendering of Yiddish folk-songs — an impromptu contest which they resumed on the return journey and carried on with resounding gusto as we careered through the night.

The most emphatic form that the cult had taken was in the establishment of Yiddish schools for children, particularly in Montreal, Toronto, and Winnipeg. These were institutions which children attended after the ordinary school-hours or on Sundays, in order to receive instruction in the Yiddish language and literature and in Jewish history. They were maintained for the most part by Jewish Labour organisations that had little or no sympathy with Zionism and the Hebrew revival, which contended that Yiddish was the Jewish national tongue, and demanded that Jewish children, even though born in Canada, should obtain a thorough grounding in it. The children attending such schools, however, were in the minority, and they were generally the offspring of parents who, on principle, did not belong to synagogues and believed that such an education sufficed for the fostering of the Jewish national consciousness. At Fort William I came across a group of native-born women who attended a Yiddish class, and who gave as the reason the desire to be able to correspond with their parents in the United States who could not write or read English. But in the Western prairies, where there were communities speaking German, Hungarian, or Ukrainian, it seemed in accordance with the local spirit that there should also be Yiddish-speaking colonies.

IX

Jewish life in Canada would hardly have been normal if it had not been afflicted with a certain amount of Anti-Semitism, but it was significant that this manifested itself mostly in those districts where there was a considerable non-British element. It was originally confined mainly to the Province of Quebec and almost exclusively to a small and obscurantist section of French Catholics. The city of Quebec itself was the scene of a trumped-up charge of "ritual murder" in 1925, and the crass ignorance of even some of its educated burghers concerning the Jewish faith was illustrated by a question put by one of the counsel for the prosecution to a Montreal Rabbi who appeared as a witness for the defence: "Are you a Pharisee or a Sadducee?" For that legal luminary Jewish religious life had not developed since the first century.

The position became worse later, after the Nazi régime in Germany began, not only in Montreal, where the German Consul was requested by the Government to cease distributing anti-Jewish literature, but in the Western provinces too. In these regions, where (with the exception of British Columbia) the British element formed less than half of the population, the people of foreign racial stocks comprised a goodly proportion of German origin, who were easily infected by the Nazi plague. That discredited forgery, *The Protocols of the Elders of Zion*, was put into circulation, Hitler's *Mein Kampf* found its way into remote hamlets, and all the baseless calumnies fabricated against the Jews by Nazi propagandists were brought into play. A check to this campaign was administered by a law enacted in Manitoba in 1934 against any libel committed against a person in respect of his race or creed,[1] and an organised crusade against anti-Jewish prejudice

[1] A similar law was passed in Saskatchewan in 1947.

A TRANSATLANTIC TOUR

was later conducted by various Christian bodies and by the Canadian Jewish Congress with satisfactory results.

X

After reaching Winnipeg on my return journey (on December 17th, 1931), I went to Chicago to have a look around in the city and to call upon the aunt of a London friend. She had formerly been a famous prima donna, known as Rosa Olitzka,[1] who had appeared in many opera-houses on the Continent and also at Covent Garden, and later achieved much success in the United States. There she married a wealthy merchant and retired from the stage. But after some years her husband's wealth rapidly dwindled in a slump and he died, leaving her poorly provided for. She invited me to lunch in her modest flat, but the meal was so meagre that after I left her I hurried to a restaurant. Her plight formed a fitting theme for a homily on the transience of fame and fortune.

I then returned to Toronto and thence to Montreal, where I was given a lunch by the National Council of the Zionist Organisation, and I reported on the state of the movement in the various cities that I had visited. Among those present at the gathering was a local historian, who told me that there was a Jew in Montreal named de la Penha, who was a claimant to the territory of Labrador. The story seemed to me so romantic that I went to see the claimant. Mr. de la Penha told me that he had inherited the claim from an ancestor Joseph de la Penha, to whom the territory had been awarded by William III of England on the ground of discoveries that he had made there and because he had hoisted there the " arms of Nassau and Orange." He showed me two elaborate parchment documents in Dutch. The first, dated March 1st, 1697, granted ownership of " Labrador, Corte Real, and Estotiland," to Joseph de la Penha, a citizen of Rotterdam, who had taken possession of those territories in the name of his King; and the second, dated January 6th, 1768, signed at the Court at The Hague by Prince William of Orange, was issued to Daniel, the son of Joseph (after the death of his brother David), confirming his right to " all the lands, forests, hunting

[1] Died in 1950.

grounds, rivers, fruits, and fisheries, situated therein and therebefore, as also the Dominion and Territorial rights, high, intermediate, and low jurisdiction, such to hold from Us and our Heirs in time, as an immortal hereditary fieff, of the nature of the Holland feudal tenures." Mr. de la Penha gave me photostat copies of the English translations of the documents, the correctness of which was certified on April 13th, 1927, by the Netherlands Consul General in Montreal, who added in the margin of the first document that " attached to the original parchment is the Great Seal of England, red wax in a case." The de la Penha family had not taken any steps to enforce or exploit their claim, and looked upon the parchments merely as historical curiosities.

I left Montreal on December 23rd for New York with a profound sense of relief. After weeks of ceaseless travelling and speaking, giving interviews and writing reports, moving into and out of hotels, packing and unpacking, meeting deputation after deputation, answering the telephone at odd and awkward moments, conveying greetings from people in one city to relatives and friends in another, and expected all the time to be good-tempered and look amiable, I was anxious for a rest. I was hardly allowed any respite in the smaller communities in the West, where I suffered from an excess of attention, hospitality, and questioning, so that I was often driven to take refuge in a cinema.

In New York, I went to see Mr. Sokolow, who had just arrived with his daughter, Dr. Celine Sokolow, for a propaganda tour in the States, and gave him an account of my experiences in Canada. I stayed in the city about twelve days, during which I visited a number of leading Jewish institutions and exchanged views with those in control of them. One of them was the Jewish Theological Seminary, where I had lunch with the Principal, the late Dr. Cyrus Adler[1], and in the course of our conversation the suggestion arose about my writing a book on " The Jews in Vilna " for the Jewish Publication Society of America. I could not help being impressed by the generous equipment and comfortable amenities of the Seminary — its library, lecture-rooms, common rooms, residences for professors and students,

[1] Died in 1940.

and dining room. On my last day, January 4th, 1932, I was entertained to lunch by a number of Jewish writers (including Louis Lipsky, Jacob Fishman[1], and Bernard Richards), who made speeches in my honour, and then I set sail on the *Majestic* for England. A week later I arrived at Southampton, early in the morning, and my wife came on board to have breakfast with me.

[1] Died in 1946.

Chapter Eighteen

PRELUDE TO CALAMITY

1932 — 1935

I

IN June, 1932, I set out for Poland again on behalf of the Zionist Executive. I had to stop in Berlin for some hours for my train to Warsaw, and therefore went to look up some friends at the office of the German Zionist Federation in the Meineke Strasse, off Kurfürstendamm, where so many Conferences of the Zionist General Council had taken place. I found them rather depressed, as though sensing some coming danger. The clue to their state of mind was provided presently by a procession of brown-shirted, jack-booted, belted, and evil-looking louts, whom I saw tramping along the Kurfürstendamm, displaying banners with the swastika, and yelling now and again:" *Heil Hitler* !"

I had dinner with my old friend, Dr. Jacob Klatzkin[1], who had been a colleague of mine more than twenty years before at the Zionist headquarters in Cologne. For the last few years he had been editing a monumental work of reference, the *Encyclopaedia Judaica*, in collaboration with Dr. Nahum Goldman[2], to which I had contributed some articles, and we discussed some further topics on which I should write. But he could not suppress the anxiety that he felt about the growing and menacing strength of the Nazis and the peril that it might mean for the Jews. He must have also been concerned not a little about his own enterprise, on which so much

[1] Died at Vevey, 1947.
[2] Now President of the World Jewish Congress and Chairman of the American section of the Jewish Agency Executive.

money and labour had been spent. It was only an infinitesimal part of the destruction soon to be wrought. The tenth volume, which went as far as " LYRA " and appeared in 1934, proved to be the last, for the flight of German Jewry had already begun the previous year and Jewish publications were forbidden.

II

My mission in Poland was not to conduct propaganda, for there were comparatively few among the three-and-a-quarter million Jews in the country who were not ardent Zionists. Its purpose was to exhort or stimulate the local organisation or rather organisations to energise their activity, particularly in regard to the collection of *Shekalim*, the obligatory annual contribution due from every avowed member of the movement to the London headquarters. The number of *Shekalim* determined the number of delegates that the Zionists in any country could elect to a Congress, and as there was a tendency to be lax in the collection in a non-Congress year the Zionist Executive suffered from a corresponding diminution in their revenue. Owing to the poor economic conditions of a considerable section of Polish Jewry the *Shekel* was fixed at a lower figure for that country than for most other countries[1], but as the community was so large it could nevertheless make a very substantial contribution if only sufficient energy were methodically applied. It was to achieve this objective that I visited not only Warsaw, but also several other cities — Lodz, Vilna, Bialystok, Czenstochau, Cracow, and Lwow. In all these places I had to have conferences and meetings which usually began late and were nedlessly prolonged, and at most of which other questions were raised that lay outside my competence. There was a general demand for a larger number of immigration certificates for Palestine, and however insistent I was in confining the discussion to the *Shekel* there was always somebody present who complained that his party did not receive its proper allocation of certificates and wanted the grievance remedied before paying attention to what was considered a humdrum matter.

How great and urgent the demand was for these certificates, I realised when I called at the Palestine Office. The stairs and the

[1] The *Shekel* in Poland was one zloty (8d.) per annum, and 2s. in Western countries.

ante-room were crowded with applicants, men and women, of all ages, some of whom had come from far-off provincial towns, and many of whom had been waiting for hours to see the secretary. The main office, in which the secretary and his assistants were fortunately separated from the public by a low partition and a sliding window, was likewise crammed. I learned that the would-be emigrants represented all sorts of occupations: there were qualified doctors and lawyers, engineers and mechanics, teachers and tailors, students and seamstresses, and scores of petty shopkeepers or pedlars — all unable to earn a living and anxious to get to Palestine, which seemed to them a sort of Utopia. But the number of certificates at the disposal of the Warsaw Office was strictly limited: it formed only part of the six-monthly quota for which the Executive in Jerusalem had always to wrangle with the Mandatory Government, and which had then to be divided up among a score of countries. No wonder that the receipt of a certificate was prized more highly than a successful lottery-ticket.

After I had been in Warsaw a few days, and, still more, after I had visited other Jewish centres too[1], I realised the compelling causes for this widespread urge to emigrate and the complexity of the conditions responsible for the prevalent distress and discontent. The Jews were the victims of political discrimination, bureaucratic chicanery and economic oppression, and their position was much worse than it had been on the occasion of my last visit seven years before. The benefits that they had hoped to derive from the clauses in the Peace Treaty safeguarding the rights of minorities had been whittled down through parliamentary reforms, and departmental Ministers had devised laws which, though apparently free from any racial bias, inflicted upon them the heaviest burden. There were grievances among all sections — the commercial element, artisans, professional people, students, and even those concerned with communal and public affairs. The Jewish businessman had to pay a higher rate of income-tax than the non-Jew, and was handicapped by the Sunday closing law. The entry of a young Jew into a manual

[1] A full account of my impressions of the Jewish communities in Warsaw and other cities in Poland will be found in my *Travels in Jewry*.

PRELUDE TO CALAMITY

trade through a technical school was impeded by various obstacles; there was a *numerus clausus* at every University; and although there was no law to that effect, Jews — with insignificant exceptions — were excluded from the public service. The Treaty stipulated that the Jews should receive " an equitable share " of the State funds available for educational, religious, and charitable purposes, but what they were given was quite a paltry sum. Their sorry plight was also due to an abnormal proportion being engaged in trade and distribution. There was a multiplicity of parties and groups, all trying to remedy the situation in their own way, but owing to their limited powers and resources and the differences that divided them their efforts were largely futile. A leading Jewish sociologist had estimated that there were one million Jews too many in Poland, and a social worker said to me: " In the little towns people live on potatoes and wonders." Indeed, if it had not been for a system of loan funds, mainly provided by the Joint Distribution Committee of America, the economic position of hundreds of thousands would have been utterly desperate.

Nowhere had I seen such misery and squalor as in the Warsaw Ghetto. It presented a drab and dreary scene of huge blocks of dwellings, honeycombed with grimy courts and alleys, upon which there frowned still dingier blocks of dwellings. The entrance to each " house " was a ponderous portal of timber and iron, and within the gloomy doorway, on the wall, were serried columns of names of all the tenants, most of which were hard to decipher. The lower strata of these dismal habitations were filled with endless rows of little shops, mostly devoted to the sale of foodstuffs and soft drinks. In many of the streets were lines of *droschkies* with Jewish drivers — some with grizzled beards — perched behind their sorry nags, and patiently waiting for a passenger who hesitated at spending even a zloty (eightpence) on a journey. There were swarms of hawkers with cheap ties, socks, combs, and similar wares, and even larger bands of beggars. It was impossible to walk more than a dozen yards in some roads without being accosted for alms. Some of the beggars were timid and probably driven to this means of livelihood quite recently; others were aggressive and not to be shaken off; and others again hunted in groups. But what impressed me more painfully were the numbers of abnormal creatures that I came across—the lame, dwarfs, and idiots, offspring of poverty and disease.

Even more distressing was the spectacle I saw in the slums in the Krochmalna and Ostrowski streets, where my nostrils were assailed by the evil odours of the garbage in the gutters. The people were unwashed and unkempt, with little more than rags on their famished bodies: they were not clad decently enough even to venture forth as beggars. The scene in the dingy courts that I entered through a gloomy alley was more gloomy still. There were huge blocks of dwellings four to five stories high, sombre as prisons, with patches of the walls crumbling away, and tattered bedding hanging from the window-sills. On a level with the ground and reaching lower still were the windows of the cellar-dwellings, dark insanitary hovels, which diffused an evil stench. On the steps of each dwelling were children of all ages, dirty yet cheerful, the older girls mothering the younger ones. One little girl told me that eleven people lived in the cellar that she was minding: her father was in hospital with cancer. Crowds of porters were lolling about in the alleys, husky fellows who seemed not to care how they kept body and soul together. As I left the dismal quarter, a friend who acted as my guide told me that one of the saddest features of the Warsaw Ghetto was the number of young children and infants who were abandoned in the streets by their mothers, and who were taken to a house for Jewish foundlings.

The burden that lay upon the Council of the Jewish community at that time was probably heavier than in any other Jewish centre in Europe, for the needs were great and growing, and the sources of income were shrinking under the economic scourge. But as the Council consisted of a variety of rival parties, its meetings were often a scene of acrimony and turbulence.

III

The other cities in Poland presented the same general pattern of poverty and distress, with some local variations. Lodz, once dubbed the "Manchester of Poland," did not impress me as possessing the least resemblance to my native city. Its industry was temporarily paralysed, its streets swarmed with pedlars, porters, and beggars, and its pale-faced children obviously suffered from rickets. In Bialystok, the birthplace of Zamenhof, the creator of Esperanto, over half of the population were Jews, yet no Jew was permitted to be Mayor. The factories had been idle for several weeks, as the workers had gone on strike to protest against the decision of the employers to reduce wages by half; but the factory-owners themselves were fighting for their existence as the orders that they obtained barely sufficed to keep them busy half of the year. An increasing number of young Jews spoke Hebrew with one another, as they saw the only solution of their troubles in Palestine. In Czenstochau, where Jews formed a fourth of the population, most of the shops on both sides of the main road had Jewish names, but business was slack and unemployment widespread. The community was strife-ridden, because the Zionists, although forming with the allied party of the Artisans a majority on the Council, were not allowed to choose one of their own members for President, as the Polish authorities insisted upon the position being held by one of the ultra-orthodox Agudas Israel. But fortunately there was no dissension among the group of young folk who were being trained on a farm outside the city with a view to settlement in Palestine.

I travelled to Lwow in greater comfort than I did in 1919, as I had a sleeper. The conductor impressed upon me to lock the door quite securely, as, only a few weeks before, a member of the Seym who had omitted to take this precaution woke up in the morning to find that his trousers, which had contained his wallet, had disappeared. In Lwow I had a long talk with a leading Zionist, who told me that the Ukrainians were proving dangerous rivals to Jews in many branches of business, especially in rural districts, and that the Jews in Galicia were faced by a bleak, blank prospect. That was why there was everywhere a passionate desire to emigrate to Palestine, and as the prospects of getting either there or elsewhere were limited, many young Jews were perforce listening to the seductive talk of the Communists. In Cracow the material depression seemed to be hidden under the romantic and picturesque aura of this ancient city. There was still a relic of the mediaeval Ghetto, for at the corner of the Slawkowska Street, where it once began, there was fixed to the wall

A JEWISH PILGRIMAGE

a huge chain, which in former ages was drawn right across the road to keep out potential troublers of Israel.

But of all the cities in Poland that I visited the one that appealed to me most was Vilna, which was a veritable citadel of Jewish tradition. Despite its poverty and depression, and its underground hovels, which were even worse than in Warsaw, it possessed a wealth of historic and cultural associations, which, at various periods, had attracted the attention of Napoleon, Sir Moses Montefiore, and Theodor Herzl. It owed its fame partly to having been the home of Rabbi Elijah, the Vilna *Gaon* (1720 - 1791)[1] who was the greatest Talmudical sage since Maimonides, and partly to the galaxy of humanists who in the succeeding decades produced a remarkable treasury of Hebrew works in verse and prose. The heart of the Ghetto was a secluded courtyard, called the *Schulhof*, which was surrounded by synagogues and houses of prayer of all sorts and sizes. Many of these bethels were known as a *Klaus*[2] and were named after the trade or craft whose practitioners gathered there for worship, the oldest dating back to the middle of the fifteenth century. Most sacred of all was the shrine on the site where the *Gaon* Elijah was born and lived: within its sombre walls, at a table on which burned a row of candles, sat ten devout scholars, who had left their wives and families to achieve perfect concentration and were always immersed in the study of sacred lore.

It was while I was in Vilna that I received a contract from the Jewish Publication Society of America to write a history of the Jews in that city. I therefore prolonged my stay to engage in research, to familiarise myself with the institutions and traditions of the community, and to buy whatever books would be useful for my purpose. I also devoted a day to a visit to Troki, a charming little town on the way to the old Lithuanian frontier, in order to acquaint myself with the colony of Karaites[3] that had existed there from the fourteenth century.

With my note-book full of facts and impressions, I was preparing to leave Vilna when the fellow-writer who had been my guide and

[1] A Hebrew title, meaning "Eminence," applied to an illustrious Rabbinical authority.
[2] From the mediaeval Latin *clusa* (cloister).
[3] A Jewish sect founded in Baghdad, in the 8th century, which opposed the Talmudical developments of Judaism and based itself on the literal interpretation of the Bible. My *History of the Jews in Vilna* appeared in 1943.

PRELUDE TO CALAMITY

instructor, and who had revealed to me so much of the cultural splendour as well as of the material squalor of the community, asked me whether I would like to see where the Jews were really at peace. He took me to the old cemetery, where no body had been laid to rest for over a hundred years.

When I left Poland in July, 1932, there were three-and-a-quarter million Jews there. By the end of the Second World War nearly three million had been exterminated in Hitler's death-camps. Among them were many who had been my personal friends.

IV

Soon after Hitler became master of Germany in 1933 and began to persecute the Jews, some leading Zionists from Berlin hurried to London with a strange mission. They had been summoned by Goering to his Ministry and told to go to London post-haste in order to do everything they could to stop the English press from printing reports about outrages committed against the Jews. One of these emissaries was Mr. Richard Lichtheim (a former member of the Zionist Executive), who, in reporting to the Executive on what took place at the interview, imitated Goering by banging on the table with his fist and said that he had been ordered to assure the Jews in England that all the stories in the papers were nothing but *Greuelmärchen* (atrocity fables). From that time we were repeatedly occupied at the Zionist Office with the tragic plight of German Jewry as well as with the affairs of the Jewish National Home. Indeed, the two became closely interlocked.

The next Congress was due to take place in the summer, so that choice of a suitable meeting-place became the subject of earnest discussion. It was finally agreed that, provided the permission of the authorities were granted, it should be held in Prague. After some correspondence, therefore, I called on the Czechoslovak Ambassador, the late Jan Masaryk. He, like his father, had always been a sincere friend of the Zionist movement and was willing to help. He told me that his Government would agree to the Congress taking place in their capital, but on one condition: two police representatives must be allowed to be present at every session in order to ensure that nothing was said that might offend " a neighbouring friendly Government." He personally greatly regretted that such a condition, which he well knew had never been imposed in the case of any previous Zionist Congress, was insisted upon by his Government, but they did not want Prague to be used as a forum from which to denounce the iniquities of Hitler.

The persecution of the Jews in Germany soon became the principal topic of the day, but the mendacious propaganda of Goebbels, who sought to justify it by accusing the Jews of having created a " Judaeo-German Reich," seemed to be making such an impression in some quarters, that I thought it necessary to present a critical examination of the whole question, in which the calumnies would be refuted by a recital of the facts. I wrote an article of 6,000 words and sent it to *The Quarterly Review*. Within three days I received a letter of acceptance from Sir John Murray, who published it as the first article in the issue of July, 1933. It was reprinted in pamphlet form for the Board of Deputies of British Jews in an edition of 10,000 copies[1]. This organisation also seriously occupied itself with the troubles of German Jewry, and as I was on its Foreign Affairs Committee and Press Committee I was kept pretty busy.

Germany was not the only country in which Jews were being subjected to persecution, although in no other land did their oppression assume such brutal and barbarous forms. Early in August, 1933, I received an unexpected visit from a leading Jewish lawyer in Bucharest, Dr. Misu Weissmann[2], who gave me an alarming account of Jew-baiting in Rumania. Anti-Semitism, which had been a constant feature of political life in that country for over half-a-century, had developed in the most virulent fashion as a direct result of Hitler's success, and all the methods and slogans of the Nazis had been imported. There were attacks upon Jews and their property in various cities; storm-battalions in Nazi uniform and Codreanu's " Iron Guard " had sprung up in increasing number; there was an organised boycott of Jewish shops in Bessarabia; the German Ambassador had attended a Congress of German Rumanians in Transylvania; and the

---

[1] It was also translated into Dutch and Italian.
[2] Later Dr. M. Amir, who was appointed Israel Ambassador in The Hague, where he died in 1953.

Premier, Vaida Voevod, had addressed a conference of Nazi students and expressed sympathy with their "national principles." Dr. Weissman told me that owing to the benevolent attitude of the Government to this anti-Semitic crusade, there was growing alarm in the Jewish community, and he had therefore come to London to see if some pressure could be exerted from here to counteract the menace. He was anxious to get into touch with two English women M.P.s, the Duchess of Atholl and the late Miss Eleanor Rathbone, who had recently been in Rumania, as he thought they might be able to influence some political leaders they had met there. I therefore promptly arranged an interview for him with those ladies and accompanied him to the House of Commons for the purpose. I also wrote an article on the subject, which appeared in the *Manchester Guardian*[1].

V

The Zionist Congress that opened in Prague on August 21st, 1933, aroused far wider interest than any previous one owing to the tragedy of German Jewry. Hitler's policy was basically an attack upon the Jewish people as a whole, to which a reply had to be made by its most representative assembly. The problem was debated in all its aspects in plenary sessions and committees, but the discretion imposed by the wish of the local Government in no way affected the dignity of the protests against Nazi barbarism or the demands addressed to the Mandatory Government and the League of Nations to help in providing a solution. There was a tense atmosphere throughout the proceedings, which was due in some measure to the feeling that the debates were being carefully followed by Goebbels and his Ministry of Propaganda, and also to the suspicion that some of his agents might be lurking about. There were no delegates from Germany, as the views of the Nazi Government had been expressed too clearly in the *Voelkischer Beobachter* for any German Zionist to take the risk. There was also missing an important personage who had dominated all previous Congresses and Conferences since the issue of the Balfour Declaration — Dr. Chaim Weizmann. He deliberately absented himself and was staying in Switzerland, where he was kept informed

[1] August 22nd, 1933.

of developments daily by telephone. The Congress decided to create a Central Bureau for the Settlement of German Jews in Palestine, of which he was elected Director.

But another matter that agitated the delegates even more deeply was the tragic fate that had overtaken Dr. Chaim Arlosoroff, the Labour member of the Executive, who had been in charge of its political department in Jerusalem. He was assassinated on the beach of Tel-Aviv two months before, and although a member of the Revisionist party, after being convicted of the crime, was acquitted on appeal, the Labour leaders were convinced that the Revisionists, their bitterest opponents, were responsible for the loss of their gifted young colleague. They had brought with them from Palestine documentary material which, in their view, pointed to the existence of a terrorist group of the Revisionists, and after it had been examined by the General Council, the proposal was made to appoint a commission that should carry out an investigation in Palestine, with a view to the necessary measures being taken. This proposal gave rise to the most stormy and violent scenes that I ever witnessed either in the General Council or the Congress, owing to the indignant protests of Jabotinsky and his followers and the more passionate counter-cries of the Labour delegates, but eventually it was adopted by an overwhelming majority. It was this tempestuous question that was largely the cause for the protraction of the Congress, which lasted three weeks and ended after an all-night sitting of eleven hours.

This Congress too was the only occasion on which I lost my passport. In the afternoon before the day on which I intended leaving for Vienna by a very early train, I began making preparations when I discovered that my passport was missing. I made the most thorough search in my room in the hotel and appealed to the manager, but all in vain. He thought it must have been stolen by a Nazi agent. It was already 4 o'clock, the British Consulate was due to close in an hour, and my train was leaving at 6.30 in the morning. How could I possibly get a new passport in time? I at once rang up the British Chargé d'Affaires, whose acquaintance I had made when he delivered a message from the British Government at the opening session of the Congress, and whom I had invited to lunch some days later. I

PRELUDE TO CALAMITY

explained to him my desperate plight, whereupon he kindly agreed to telephone the Consul at once to await my visit and to remain in his office until he could issue me a new passport. I also telephoned the Consul and he advised me to lose no time in hurrying to a photographer to get the requisite photographs. Within an hour I had copies of what purported to be my portrait and rushed with them to the Consul, and after the usual formalities were discharged I emerged with a new passport.

I went to Vienna to see a brother of mine, who was living there at the time, and found the once proud capital of a former powerful Empire looking frowsy and doleful, although its restaurants still provided appetising fare. From there I continued my journey to Rimini, to join my wife for a holiday. We stayed in that historic city for over a week, during which we made trips to Ravenna, to see its Byzantine colonnades and mosaics, and then to the little, comic-opera Republic of San Marino, on a mountain-side, which presented a picturesque scene in all its mediaeval panoply. We also witnessed the unveiling of a new bronze statue of Julius Caesar, which had been presented by Mussolini to perpetuate the association of the founder of the Roman Empire with the city. It was placed on the column in a public square from which Caesar, after crossing the Rubicon, set out on his successful march to Rome. It was from the same spot that Mussolini set out on his own triumphant march to the capital in 1922, and he was expected to be present at the festive ceremony. But the public, who had decorated the square with flags and bunting, had to be content with the speech of a bemedalled General, who eloquently dilated on a comparison between the achievements of the great Caesar and those of his modern counterpart, and was richly rewarded by the plaudits of soldiers and Fascists.

From Rimini we went to Rome, where I called on the Chief Rabbi, Dr. Sacerdoti, to inquire about the position of the Jews in Italy. We naturally touched on the persecution of the Jews in Germany, and he told me that many of them had already migrated to Italy and received a sympathetic welcome. Dr. Sacerdoti was at that time on friendly terms with Mussolini, and he informed me that when the Nazi Government, at the end of March, 1933, decreed

A JEWISH PILGRIMAGE

a three days' boycott against the Jews, Mussolini telephoned to Hitler and by his personal intervention secured the reduction of the boycott to one day. But within a few years Mussolini had succumbed to the wiles or spell of Hitler, abandoned his pro-Jewish attitude, and swallowed all the noxious principles and practices of the Nazi ideology.

VI

The disappearance of German Jewry from the contributors to the funds for Palestine and the need of augmenting these funds owing to increased requirements made it desirable to discover some new source of revenue. I was therefore asked by the Directors of the Keren Hayesod (Palestine Foundation Fund) in November, 1934, to undertake a tour in Spain and Portugal. Although the total number of Jews in those countries at that time was estimated to be only about five thousand, and comparatively few were distinguished for their financial support of the Jewish National Home, it was nevertheless thought that such a tour would prove worth while. I might be fortunate enough to evoke a generous response, and in any case my visit might prepare the way for other emissaries in the future.

I found that the Jewish community in Madrid was much smaller than I had anticipated. The total number of registered members of the religious congregation was under fifty. There were more Jews than that in the city, but most of them did not wish to be associated with the synagogue and many did not wish even to be known as Jews. They lived in seclusion and isolation. So invisible were they that a Polish Jew told me that he had lived in the city three years before he accidentally discovered the existence of other Jews by overhearing them behind him in a cinema talking Yiddish. Mixed marriages were frequent. There were certain families of which some members were openly Jewish, while the others professed either Protestantism or Catholicism. The language spoken by most of the Jews among themselves was German, due to the majority having come either from Germany or from other parts of Central and Eastern Europe.

The poverty of the community was sufficiently evidenced by the fact that it had no synagogue. Its conforming members met for

PRELUDE TO CALAMITY

religious worship in a couple of rooms on an upper floor of some premises in a business street near the famous Puerta del Sol, and when I went there on a Sabbath morning I had to mount some seventy steps of a narrow staircase. There was no notice or emblem of any kind to mark the entrance to the place of worship, but after I pressed an electric button the door was opened and I found myself in the midst of a small congregation of the faithful. It was strangely reminiscent of the middle ages, when Jews met for prayer secretly to escape the eyes and the arm of the Inquisition. The service was conducted by a layman, for the community could not afford to have a Rabbi or a cantor[1]. I had, therefore, to scale down my expectations very drastically when I spoke to a modest gathering in the same place the following day. It was quite out of the question to meet in an hotel or public hall, because there was no money to pay for the hire and, above all, because it was the general wish that no news of the meeting should leak out.

But for my disappointment at the scanty fruits of my visit I was consoled by the opportunity of seeing the sights of the Spanish capital, especially the art treasures of the Prado. And I was more than richly rewarded when I spent a day in the neighbouring city of Toledo, which, in mediaeval times, had given birth to the greatest Hebrew poet since the close of the Bible, Judah Halevi, and to a veritable galaxy of Jewish scholars and statesmen, physicians and astronomers. Two venerable buildings still survived as testimony to the glorious age of Spanish Jewry — the imposing and ornate church, Santa Maria la Blanca, originally a synagogue in the fourteenth century, and the " El Transito " Synagogue, erected at the same time by the ill-fated treasurer of Pedro the Cruel, Samuel Halevi, whose stately home later became the abode of El Greco.

From Madrid, after a train journey of fourteen hours I reached Lisbon, where I found a community that was alive and with a sense of responsibility. The Sephardim had come originally from Morocco, partly from Gibraltar, and some *via* the Azores, while the Ashkenazim had trickled in before the First World War from Germany, Austria,

[1] The first Jewish religious service in Madrid conducted by a visiting Rabbi since the expulsion of the Jews from Spain in 1492 took place, with the official cognisance of the authorities, on New Year's day in September, 1953.

and Poland. They had separate places of worship, but met together in a social club, where I addressed a fair-sized meeting. The financial response was satisfactory, especially from some of the Sephardim, who formed the wealthier section of the community, and many of whom also had houses at Estoril. They had produced some notable scholars and scientists, one of whom, Professor M. B. Amzalak, economist, Orientalist, and a prolific author, was the acknowledged head of the community.

The next city where I tried my fortune was Gibraltar. It took me nearly a day-and-a-half to get there, as I had to travel, *via* Seville and Cadiz, by train, motor-coach, and ferry, but I no sooner arrived than I realised that my journey was in vain. For the Jews of Gibraltar, although they prayed in four synagogues for the restoration of Zion, either could not or would not give any money for the purpose. So I lost no time in returning to Seville, in order to make for my final destination, Barcelona. I stayed in Cordova *en route*, the birthplace of Maimonides, whose memory, after eight centuries, was shortly to be honoured by the Spanish Government by holding an impressive ceremony, to which representatives of the universities of many lands were being invited. A little quiet cobble-paved square had recently been renamed " Plazuela de Maimonides," and from it stretched a narrow straggling lane, called " Judios," which formerly bore the name, " Calle Maimonides," because in it was reputed to be the house in which the philosopher was born. It was in this lane that I saw what still remained of a mediaeval synagogue in Moorish style, with a recess that once contained the Ark of the Law, and the walls decorated with florid arabesques, alternating with the traditional motifs of the " Shield of David," the palm-leaf, and the tree of life.

Barcelona proved to possess the largest Jewish community in the whole of Spain. It consisted entirely of immigrants, who had come from various parts of Europe as well as from Morocco and Egypt, but owing to their diversity of origin as well as of social status and religious outlook it was difficult to establish any proper unity. Nevertheless a synagogue was maintained on the ground floor of a large private house, which was a more commodious and attractive place of worship than the one in Madrid. It was there that I addressed a

PRELUDE TO CALAMITY

meeting in German with a satisfactory result, which was considerably augmented after I had made a number of personal visits.[1]

After five very interesting, and, for the most part, pleasant weeks in the Iberian Peninsula, I was back in London before the end of December, 1934.

VII

The Congress in the summer of 1935 marked the return of Dr. Weizmann to the Zionist scene and likewise his return to the official leadership. It was held in Lucerne, which was quite immune from any sort of Nazi influence, direct or indirect, and where the delegates were free to express themselves on the increasing tragedy of German Jewry without any inhibition. Dr. Weizmann, who, at the beginning of the deliberations, was not a member of the Executive, was elected President of the Congress, but the burdens of that office were shared in turn by a number of vice-presidents. Mr. Sokolow, who gave a critical address on " The Situation of the Jewish People," delivered a scarifying indictment of Nazi barbarism and demanded that the disfranchisement and degradation of a race should be forbidden by international action just like slavery. Dr. Arthur Ruppin, the sociologist, in his survey of the German problem, stated that 25,000 Jews from that country had already settled in Palestine and brought £8,000,000 with them. The most serious Palestinian question discussed was the Government's proposal to set up a Legislative Council, which was very strongly deprecated by Dr. Weizmann on the ground that it would engender friction and bitterness and obstruct the efforts to increase Jewish immigration and colonisation.

Owing to the feeling of revulsion for all things German, the German language was hardly spoken by any delegate from the rostrum. For the first time Hebrew became the official language in practice as well as in theory, and far more delegates than on previous occasions used Yiddish. The change meant some relief for me, since no translations into German were called for. It was a much quieter Congress than that of 1933, as Jabotinsky and his Revisionist party had seceded from the Zionist Organisation a few months before owing

[1] I revisited Barcelona in the summer of 1950, when I found that the Jewish community had developed considerably (see my *Travels in Jewry*). A Synagogue has since been built and was opened in 1955.

to their unwillingness to refrain from indulging in their independent political activity and their refusal to conform to discipline. Their absence made it easier to arrange for Weizmann to return to his former office. When he was sounded on the matter he replied that he would agree to resume the Presidency only on condition that he was free to choose his own Executive, otherwise he would serve as head of the Political Department under the continued presidency of Sokolow. There was a general desire, however, to see Weizmann back again in his former position of dignity and authority. He was, therefore, re-elected President of the Organisation on his own terms, and Sokolow was elected Honorary President. It was a bitter pill for Sokolow to swallow, and he did not survive it for even a year.

VIII

Immediately after the Congress my wife and I left for Trieste to sail to Palestine. I had not been there since 1921, and my wife had never been there at all, so that we looked forward to the visit with equal enthusiasm. We travelled on the *Galilea*, the captain of which was an Italian Jew, and as many of the passengers had also come from Lucerne the voyage seemed an extension of the Congress debates. Indeed, one member of the Executive gathered around him on the deck a large group of young people, to whom he discoursed at length on the developments in the Land of Israel.

Such tremendous progress has since taken place in Palestine, particularly since the establishment of the State of Israel, that there is no need to describe here in detail the conditions that we found in September, 1935.[1] It must suffice to summarise our experiences and impressions. We landed at Jaffa and stayed a week in Tel-Aviv, from where we made excursions to over a dozen rural settlements, including both the earliest, Rishon le-Zion, Rehoboth, and Petach Tikvah, as well as some of the new ones, Ramath Gan and Ramath Hashavim, where we saw how German lawyers had rapidly developed into successful farmers. There was everywhere an air of bustle, animation, and ceaseless industry, which speedily gave way at the approach of Friday evening to the perfect peace of Sabbath, when

[1] In 1935 Palestine had 310,000 Jews in a total population of 1,195,000. In January, 1956, Israel had 1,591,000 Jews in a total population of 1,789,000.

PRELUDE TO CALAMITY

traffic vanished from the streets as though there were a general strike. From Tel-Aviv we drove through the picturesque village of Zichron Jacob to Haifa, where we stayed for a time in a pension on Mount Carmel, the inspiring associations of which blended harmoniously with a magnificent view of the Mediterranean. We then passed through a few pleasant villages, including Balfouria, a thriving memorial to the author of the Balfour Declaration, and reached Jerusalem a day before the Jewish New Year.

We were impressed by the fortress-like building which contained the offices of the Jewish Agency and of the Zionist Organisation and its affiliated institutions, and spent some time in going from room to room and chatting with members of the Executive and officials. On the eve of the New Year we were conducted through the narrow tortuous alleys, past a buzzing Arab bazaar, to the imposing remnant of the Second Temple, the Western Wall, before which stood, in reverent mood, a group of devout worshippers, pouring forth their supplications for the restoration of Zion, as countless generations before them had done for close upon two thousand years. We attended the Bnei Jeshurun Synagogue, where the service was conducted, more movingly than by a professional cantor, by the late Dr. Mordecai Eliash, who was afterwards appointed the first Minister of Israel to the Court of St. James's.[1]

Our days in Jerusalem were brimful of varied interest not only because we visited the Hebrew University, the Mosque of Omar, and other notable institutions, but also because it formed the starting point from which we went to see the Tomb of Rachel and the Pools of Solomon, the sacred cities of Bethlehem and Hebron, and, even more awe-inspiring than these, the grandiose and ravishing spectacle of the Dead Sea, whose torpid, azure-coloured waters had been turned as by magic into a source of life. On our final tour we visited the forlorn-looking Samaritans at Nablus, saw the remains of an ancient synagogue at Beth Alfa, stayed overnight at Tiberias, viewed the recently recovered relics at Capernaum, drove up steep mountain-roads to the city of the mediaeval Cabbalists, Safed, and returned through the model village of Nahalal to Haifa, where we waited

[1] He died in 1950.

for the luxurious *Esperia*, which was to take us back to Europe. But we not only saw scores of places of historic or modern interest, and countless scenes of ineffable beauty under a radiant, blue sky, but also had innumerable talks with people who had either already played a part in the evolution of the new Judaea, like Max Bodenheimer,[1] a fellow-worker of Herzl, and Meir Dizengoff,[2] a founder and first Mayor of Tel-Aviv, or with others who became famous in later years, like David Ben-Gurion, the first Prime Minister of Israel, and Professor Sukenik,[3] the discoverer of the Dead Sea Scrolls.

The *Esperia* docked at Alexandria, where, on attending the synagogue for the Feast of Tabernacles, we were welcomed by the Chief Rabbi, the late Dr. David Prato, whom I had known in Milan in earlier years, and who invited us into the beautifully adorned congregational *Succah*.[4] Just before the ship was to leave for Naples a large number of young and ardent black-shirted Italians, who were seen off by relatives and friends with much kissing and hugging, came on board laughing and shouting. They were volunteers for the war against Abyssinia. They listened intently to a short and rousing speech by an officer, and replied with resounding cheers for Mussolini. Their journey homewards was not only an overture to winning a spurious and fleeting glory for the ambition-intoxicated Duce. It was also a prelude to the great calamity that was to break out upon the world.

---

[1] Died in 1938.
[2] Died 1936.
[3] Died 1953.
[4] Tabernacle.

Chapter Nineteen

IN THE SHADOWS

1935 — 1939

I

THE return of Dr. Weizmann to the Presidency was marked by a reduction of the administrative machinery in Great Russell Street, partly because the Lucerne Congress decided that there should be only one other member of the Executive in London, namely, Professor Brodetsky, and partly because the Organisation Department was transferred to Jerusalem. The shrinkage of the London Executive inevitably meant fewer formal meetings, especially as Weizmann was not fond of them, but this lull was only temporary. There soon began a succession of political developments of the highest importance in connection with Palestine, which brought the leading members of the Jerusalem Executive, David Ben-Gurion and Moshe Shertok (now Sharett), as well as non-Zionist representatives of the Jewish Agency Executive, to London for prolonged conferences and momentous decisions.

The resumption by Weizmann of the leadership also meant the gradual effacement of Sokolow. Although the latter had been elected Honorary President, he knew full well that this was an empty title, and although also appointed President of a new Cultural Commission for the furtherance of a knowledge of Hebrew culture among Jews throughout the world, he was not provided with the requisite means for the discharge of this onerous task. Since he was fond of travelling the Directors of the *Keren Hayesod* (Palestine Foundation Fund) invited him to undertake a propaganda journey to the Argentine, where he was sure to be welcomed with every mark of honour and the plaudits of large communities. The journey was planned for the early summer in 1936, and he looked forward to it eagerly. Meanwhile he wrote (in a tiny yet remarkably clear calligraphy) for the Hebrew press in Palestine and the Yiddish press in Poland, while continuing to work methodically at a Hebrew Dictionary, upon which he had been engaged for several years, and which accompanied him on all his travels. But all these offices, plans, and activities failed to console him for the feeling of diminished prestige and increasing isolation. The last straw had been the transfer of the official Hebrew weekly, *Haolam*, to Jerusalem, which took place immediately after the Congress. It had been decided upon without previous consultation with him, and he felt it acutely as a personal blow because that journal had been his own creation. He had brought it into existence in the early days of the movement, watched over it with paternal solicitude, and now, in his old age, after being deprived of the Presidency, he was robbed of this last remaining symbol of influence and authority. Throughout the thirty years that I had known him I had always found him calm and imperturbable in the face of even the sorest trial and provocation. But when *Haolam* was taken away he gave vent, before a small circle of friends, to a pitiful outburst of anger and resentment such as I had never seen before. He survived it for less than twelve months.

On a Sunday afternoon, May 17th, 1936, I had a reception at my house on the occasion of the *Bar-Mitzvah*[1] of my younger son, Jonathan, at which I expected Sokolow and his daughter, Dr. Celine Sokolow. When the latter came she told me that her father would be following later. But after a while the telephone rang and Dr. Sokolow was asked to return home immediately. When she arrived there, her father had already passed away. He met with an ideal end. He was seated at his desk, with a pen in his hand, when death stole upon him unannounced.

Nahum Sokolow had been a dominating figure in the Jewish world during the last twenty-five years of his life and a notable personality, before that period, for an almost equal number of years. He was unquestionably one of the great Jews of his time, a distinction

[1] Confirmation at the age of thirteen.

that he attained solely by means of his original and prodigious achievements. He possessed a singular combination of gifts and talents, by virtue of which he rose to the position of eminence that he adorned. A partial bibliography shows that between 1878 and 1936 he wrote thirty-six books, edited ten periodicals and annuals, and wrote thousands of articles. He was equally at home in the company of statesmen and scholars, of Rabbis and journalists, ready to engage in spirited conversation with any of them on any topic they might choose and in almost any language they might speak. Although he had never attended a university, he was more of the savant than many a professor, and although in the political maelstrom of the Zionist world for nearly forty years he was never identified with a party. Throughout his life he preserved a mood of serenity that was but seldom broken, and up to the day of his death, beneath an apparently Olympian exterior, there breathed an air of undying optimism.

II

Among the questions about which Mr. Sokolow was particularly concerned was the tragic plight of the Zionists in Russia. Before the First World War the Zionists in that country had not only formed the largest proportion of the movement, but also provided some of its most important and influential leaders. But soon after the Bolshevik Revolution they began to be frowned upon by the Government, and from 1922 they were subjected to systematic and relentless persecution. The reason given for this oppression was that Zionism was regarded as a counter-revolutionary movement and an agency of British Imperialism, and although the caustic criticism of British policy in Palestine by the Zionist leaders should have convinced the Soviet Union of the baselessness of this charge it was either ignored or dismissed as of no account. The arch-persecutors of Zionism were the *Yevsektzia*, the Jewish section of the Communist party, who were invested with full authority to deal with Jewish affairs, and whose main activity consisted in combating the Zionist adherents with the fanaticism and cruelty of the Inquisition until they were disbanded. They began their campaign by branding Hebrew as an instrument of clerical reaction, and accordingly they forbade the teaching of the language and the printing of Hebrew books. Before long Zionists were hunted down like enemies of the State; they were clapped into jail and kept there, in the company of thieves and murderers, for months without trial; and then sentenced, as in the worst days of Tsardom, to years of banishment in remote and inclement regions. They were confined in special political prisons, called *politisolators*, or deported to Northern Russia, Siberia, or Turkestan, and even after their sentences had expired they were doomed to idleness, privation, suffering, and slow but sure demoralisation.

Despite their knowledge of the dangerous risks that they ran, Zionists in Russia continued to engage in underground propaganda, and in the early 'twenties they were estimated to number about 30,000. Their leaders met from time to time in secret conference, known to one another only by a pseudonym but not by their real names (to avoid the risk of betrayal), for the purpose of considering plans for further activity, and then they dispersed to various provinces. Even when discussing how to further their ideal in the face of peril, they were divided in their views as to its realisation in Palestine, for some belonged to the Right and others to the Left Wing of the Socialist party, while others were General Zionists. Now and again the Soviet Government allowed a few of them to go to Palestine: to use its own language, it "banished" them to that country. But before those fortunate beings could get away they had to pay an exorbitant fee for a passport, and then endured a tantalising ordeal until they could find the money.

It was partly from those who succeeded in leaving or escaping from Russia, that the Zionist Executive learned of the martyrdom endured by the devotees. They provided money for their relief or rescue without being sure that the money would reach its destination. It was particularly at a Congress that attention was called to this tragic problem, when resolutions would be adopted expressing sympathy with its victims and appealing to the Soviet Union to cease its persecution. It was on such occasions that I would be furtively approached by a representative of the Russian Zionists with a request that I should keep the Executive ever mindful of their plight, so that his comrades might be saved before it was too late. Their numbers had gradually dwindled, either by death hastened by suffering or — as in some cases — self-inflicted, or owing to despair that had triumphed over faith; but even in the years immediately before the Second World War there were still a few thousand who clung passionately to the conviction that they would be privileged to take part in the rebuilding of Zion.

III

Meanwhile the very existence of the Jewish National Home was threatened by the Arabs, who began an armed revolt against the Mandatory Government, which lasted for three years, until the outbreak of the Second World War. They demanded the stoppage of Jewish immigration, the prohibition of land-sales to Jews, and the creation of "a national representative government," and as these demands were rejected they organised a campaign of murder and outrage, which became so widespread and destructive that military reinforcements had to be despatched to suppress it. The increasing gravity of the situation impelled the British Government, in the autumn of 1936, to send out the Peel Commission to ascertain the causes of the disorders and make recommendations for the prevention of their recurrence. The Commission, after months of inquiry and deliberation, made the sensational proposal that Palestine should be partitioned into a Jewish State and an Arab State, with a separate British enclave including Jerusalem. The Government declared that they would take steps to implement the scheme, but Parliament resolved that it should first be brought before the League of Nations, and when this was done the Council decided to defer consideration of the question.

When the Twentieth Zionist Congress met in August, 1937, in Zurich the delegates were sharply divided in their views on the projected Jewish State, as its advantages and attractions were counterbalanced by the smallness of the territory offered and the loss of the major part of Biblical Palestine. After days of vehement discussion, in which all aspects of the plan were criticised by the spokesmen of all parties, it was resolved by a large majority that negotiations should be conducted with the Government with a view to securing a scheme that would enable the Jews in Palestine to live their own independent national life and that would contribute to the solution of the Jewish problem in other countries. It was for me a harassing and fatiguing Congress, as, in addition to my official duties, I had to telephone to the London office of the *Manchester Guardian* daily from 600 to 1,000 words, besides sending articles to four other papers.

I therefore felt no little relief when I set out for Abano, near Padua, where I took the mud baths for my rheumatism, and where I was joined by my wife for a subsequent holiday on Lake Garda. We renewed our acquaintance with the fascinating city of Padua and attended the Jewish New Year service in its quaint synagogue, and one afternoon the committee of the community held a reception in my honour, at which my health was drunk in " Asti Spumante." But after the speeches were over some of the members spoke to me with anxious looks about the first pinpricks of Anti-Semitism from official quarters that they began to feel and which, they feared, would grow worse. Those fears were realised only a year later, when Mussolini fell under the yoke of Hitler and adopted his anti-Jewish policy.

The reaction of the Arabs to the proposal for the partitioning of Palestine was to resume their campaign of assassination and sabotage, which continued until the outbreak of the Second World War. Their rebellion was the most terrible and sanguinary event, until then, in the history of the Zionist movement, and one that I can recall only with a shudder, even though I was not in Palestine at the time. For cables with news of murders and atrocities came pouring into the Office at all times of the day, day after day and month after month. The Zionist Executive in London at that time maintained a telegraphic news agency, called " Palcor," for the transmission of news from Jerusalem to New York and *vice versa*. In order to save time an arrangement was made with Cable and Wireless that they should immediately forward to New York every message that was received in London, and in the case of cablegrams arriving at night or in the early hours they were read over the telephone to an official at his home for assent to be given for the further transmission. On several occasions during that troubled period it fell to my lot to discharge that function, when I would be aroused by the telephone at my bedside to receive news of the latest Arab outrage before it was

DR. WEIZMANN ADDRESSING THE TWENTIETH ZIONIST CONGRESS, ZURICH, 1937
The Author is in the foreground.

despatched to New York. After that further sleep was impossible.

IV

Parallel with this orgy of slaughter, Hitler's reign of terror was being intensified in Germany and suddenly spread to Austria on his invasion of that country in the spring of 1938. The Zionist Executive were anxious to know what had happened to our friends in Vienna and the Jewish community in general, and sent me to find out and to convey a message of comfort. I was advised to buy a little Union Jack and pin it to my lapel so as to ward off any possible molestation by the Nazis: it proved an effective charm. I travelled *via* Berlin, where I was met by the secretary of the German Zionist Federation, who had reserved for me a sleeper to Vienna. I arrived there on Friday, March 25th, and took a room at the Hotel Metropole, near the Francis Joseph Quay, purposely avoiding the more fashionable hotels near the Opera House, as they were known to be occupied mainly by German officers. I first called upon Dr. Siegfried Schmitz, the journalist who used to edit the *Kongress-Zeitung* and who lived near by. In response to my ring at his flat an eye peered through the peep-hole in the door before I was admitted.

Schmitz was surprised to see me. He whispered to me to speak as softly as possible, and then gave me news of all the evil happenings that had already taken place. He told me that all Zionist offices had been closed and all Zionist activities suspended by order of the Gestapo. All Zionist officials had to present themselves at eight o'clock that morning at the Palestine Office, where they were interrogated by a Nazi official named Eichmann[1]. This individual, who was in charge of all Zionist affairs in Germany, was an expert: he was born in the German colony of Sarona in Palestine, knew Hebrew, and had made a special study of the Jewish problem. He questioned the Zionists not only about their respective activities and hours of work, but also about the party to which they belonged. Among those present was Adolf Boehm (1873 - 1943), to whom Eichmann said that he was pleased to see him, as he had already read the first volume of his history of the Zionist movement, but had not yet found time to read the second. He objected to the existence of so

[1] See Gerald Reitlinger, *The Final Solution*, London, 1954.

many different Zionist bodies and offices, announced that they must all be co-ordinated under a central direction, and ordered Boehm and Schmitz to draw up a plan and submit it to him at eight o'clock on Monday morning. The Nazis could not begin their acts of oppression too early.

On the following day Schmitz accompanied me on a visit to Boehm, but thought it prudent that we should not enter his flat together. Boehm showed me the plan that he had already drafted, but would not give me a copy in case it should be discovered that he had been in touch with me. He had at first declined the request to undertake the task of reorganisation on the ground of inexperience in such matters, but Eichmann insisted, saying that if he had previously worked fourteen hours a day he would have to work sixteen hours in future. The Nazi Commissar had also forbidden him to continue publishing his monthly journal *Palästina*, which he had devotedly edited for many years, a prohibition that had plunged him into a state of depression. Schmitz and I left as we had entered, with an interval of five minutes between us.

In the evening Field-Marshall Goering delivered his widely advertised speech to inaugurate the campaign for the German plebiscite to settle the future of Austria. He spoke in the vast hall of a disused railway station, and the newspapers announced that the speech would be relayed to all restaurants and cafés. As I had no desire to hear it I deferred my supper until half-past nine, by which time I expected that it would be over. But as soon as I entered a somewhat deserted eating-establishment, I heard a thunderous voice, to which about a dozen guests were listening with tense faces. A waiter sidled up to me, whispered that the speech had already lasted an hour-and-a-half, and took my order. For the next half-hour I was condemned to listen to the concluding part of the furious tirade: it was the most menacing part.

" All Jews must leave Austria," bellowed Goering. " Vienna has no longer a right to call itself a German city . . . It has to fulfil tasks in the cultural and economic fields, and in neither can Jews be employed. The Jews must get out, not because of hatred, but because of necessity. The Jews must get out quickly . . . Let the Jews take note that by the end of the four-year plan Vienna will be a German city again. Jews are in control of trade, finance, art, everything. But I am going to alter that. We don't like Jews and they don't like us. We shall make them glad to go away. Vienna shall be free from Jews ! "

It sounded like a death-sentence, and tens of thousands of Jews shuddered behind their darkened windows as they heard it on their radios. Even if Goering had not pronounced their doom, there were too many evidences of Nazi might and malignity to leave them in doubt of their fate. The city was plastered all over with swastikas in all sizes. The black and red hooked-cross was on flags and banners on every public building, in shop-windows and over house-fronts, on military lorries and taxi-cabs. Large portraits of Hitler glared at you from every hoarding, and smaller photographs of him, as well as of Goering and Goebbels, stared at you from most of the shop-windows in the Ring and the Kaerntner Strasse. Kerb-side hawkers were doing a busy trade in the Nazi emblem, and most of the people in the streets were wearing it, if not from conviction, at least as a protection against molestation.

The invaders carried out a systematic campaign of plunder. They had come prepared with lists of Jews whom they intended to arrest, and showed a partiality for those engaged in the jewellery trade. The Gestapo even sent telegrams in the names of their Jewish prisoners to banks or business-firms abroad to secure money, and the fact that they proved so well informed about the financial position of many Jews seemed to show that they had carried out a system of espionage at many leading banks in foreign countries. The Storm Troopers raided both shops and houses of Jews and stole everything of value — money, jewellery, furs, securities, bank-notes, motor-cars, typewriters. While I was in Vienna at least a few thousand Jews in the city were plundered, apart from thousands in the provincial districts. Moreover, not only were all Jewish employees dismissed by Christian firms, but all Jewish firms were compelled to discharge their " non-Aryan " employees, even if they were members of their own family. The wholesale robberies and physical ill-treatment caused an epidemic of suicides, which were already believed to amount to over six thousand, and owing to their number burials were allowed only at night.

The leaders of the Jewish community had been arrested for taking part in the collection in aid of the Schuschnigg plebiscite. They included the President, Dr. Desider Friedmann, and the Zionist leader, Robert Stricker, who were doomed to suffer nearly seven years of agony before meeting their end, like millions of others, in a death-camp in Poland. The Gestapo also compelled the Jews to raise for them an amount similar to that which they had contributed to the Schuschnigg Fund, 800,000 schilling (about £32,000), as proof that they were equally well-disposed to their new masters. Those who were allowed to administer the affairs of the Jewish community were ordered to hasten the emigration of the poor, while the Gestapo continued despoiling all who still had any possessions. One of the leaders still free was Dr. Plaschkess, but he was ill, and when I went to see him in the Rothschild Hospital I found him in pain and anxious about the fate that awaited him after he would be discharged.

There were about 10,000 Polish Jews in Vienna, besides some thousands from Czechoslovakia, Hungary, and Rumania. All Polish Jews who went to the Polish Consulate for visas to enable them to return to their native country had their passports withdrawn if they had been abroad for over five years. The Gestapo threatened that they would gather those Polish Jews together and drive them over the frontier into Poland.

Thousands of Jews were besieging different Embassies and consulates in frantic efforts to obtain visas. They began queuing up at midnight, members of a family relieving one another, so as to make sure of being admitted the following day. At the British Consulate I found the courtyard, the staircase, and the waiting-room crammed with anxious-looking men and women; and I was told that over six thousand had already applied for permits for Palestine and the British Dominions, especially Australia. The feeling of terror could be sensed most keenly in the cafés, where the light-hearted hubbub of conversation of former days had sunk to a timid whisper, for everybody suspected his neighbour, and nobody spoke without first glancing over his shoulder. I met the brother of a friend of mine in a café: he muttered a message while drinking his coffee, asked me nervously whether I was sure that we were not being watched, and disappeared after imploring me to deny, if questioned, that I even knew him. After five days of what seemed to me a prelude to the inferno, I was handed by one of the hotel clerks a cyclostyled note requesting me " most politely " to vacate my room by the following midday " as the Gestapo were coming in." I was not surprised that the Hotel Metropole was to become their headquarters, as I had noticed a gradual infiltration of arrogant-looking German officers about the place. I decided not to wait until the last moment.

Before leaving the city I went with Dr. Schmitz to the Doeblinger Cemetery, to pay a silent tribute to the memory of Theodor Herzl. His grave had been the scene of imposing pilgrimages for over thirty years, and it was feared that Nazi vandals might have desecrated it. We were relieved to find that it had not been touched, and as we walked away we could not help thinking how different the fate of Vienna Jewry, and, indeed, of many other Jewries, might have been if only Herzl's appeal had met with greater understanding and wider support.

V

Early the following morning I took the first train to Prague. On my way to the station I entered into conversation with my taxi-driver and was astonished at his courage in expressing sympathy with the Jews. " Those who are persecuting them will themselves be one day persecuted," he said. " Read the Book of Daniel, chapter 8, verses 23 to 25, and you will find a true description of Hitler:

. . . *There shall stand up a king of fierce countenance, and understanding stratagems. And his power shall be mighty, but not by his own power; and he shall destroy wonderfully, and shall prosper and do; and he shall destroy the mighty and the holy people. And through his cunning he shall cause craft to prosper in his hand; and he shall magnify himself in his heart, and in time of security shall he destroy many; he shall also stand up against the prince of princes; but he shall be broken without hand.*

I could not help marvelling at the Scriptural knowledge displayed by my bucolic-looking driver, who told me that he was an assiduous student of the Bible but never went to Church. He went on quoting other texts foretelling the day when Jehovah would triumph, and excused the swastika on his windscreen on the ground that he would otherwise lose his livelihood.

When the train neared the Czech frontier, and after all customs and passport formalities were over, two plain-clothes officials went from one compartment to another, carefully comparing passengers' names with the entries in a little black book that one of them carried. I breathed more freely after they had gone. I presume that my name was added to the Gestapo's "black list" at a later date.[1]

I spent a day in Prague, during which I was taken by Dr. Angelo Goldstein, a member of the Czech Parliament, to the building of that assembly. He showed me the room that was specially reserved for the use of Jewish members, and I watched a debate from the visitors' gallery. I was also present at a meeting of the Executive of the Zionist Federation, which was attended by some representatives from the Sudetenland, and at which there was an animated discussion of the steps that should be taken in the interests of the Jews of that region who had begun to flee to Prague from the Nazi peril.

I travelled back by the night-train to Berlin, where I also stayed a day. It was long enough to be seized with a sense of the gloom and depression that hung over the city and of the gnawing anxiety that gripped its Jewish community. When I called at the Zionist Office I was informed that most Zionists of the older generation, and very many Jews who had formerly derided the movement, had already left for Palestine, and gradually those of the younger generation were following them. In the general atmosphere of dejection and dread, there was still one place where the Jews sought to banish all care and find relaxation or entertainment. It was the theatre that they were allowed to have exclusively for themselves, and that was intended as some consolation for being strictly forbidden to enter any place of

---

[1] In the summer of 1945 the British military authorities in Berlin discovered, among other documents, a "black list" drawn up by the Gestapo of hundreds of persons, both Christians and Jews, occupying positions in British public life, with a view to their immediate arrest after the planned German invasion of England. The list was published in the *Daily Mail*, September 14th, 1945, and as it was arranged alphabetically my name was in the same paragraph as those of Winston Churchill, Lord Robert Cecil, Sir Stafford Cripps, R. H. S. Crossman, and others.

amusement open to the general public. It was situated in a drab and dismal thoroughfare in the East End, and the entrance was shabby and plebeian. I witnessed a play there — a piece set in ancient Greek times, but relieved by some sly and subtle allusions to contemporary conditions. I was more interested in the audience, however, than in the performance: they all looked sad and dowdy, and seemed reluctant to talk to a stranger. I was impressed above all by the pictorial posters on the walls of the foyer, which gave a glowing account of the life in Palestine enjoyed by the thousands of Jewish children who had gone there from Germany, and which appealed to parents who still had any children at home to secure for them a like happiness without delay.

When I returned to London I reported to the Executive my impressions of the Jewish situation in the countries that I had visited. They realised full well that the only way in which they could help was by rendering possible a much larger influx into Palestine. That was why they looked forward with such impatience to the outcome of the visit to that country of the Woodhead Commission, who were instructed to draw up a scheme of partition that would be " regarded as equitable and practicable." But when the Commission's Report appeared in November, 1938, and the Government declared that the solution of the problem by partition was impracticable, the disappointment in the Zionist world was profound, and it was all the more galling because of the orgy of pogroms that took place in Germany and Austria at the same time. The Executive then requested the Government to allow an increased immigration into Palestine, so as to provide a refuge for the tens of thousands whose lives were threatened. But it was all in vain. The Government responded by convening a Conference of Jews and Arabs, including among the latter representatives of five states neighbouring upon Palestine; and by way of a counterpoise the Executive organised a large Jewish delegation, which included representatives of the anti-Zionist organisation, the Agudas Israel, and of the principal communities. It was a worthy delegation of world Jewry, among the representatives of British Jewry being several men of eminence.[1]

[1] They included Lord Justice Cohen (then Mr. Lionel Cohen, K.C.), the Marquess of Reading, K.C., Mr. James de Rothschild, M.P., and the late Viscount Bearsted.

The Conference was held in February and March, 1939, in the spacious and magnificent rooms of St. James's Palace, whose walls are adorned by impressive paintings of historic interest. Unfortunately it was rendered abortive from the very outset by the refusal of the Arab delegates to meet the Jews, so that the Government had to conduct talks with each side separately. The meetings were presided over by the Colonial Secretary, Mr. Malcolm MacDonald, and as I listened to him calmly and suavely expounding views designed to justify the Government's intended retreat from the Mandate, I could not help wondering whether it was the same man who had taken up a determined stand against the Passfield White Paper nine years before. It soon became evident that the Government had made up its mind to ignore its obligations in order to placate the Arabs, with a view to ensuring their support in the event of war: and when I heard the Foreign Secretary, Viscount Halifax, remark — rather *sotto voce* — that there were times when questions of justice must give way to considerations of expediency, I was astonished at the spectacle of this distinguished High Churchman deliberately donning the cloak of a Jesuit. The outcome of the whole business, as will be generally recalled, was the notorious White Paper of May, 1939, which provided for the establishment of an independent Palestine within ten years, in which the Jews were to be a permanent minority.

When the Zionist Congress assembled in the following August, in Geneva, to consider the White Paper, the shadow of war was already approaching. Dr. Weizmann painted a sombre picture of the suffering and destruction wrought among the Jewish people by the Nazi terror and of the futile efforts of the Evian Conference to devise any measure of relief. He emphasised the fact that when the Jewish Agency submitted to the Conference a plan for the absorption of 100,000 regugees in Palestine within a short time, it was thwarted by the very Power whose duty it was to facilitate the immigration of Jews into that country. He accused the British Government not only of a lack of practical sympathy but of bringing the return of Israel to a standstill at the very moment when the Jewish people was faced by the most appalling and tragic crisis in its history.

The tone and temper of Dr. Weizmann's speech were fully shared

IN THE SHADOWS

by the five hundred delegates at the Congress, who were particularly incensed by the Government's suspension of immigration during the next six months, thus depriving Jews under Nazi tyranny of their only sure means of escape. It was originally intended that the Congress, like most of its predecessors after the First World War, should last a fortnight, but owing to the inexorable approach of the new war it had to be cut short. After it had been in session only a few days I bought a midday edition of the *Journal de Genêve* and read a report of the agreement that had been concluded between Hitler and Stalin. It could not be many days before the first shots would be fired, but such was the absorption of some of the committees in their discussions of resolutions that the precise formulation of an amendment seemed to them at the moment to be of the most supreme and vital consequence. But it soon dawned upon all that the time for arguing about niceties of expression and gradations of emphasis, however strong the indignation that moved them, was now over and the Congress must be brought to a close.

The final session took place on Thursday night, August 24th. There was a tense stillness in the hall when Weizmann, speaking under the stress of deep emotion, said that he hoped that they would all survive the impending conflict and that their work would continue. Then, rising above the grievances with which they had been so intensely concerned, he declared that there were higher interests that were common to them and the Western democracies, and "their fight is our fight." He was followed by the dour, grey-bearded President of the Congress, Menahem Ussishkin, who, in closing the proceedings, dwelt on the world catastrophe that was about to break out and the fate that was awaiting the Jews in the lands of Central and Eastern Europe as well as those in Palestine. Then, as though glimpsing a vision of the colossal extermination that was to take place, he uttered the hope that the Jews of Poland would not have to suffer too much in the disaster that threatened. In the traditional Hebrew phrase, he bade them all: "Go in peace." Thereupon the vast assembly — delegates, visitors, and journalists — rose and fervently sang "Hatikvah," and with mutual good wishes that they would meet again in better times, accompanied in many cases by an

A JEWISH PILGRIMAGE

embrace and even a kiss, they streamed out of the building at one in the morning to hasten back to their homes in all parts of the globe.

Chapter Twenty

A VARIED CAVALCADE

1919 — 1939

I

DURING the twenty-one years that I was at the Zionist headquarters in London I witnessed a constant procession of persons and personalities, who ascended either to the first floor, to see Weizmann or Sokolow, or to the next floor to see me or somebody else. They were of all degrees, from the most eminent to the lowly; they came from over a score of countries; and they spoke a variety of tongues. Some of them came to give advice, others to gather information, others again to secure favours, and still others to attend the succession of Conferences that helped to fashion Zionist history. They included Peers and politicians, Chief Rabbis and communal leaders, Generals and lawyers, authors and artists, journalists and detectives, philanthropists and concession-seekers, as well as men who afterwards became Premiers and judges. Several of them have already been mentioned in the course of this book; of the others only a selection can be given here.

A year after Lord Samuel retired from the position of High Commissioner for Palestine, he, in conjunction with Dr. Weizmann, convened an important Conference (in 1926) at the Office for the purpose of dealing with the economic and financial aspects of the upbuilding of the Jewish National Home. It was at a time of one of the recurring economic crises in Palestine, and it was thought that only a gathering of the best available experts, meeting for a four days' private and thorough discussion, could devise the requisite measures to remedy the disquieting situation. Among the authorities who came from various lands were Leon Blum (later three times Premier of France), Oscar Wasserman, the Berlin banker, Judge Visser, of the Hague, Senator della Torre, a big industrialist from Milan, Ernest Kahn, the Financial Editor of the *Frankfurter Zeitung*, Dr. Arthur Ruppin, the economic expert from Palestine, besides Mr. James de Rothschild, M.P., and others from London. It was no part of the business of the Conference either to provide money or even to initiate an appeal for funds. It limited itself to examining the adequacy of the resources of the Zionist Organisation and of its financial institutions for its manifold tasks, and to formulating proposals whereby those resources could be increased or supplemented. The discussions, under the chairmanship of Lord Samuel, were strictly business-like and free from long or passionate speeches, which were more usual in the Conference Room; and it was gratifying to see how the Socialist Blum and the capitalist Wasserman debated different points in the most friendly manner and the most harmonious spirit.

Probably the two most famous men who honoured the Zionist Office with a visit were Field-Marshal Smuts and Professor Einstein. Smuts was a staunch and valuable friend of the Zionist movement from the inception of the Balfour Declaration. He was once (in 1928) offered the position of High Commissioner in Palestine, but refused it because he would not leave the political scene in South Africa for a few years. He could always be relied upon to make strong representations to the British Government when Jewish interests were threatened, and his talk with Dr. Weizmann was in private. Einstein's only visit took place in 1933, soon after Hitler seized power. He had just returned from lecturing in the United States, and as press attacks against him had already been made in Germany it was obviously impossible for him to go back to that country. I could not help being struck by the air of simplicity and other-worldliness that emanated from him. When he spoke to you he seemed to look far beyond you to remote astral spheres. While he was in London I was rung up by an official of the Spanish Embassy, who told me that his Government wished to offer Einstein a Chair at the Madrid University and would be honoured if he would accept it. I replied that similar offers had already been made by other Governments and I would be pleased to convey his proposal to the Professor. He seemed quite annoyed with me for not holding out any hope that it would certainly be accepted.

II

Apart from Justice Brandeis the two most outstanding American Jews whom I met were Louis Marshall (1856 - 1929) the famous lawyer, and Felix Warburg (1871 - 1937), the financier, who were brought into close contact with the Zionist Organisation through its extension as the Jewish Agency. Marshall was then not only President of the American Jewish Committee but also the undisputed leader of American Jewry in a sense that none of his successors as President could claim to be. It was largely thanks to Weizmann's success in winning Marshall over to his ideas that the support of the wealthy and influential section of American Jewry was secured, with the result that it was comparatively easy thereafter to obtain the active cooperation of non-Zionist circles in other countries. Weizmann's meetings and conferences with Marshall were all brought to a satisfactory consummation in the United States, so that it was not until the summer of 1929 that the American leader first came to the Zionist Office in London, on the way to Zurich, where the formal inauguration of the enlarged Jewish Agency was to take place. It was his only visit, as he died in Zurich almost immediately after the Conference.

Felix Warburg, on the other hand, was at the Zionist Office several times both before and after the founding of the Agency. He was fifteen years younger than Marshall, but outlived him only by eight. He was a millionaire and looked like one in dress and deportment — with his well-cut elegant clothes, carefully curled black moustache, and a white rose always in his button-hole. He presided over the Administrative Committee of the Agency in a business-like fashion, and as he spoke German as well as English he did not need help from me as much as did other chairmen.

There were two men of strongly marked individuality who came to the Office a number of times in the early twenties in connection with important projects in Palestine, and whose discussions with the Executive, and especially with Dr. Weizmann, usually generated a certain amount of heat. One was Pinchas Rutenberg, a man of massive frame and iron will, who had played a part in the revolutionary movement in Russia in the last years of the Tsardom, and whose name was whispered in connection with the fate of Father Gapon; the other was Sir Elly Kadoorie, a native of Baghdad who had become a millionaire in Shanghai. Rutenberg, an engineer, was busy drawing up plans for harnessing the Jordan for electricity and was intent upon obtaining a concession from the Mandatory Government as well as securing the capital requisite for its fulfilment. He needed the political support of the Executive for the former and the co-operation of the *Keren Hayesod* in connection with the latter, and there were repeated exchanges of views — in an increasing temperature — about the proportion of control to be allotted to those bodies on the board of the company to be entrusted with the concession.

Kadoorie[1], the Oriental philanthropist, short, well-groomed, paunchy, with close-clipped grey moustache, and oozing with opulence, was anxious to immortalise himself by the establishment of a " colony " or settlement in Palestine bearing his name. He drew a roseate picture of its distinguishing features as visioned in his fantasy, with beautiful gardens and plashing fountains to please the eye, but the amount of money that he was prepared to give for the realisation of his dream and the conditions attaching to his gift made it difficult to come to an agreement, especially as the Executive were afraid of becoming saddled with a heavy financial liability. As a last resort, Sir Elly invited me to lunch at his princely mansion at Princes' Gate to discuss the project, in the hope that I might talk the Executive round. But the scheme never materialised.

III

Among the many people who called on me at the Office were men whom I had previously met in the course of my varied travels in the interests of the movement; others whom I had known when I lived abroad before the First World War; and others again whose friendship I had enjoyed in my student days. Most of them have long

---

[1] Not to be confused with his brother, Sir Ellis Kadoorie, of Hongkong, who died in 1922 and left £100,000 for Palestine, which was used to build separate agricultural schools for Jews and Arabs.

gone the way of all flesh, and all have left for the most part a pleasant memory.

One who had played an authoritative part in Zionist affairs for several years from the days of Herzl was Jacobus Kann (1872 - 1944), who had helped very substantially in the founding of the first Zionist bank — the Jewish Colonial Trust. He was a leading banker at The Hague, but with his fair beard and butterfly-tie looked more like a Bohemian artist. I first made his acquaintance when I was at the Zionist headquarters in Cologne, to which he used to come for meetings of the Executive. After the outbreak of the First World War, when I was in Berlin, I was able to communicate with my family in England (before my internment) by addressing letters for them to Kann, who forwarded them, and I received replies through the same medium. When the war was over he came to London from time to time to attend meetings of the Board of the *Jewish Chronicle* of which he was a director, and invariably looked into my room for a chat about old times and comments on the new. Unfortunately, when the war began in 1939 he did not escape from Holland when he could have done so, and he ended his days in a concentration camp.

Another Zionist veteran who looked in once or twice was Dr. Alfred Klee, who had been one of Herzl's most devoted and eloquent supporters. He was a popular lawyer in Berlin in the days when I lived there, and I often enjoyed his stimulating company. Soon after Hitler seized power, Klee went to Hanover on some legal business, and from there telephoned to his son in Berlin to let him know when he would return. The son thereupon impressed upon his father not to return in a hurry, as " the state of his health " surely made it necessary for him to go abroad for a " cure," Alfred Klee, who was a prominent leader of the Jewish community in the German capital, understood that this was a hint not to return and risk arrest, and therefore immediately got a reservation in a sleeping-car for Holland. He told the conductor that he was very tired and unwell and did not wish to be awakened at the frontier, and as he pressed a handsome tip into his hand he was allowed to leave the country undisturbed. I advised him to remain in England, although there was no talk of war

A JEWISH PILGRIMAGE

at the time, but there was nothing with which he could have occupied himself here. So he returned to Holland, where he was eventually caught by the Nazis, and he also died in a concentration camp.

Two men from Palestine whom I was particularly pleased to welcome were Chaim Nachman Bialik (1873 - 1934), the national poet, and Meir Dizengoff (1861 - 1936), the founder and first Mayor of Tel-Aviv — both natives of Russia. Bialik, who had already become famous before the First World War as the greatest Hebrew poet since the middle ages, was often in London either to attend a conference or on his way to and back from America, where he addressed public meetings in aid of a fund-raising campaign. He owed both his life and his freedom to Maxim Gorky, who intervened on his behalf when his protests against the Bolshevik persecution of Hebrew and the Jewish religion exposed him to arrest. He had written his best and most passionate poems in the days of the Tsardom, when the barbarous pogroms wrung from him a flaming denunciation in the language of Isaiah of the miscreants who had committed them and a bitter reproach against his own fellow-Jews for lack of courage in their self-defence. But by the time he came to London he had passed through the worst anguish of his life, His rotund, clean-shaven face and bald head made him look anything but poetical, but he spoke softly, slowly, reflectively, like a man of sorrows.

Dizengoff was quite a different type, a blend of the idealist and man of action, who joined the " Lovers of Zion " movement at the age of twenty-one at the risk of imprisonment, laid the foundations of Tel-Aviv in 1906, and adopted such a bold attitude towards the Turkish Generalissimo, Djemal Pasha, during the First World War that he was banished from Palestine. The town that he brought into existence, and which is now the largest city in Israel, was still in its infancy when he came to my house one day for lunch, and as I took him later through Golders Hill Park he was full of admiration and said he would be happy to see even a small park some day in Tel-Aviv. He studied with interest the particulars itemised on my Rate Demand from the Borough of Hendon, and I gladly gave him some receipted Demands so that his Town Clerk could use them as a model.

A VARIED CAVALCADE

IV

Quite a bevy of distinguished professors came to the Office from time to time. From Budapest came Professor Adolf Strauss, who had been of such valuable service to me in connection with the purchase of the Goldziher Library for the Hebrew University.[1] Before the First War he used to visit Sofia to lecture at its University, and he entertained me with stories about King Ferdinand, who often invited him to his palace. His visit to London was solely to satisfy his curiosity about the English metropolis, and he was too old to repeat it. From Berlin came Professor Franz Oppenheimer (1864 - 1943) to give three lectures at the London School of Economics. He was a well-known economist and sociologist, with a sabre-slashed cheek due to a duel fought with an Anti-Semite in his student days. He was first introduced to the Zionist world by Herzl at the Sixth Congress (in 1903), and he afterwards drew up the plans for the first co-operative settlement at Merhaviah, in the Vale of Jezreel. I saw a great deal of him when I lived in Berlin, and it was he who introduced me to the ill-fated Dr. Matthias Erzberger.[2] After the outbreak of the Second War Oppenheimer passed through London on his way to the United States, where he died, in 1943, at San Francisco in poverty and isolation.

From Lisbon came Professor Moses B. Amzalak, also to lecture in London. I had made his acquaintance when I was in the Portuguese capital, in 1934, and was much impressed by the wide range of subjects on which he lectured with authority, extending from economics to Oriental lore. He is the author of an imposing list of books and monographs, and has long enjoyed general respect and regard as the head of the Jewish community in Lisbon.

Two other professors call for mention here. One is Alfred E. Zimmern, author of numerous learned works, who was once Professor of International Politics at Aberystwith University and later Deputy-Director of the League of Nations Institute of Intellectual Co-operation. His Jewish blood prompted him to pay a visit to Palestine very soon after the First War, and when he returned to

[1] See Chapter XIV.
[2] See Chapter V.

339

England he gave an account, to a select gathering in the Office, of his impressions and experiences, delivered with engaging fluency and unrestrained enthusiasm. The other is Professor Hersch Lauterpacht, F.B.A., who was born in Poland. While still a student at the London School of Economics he was temporarily engaged in the Office of the Zionist Organisation to assist my colleague Dr. Leo Lauterbach (the similarity of their names caused some amusement), in connection with the elaborate preparations for a Zionist Congress. It is probably not generally known that when this eminent authority on international law was a candidate for the Chair in this subject at the University of Cambridge, the body responsible for the appointment sounded the Foreign Office on his suitability, as it was customary for the Government to engage or consult the occupant of that post in connection with important matters involving international law. The Foreign Office took exception to his appointment, presumably because of his foreign birth; but the University authorities were so impressed by his superiority over all other candidates that they nevertheless elected him, and when the Foreign Office was informed of the *fait accompli*, a message of congratulation was at once sent to Professor Lauterpacht. He was appointed a member of the Permanent Court of Justice at The Hague early in 1955.

V

From the very beginning the Zionist cause enjoyed the support of many Christian friends, who were influenced either by their study of the Bible and their belief in the prophecies about the restoration of Israel, or by their sympathy with the sufferings of Jewry and their desire to see them ended through the recovery of national independence, or by their conviction that the Jewish settlement in Palestine was of vital service to British policy. It is superfluous here to refer again to Arthur James Balfour, David Lloyd George, and Winston Churchill. I shall confine myself only to those with whom I came into personal contact at the Zionist Office, and who have not already been mentioned in this book.

One of the first to volunteer his aid, who has remained a devoted friend of the movement throughout all the vicissitudes of the last thirty years, was Brigadier-General Sir Wyndham Deedes. He was Lord Samuel's first Chief Secretary in Palestine, and when he left after only two years to return to London, there was sincere regret in Jewish circles, which was all the keener because so many officials in the Administration made no secret of their hostility to the Mandatory policy. Sir Wyndham had given evidence of his attitude even before taking up his appointment in Palestine, for during the 1914 - 18 War he had held an important military post in Constantinople, and when he heard that a Rumanian Jew had been carried off forcibly to the Rumanian Consulate he sent a couple of stalwart " Tommies " to secure his release. Soon after his return to England he gave an address at a meeting in the Hotel Great Central, and never shall I forget the impression it produced. He showed a deep understanding and appreciation of the Zionist philosophy, and I felt as if I were listening to a disciple of Ahad Ha-Am. Not only did he address many meetings in this country, of both Jews and Gentiles, but he also went to Poland, Czechoslovakia, and other lands, where his speeches were applauded at crowded gatherings. He founded the Anglo-Palestine Association, which was afterwards converted into the Anglo-Israel Association, for the furtherance of friendly relation between Jewry and Britain, and devoted much time and energy to its activities.

Two other Generals also made an appearance at the Zionist Office. One was Sir Gilbert Clayton, a dapper figure, who had been Political Officer of the British forces in Palestine under Field Marshal Allenby and afterwards succeeded Sir Wyndham Deedes as Chief Secretary. The other was Sir George Macdonogh, who had been Chief of Intelligence in the First War, and once presided at a private meeting in the Zionist Office — after the war, of course. He was tall, thin, with a slight moustache, and relaxed from his usual professional sternness into the amenities of friendly discussion. There was one other military personage whom I met — Colonel J. H. Patterson, who had been in command of the Zion Mule Corps at Gallipoli and afterwards of the " Judaeans " in the Palestine Campaign. But when the war was over he was doomed to disappointment, as he had hoped to receive a post under the Palestine Administration. Perhaps he had been too friendly with Jabotinsky, who was anything but a *persona grata* with the authorities. He was given to understand that he was not wanted in Palestine, so, after addressing some public meetings in England he went to the United States, where he died a few years ago.

The most resolute and militant Christian champion of the Zionist cause whom I knew was undoubtedly Colonel Josiah Wedgwood, M.P. (afterwards Lord Wedgwood). "Josh," as he was familiarly called by his Zionist as by other friends, was particularly intimate with Weizmann and Joseph Cowen, and usually walked up the stairs of the Office unannounced, as though he were quite at home there. No debate on Palestine in the House of Commons ever took place in which he did not deliver a striking and provocative speech, and there was no searching or critical question in regard to the Jewish National Home that he was not prepared to put either to the Prime Minister or to the Colonial Secretary, and to follow it up with an embarrassing supplementary. No Jewish M.P. ever ventured to indulge in such scathing attacks upon anti-Zionist or anti-Semitic officials in the Palestine Administration with such courage and candour as he generally displayed. Indeed, the Zionist Executive sometimes felt uneasy because of the language that he often used, fearing that he might thereby do the cause more harm than good; and they often withheld information from him lest his use of it might prove detrimental. But no considerations could restrain him from his wholehearted advocacy of the Zionist cause at all times and in all places. He addressed countless public meetings and dinners both in this country and in America, and was a fighter to the last. He founded "The Seventh Dominion League" in the hope that the British Government would favour the evolution of Palestine into a Jewish State on condition that it became a constituent of the British Empire,[1] but his idea, even though promoted and proclaimed at a public meeting, remained still-born.

There was also a woman, who, as the niece of Lord Balfour, felt that it was her mission to do her utmost to ensure the maximum implementation of the Balfour Declaration. Thanks to her social and political connections, Mrs. Blanche Dugdale was able to be of

[1] He expounded his views in a little book, *The Seventh Dominion* (1928).

useful service to Dr. Weizmann and belonged to his little circle of political advisers. She was welcomed occasionally to a meeting of the Executive when some momentous question was under consideration, and I could not help noticing how even Leo Motzkin — always jealous of the rights and prerogatives of the Executive — smilingly deferred to her advice on a matter of tactics or her suggestions for the stylistic improvement of a memorandum or resolution. " Baffy " Dugdale, as she was familiarly called (although her aristocratic bearing hardly encouraged familiarity), was a constant, and for some time even a daily visitor at the Office, and was eventually provided with a room of her own. She was in frequent demand at public meetings, and for some months contributed regularly to the weekly *Zionist Review*.

It was an important requisite of the movement to have influential and well-informed support in the Press, and in this field there was one distinguished journalist in particular, Herbert Sidebotham, who rendered invaluable service. He began his reasoned and cogent advocacy of the cause in the middle of the First World War, when he was on the *Manchester Guardian*, whose editor, C. P. Scott, was a friend of the movement until his death. When he joined *The Times* he continued his championship in its leaders, and later, both as " Scrutator " in the *Sunday Times* and as " Candidus " in the *Daily Mirror*, he was indefatigable in his demonstration of the advantages to Britain of her espousal of Zionist aspirations and infinitely resourceful in his demolition of arguments from the enemy camp. He also wrote the leader in a little weekly journal, *Palestine*, whose combativeness was a thorn in the sides of some of the high officials at the Colonial Office. His unexpected death in 1940 left a gap that was never filled. Another journalist of ability and wide experience, Sidney Dark, took charge of *Palestine*, but he had neither the extensive political knowledge nor the literary skill and logical persuasiveness of Sidebotham. Dark, who closed his career as editor of *The Church Times*, wrote a multitude of books on all sorts of subjects, one of which was entitled *The Jews of To-Day*. In the course of a conversation that he had with me for the purpose of obtaining elucidation of some points, I asked him why he was interested in the Jewish question, whereupon he told me that his grandmother had been a French Jewess.

There were many other Christian friends of the movement with whom I had talks in my room — authors and journalists, politicians and Christadelphian preachers — but their names are too numerous to record and they sought no mention of them.

VI

There were also many people who came to the Office to see me, not because of any interest in the movement, but for the most varied of other reasons — because they wished to seek some favour for themselves or for an institution with which they were connected, or because they wanted some special information that they thought I could provide. A well-known M.P., who had never previously betrayed any sympathy with the movement or any special knowledge of it came to me after he had been defeated in a General Election and asked me if he could be engaged as a propagandist. A former official in a Government department, who had been " axed " on grounds of economy, came to me with a letter of introduction from a Cabinet Minister and offered his services as a publicity expert. A representative of a " Safety First " organisation told me of the difficulties that he had to obtain large donations from the public, and asked if I could furnish him with the names of a dozen wealthy Jews who could be counted upon to make a generous response. And a director of a big insurance company called upon me to inquire if I could let him have the names of two or three energetic Jewish insurance agents, as he had heard that Jews were so much more successful than non-Jews in this branch of business.

One day two Jews from Rumania, with long black beards, long black coats, and big round black hats, were ushered into my room. They told me that they had come from a little town in Transylvania to raise money in London for the building of a Talmud Torah (Hebrew religious school), and showed me a euphuistic Hebrew letter of introduction from their Rabbi, with florid signature and imposing seal, invoking the blessing of Heaven upon all who would contribute to the holy cause. All that they wanted from me was a list of the names and addresses of about two or three dozen rich Jews, such as Rothschild and Montefiore, and they would do the rest. They were convinced that their appeal to the kind-hearted philanthropists in London, " surely all lovers of the Torah," would be rewarded with rich donations, and that they would complete their mission with success in a few days. Neither of them had ever been in London before, and neither could speak a word of English. When I told them that their quest was utterly hopeless and that the best thing that they could do was to return home without delay, they were dumbfounded. They explained that their community had been split for weeks over the question whether they should come to London, and only after the most stubborn and bitter struggle had they triumphed. How could they now return to Transylvania empty-handed ? What shame and humiliation ! They left with bowed heads and broken hearts.

Another day the reception-clerk telephoned up to me that a lady wished to see me and gave the name of a well-known Jewish actress. Presently she came sailing into my room with a sweet, alluring smile and a seductive perfume, and as she took a seat opposite me she revealed a rather larger expanse of *décolléte* than was warranted at that time of the day or was justified by the temperature. She told me that she wished to produce a great and important play, and as she " didn't have the needful " she felt sure that, if she explained the situation, the Zionist Organisation would be only too pleased to help her. She didn't think that she would need more than a few thousand pounds, which must be a trifle to " a great and wealthy organisation." As I listened with apparent sympathy she opened her bag and produced the manuscript of the play, which she offered to leave with me to study. What the title was I have long forgotten, but I quickly realised that the play had not the remotest connection with Palestine or even the very slightest Jewish interest. She rambled on about its wonderful merits, and as soon as I could edge a word in I told her that the funds of the Organisation were not available for her purpose. " But surely, surely," she exclaimed in a melodramatic voice, with beseeching eyes, " for the sake of Zion ! " She must have left a confirmed anti-Zionist.

A JEWISH PILGRIMAGE

A couple of years after my return from the Far East I had a visit from a native of that region — from Korea. He was a short, squat individual, in a rather soiled raincoat, and as he took a seat he began to speak in German. He explained that he had been a student at the Berlin University for some years, and was therefore able to speak German better than English, having been in this country only a short time. When I asked him what he wanted to see me about, he said that he was a member of the Korean revolutionary movement to get rid of the Japanese tyrants, and as the Jews in Palestine also looked forward to regaining independence, he thought I might be able to give him some secret information about our proposed methods and plans. When I told him that we had no such plans he was disappointed and looked rather incredulous. He was pleased, however, when I mentioned that I had been in Korea. His name was Kolu Li, and he gave me two pamphlets that he had written on Korea's struggle against Japanese Imperialism, both in German.

One day I was surprised on being informed on the telephone that a man from Scotland Yard wanted to come up to see me. Not being conscious of having committed any offence myself, and not having heard of any perpetrated by a colleague or a member of the Executive, I wondered what the reason could be for this unusual visit. When the six-foot detective strode into the room and took a seat, he said that he had come to make inquiries about Nahum Sokolow, who had applied for naturalisation. I then remembered that Sokolow had asked me many months before to act as one of his sponsors for this purpose. I also remembered that he had told me that Lord Balfour had also agreed to act as a sponsor. I therefore asked the Scotland Yard man whether he was aware of this notable fact and whether this should not render any further inquiries about Sokolow's qualifications for British citizenship quite superfluous. He replied that he had instructions to follow the usual routine and "check up." The following evening he came to see me at my house, to make sure that I was identical with the person whom he had seen at the Zionist Office. Again, he merely wanted to "check up."

Chapter Twenty-one

ON GUARD

1919 — 1939

I

EVER since I began to take an interest in Jewish affairs I was dominated by a passion to defend any Jewish cause to which I was attached, to repel any attack that might be made upon the Jewish people, and to correct any misrepresentation or untruth that might be published about them. Such was the feeling that animated me from the day that I entered upon the life of a journalist and that continued to possess me throughout the years of my official connection with the Zionist movement and after.

When the Balfour Declaration was published after three years of war, it was greeted by all sections of the British press and public opinion with a unanimous chorus of praise as an act of the wisest statesmanship. I contributed an article on the subject, under the title of "The Development of Political Zionism," to the *Fortnightly Review*,[1] to show that the Declaration formed an epoch-making landmark in the movement for the realisation of an ancient national aspiration. But after the first Arab disorders in Palestine in the spring of 1920, British policy in that country became a subject of controversy, which varied from time to time in extent and vehemence, and which seldom disappeared for any appreciable interval until the end of the Second War, when the dispute broke out afresh in a much more acute and violent form than before. The attacks upon British policy which began in the early 'twenties were largely concerned with Britain's alleged promise of independence to the Arabs in

[1] January, 1918.

Palestine, but although this allegation was officially repudiated by Sir (then Mr.) Winston Churchill, as Colonial Secretary, in 1921, it was repeated over and over again in letters and articles in various newspapers and journals. No sooner did I note this legend in a paper than I immediately sent in a reply to disprove it by referring to the terms of the McMahon Correspondence of 1915, the Feisal-Weizmann Agreement of 1919, Feisal's letter of 1919 to Professor Felix Frankfurter, and the Syrian Delegation's statement to the Peace Conference, supplemented later by the testimony of T. E. Lawrence himself.[1]

There were two other main themes upon which the anti-Zionists used to play: one was the supposed cost of the administration of Palestine to the British tax-payer, and the other was the rumoured connection and even identification of Zionism with Bolshevism. There were various other grounds of objection too, but these were the principal. I had no difficulty in disposing of the first of these objections by showing that the cost of administration was covered by the internal revenue of Palestine. The critics, especially in some London morning papers (notably the *Daily Mail* and the *Daily Express*) usually lumped together Palestine and Iraq (for which Great Britain held a Mandate until 1932), made a clamour about these countries costing the British tax-payer hundreds of millions a year, and agitated for Britain to clear out of them " bag and baggage." Whenever Arab disorders broke out, the demand for British evacuation on the ground of expense was revived. In addition, therefore, to sending dozens of letters at that time to the press I wrote, in 1929, a pamphlet entitled *Palestine and the British Tax-Payer*,[2] in which I showed, not only that the British tax-payer had not contributed a single penny to the creation of the Jewish homeland or the maintenance of the Palestine Administration, but also that the annual cost incurred by the British Exchequer in respect of military and air forces in Palestine and Transjordan had been reduced between 1921 and 1929 from £3,339,000 to £100,000. I also showed that Palestine herself defrayed the excess cost of the British forces stationed

[1] See the author's *The Zionist Movement*, pp. 118-119.
[2] Published by the Jewish Agency for Palestine, London.

in Palestine and Transjordan over the cost of such forces if stationed in Great Britain.

The agitation for abandoning Palestine reached its climax during the three years of Arab rebellion that began in 1936. It was then based not only upon the legendary waste of British money but also upon what made a much stronger appeal to popular sentiment — the loss of British lives. I therefore wrote an article[1] in which, while pointing out that the loss of lives would have been far less if prompt and drastic steps had been taken to suppress the revolt when it first broke out, and if the Jews had been allowed to take an adequate part in their own self-defence, I showed that not only had the disorders not entailed any expense to the British Treasury, but both Treasury and Britain had benefited from the Mandate financially. By the spring of 1936 the Palestine Government had an accumulated surplus of £6,500,000, thanks to the influx of Jewish settlers and Jewish capital and to the prosperity created by Jewish industry and enterprise, so that it was able to dispense with the loan of £2,000,000 which Parliament had voted for the resettlement of " displaced Arabs "[2] and a variety of public works. Moreover, I called attention to the benefits that Britain had derived from her trade relations with Palestine, to the income-tax she received from several Palestinian companies registered in London, to the indirect benefit resulting from the loans given and investments made in Palestine by British banks and insurance companies, to the salaries and allowances amounting to over £400,000 received by British subjects from the Palestine Government, and to the income tax presumably payable by Palestine herself in respect of the substantial portfolio of securities in which her surplus was partly invested. In short, I exploded the current legend that England was pouring treasure into Palestine, and concluded: " The golden tide is flowing in the opposite direction."

The charge about Zionism being connected and even identical

[1] Published under the title, " What Britain makes out of Palestine," in the *Jewish Chronicle*, July 29th, 1938, and reprinted as a pamphlet.
[2] The term " displaced Arabs " was officially defined as " such Arabs as can be shown to have been displaced from the lands which they occupied in consequence of the land passing into Jewish hands, and who have not obtained other holdings on which they can establish themselves, or other equally satisfactory occupation." See *The Zionist Movement*, pp. 195 and 228.

with Bolshevism was so utterly absurd and fantastic that it was astonishing that it was seriously advanced by apparently intelligent people. Even the late Lord Sydenham believed in this nonsense.[1] I had therefore repeatedly to demonstrate its falsity by calling attention to the Soviet Government's suppression of the Zionist movement and persecution of its followers.

II

It was a singular and disquieting feature of the crusade against British policy that its most zealous spokesmen were men who had been appointed and paid to carry out that policy, namely, former officials of the Palestine Government. One of the first was Colonel Vivian Gabriel, who had been Financial Adviser and Assistant Administrator in Palestine in 1918 - 19. In an article in the *Edinburgh Review*,[2] entitled " The Troubles of the Holy Land," he attributed the Arabs' loss of " faith in the sincerity of British promises " to the appointment of Sir Herbert Samuel as High Commissioner and vilified the Jewish National Home in the sentence:

> *The Jews now entering Palestine are not the Rothschilds, Montagus, and Samuels, but the sweepings of the ghettos of Eastern Europe, with no money, no energy, and no ability.*

The next critic was Captain Chisholm D. Brunton, who had been connected with the Military Administration, and who wrote two articles in the *Fortnightly Review*.[3] In the first he betrayed both ignorance and prejudice by asserting that " among Zionist aims is the eventual inclusion of both Syria and Mesopotamia within the Jewish National Home," and in the second he wrote that Sir Herbert Samuel was " a nominee of the Zionist Committee " and that " the real aim of the Zionists is to set up a Communist Jewish State in Palestine." A former Civic Adviser to the City of Jerusalem, Mr. C. R. Ashbee, wrote in *A Palestine Note-Book*, 1918 - 1923 the following sweeping condemnation:

> *The policy of the Balfour Declaration is an unjust policy, and Zionism, as understood and as sometimes practised in Palestine, is based*

[1] See his article, " The Tragedy of Palestine," in *The Nineteenth Century*, May, 1930.
[2] January, 1922.
[3] May, 1923, and January, 1924.

upon a fundamental injustice, and therefore dangerous both to civilisation and to Jewry.

The best known and most relentless assailant of the Mandate policy was Mr. H. St. John Philby, who was chief British Representative in Transjordan in 1921 - 1924. On the occasion of Lord Balfour's visit to Palestine and inauguration of the Hebrew University he contributed an article to the *Nineteenth Century*,[1] in which he stigmatised the University as " the Temple of Mammon " and referred to Balfour as " one who is publicly and peculiarly identified with an act of betrayal for whose parallel, with the shekels and the kiss and all the rest of it, we have to go back to the Garden of Gethsemane." I immediately wrote an article in reply, which was published in the following number of the same review.[2] By far the most cynical and savage onslaught was delivered by Mr. Ernest T. Richmond, Political Secretary to the Palestine Government, also in the same review.[3] He accused the British Government of being " blind to ordinary standards of conduct " and of " appropriating without their consent the revenues of an unoffending people and using their revenues for paying an Administration whose primary duty is to attend not to the welfare and wishes of the taxpayers, but to those of aliens." The climax of his denunciation was in the following terms:

International Jewry and British crankiness . . . combining together, were able to impose upon the League of Nations outward responsibility for the iniquitous document known as the Mandate of Palestine.

Yet despite this abusive outburst, Mr. Richmond was shortly afterwards appointed as Director of the Antiquities Department of the Palestine Government.

These are just a few typical examples of the malignant attacks on Zionist policy and achievements committed by ex-officials, which kept me busy.[4] And lest it should be thought that they were exceptional among the members of the Palestine Administration, I should like to cite the testimony of Mr. Beverley Nichols, who, in

[1] June, 1925.
[2] July, 1925.
[3] July, 1925.
[4] A more detailed account is given in an unsigned article that I contributed to the *Jewish Chronicle*, December 18th, 1936 (pp. 19-20).

his book *No Place Like Home*, describing his impressions of Palestine, wrote that he found the English community " pro-Arab " — " some because they were frankly anti-Semitic." Mr. Nichols went on to say that when he asked an English officer in a very responsible position why he was anti-Jewish, the reply was: " Because the Arab is a gentleman and the Jew is not "; and the cultured answer from an official in the Education Department was: " Because the minute you cease to kick them [the Jews] then they get uppish."

I never kept a detailed record of all the letters and articles that I contributed to the Press in defence of the Zionist cause, but believe that I am not making an overestimate when I say that during the twenty-one years from the beginning of 1919 to tne end of 1939 I must have written about a thousand letters — to morning, evening, weekly and Sunday papers, London and provincial, as well as Colonial and foreign papers. With very few exceptions, they were all published. During one period alone, for which I have a list, from December, 1935, to October, 1936, I wrote over sixty letters, which were all printed. The polemics about Palestine and the frequency of my replies once prompted the editor of *The Jewish Guardian*[1] (the late Laurie Magnus) to devote a leader to the subject, in the course of which he wrote:

Lord Raglan's reply to Mr. Israel Cohen in the English Review, *on 'Lord Balfour in Palestine,' we mention in another column, with very faint admiration; and here we have further to mention a reply by Mr. Israel Cohen to Mr. St. John Philby on ' Palestine and Lord Balfour' in the current* Nineteenth Century. . . . *Moreover, Mr. Israel Cohen is always armed, cap-a-pie, for the Palestine joust. If he is not replying, he is being replied to, and we venture to hazard the conjecture that he is already meditating a reply to Mr. Richmond's article in the* Nineteenth Century.

Apart from the articles already mentioned I also wrote several others (before the war) for monthly reviews,[2] besides two further

[1] July 10th, 1925.
[2] " The Conflict in Palestine," *Eastern Europe*, June, 1922.
" Lord Balfour in Palestine," *English Review*, June, 1925.
" The Tragedy of Palestine," *Nineteenth Century*, June, 1930.
" The Situation in Palestine," *Contemporary Review*, December, 1933.
" Palestine Strides Forward," *The Fortnightly*, January, 1935.
" The Future of Palestine," *Nineteenth Century*, July, 1939.
" Die Zionistische Bewegung," *Süddeutsche Monatshefte* (special number entitled *Die Judenfrage*), Munich, September, 1930.
" A New Crisis in Zionism," *Current History*, New York, December, 1930.

pamphlets.¹ Unfortunately the frequent appearance of my name in the press brought me many abusive letters, usually anonymous and probably from Fascists, while I was even disturbed by midnight calls on the telephone at home by malevolent vulgarians, whose rude words I soon cut short. On one occasion there arrived for me at the Zionist Office a large oblong-shaped parcel, containing a carefully packed model of a coffin, which bore a maledictory inscription.

On the other hand, I received many letters of approval and good wishes from all sorts of people — sincere believers in the Biblical prophecies, Christadelphians, British Israelites, and Christian missionaries, who sent me tracts with quotations from Isaiah and the Acts of the Apostles, sometimes accompanied by elaborate charts and diagrams, forecasting, on the basis of some fantastic system of chronological calculation, the year in which the restoration of Israel to his ancestral land was to take place.

The strangest epistle that I ever received — six large pages in small bold script — came in the early twenties from a lady in Salisbury. She wrote that she had been intimately interested in the Jews since her childhood and that her father, who had died when she was very young, had taught her that " the Jews still await the Living Presence of the Holy Uncreated Father on earth." I had not to read far before I realised that the lady was mentally unbalanced. She stated that she had been in correspondence with Sir Philip Sassoon,² at the time when he was secretary to General Sir Douglas Haig, and had learned to honour and love him. She then went on:

> I love Philip with all my being and I am quietly awaiting the glorious moment when my Holy Father in Heaven shall gloriously guide me to the delight of happy personal companionship with him. I have told you because I want you to share my knowledge of coming heavenly joy. And I want you to love Philip and constantly pray for the holiest consummation of my perfect love on earth. . . I'm going to give my Jews a first son, my first son and Philip's, and when that dear baby-boy is of full age then the spirit of David your King will dwell in that first-born Son.

¹ *The Progress of Zionism*, 1929. Eighth Revised Edition, 1947.
Les Progrès du Sionisme (French edition of 2nd Revised Edition), 1935.
Points about Palestine (Facts and Figures), 1936.
² Died 1939.

Although the poor woman concluded by addressing me as "dear Israel" and "commending" her love to me, I did not reply and never heard from her again.

III

Besides all this multifarious activity with the pen, I addressed countless meetings, clubs, University and other societies, and institutes of all kinds. I received repeated invitations from Rotary Clubs in all parts of London and in various parts of the country, and always gladly responded, as I knew that I should meet with a friendly and attentive hearing from an intelligent audience representing a cross section of the professional and business world. As these were all luncheon gatherings, I was usually limited to twenty minutes, but I found this long enough to provide the reporter of the local press with an adequate statement on the current situation. There were much larger meetings at Friends' House, Conway Hall, and Toynbee Hall, where my address was generally followed by a barrage of questions; and I felt equally at home whether I spoke from the pulpit in the Ethical Church or in Whitefield's Tabernacle, or from the platform at a Salvation Army prayer meeting in Clapton.

The most fashionable assemblies in which I spoke were the meetings of the Near and Middle East Association, the President of which for many years was the late Earl of Lamington. This was a society that always met in a large house of a wealthy hostess in Mayfair or Kensington, where many of those present were Government officials or members of the diplomatic world, the wearing of evening dress was *de rigueur*, and lavish refreshments were served from a buffet by stalwart flunkeys in coat-tails. Women were usually predominant, and their elegant gowns and pervasive perfumes were often more suggestive of a *foyer* at the Opera than of a meeting of a quasi-political society. Palestine was a frequent topic of the papers read, and the pro-Arab attitude of the majority was unmistakable. Nevertheless I was always allowed to put the Zionist point of view, and was listened to with attention, if not with sympathy. There were two occasions in particular, of which I retain a vivid memory.

At the first of these, which took place in June, 1925, at a house in Wilton Crescent, with Major-General Lord Edward Gleichen

ON GUARD

in the chair, addresses on Palestine were given by Captain (later Sir) Ernest N. Bennett and Mr. Ernest Richmond, and in the subsequent discussion Lord Raglan, Mr. Philby, and I took part.[1] Both of the principal speakers made the most fantastic statements. Captain Bennett attributed the origin of the Balfour Declaration to the alleged fact that the Government angled for the support of the Jews of high finance, and maintained that Zionism was based on fallacies, misrepresentation, and hypocrisy. Mr. Richmond accused the Government of perfidy to the Palestinian Arabs and complained that the teachings of the ancient prophets of Israel were being displaced by the subversive doctrines of Bolshevism. A General Blakeney went even further: he said that he had heard from "a well-informed source" that Zionism, Bolshevism, and Pan-Islamism were all interconnected and run from the same office ! When the chairman invited me to state the Zionist case, I had no difficulty in making mince-meat of all these and other preposterous fabrications.

At the end of the meeting Mr. Philby rose and challenged me to a public debate on Zionism. I promptly accepted the challenge. A few days later I wrote to him to inquire when and where we could meet to discuss arrangements for the debate, and he replied that as he had to go out of town we should leave the matter over for a bit. I wrote to him again about ten days later, and received a reply that he would shortly have to go out to Saudi Arabia. I therefore answered that I would be ready to take up his challenge when he returned to England, but I never heard from him on the subject again. However, I had later opportunities of crossing swords with Mr. Philby,[2] both at Chatham House (Royal Institute of International Affairs) and in the correspondence columns of the *Manchester Guardian*.

The other meeting of the Near and Middle East Association that I vividly recall took place in January, 1930, in the lovely and artistic home of Mrs. Rosita Forbes (Mrs. McGrath), the well-known traveller and author, in Great Cumberland Place. It was convened for the purpose of hearing an address by Jamal al-Husseini, Secretary of the Supreme Moslem Council of Palestine (and a cousin of the

[1] *Jewish Chronicle*, June 26th, 1925.
[2] During the Second World War Mr. Philby became in favour of the creation of a Jewish State under certain conditions. See Chaim Weizmann's Autobiography, *Trial and Error*, pp. 526, 531-2.

355

notorious Mufti of Jerusalem), who was in England on a propaganda mission. After he had spoken I was allowed ample time to reply, and when Mrs. Forbes acknowledged the motion of thanks for her hospitality she tactfully observed that she would reserve her judgment as to who was right. That was not by any means the only occasion when I debated with Jamal al-Husseini as we had two more encounters in the summer of 1937 — at another meeting of the Near and Middle East Association and at a public meeting of a women's political organisation in Liverpool. My first debate with an Arab speaker was in 1922 with Shibly Jamal, who came to London with the delegation headed by the venerable Musa Kazim Pasha for the purpose of conferences at the Colonial Office.

It was quite a different sort of experience to speak in Hyde Park. I had often listened, from the remote days of my arrival in London, to the political and religious apostles who attracted crowds near Marble Arch as they held forth from overturned boxes in zealous emulation with one another, and was usually impressed by their courage and endurance more than by their views and arguments. At last, in the summer of 1936 it was my fate to join the band of orators. The Arab rebellion in Palestine that broke out in that year made it more necessary than before to adopt all forms of propaganda for the purpose of bringing home to the public the Zionist point of view, and it was therefore decided to have a " platform " near Marble Arch on Sundays. Despite my age, for speaking in the open air, in close proximity to other loud-voiced expositors, entailed no little physical effort, I joined the panel of speakers. A little throng had already been attracted by my predecessor, a much younger man, who stood on the top step of a specially constructed ladder surmounted by the blue-white Zionist flag, gripping a miniature desk with his left hand while emphasising his arguments with his right, and when I followed him and got under way I was gratified to see the crowd slowly growing, with Lady Samuel on the outskirts. After I had spoken for about an hour I answered a spate of questions for another half-hour, and then descended to cool off. I repeated the experience the following summer with undiminished zest, and welcomed some heckling as it kept the crowd interested.

ON GUARD

The controversy about Palestine raged almost as fiercely in Dublin as in London, although Eire was politically unaffected, and after a pro-Arab talk had been given from Radio Athlone I was urged by some friends to go over and deliver a reply. The broadcasting authorities readily agreed and approved of my script, and I went over to give my talk on May 18th, 1937. While in Dublin I had lunch with the Editor of the *Irish Times*, Mr. Robert M. Smyllie,[1] who had been interned with me at Ruhleben. We relived some of our experiences in the German Prison camp, besides discussing the situation in Palestine, and I amused him by recalling some of the friendly rough-and-tumble scraps in which he indulged to release his animal spirits when he was twenty years younger.

IV

For the most part I confined my defence activities to attacks or misrepresentations that were made in the press or at public meetings. In general, I left the House of Commons alone, as there was usually a Jewish M.P. competent to deal on the spot with any such case that might arise there. But on one occasion I felt impelled to take action. In the course of the debate on the Palestine Loan in the House of Commons on May 11th, 1934, Earl Winterton made the following astonishing statement:

> In Europe land that was expropriated after the war and given to the peasants had nearly all fallen into the hands of Jewish money-lenders; practically the whole of the land of Czechoslovakia belonged to Jewish money-lenders.

I was so aghast at this allegation made by an old and well-known member of the House, who might have been expected to exercise elementary care in his utterances, that I immediately wrote to a member of the Czechoslovak Parliament, the late Dr. Angelo Goldstein, who was a friend of mine, for his comment. His reply was a complete refutation. He wrote that the extent of agricultural land in Jewish ownership in his country, which had never been considerable, had greatly diminished during the past ten years in consequence of the general flight of the Jewish population to the towns; that, owing to the Land Reform, the number of Jews who

[1] Died 1953.

had leased estates from large landowners and the nobility had been greatly reduced; and that in the distribution of the large estates the Jews received scant consideration, as they formed only a tiny proportion of the peasantry. Dr. Goldstein added that the entire agricultural credit system was in the hands of Co-operative Societies and Funds, in which the Jews took no part, and that the small amount of private capital used for lending on agricultural land came mainly from people in the little towns and rural districts, where there were very few Jews. He observed in conclusion that no complaint had ever been made publicly, even in anti-Semitic quarters, that landed estates were indebted to Jewish capital to any extent — a grievance that would certainly have been widely exploited if it had had even " a glimmer of justification."

I sent a copy of Dr. Goldstein's letter to Lord Winterton, who replied that his statement in the House of Commons was " perhaps an exaggeration " and that it would be more accurate if he had said " a large proportion," but he was " not impressed " by the letter on account of its author. I thereupon wrote again to Dr. Goldstein, who arranged that an interpellation on Lord Winterton's statement should be addressed to the Czechoslovak Premier by two non-Jewish deputies (one of whom, Deputy Srba, was a former Minister). The official reply, given in writing by M. Bechyne, Deputy Minister-President, was a complete confirmation — with statistical details — of the answer I had received from Dr. Goldstein. It stated that out of a total of 628,000 new purchasers of land under the Reform scheme there were only 718 Jews, who were allotted less than one-half per cent of the total area distributed, although the Jews were nearly two-and-a-half per cent of the population. It also denied that " almost the whole of the land of Czechoslovakia belongs to Jewish financiers," pointed out that credits for land purchase were provided mainly by the State with the aid of various funds administered by the Government Land Office, and that it was only in certain parts of Slovakia and Carpathian Ruthenia that private loans on land were provided by Jews, but " this local phenomenon amounts hardly to a fraction of one per cent of the total sum of the credits effected in connection with the execution of the reform." I transmitted a copy of this statement to Lord Winterton, but he took no steps to withdraw his monstrous calumny.

V

While devoting my days to Zionist affairs, I dedicated my nights to the Jewish world in general. My *Jewish Life in Modern Times*, which was published in 1914, had become quite out-of-date after the First World War owing to the manifold and far-reaching changes that had taken place in the conditions of the Jewish people. Besides, it had become out of print, and second-hand booksellers were demanding a fancy price for the few copies that drifted into their shops. I therefore decided to revise it and bring it up-to-date, a task that entailed the jettisoning of many parts that had become obsolete and replacing them by new chapters, besides countless alterations. The political settlement, the redistribution of Jewry in the new Europe, the fate of the large community in Russia, the institution of Minority Rights, the developments in Palestine under the Mandate, the progress in the sphere of culture, the numerous changes in the tides of emigration, population, and economic conditions generally, and the conflicting currents of assimilation and conservation — all these and many other aspects had to be carefully surveyed and examined and methodically and critically presented. I worked assiduously at the task every night from eleven o'clock for two to three hours, besides week-ends and occasionally on holidays, and after three years completed a revised and enlarged edition, which was published by Methuen and Co. in 1929. I had every reason to be satisfied with the reception accorded to it by the press.[1]

Even while I was passing the proofs, the position of the Jews in the greater part of Central and Eastern Europe began to deteriorate. The faith that had been put into the Minorities Treaties proved a phantasm, the plague of Anti-Semitism spread from land to land, and the advance of Hitler to power was the prelude to a sequence of calamities of ever increasing barbarity. Although reports of Jewish oppression appeared in the papers and there were occasionally leading articles on the subject, I did not think that they conveyed an adequate

[1] The *Manchester Guardian* wrote: "For the student of the Jewish Question in any of its aspects the book is indispensable."

sense of the tragedy that was taking place or of its incalculable consequences. I therefore considered it necessary, for the enlightenment of the intelligent or the intellectual world, to write an account of each successive phase of persecution, as it manifested itself in one country after another, with an explanatory background and critical commentary. I began by writing an article on " The Reign of Anti-Semitism," which appeared in the *New Statesman* of July 22nd, 1932.[1] Six months later Hitler was in control of Germany and initiated his campaign of Jewish persecution, which began with the destruction of German Jewry and was systematically extended to the various countries that fell under his yoke. As Goebbels's Ministry of Propaganda, with all the vast resources and money at his disposal, was busy deluding the world about the facts of the situation I contributed a long article on " The Jews in Germany " to the *Quarterly Review* of July, 1933. This was reprinted as a pamphlet in an edition of 10,000 copies at the expense of the Board of Deputies of British Jews, and was also translated into Dutch and Italian. As the affliction of the Jews spread to other parts of Central and Eastern Europe, and the activities of Nazi agents disturbed the peace and security of Jews in many other parts of the world, I wrote another comprehensive article, " The Jewish Tragedy," which appeared in the *Quarterly Review* of October, 1934, and was also reprinted as a pamphlet. After this followed a number of articles in other periodicals, dealing with the situation in different countries.[2]

The culminating article in the *Quarterly* appeared in the issue of October, 1938, under the title of " The Nazi International." It was a world-wide survey, based upon numerous quoted sources, English and foreign, of the subversive methods and maleficent activities of Goebbels's Ministry, which enjoyed the same rank as the German War Office or Foreign Office and often dominated them both in

[1] This was preceded by an article in *The Student World* (" The War against the Jewish Student "), July, 1927.
[2] " The Jews in Poland," *Contemporary Review*, December, 1936.
" University Hooliganism," *New Statesman*, March 20th, 1937.
" The Jews in Rumania, *Nineteenth Century*, March, 1938.
" The Doom of Austrian Jewry," *Contemporary Review*, June, 1938.
" Mussolini and the Jews," *Contemporary Review*, December, 1938.
" The Jews in Italy," *Political Quarterly*, July-September, 1939.
" The Jews in Hungary," *Contemporary Review*, November, 1939.

authority and policy. The editor, Sir John Murray, showed the importance that he attached to it by placing it as the first article in the *Review*, and we agreed that in view of the prevailing circumstances it should appear without my name. It attracted wide attention, was reprinted as a pamphlet, and was quoted in the House of Commons in a speech by Mr. Philip Noel Baker. It was also printed as a pamphlet in Alexandria, and condensed in the Canadian *Magazine Digest*.[1]

VI

The disquieting situation on the Continent engaged a great deal of the attention of the Foreign Affairs Committee of the Board of Deputies of British Jews, of which I had been a member for several years. It also occupied much time of the Board's Press Committee, of which I was also a member and the late Philip Guedalla was the chairman. The Press Committee had to consider the numerous articles and letters on the Jewish situation published in the papers and to decide in which cases replies should be sent in. Guedalla was usually in favour of ignoring anti-Semitic misrepresentations on the ground that a reply might provoke further unpleasant letters, but when a majority insisted that a rejoinder should be sent in he invariably turned to me with an ingratiating smile and a flattering phrase as he said: " I think that's just up your street."

The persecution of the Jews in Germany often formed the subject of addresses at Chatham House from 1933. Those addresses were sometimes given by German visitors, who naturally tried to make out a good case for their country and dismissed the English newspaper reports of outrages against the Jews as *Greuelmärchen* (atrocity fables). I always took part in the discussions that followed for the purpose of refuting the statements of these Nazi apologists and was listened to with sympathy. On one occasion the speaker was an official from the German Embassy, who said that his Government's acts of repression were directed only against the East European or Polish Jews who had swarmed over the frontier. I therefore reminded him that those Jews had been officially invited or deported into Germany

---

[1] It was reprinted a third time as a pamphlet, with a Foreword by Sir John Murray, as one of the " Friends of Europe " Publications.

in the 1914 - 18 war to provide needed labour, and that when General Ludendorff invaded Poland he actually issued a manifesto in which he called them " *Meine lieben Juden* ! " The outburst of applause and laughter that followed caused the speaker such discomfiture that I could not help feeling a little sorry for him. On another occasion (in October, 1937) the visitor was Henlein, the Sudeten leader. I had taken the precaution of previously writing to a journalist friend in Prague, who sent me a batch of cuttings from the *Prager Presse* containing disclosures about Henlein's subversive activities. I was therefore able to disprove his statement that he had had no relations with Hitler or with any of his representatives, and put to him some embarrassing questions.

When the exodus from Germany and other parts of Europe was assuming alarming and panicky dimensions an international Conference was held in 1938 at Evian on the proposal of President Roosevelt, to ascertain which countries were prepared to accept the victims of persecution in appreciable numbers. The British Government insisted that Palestine must be excluded from the agenda, although that was the one country where the refugees would have received the most friendly welcome. I wrote an article on the subject, entitled " New Homes for Jews," which appeared in the *New Statesman* of July 2nd, 1938, to show that all the varied proposals for settlements in other lands were hopeless.

Among the thousands of fugitives who swarmed into England there were also many distinguished scholars and scientists, of whom probably the most famous was Professor Sigmund Freud, who fled from Vienna. There was an appeal campaign for the Palestine Foundation Fund at the time, and it occurred to me that a message from this international celebrity would serve as an inspiring incentive. I therefore wrote to him to let me have a letter in support of the appeal, and received a reply in German in his own hand, in rather jerky Gothic script, of which the translation is as follows:—

While thanking you for welcoming me to England, I should like to ask you not to treat me like ' a leader in Israel.' I should like to be considered only as a modest scientist and not figure in any other manner. Although a good Jew, who has never denied his Judaism, I nevertheless

> *cannot overlook the fact that my absolutely negative attitude to every religion, including the Jewish, separates me from the majority of our fellow-Jews and makes me unsuited for the role that you would assign to me.*

But although Freud wrote in these terms, it is only just to his memory to add that he was keenly interested in Jewish progress in Palestine and served on the Board of Governors of the Hebrew University in Jerusalem.

After the outbreak of war there was a sudden diminution in the influx of refugees into this country, and only those of political importance were admitted without difficulty. Among these was Mr. August Zaleski, who had been Poland's Foreign Minister and also Ambassador in Rome. As I had known him since his first arrival in London as a poor refugee in 1906, I went to see him at Claridge's Hotel, on November 16th, 1939. He looked a figure of indescribable distress, mirroring the tragedy that had overwhelmed his country. He gripped his coat by the two lapels as he said to me sorrowfully: "This is all that I have left." After we had been talking for some time my visit was brought to an end by the entry of the Polish Ambassador, Count Eduard Raczynski, to whom he introduced me as one of his earliest friends in London. Mr. Zaleski is now the recognised head of the Polish exiles in Britain, one of the few liberally minded statesmen of pre-war Poland.

Chapter Twenty-two

IN RETIREMENT
1939 - 1945

I

THE outbreak of the Second World War caused a sudden diminution of activity at the Zionist headquarters in London, the duration of which it was impossible to foresee. Correspondence from abroad shrank to a trickle, meetings of the Executive became fewer, Palestine disappeared from the headlines in the press, and the Office became strangely silent. In the cataclysm that had shaken the world the Jewish national idea seemed momentarily eclipsed, and there was apparently little left for me to do in my official position. I therefore carefully reviewed the situation and came to the conclusion that a suitable moment had arrived for me to retire. The thought that I could utilise my time to greater advantage in the interest of both Zionism and the Jewish cause in general if I were free from the trammels of office, and, above all, the desire to have more leisure for literary work, determined me to leave.

I therefore had a talk with Dr. Weizmann in October, 1939, and we came to a friendly arrangement that I should retire at the end of the year. I subsequently wrote him a formal letter, in the course of which I said:

> I believe that, after having devoted half of my life, in an official capacity, to the furtherance of our national cause, I can now retire with a feeling that I have played no unworthy part in the progress of our movement, although I consider that my powers for continued usefulness are in no way impaired. My leaving this Office will mean for me a very painful wrench, as I have grown up in the Zionist movement and been devoted to it from its earliest beginnings. I have been in intimate

IN RETIREMENT

association with all who have guided its destinies for over a quarter of a century, and helped to spread the cause to some of the remotest parts of the world. I, therefore, need hardly say that I shall always be willing to undertake any special task or carry out any mission with which you or the Executive may entrust me.

In his reply, dated December 18th, 1939, Dr. Weizmann wrote:

My colleagues and I desire to convey to you their sincere appreciation of the devoted service which you have given to the Zionist Organisation and the Zionist cause for so many years and in so many fields. In addition to your work in this Office, you have brought the Zionist idea to Jews in many countries, and defended our cause, both in person and by your pen, before the bar of English public opinion. The contribution you have thus made to Zionist history has been a truly remarkable one and will long be remembered; our grateful thanks go out to you for these many years of loyal service.

We deeply appreciate, too, your kind offer to continue to serve the cause, even though your official connection with this Office is now coming to an end, and trust that whenever occasion may arise, we may still have the benefit of your great experience and high abilities.

I was given a farewell luncheon by the Zionist Executive on January 2nd, 1940, which was attended by a large gathering of representatives of all the Zionist bodies in this country and other Jewish organisations. Professor Brodetsky, who was in the chair, and other speakers delivered a series of panegyrics, which were followed by the reading of messages in a similar strain from people who were unable to be present. In my reply I briefly recalled some of the more outstanding events in my career, emphasised that Zionism had given to me far more than I had given to it, and paid tribute to the sympathy and co-operation that I had always received from my wife (who was present with our sons) and the comfort she had afforded me in times of anxiety (to which I have deemed it unnecessary to make any allusion in this record).

The news of my retirement brought me dozens of letters from friends in several countries, all expressing regret, and some surprise and incredulity. There were also complimentary comments in various papers. *The New Palestine*, the organ of the Zionist Organisation of America, wrote:

> Devoted to his task, a hard worker, he filled an important place in the field of Zionist propaganda. . . . He had the dogged persistence and obstinacy of the early English Zionists, always ready to engage in controversey, always pugnaciously defending their ideas. His presence will be missed in Zionist circles. He may be retired, but now that his civil service life is over, he will in all probability devote himself to writing the history of Zionism, with regard to which he is so well informed.

The South African *Zionist Record* published a flattering article, in which it said: " Israel Cohen has been for over a quarter of a century a landmark in English Zionism " And the Shanghai monthly, *Israel's Messenger*, after recalling my visit to China in 1920, indulged in Oriental hyperbole by referring to " the presence of a most attractive personality . . . possessed of benevolence, sagacity, and cheerfulness " and to " his courageous individuality, his plodding and indomitable industry."

II

I soon adjusted myself to my new life. I had long been anxious to begin writing a *History of the Jews in Vilna*, for which I had received a contract from the Jewish Publication Society of America when I was in Vilna in 1932. I had already collected a lot of material and accumulated notes, but was prevented from settling down to the task by my official duties and the contributing of so many articles to periodicals on the developments in Palestine and on every fresh phase of the Jewish tragedy in Europe. No sooner had I finished the first chapter, however, than I was called upon to assist in an appeal campaign for the *Keren Hayesod* (Palestine Foundation Fund) by taking charge of the organisation in Brighton and Bournemouth. I therefore packed my books, notes, and writing material in my suit-case, so as to be able to continue with the work in my hotel bedroom in whatever intervals I could find. After the campaign was concluded in Brighton with a public meeting, which Mr. Anthony de Rothschild joined me in addressing, and at Bournemouth, where my fellow-speaker was to have been Mr. Lionel Cohen, K.C. (now Lord Justice Cohen), whose absence, owing to illness, was com-

IN RETIREMENT

pensated by the arrival of Mr. Barnett Janner, M.P., I returned to London.

Shortly after the beginning of the war the Rev. Ephraim Levine, Minister of the New West End Synagogue, and I arranged to conduct a religious service for the Jewish boys of St. Paul's School, which had been evacuated to Easthampstead. We both had a son at the school and thought it necessary that the Jewish boys, who were likely to be away from their homes for a long time, should not be deprived entirely of spiritual communion and Jewish teaching. The High Master, Mr. W. F. Oakeshott, readily agreed to place a room at our disposal. Mr. Levine and I travelled up together to Easthampstead on Sunday morning, November 5th, 1939, to hold the first service, and I gave a short address. Thereafter we took it in turn to hold the service every Sunday.

I worked steadily at my book on Vilna until the summer of 1940, when the sudden breakthrough of the German Army to the Channel Ports brought me an urgent telephone call early in July from the Zionist Office. I was informed by Mr. Berl Locker, a member of the Executive, that there had been consultations with the Foreign Office on the question of the possibility of a German invasion and the precautions that should be taken by the Zionist Organisation. They were already transporting the archives of the Organisation to Canada, and had been advised to ascertain whether certain persons prominent in Jewish public life, who were known to have criticised Nazi policy and were therefore exposed to danger in the event of an invasion, were desirous of crossing the Atlantic too while facilities were still available. I discussed the matter with my wife, but she was firmly and bravely opposed to our leaving England. We, therefore, remained in London until the middle of September, when the air-raids began in full fury. As there was no need for my presence in London and I was anxious to get on with my book, I decided to go to Droitwich, and my wife accompanied me.

My reason for choosing Droitwich was that I was very familiar with that health-resort, having gone there for its brine-baths at intervals for over twenty years. Indeed, I had only just returned from there after a couple of weeks, and was thus attracted by the quietude that it offered for my literary work. Our son Jonathan, who had won an open Classical scholarship at Balliol at the beginning of the year, stayed with us for a short time until he went up to Oxford. I had a good part of my library transferred to Droitwich, and many of my books found shelter at Balliol.

Despite cramped lodgings, I was able to make steady progress with my book, especially as there were no local distractions. Most of the hotels had been requisitioned by the Government for offices or hostels for officers in training, and the principal diversion consisted of watching batches of young A.T.S., in their new uniforms, marching smartly through the quiet streets. My wife lost no time in joining the local Air Raid Wardens' Post, but although there was seldom an alarm she was most regular in her attendances. She also joined the Women's Volunteer Service and the local Choral Society, and soon made many friends.

I could not help feeling conscious of the incongruity of the milieu in which I wrote my book, as for months I was mentally engrossed in the company of the pious Talmudists, Hebrew poets, and political revolutionaries of the city famed as "the Jerusalem of Lithuania," while around me was the peaceful landscape of a slumbering English spa, whose tranquillity was disturbed only on a Sunday afternoon by a Salvation Army band. I had taken with me all the reference books that I needed except the twelve ponderous volumes of the *Jewish Encyclopedia*, which I had stored in my son's rooms at Balliol, but fortunately, and to my great surprise, I found a set in the Reference Library at Worcester, which I reached after a twenty-minute journey in a comfortable bus along a beautiful country-road bordered by green meadows. As I finished each chapter I had it typed and sent a copy in an envelope addressed to the Jewish Publication Society in Philadelphia, enclosed in a larger envelope addressed to the Chief Censor in London, with a request that he should despatch it with a minimum of delay. In this piecemeal fashion I forwarded all the chapters in succession until I completed the book early in January, 1941. Despite the hazards of the Atlantic not a single chapter was lost and the book was published two years later. It was hailed as the first comprehensive history in any language of the Jewish community in Vilna from the earliest times to the present day.

I was again called upon to take part in fund-raising for Palestine, and addressed meetings in various cities from Cambridge and Leicester to Newcastle and Sunderland, with a détour to Llandudno. During 1941 I also spoke on "Palestine and the War" at over a dozen Rotary Clubs, beginning with Droitwich and Worcester, and travelling all over the country from Cheltenham and Hereford to Southport and Blackpool. In the course of these journeys I found that there was a great deal of ignorance with regard to the part that the Jews were playing in the war, and thought that the best way of dissipating it was to write a little book on the subject. In view of its proposed contents I went to the Ministry of Information for a preliminary discussion with Mr. (now Professor) C. Day Lewis, who was in charge of publications, and after submitting a synopsis received official approval.

I kept the book short, so that it should appear as soon as possible. I first of all explained the Jewish issue, for however much the lives and liberties of other nations might be threatened by Hitler, they would nevertheless survive and rebuild their countries anew, whereas the Jews in Europe, who formed half of the entire Jewish people, were menaced in their very existence. I then described Hitler's first war — his war against the Jews, begun in 1933 and waged with ever-increasing barbarity until 1939; presented a systematic and detailed account of the destruction of European Jewry; and recounted the contributions — military, economic, and technical — that the Jews of the Allied countries were making to the overthrow of the Hitlerite despotism. As an appendix I included a list of the British Jews in the Navy, Army, and Air Force, who had received decorations, and also of those engaged in Civil Defence to whom honours had been awarded. *The Jews in the War*[1] appeared in July, 1942, and thanks to its success a second and revised edition was necessary the following year.

A smaller booklet that I also wrote in Droitwich was entitled *Britain's Nameless Ally*. It dealt with the persistent and tantalising efforts of the Zionist leaders to secure the assent of the British Govern-

[1] Published by Frederick Muller, Ltd.

ment to the raising of a large Jewish fighting force of volunteers to help in the defence of Palestine and the support of the Imperial troops in the Middle East, as well as to fight wherever they might be required in other regions. A formal offer to this effect had been made to the Government at the very beginning of the war, and after nearly two years was agreed to, but in October, 1941, it was definitely rejected. The Jews of Palestine had indeed been allowed to join the British Army, but they were accepted only in strictly limited numbers (so as not to exceed the Arabs, who were very reluctant to volunteer) although they fought gallantly in every sector in which they were engaged. The purpose of my booklet was to relate the disappointing story of the frustrated attempt to create a military contingent under the Jewish flag, as well as the impressive record of the manifold services rendered by Palestinian Jewry to the war effort. It was published[1] in April, 1942. Not until more than two years later, in September, 1944, did the British Government agree to the formation of a Jewish Brigade Group, based on the Jewish battalions of the Palestine Regiment, and displaying a distinctive shoulder flash, with the traditional " Shield of David " in gold.

We returned to London in the spring of 1942. I was thus able to attend regularly the meetings of the Board of Deputies of British Jews[2] and of its committees of which I was a member, and likewise to keep in closer touch with the Zionist Office, although my activity was interrupted for some months by a depressing illness. The developments in connection with Palestine prompted me again to write some articles for the reviews,[3] but I was increasingly impressed by the need for a history of Zionism. My pamphlet on *The Progress of Zionism* (1929) had expanded into a brochure three times as large when it reached a sixth revised edition early in 1943,[4] but this was still inadequate as a record of the movement which had had such a

---

[1] By W. H. Allen & Co.
[2] The representative organisation of British Jewry, founded in 1760.
[3] " Palestine: " New Land Policy," *Contemporary Review*, May, 1940.
" Palestine, the Jews and the War," *Contemporary Review*, March, 1942.
" The Balfour Declaration: Twenty-Five Years After," *Contemporary Review*, November, 1942.
" Palestine and the Jewish Future," *Quarterly Review*, July, 1944.
[4] The 8th revised edition appeared in 1947.

romantic and eventful past, nor was there one in existence at that time in any language. I therefore devoted the year 1943 to the writing of *The Zionist Movement*, presenting for the first time a comprehensive history of the evolution of the Jewish national idea from the earliest times to the present day. It was a task that I should have found very difficult of accomplishment, had I not been favoured with the special knowledge gathered in the course of a long and intimate connection with the movement. My old friend, Sir Leon Simon, who ably combined the cultivation of Hebrew letters with the administration of the Telegraphs and Telephones of the General Post Office, kindly read through the typescript, but owing to the delay due to war conditions, the book was not published until 1945.[1] It met with a friendly reception not only in England but also abroad.[2] American and French editions appeared in 1946, a Spanish edition in the following year, and an Italian version in 1953. A Hebrew translation has also been made and is to be published in Jerusalem.

In the autumn of 1944 the Executive of the Zionist Federation of Great Britain, realising the need of enlightening the Jewish public on the history of the movement, invited me to give a course of six monthly lectures on the period from 1860. I delivered them in both London and Birmingham, and they were afterwards printed under the title of *A Short History of Zionism, 1860 - 1944*.

III

From the very beginning of the war I closely followed its effects upon the Jews in Europe, so far as they could be learned from reports in the Jewish press, and wrote review articles on their tragic plight from time to time. The first was an article on " The Jews in France," describing the persecution under the Vichy régime, which appeared in the *Contemporary Review*.[3] Then followed a longer contribution, giving a harrowing account of " Polish Jewry under Nazi Tyranny," in the *Quarterly Review*,[4] and a survey of Hitler's plan of wholesale

[1] By Frederick Muller Ltd.
[2] *The Manchester Guardian* called it " a competent book written by a man who is master of his subject "; and *La Renaissance Juive* (Paris), " *un tour de force réussi*."
[3] October, 1941.
[4] January, 1942.

extermination, "The Doom of European Jewry," in the *Contemporary*.[1]

One of the effects of the war in England was the aggravation of Anti-Semitism, which was partly due to the disproportionate publicity given in the press to prosecutions for "black market" trading by persons with foreign-looking names, as compared with those in which persons with purely British names were involved. I therefore thought it necessary to contribute to *The New Statesman*[2] an article entitled " Anti-Semitism and Treachery," in which I related some striking instances of the realisation of Hitler's boast that " Anti-Semitism is a useful revolutionary expedient and beyond question the most important weapon in my propaganda arsenal and almost everywhere of deadly efficiency," and stressed the fact that " in Great Britain, too, the Anti-Semites are largely identical with those who are regarded as dangerous to their country, for all the Fascists and most of the others interned under Regulation 18B have been guilty of Jew-baiting." I therefore pointed out that after Hitlerism was crushed and Anti-Semitism would presumably be no longer serviceable as an instrument of treachery it would " still possess an infinite capacity for generating political discord and social unrest," and accordingly concluded that it would " be necessary, in the interests of peace, not only of Jewry but of the world in general, that the most effective means should be adopted for its suppression."

This article immediately provoked a reply, in the form of a full-page article under the same title, in *Truth*[3], by its editor, Mr. Collin Brooks, which consisted of a laboured defence of Anti-Semitism, reeking from beginning to end of the ideology and terminology of Nazism. I therefore sent in a rejoinder,[4] in which, after refuting his charge that Jews were trying " to wrest the control of British affairs, whether political, social or industrial," I went on to say:

> In his emphasis upon ' the race which is native to this land,' Mr. Brooks has apparently forgotten that the Angles and Saxons were not natives of this island at all, but arrived here only some fifteen hundred years ago. The worst expression that he can use about the Jews is that they are Oriental, for he says: ' This is our land, these are our traditions,

[1] February, 1943.
[2] May 30th, 1942.
[3] June 5th, 1942.
[4] June 19th, 1942.

and we wish neither to be orientalised.' Since the Jews have been in Europe at least 2,000 years, they surely have the same claim to the name of Europeans as the descendants of the Anglo-Saxons. In any case the use of ' orientalised ' as a term of disparagement is a very questionable way of appreciating the importance of Britain's vast possessions in the Orient, from the Near East to the Far East.

I concluded:

> Not only is the attitude of Mr. Brooks disloyal to British tradition, but also to the tradition of Truth, for his reactionary article is enough to make its famous founder, that robust Radical, Henry Labouchere, turn in his grave. And Mr. Brooks is equally disloyal to Christian doctrine, for in the New Testament there is no principle of social conduct that is stressed so often by his Saviour as the rule: ' Thou shalt love thy neighbour as thyself.'

My article also attracted the notice of the traitor, William Joyce, known as " Lord Haw-Haw," who referred to it jeeringly in one of his anti-British broadcasts from Germany.

It was in the hope of helping to stem the tide of Anti-Semitism that I contributed an article on " The Economic Value of Refugees " to the *Contemporary Review*.[1] The settlement in England of some thousands of fugitives from Nazi oppression had given rise in some quarters to the fear of economic competition and a feeling of antagonism. I therefore collected all the material data available, and showed that the capital, skill, knowledge of patent processes, and information about the export trade to oversea countries, which they had brought with them, and the hundreds of factories in a variety of industries that they had established, had provided work and food for several thousand British unemployed. My article also gave an account of the economic benefits that had been conferred by refugees upon the British Dominions, the United States, and parts of South America.[2]

IV

During the latter part of the war the Board of Deputies of British Jews occupied itself to an increasing extent with the tragic fate of the Jews in Europe. From time to time we received confidential

[1] February, 1945.
[2] The article was reproduced in *The World Digest* and the New York German weekly, *Aufbau*.

information through underground channels of the death-camps and gas-chambers that Hitler had constructed in Poland for the murder of millions of Jews, but the news seemed to us so horrible and fantastic that some of us felt rather sceptical, or at least thought that the reported numbers of the victims were grossly exaggerated. These confidential reports were usually brought to the meetings of our Foreign Affairs Committee by Dr. I. Schwarzbart, a former member of the Polish Parliament, who took refuge in London after Europe was overrun by the Germans, and had close relations with the Polish Government in Exile. At one meeting, in July, 1942, we had a visit from Mr. S. Ziegelbaum, a leader of the Bund (Polish Jewish Socialist Party). He was also a refugee, a haggard-looking man in the late forties. He showed us some thin foolscap sheets containing lists of towns in which Jews had been shot or slaughtered in tens of thousands, the total already amounting to over one million. He appealed to us tearfully to make immediate and urgent representations to the British Government, that they should take concerted action with the United States and Soviet Governments to restrain Hitler from continuing his maniacal orgies of massacre and do everything in their power to save all who could still be rescued.

The three Governments published solemn declarations of warning of the retribution that they would inflict upon Hitler if he did not desist from his " bestial policy of cold-blooded extermination." But the unparalleled barbarities continued uninterruptedly and even on a larger scale than before. The Allied Governments would not be deterred from their concerted strategy to undertake any scheme of rescue. It was even reported that an important member of the British Government had said that if Hitler were indeed to release the millions of Jews still in his clutches, they would cause the Allies a very serious embarrassment. In his despair and distress at failing to bring any succour to his martyred brethren in Poland, Ziegelbaum in 1943 committed suicide in his lodgings, leaving a note expressing the hope that he might achieve by his death what he had been unable to accomplish in his life.

At the meeting of the Board of Deputies on Sunday, November 21st, 1943, a sensation was caused by the presence on the platform

IN RETIREMENT

of two Jewish emissaries from Soviet Russia. They were Solomon Mikhoels, a distinguished actor, and Itzik Feffer, an equally eminent writer, the heads of the Soviet Jewish anti-Fascist Committee. They had already addressed Jewish public meetings in the United States to appeal for increased material collaboration in the struggle against the Nazis, and they had now come to England for the same purpose. They were the first Jews who had been permitted by the Soviet Government to emerge from behind the Iron Curtain that had cut off the Jews in Russia from their brethren in the rest of the world for twenty-five years. They delivered eloquent speeches in Yiddish, in which they painted a reassuring picture of the religious liberty and cultural progress enjoyed by the Jews in Russia. They expressed the hope that their coming to England would be reciprocated by a visit of Anglo-Jewish leaders to Moscow. It was a vain hope, as the Kremlin refused to consider the idea. On the contrary, a few years after the war the Soviet Government dissolved the Jewish anti-Fascist Committee and embarked on a campaign for the suppression of Jewish culture. Jewish theatres were abolished, the Yiddish press and publishing houses were closed down, Yiddish writers were reduced to silence, and the Jewish " intelligentsia " were purged on the ground of " cosmopolitanism." In short, the roseate picture that had been drawn for us, in all sincerity, by the Moscow emissaries in 1943, had not only become defaced but was deliberately destroyed[1].

In the latter part of 1944 the Executive of the Board and its Foreign Affairs Committee, after repeated discussions on the plight of the Jews in Europe, and on plans and proposals that should be formulated in the interests of the surviving communities, decided that a comprehensive document should be drawn up, which would recount their vicissitudes in the various lands since the end of the First World War and outline the policy that should be adopted at the close of the Second. They entrusted me with the writing of the document. As it

[1] Mr. Leon Crystal, correspondent of the New York *Jewish Daily Forward*, after returning to Paris from an extended tour of Russia, stated that twenty-six Soviet Yiddish writers (including Feffer, David Bergelson, and Peretz Markish) were shot on Stalin's orders on August 12th, 1952 (*Jewish Chronicle*, March 16th, 1956). The Congress of Jewish Culture held in New York on April 4th, 1956, sent to the Soviet Ambassador in Washington a list of 450 prominent Russian-Jewish writers, poets, and artists who have been " missing " since 1948 (*Jewish Chronicle*, April 6th, 1956).

was an exacting task that demanded freedom from all disturbance and interruption, I betook myself to the tranquillity of Winchester, where I secured a room in a house occupied by the Jewish minister of Southampton, whose family had been bombed out of their home. American Jewish soldiers from a neighbouring camp used to meet there on Sunday afternoon for a religious service, and the melody of their hymns that rose to my room evoked in me a sort of nostalgia. There I was able to concentrate and produced a booklet of about 30,000 words, which was published in 1945 by the Board of Deputies under the title of *The Jews in Europe: Their Martyrdom and Their Future*. I also spoke at a meeting of the local Rotary Club, which was attended by most of the dignitaries of the city.

My wife, who remained in London to look after our home and carry out her duties as an Air Raid Warden, came to me occasionally for week-ends; and as we strolled through the lawns of the Cathedral and the cloisters of the College, enjoying the mediaeval quietude of the ancient capital of England, we talked of the happenings of the years that had passed and looked forward to the dawn of peace.

Chapter Twenty-three

POST-WAR EVENTS

1945 — 1955

I

THE Zionist Conference that took place in London in August, 1945, was an event of outstanding importance, as it was the first gathering of the kind to be held after nearly six years of war. It afforded the first opportunity of finding out the facts about the tragic situation in which the Jewish people in Europe had been left after the colossal losses it had suffered by organised mass murder. It also provided the first occasion on which authoritative decisions could be taken on the policy to be adopted in the interests of the survivors and, above all, in the endeavour to achieve the realisation of Zionist aims. The Conference was attended not only by all members of the Executive of the Zionist Organisation and the Jewish Agency,[1] but also by many representatives from all parts of the world, both near and far, including even South America, South Africa, and Australia. Enthusiastic as was the applause that greeted Dr. Weizmann and Mr. Ben-Gurion on their appearance, it was surpassed by the ovation given to the bent and grey-bearded figure of Dr. Leo Baeck, the former Chief Rabbi of Berlin, who had lived through all the horrors of the concentration camp at Theresienstadt. But loudest and longest of all were the resounding cheers with which the delegates from Poland — seven men and a girl — were acclaimed, for they were among the leaders of the Partisans, who had fought desperately for years as guerrillas and in the underground movement.

[1] From 1945 the Executive of the Zionist Organisation and the Jewish Agency became practically synonymous.

A JEWISH PILGRIMAGE

For the first time after more than thirty years I was at a Zionist Conference without having any official duties, and I was therefore able to use my liberty and my leisure in chatting with delegates from different countries and hearing of their dangerous and thrilling experiences in the war. I spoke with some of the leaders of the Resistance Movement in France, and with delegates from Sweden who had helped in the rescue of Jews from Denmark; I spoke with a delegate from Athens who told me of the vast deportations from Greece, and with another from Rome who related a similar story of the deportations from Italy. I also had a talk with the girl, Chaya Grossmann — fair-haired and frail — from the Warsaw Ghetto, who made light of the furious battle in which she had been engaged and modestly remarked that she had found it easier to handle a gun or lay a mine than to make a speech.

It was with high hopes that the Conference had assembled, for a Labour Government had just been returned at the General Election. Ever since the Balfour Declaration the Labour Party had repeatedly affirmed its sympathy with Zionist aspirations, and even as recently as May, 1945, its National Executive Committee had pronounced in favour of a Jewish State in Palestine. What else, therefore, after the Labour victory, could the entire Jewish people expect but that the new Government would immediately scrap the White Paper of 1939 and proceed to carry out the Party's oft-reiterated promises ? They were grievously disappointed, for the Government turned a complete somersault. Palestine was removed from the sphere of the Colonial Office and placed under the control of the Foreign Office, and the new Foreign Secretary, Ernest Bevin[1], showed himself a most implacable and rancorous enemy of Zionism. His hostility provoked the most stubborn and reckless resistance on the part of the Jews in Palestine, who were determined to use all possible means and devices to secure the entry of thousands of hapless refugees from Europe, so-called " illegal immigrants," with the result that a bitter, inglorious war, involving the loss of many lives, dragged on for nearly three years.

[1] Died 1951.

II

A new phase developed, towards the end of 1945, with the appointment by the British and United States Governments of a Joint Committee of Enquiry to investigate the problems of Palestine and European Jewry and to propose recommendations for their solution. The Committee, after hearing witnesses in Washington, came to London, where it held several sessions in February, 1946, before proceeding to the Continent and thence to Palestine. As it was open to all official bodies interested in the question to submit memoranda, the Board of Deputies of British Jews decided to have a statement drawn up, giving a comprehensive survey of the Jewish conditions in the various countries of Europe, the writing of which was entrusted to me. I produced a brochure (of about 15,000 words) entitled *The Jews in Europe: Their Post-War Situation*, copies of which were distributed to members of the Committee, as well as to the Foreign Office and other Government departments. I also spoke to certain members of the Committee and furnished them with information on particular matters, which they found useful in putting questions to anti-Zionist witnesses.

The problems resulting from the catastrophic plight of the Jews in Europe engaged the serious consideration of all Jewish representative organisations on both sides of the Atlantic. In the last week of February the American Jewish Committee, jointly with the Anglo-Jewish Association, sponsored a conference in London, which was attended by delegates from fifteen countries in Europe, North and South America, and Australia. The officials of the American Committee were so anxious to ensure that no material hitch of any kind should hamper the success of the deliberations that they even brought with them a large stock of stationery, note-books, and pencils, for the use of the delegates. The Board of Deputies was invited to send two fraternal delegates, of whom I was one. There was a free exchange of information and views on such matters as rehabilitation, restitution, resettlement, human rights, Palestine and cultural reconstruction, as well as Anti-Semitism and the methods of combating it in the various countries. A profound impression was produced by the revelation that in the United States as much as five million dollars a year was spent on fighting anti-Jewish defamation. The conference was rendered particularly interesting by the presence of representatives from the Balkan regions, who were at pains to convince us that the Jews in those lands felt quite happy under their new Governments. Indeed, the delegate from Bulgaria seemed so anxious to impress us that the Jews in his country enjoyed all rights and liberties that he emphasised that none of them wished to emigrate to Palestine. But before long it became evident that he had protested too much, for within a few years as many as 40,000 Jews from Bulgaria emigrated to Palestine, leaving only a residue of about 7,000.

Presently I found myself returning to the Zionist Office in Great Russell Street. It had been decided that the next Congress should be held in December, 1946, and the Executive wanted to have a report drawn up on their political activities since the outbreak of the war. They entrusted me with the task and placed at my disposal an accumulated mass of records, memoranda, correspondence, and papers of all kinds. I worked at the job daily for weeks in the room of Dr. Weizmann, who was then in the United States, and as I plodded through the material and made notes I learned something of the heart-breaking struggle that he and his colleagues had had with the British Government, of promises violated and hopes frustrated, throughout the dismal years of the war.

III

In June, 1946, the Council of Foreign Ministers of France, Soviet Russia, the United Kingdom, and the United States, met in Paris for the purpose of drafting the Peace Treaties with the ex-enemy countries (Italy, Hungary, Rumania, Bulgaria, and Finland). As it was of great importance that these Treaties should include articles that would guarantee the rights and satisfy the claims of the Jews in those countries, the Board of Deputies of British Jews sent me to Paris to collaborate with representatives of the World Jewish Congress and the American Jewish Conference[1] in formulating proposals for this purpose. After a fortnight's labours we drew up and presented two joint documents:

[1] The American Jewish Conference was established in 1943 to carry out a programme of Jewish post-war reconstruction, and consisted of delegates of over 60 national Jewish organisations and of every Jewish community in the United States. It was dissolved in 1948 owing to internal differences.

one containing proposals that were considered essential to establish the rights, liberties and status of the Jews, and the other consisting of supplementary statements dealing with each of the Treaties, as the conditions in the different countries varied.[1] It was deemed unnecessary to submit any recommendations on behalf of the Jews in Finland, as they were so few in number and had been treated justly by their own Government as long as it was free from German pressure.

Soon after my return to London I was appointed by the Foreign Affairs Committee of the Board of Deputies head of its delegation to the Peace Conference[2], to collaborate with representatives of other Jewish organisations in an endeavour to secure the inclusion in the Peace Treaties of the proposals already submitted. Before the Conference was to begin there was time for a short holiday, so my wife and I left London in the middle of July for Lugano. We had not been there for twenty-five years, and in the atmosphere of the first post-war year we thoroughly enjoyed our fortnight together in the delightful surroundings of the picturesque lake-side under a sunny, blue sky. At the end of the month I was back again in Paris, and my wife returned home.

The Peace Conference brought to the French capital delegates from seven other Jewish organisations (from Europe, America, and South Africa), besides the three already mentioned, but all agreed to confer and co-operate together and to present their proposals to the Conference in a single document. We were faced by a formidable task, for when the draft Treaties were published they were found to contain only two articles based on the statements submitted to the Council of Foreign Ministers, and even those articles, in our view, were formulated unsatisfactorily. We were therefore obliged to present our proposals afresh; but this time, in order to comply with the procedure of the Conference, we had to frame them either as amendments in the draft Treaties or as supplementary articles. The discussions were conducted quite harmoniously, considering that some of the delegations represented divergent standpoints on such

[1] For details see the author's *Contemporary Jewry*, pp. 266-269.
[2] Other members of the Delegation of the Board of Deputies of British Jews, who attended for various periods, were Professor S. Brodetsky (President), Mr. Barnett Janner, M.P., Mr. A. G. Brotman (Secretary), Dr. D. Mowshowitch, and Dr. J. L. Talmon.

questions as religious conformity and Jewish nationalism, and that speeches were delivered in three languages (English, French, and German), with an occasional one in Italian, necessitating frequent translation and repeated exposition; but when Jewish delegates from the four ex-enemy States also arrived and insisted on pressing the wishes of their respective communities, the deliberations over each paragraph and sometimes over a sentence were not only protracted but often became extremely involved and even heated. Among all the knotty points over which we debated, perhaps the most stubborn was a term that would clearly indicate the Jews as a corporate body and that would satisfy all parties. The French delegates were aghast at the suggestion that we should use the term " *le peuple juif*," as in their view there was no such thing and, if used, it would reflect on their patriotism. They only recognised " *la réligion israélite*," but finally compromised on the ugly expression, " Jewish collectivity." At last, after weeks of exhaustive discussion, conducted with the aid of legal experts, and, in the final stage, with the co-operation of the Professor of International Law at the Cambridge University, Dr. Hersch Lauterpacht, agreement was reached on an imposing document containing more than forty amendments, which occupied over thirty octavo printed pages.

The next problem was to secure consideration for this document by the Peace Conference. An inquiry on this point addressed to the chairman of the Committee on Procedure (M. Spaak, the Belgian statesman) and to the Secretary-General of the Conference elicited no reply. The document was therefore distributed to all the twenty-one Government delegations at the Conference, but as it was acknowledged only by a few it became necessary to try to induce some of them to sponsor particular amendments. All efforts towards this end, however, whether among the delegations of the so-called Western *bloc* or those of the Slav *bloc*, were, with two exceptions, in vain. The Government delegations were all approached by some or other of the Jewish delegates, with the same negative result. I called upon the head of the Indian delegation, Sir Samuel Runganhan, but although received with courtesy and sympathy, was told that he would have to communicate with his Government in Delhi before he could do anything, and it would be a few weeks before he had a reply. I next called upon the head of the Canadian delegation, Mr. Brooke Claxton, with whom I had a half-hour's interview, but his reply was that if I could reduce the Jewish proposals to *fifty words* he might be able to do something about it. I then had a talk with a high official of the British Foreign Office in the sumptuous lounge of the palatial Hotel Georges V, where the Britiah Delegation were quartered. As we sat and conversed on a luxurious couch I could not help being struck by the ceaseless hand-sawing and finger-pointing with which he emphasised his every remark, while I, more seriously concerned than he, sat immobile with clasped hands resting on my knees. Had anybody watched us from a little distance, he would have thought that the official, whose figure, face and name testified to unquestionably Anglo-Saxon ancestry, was of excitable Semitic stock and that I was of phlegmatic British breed.

The result of the talk was that a few days later (on August 20th, 1946) Mr. Hector McNeil, M.P., Under-Secretary for Foreign Affairs,[1] who was head of the British Delegation in the absence of the Foreign Secretary, Mr. Ernest Bevin, received a deputation of British Jews. He informed us that as the draft Treaties represented the unanimous decisions of the Council of Foreign Ministers, none of them could sponsor any of the Jewish amendments. On the other hand, he stated that the United Kingdom delegation contemplated introducing an amendment concerning the restitution of confiscated property, which should prove very helpful to the Jews affected. In the end, the United Kingdom delegation secured the adoption of a very comprehensive amendment in the Treaty with Rumania, as well as in those with Hungary and Bulgaria, to ensure the prohibition of any kind of discriminatory legislation in reference to " persons, property, business, or financial interest, status, political or civic rights, or any other matter." Similarly, some of the American Jewish delegates had talks with the heads of the United States Delegation, who eventually combined with the United Kingdom Delegation to secure the adoption in the Treaties with Rumania and Hungary of a dual amendment for the restoration of confiscated property and for the

[1] Died in 1955.

transfer of property that remained heirless or unclaimed. These three amendments were the only ones adopted by the Conference (against the minority vote of Soviet Russia, the Ukraine, and Byelo-Russia) out of the whole of the elaborate document submitted by the Jewish delegations after three months' hard labour. In view of the later political developments in Eastern Europe one might as well describe it as "love's labour's lost," for the Treaties with Hungary, Rumania, and Bulgaria, after being duly signed and sealed, were afterwards discarded when these countries became satellites of the Soviet Union.

Our discussions took place for the most part in a suite of offices on the fourth floor of some old premises in an arcade off the Champs Elysées. There was a defective and decrepit lift which we used at first, but as it sometimes stopped midway and always bumped the ceiling with a dreadful thud, I preferred safety to speed and walked up the sixty-odd steps — an ordeal that I had to perform three times on most days. But a counterbalancing advantage was our proximity to the beautiful boulevard, where we had a choice of open-air cafés and restaurants and could take a stroll to the Arc de Triomphe.

It was in the summer of 1946, after Bevin had brushed aside the Report of the Anglo-American Committee of Enquiry, that the violent resistance of the Jews in Palestine to the repressive measures of the Government led to the internment of members of the Jewish Agency Executive (including Mr. Moshe Sharett) and other Jewish leaders who were in the country. Fortunately Mr. Ben-Gurion was then in Paris, and he and other Zionist leaders (some of whom were in the delegations engaged in discussing the Peace Treaties) held frequent and prolonged meetings to consider their attitude to the British Government's scheme for provincial autonomy in Palestine (called the Morrison plan[1]). Whenever I met the future Prime Minister of Israel in the corridors of his hotel his brow was furrowed and his arms were laden with books on constitutional law.

---

[1] This plan proposed the division of Palestine into four areas — a Jewish province, an Arab province, the district of Jerusalem, and the district of the Negev. The Jewish and Arab provinces would each have an elected legislative chamber, from whose members the High Commissioner would appoint two separate executives. Bills passed by either chamber would require the assent of the High Commissioner. See the author's *A Short History of Zionism*, pp. 188-191.

POST-WAR EVENTS

It was at the same time that the Palestine Government had issued a warrant for the arrest of Dr. Moshe Sneh, the head of the Haganah (Jewish self-defence organisation). All the military and police authorities were mobilised to track him down, and the news of the hunt and of false alarms figured in big head-lines in the world's press. At the moment when public interest had risen to fever-heat I walked into a small restaurant not far from the Etoile and saw a man at a table who had a very strong resemblance to Sneh. The only difference was that his black hair was cut short and his upper lip had only a few days' growth. I eyed him at first somewhat dubiously, but a slight responsive smile at once dispelled all doubt. I greeted him with " *Shalom* (Peace) ! ", and over a cup of coffee he told me of the simple yet ingenious way in which he had slipped past the frontier and port patrols of Palestine and sailed safely to Marseilles.

After being in Paris more than six weeks I returned home in the middle of September, leaving behind a diminished delegation, but still adequate enough to watch over Jewish interests. I delivered a verbal report a few days later at a plenary meeting of the Jewish Board of Deputies.

IV

From time to time I was summoned to serve on a jury, but shortly before the day of the trial I would receive a letter to inform me that my attendance in Court would be unnecessary. About a month after my return to London, I received a summons to serve on a Grand Jury at the High Court, and looked forward to the experience eagerly. But unfortunately I had a recurrence of dermatitis at the time which had plagued me a few years before, and it became doubtful whether I would be able to leave the house. I therefore wrote to the Sheriff's clerk, who replied that I would be exempted only if I sent him a medical certificate. I then consulted my doctor, who said that it would be quite impossible for me to go to the Court and gave me the required certificate, which I sent on.

On the very morning when I received the letter of exemption I read in *The Times* that the case for which I had been required to serve on the Grand Jury was that in which the late Professor Harold

Laski was suing the *Newark Advertiser* and other papers for libel, arising out of a speech that he made during the General Election of 1945. I was profoundly disappointed at being unable to attend the trial. When the reports of the proceedings appeared in *The Times* I read them with meticulous care, and so far as the evidence as recorded in its columns showed, I came to the conclusion that Professor Laski was justified in maintaining that no words of his could be rightly interpreted as meaning that he actually advocated the adoption of violence for political purposes. It is possible, that, had I been on the jury and heard other pieces of evidence not given in the paper, I might have come to a different conclusion. But as I accepted the *Times* report as containing all the material evidence I formed the definite view that Professor Laski had been libelled, and had I been on the jury that was the view that I would have advanced. Whether I would have convinced my fellow-jurymen or succeeded only in dividing them must remain a matter for speculation.[1]

V

The Twenty-Second Zionist Congress was due to begin on December 9th, 1946, at Basle. My wife was going there to attend a conference of the Women's Zionist Organisation, and although I felt somewhat listless after recovering from my ailment, I was persuaded by her and advised by my doctor to go too. I was glad that I went, not only because I thus maintained the record of attending every Zionist Congress since 1903, but also because it was an instructive and thrilling experience.

The assembly presented a sadly different aspect from that of the Congress of 1939, for the war had wrought terrible ravages in the movement and there were many familiar faces missing. Most of the countries of the Continent were represented by many fewer delegates than ever before, and scores of prominent Zionists of pre-war days, who had been leaders in their own land and played a decisive part in previous deliberations, were no more. Just as the Russian delegation was missed after the First World War, so now I missed the Polish delegation, even though it was still represented by a small group,

[1] Professor Laski lost the case and had to pay about £13,000 costs, for which his friends raised a fund.

and likewise the delegations from Rumania and Hungary, from Austria and Germany, although these countries too were represented by tiny groups, in some cases coming from the Displaced Persons' Camps. On the other hand, for the first time there were delegations from Mexico and Cuba, indicative of recent developments in the extension of the Diaspora. By mere chance I met the two delegates from Mexico when I took a seat at their table in a restaurant and was attracted by their Spanish conversation. One had emigrated from Poland and the other from Greece, and both had lived in Mexico for nearly twenty years. They told me that the country already contained 20,000 Jews, consisting of large groups not only from Central and Eastern Europe, but also from Damascus and Aleppo; and they had a Yiddish paper that appeared three times a week, as well as a Spanish monthly.

Many delegates had not seen one another for seven years, during which time had wrought changes. Some had grown grey, others greyer still; some had increased in girth, but far more had shrunk and bore sad traces of the privations they had endured. I was shocked when I caught sight of an old friend, who had formerly lived in Zagreb. He had been a leading lawyer, president of the Zionist Federation of Yugoslavia, a man of substance, and accustomed to command. He had shrivelled into a wizened old man, his rotund cheeks had become hollow, his eyes looked bleary, his shoulders were bent, and his once upright gait was humbled. He told me of the months of suffering he and his wife had borne in Gestapo prisons, and of the perils and hardships they had endured before they succeeded in escaping over the frontier into Italy and from there into Switzerland.

There were scores of men, and many women too, who had lived under the Nazi occupation in their various lands and played a brave part in the Resistance movements. They had been hardened by their terrible experiences and developed all the toughness and resourcefulness needed for settlement in their ancestral home, to which their entry was still barred. One of them, young Zivia Lubetkin, a heroine of the Warsaw Ghetto, was honoured by being included in the *Praesidium*, and when she took the chair she was given a warm and prolonged ovation. Among the vast concourse of delegates, visitors, and press correspondents, I came across knots of sturdy young men in khaki uniform and peaked caps, with letters in blue on their shoulders indicating that they were the *Shelichim* (couriers) of the Jewish Agency for Palestine, charged with the task of bringing succour and hope to the Jews in the liberated regions, who were impatiently awaiting the day when they could set forth for the land of their dreams.

There were many languages spoken by the two thousand who filled the Congress hall and swarmed through the numerous corridors, offices, and committee rooms of the vast "Mustermesse" (Trade Fair building). But from the Congress tribune only three languages were heard: Hebrew, English, and Yiddish. English was spoken far more than at any previous assembly, an inevitable consequence of the large proportion, amounting to one-third, that the delegates from America formed of the total composition of the Congress. I remembered the times when Russian predominated and then the times when German was general, but the political cataclysms of thirty years had reduced those tongues to silence in the Zionist Parliament. One delegate who could express himself freely only in German prefaced his remarks with an apology in perfect Hebrew, so as to disarm criticism; and Mr. Sharett, who spoke Hebrew more fluently than English, after a brief preface in Hebrew delivered his political report in English.

I met scores of old friends (with older faces), from whom I was able to gather information about people who were not there and about places in different parts of the globe that I had visited many years before. I saw friends from Buenos Aires and Johannesburg, from Vancouver and Wellington, from Budapest and Athens, from Bucarest and Jerusalem, and from dozens of other cities, and was able to renew memories and impressions that have gone to make up my Zionist life. Some of the information that I got was heartening and some depressing, for the effects of the war had varied from place to place. In the British Dominions, whether Canada or South Africa, Australia or New Zealand, Zionist sentiment was on the ascendant, partly because of the astounding progress made by the Jews in Palestine, partly because there was no satisfactory solution for the problem of the surviving victims of Hitler except settlement in that country.

Most distressing were the bits of information that I picked up about conditions among the Jews in Central Europe and the Balkans. I learned that the Jewish emigration from Poland, although it had lessened owing to the rigours of winter, would increase in the following spring, when travel conditions would become easier, for the combination of political intolerance and anti-Semitic violence did not act as a magnet. In Hungary, I was told that there were about 50,000 baptised Jews besides 150,000 more or less conforming members of the Jewish community, and it was, therefore, impossible to give a simple answer to the question: "How many Jews are there in Hungary?" A large proportion of the converts had become baptised during the war not from conviction but as a measure of safety; and many of them, whether their apostasy dated from the Second World War or the First, still regarded themselves as Jews, paid the communal taxes, and even attended the synagogue on the high Festivals. On the other hand, the once proud and populous community of Vilna had been reduced to such a tiny fraction of its former self, that it was indulging in a delusion to expect any revival there of Jewish culture.

A friend from Yugoslavia told me that Jewish life there was at a low ebb. It was true that a few thousand Jews had been left alive and that Zionism was allowed, but there was no Zionist activity there, nor did any seem possible. The Jewish youth were all ardent followers of Communism, which meant that they were lost to Judaism. I heard that the same thing had happened to most young Jews in other Balkan lands that had fallen under the yoke of the Kremlin. A delegate from Greece surprised me by rolling off without a pause a full list of the thirteen cities in that country where there were still Jews, and the exact number in each. One evening, in a restaurant, chance brought me face to face with two young men who told me that they were on the way to Palestine. They originated from different parts of Poland and had been through all the horrors of war and the privations of captivity. One of them had fought in the Polish Army at the beginning of the war and was taken prisoner to Russia, where he worked for some years in a munitions factory.

He was afterwards repatriated to Poland, where he met the other young man, and then they, together with hundreds of others, trekked through one country after another and smuggled their way over frontiers, until they arrived at Basle. The former prisoner of war had had to change his name so often that he sometimes forgot what his real name was. They had been helped during part of their Odyssey by motor-trucks, but had travelled the greater part on foot, and that was how they were going to get to the port from which they would sail to *Eretz Israel*.

The main question debated in the Congress was whether the Executive should accept the invitation of the British Government to take part in an adjourned conference to consider the Morrison plan. The delegates were divided into two main groups, but not on party lines, nor according to countries. Many, long and passionate speeches, with stormy interruptions, were delivered on both sides for over a week. Dr. Weizmann looked frail and tottery as he pleaded in favour of attending the Conference, but was heckled with angry interjections as though he were the representative of the accused British Government, and when he concluded he asked to be allowed to leave the platform owing to the state of his health. There were many who supported his view, while emphasising their antagonism to the Morrison plan; there were many others who would agree to go to the Conference only on condition that the Government were willing to consider the establishment of a Jewish State. Finally, the crucial vote was taken in the early hours of the morning: by a small majority it was decided not to take part in the conference. Since the policy urged by Dr. Weizmann was defeated, his name was not submitted for re-election as President, and the position that he had held for over twenty years was left vacant. But although deprived of office and responsibility, he continued to enjoy the esteem and veneration of the greater part of the Zionist world, and when the State of Israel at last came into being eighteen months later, nobody else was conceivable or acceptable as the first President.

I returned to London in a somewhat puzzled frame of mind, as it was not clear what the new Executive would do. But a few weeks later Mr. Ben-Gurion and some of his colleagues had talks in London with Mr. Bevin about fresh proposals, even less favourable than the Morrison Plan, which they straightway rejected. Thereupon the Government decided to refer the whole problem to the United Nations.

VI

Early in the following year I was invited by the authorities of Jews' College to deliver a course of ten weekly lectures on " The Jews in the Modern World " as part of the Extension Courses of the University of London. After spending some time on drawing up the syllabus and realising that the task would involve considerable research, I thought that I might as well utilise the extensive material that I had to collect for the benefit of a much larger public than my class of students. I therefore decided to write a new book on *Contemporary Jewry*. The revised edition of my *Jewish Life in Modern Times*, which had appeared in 1929, had now become as much out-of-date as the original edition of 1914 had become fifteen years later, and although there was a continued demand for it the numerous and fundamental changes in the Jewish world that had taken place in consequence of the Second World War made it necessary to replace it by a new work. Owing to the multitudinous facts and statistical data that had to be collected from manifold sources, the labour of composition, rendered all the more tantalising by the march of events that was taking place all the time and often necessitated alterations, kept me occupied until nearly the end of 1948. My *Contemporary Jewry* covering all the main aspects of Jewish life, was published by Methuen & Co. eighteen months later, and met with considerable praise.[1]

In the summer of 1947 I interrupted my work to go for a holiday with my wife to Florence, where she wished to revive her lingering memories of its wealth of art and beauty. She also went to see the splendours of Siena, to which I confess I did not accompany her, as it meant getting up at five in the morning. We then travelled back to Stresa, where, besides strolling and reading on the shore of the beautiful Lake, we had two unusual experiences. One was to see the

[1] Dr. James Parkes wrote: "This book is probably Mr. Israel Cohen's masterpiece. It is an admirable work of reference . . . A book which is remarkable, indeed irreplaceable, in its own field" (*Jewish Chronicle*).

making of parts of the well-known film, *One Night With You*, with its stars Patricia Roc, Nino Martini, and Bonar Colleano in action. Martini would sing his songs in his mellifluous tenor voice in the hotel lounge every morning, with the guests listening in hushed admiration. The other and more thrilling experience was the discovery, on the main road between Stresa and Milan, of a palazzo in Palladian style, which was being used as a training centre or *Kibbutz* for some two hundred young Jewish refugees and " displaced persons " from Eastern Europe, who intended settling in Palestine.[1] About half-a-mile further on we saw a memorial of Nazi barbarity. It was a grey marble tablet fixed against the wall, bearing the names of fifteen Jews who had been murdered by the Nazis in April, 1943, and thrown into the Lake. The victims had formed the entire Jewish community of the townlet of Meina, and the memorial had been placed there by their Italian friends who always laid fresh flowers at the foot of it.

In the following summer we went to Montreux to attend a plenary session of the World Jewish Congress. I was a fraternal delegate of the Board of Deputies of British Jews, which meant that, apart from delivering a speech of greeting on behalf of the Board, I was merely a passive observer. I was struck by the fact that it was a sort of Zionist Congress in miniature, not only because its delegates had come from many lands on both sides of the Atlantic but also because of the similarity of procedure. Many sections of Jewry were represented, except the assimilationists, to whom, of course, the holding of such a gathering was anathema; but what distinguished it from other international or inter-territorial Jewish assemblies was the participation of several Communists and a Bundist. The presence of Communists was due to the change of political régime that had taken place throughout Central and Eastern Europe and that had also affected Jewish life in those regions. The language used mostly was Yiddish, and it was indicative of the active interest displayed by Jews of South America — the sons of Yiddish-speaking parents — that so many speeches were delivered in Spanish.

It seemed to me a tribute to the sense of Jewish solidarity

[1] See the author's *Travels in Jewry*, pp. 290-293.

animating the delegates from both the East and the West that, although divided profoundly in their political views, they, outwardly at least, presented a united front to the outside world. After a series of speeches by delegates from Eastern Europe depicting the blissful conditions prevailing in their countries — as a result of the defeat of the forces of Fascism, it was refreshing to hear one from Poland remark that the delivery of so many eulogies by speakers on their respective Governments was rather undignified. It was disappointing, however, that the Communists, forming about one-tenth of the total assembly, made no attempt to explain the absence of delegates from Soviet Russia, or why it was that, although the Soviet Government had been so vigorous a champion at the United Nations of the State of Israel, there were still a few thousand Zionists in Russian gaols and concentration camps.

We soon learned that the semblance of harmony between the Communists and the majority, which was manifested in the public sessions, entirely broke down behind the scenes in the attempt to reach an amicable arrangement about the composition of the new Executive. We were kept waiting for hours while negotiations were going on to come to an agreement; but, in the end, all endeavours were fruitless, and an Executive was elected with several empty places for the Jewish communities behind the Iron Curtain to be filled at a later stage. Within a year or two, however, all those communities were ordered by their Governments to sever all relations with the World Jewish Congress, which was denounced as a servile instrument of the " war-mongering " West.

VII

From New Year's day in 1949 I looked forward to the 24th of April, when I would be seventy. Before long my wife began to discuss arrangements to celebrate the anniversary, and a few weeks before the event invitations were sent out to a very large number of friends. But at the same time I began to suffer from a recurrence of gastritis, followed by vomiting and half a week of hiccoughing. My doctor had me taken to a hospital, with the assurance that I would soon be better, but a few days after I was admitted an urgent operation was performed on me by a surgeon, who declared that it was necessary to save my life. My seventieth birthday was thus spent on a sick-bed, with a room full of glorious flowers from friends. There followed day after day of varying discomfort, many days of pain, and some of agony. Every afternoon my wife came to comfort me with her cheerful company, bringing me books, papers, letters, and food to relieve the hospital's monotonous diet, while I was fortunate in having a young Irish nurse, whose devotion, skill, and patience were beyond all praise. At last, after ten wearisome weeks I was brought back home still in need of medical attention and nursing and two months later I was taken to another hospital, where I underwent another operation and was restored to a state of normalcy. Even then there followed an aftermath that necessitated several weeks' further medical treatment, so that it was not until towards the end of the year that I felt really well and was able to resume my activities.

The abandoned celebration of my seventieth birthday was observed a year later with grateful enjoyment. But what pleased me much more was that I was able to work in my study again and to travel abroad. I was asked by the family of my old friend, Paul Goodman, who had died in the previous year, to revise and bring up-to-date his *History of the Jews*, the last edition of which had appeared in 1939. In agreement with the publishers, Messrs. J. M. Dent and Sons, Limited, I gladly undertook the task, thus paying a personal tribute to his memory by continuing where he had left off. I not only revised the book but enlarged it by the addition of three chapters to bring it up to 1950. In the summer my wife and I went to Barcelona and the neighbouring sea-side resort of Sitges, and on our return stayed at Narbonne to look up the mediaeval Jewish relics,[1] and also visited the interesting old city of Carcasonne, with its mediaeval fortifications.

In 1950 I wrote my *Short History of Zionism*, so as to cover all the momentous events, including the establishment of Israel, that had occurred since the end of the war. It met with a good reception, was translated into Hebrew, and — what gratified me above all — it was transcribed into Braille, making four large volumes. In the following year I was busy with two other books. One was *Travels*

[1] See *Travels in Jewry*, p. 327.

THE AUTHOR'S WIFE, BARCELONA, 1950

in *Jewry*, which contained accounts of my experiences in thirty Jewish communities in twelve different countries in Europe (and all of which had previously been printed in various journals).[1] The other, which I edited, was a miscellany, *The Rebirth of Israel*, intended as a memorial to Paul Goodman: I wrote his memoir, and there were contributions on important aspects of the Zionist movement and the State of Israel by twenty-three writers of authority. Both books appeared in 1952 and met with friendly appreciation.

VIII

Now, as I complete my latest book, I cannot help looking back, not so much at the events in my own life, as at those in the Jewish world that I have witnessed since I first began to study them with an observant eye, and which have found some reflection in these pages. For some of those events have been revolutionary and cataclysmic, and the map of the Jewish world is now totally different from what it was sixty years ago. Outbreaks of persecution and massacre, tides of migration in all directions, falsified assurances that followed the First World War, Nazi barbarities that preceded the Second and orgies of sadistic extermination that accompanied it, all resulted in radically transforming the composition and complexion of Jewry. For one-third of the Jewish people were wiped out within a few years, one-fifth of the remnant are immured behind the Iron Curtain, countless communities once famed as centres of culture and citadels of religious tradition have been decimated and desolated, and the major part of Jewry is no longer in Europe but in America. How many millions of Jews have been slaughtered since I first began to read the reports of Russian pogroms in my boyhood, how many edicts of intolerance and ukases of oppression have been enacted, how many outrages, tragedies, and crimes have been committed, how much material wealth has been plundered or destroyed, and how much potential genius has been murdered — all these things await the careful examination and judicial appraisement of some future historian of civilisation.

[1] *John O'London's Weekly* wrote: "Pathos and humour and good writing have enabled Israel Cohen to make his *Travels in Jewry* a memorable book."

A JEWISH PILGRIMAGE

On the other side of the account is the fulfilment of the Jew's two thousand year old dream of the restoration of his national independence in his ancestral land. It is a consummation for which he had to labour long and heroically and, despite the United Nations' decision, to fight desperately against overwhelming and better equipped forces; and yet, such as it is, it forms only a partial attainment of the age-old aspiration and is still exposed to the menace of attack. Moreover, great as are the achievements of those who have combined to build the State of Israel, and real as is the pride of those beyond its frontiers who help to support it, both are fully conscious that what has been created is still far from the ideal that nourished the hopes and strengthened the endurance of their forefathers through the centuries, not only because the State cannot form the home of the entire Jewish people, but because an essential factor in the vision of Messianic salvation — peace and security from all kinds of hostility — is still acutely lacking. How soon that vision will be realised in all its fullness will depend less upon the efforts of the Jew than upon the goodwill and sense of justice of his neighbours in all lands, as well as upon the dawn of true amity among mankind in general. Meanwhile he can but hope and pray for the arrival of that moment with all the fervour with which his ancestors yearned for the coming of the Messiah, for he still believes, as they did, that

> *One people ariseth, another disappeareth.*
> *But Israel endureth for ever.*[1]

---

[1] Midrash Commentary on Psalm XXXVI.

Index

Aaronson, Aaron, 85
Abano, 322
Abbazia, 277
Abdul Hamid, 78
Aberdeen, 119
Abrahams, Israel, 26, 30, 31, 37
Abyssinia, 67
Acre, 181
Acton, Lord, 134
Actress, 345
Adelaide, 184
Adler, Cyrus, 296
Adler, Elkan N., 62
Adler, Dr. Hermann, 20, 30, 33
Adler, Jacob P., 61
Adrianople, 252
Aga Khan, 275
Agate, James, 15
Agra, 213
Agudists, 242; Agudas Israel, 242, 246, 303
Ahad Haam, 74-5, 76, 91, 341
Alberta, 290, 292
Aldgate, 21, 26, 62
Aleppo, 387
Alexander, David L., 124
Alexander, Michael Solomon, 200
Alexander, Samuel, 17, 122
Alexandria, 179, 216, 316, 361
Aliens Act, 59
Alkalay, Chief Rabbi, 250-1
Allen, W. H., and Co., 370
Allenby, Field-Marshal, 341
Alston, Sir Beilby, 206
Altneuschul, 249

Ambassador, American, 103
Amber trade, 246-7
America, 4, 24, 42; Zionists of, 82
American Embassy, 99
American Jewish Committee, 379
    Conference, 380
Amery, L. S., 274
Amir, Dr. M., 306
Amsterdam, 46, 47, 114
Amulet, 2
Amzalak, Prof. M. B., 312, 339
Anarchists, 52
Anatolia, 215
Angelescu, M., 235
Anglicisation, 29
Anglo-American Committee, 379, 384
Anglo-Israel Association, 341
Anglo-Jewish Association, 123, 124, 379
Anglo-Palestine Bank, 81, 90, 121
Anti-Semitism, 62, 104, 127, 129, 130, 139, 141, 142, 158, 160; in Greece, 53; in Bulgaria, 254-5; in Rumania, 256-7, 306-7; in Canada, 294; in Palestine, 352; in Europe, 359; in England, 372
Antwerp, 241
Arab Delegation, 221
Arabia, 38, 212
Arabs, 216; attacks by, 269, 347; revolt of, 321-2, 349, 356; "displaced," 349
Arc de Triomphe, 206, 384
Archer, William, 58
Argentina, 124, 317

Arlosoroff, Dr. Ch., 308
Art, Jewish, 46
Asch, Sholem, 62, 268
Ashbee, C. R., 350
Astor, John J., 42
Athens, 244, 252-3, 388
Atholl, Duchess of, 307
Atonement, Fast of, 6
Auckland, 187-8
Aufbau, 373
Auschwitz, 146
Australia, 182-7, 191, 326, 379, 388
Austria, Zionist Congress in, 92; declares war on Serbia, 96; invaded by Hitler, 323-7
Austro-Hungarian Monarchy, 137
"Awakening Magyars," 173, 177-8
Azores, 311

Bad Godesberg, 84
Baden, Grand Duke of, 170
Baden-Baden, 44
Baeck, Dr. Leo, 377
Baghdad, 194, 199, 207, 208, 209, 211, 304
Baker, Philip Noel, 361
Bakunin, 51
Baldwin, Stanley, 274
Balfour, Arthur J., 77, 122, 134, 221, 223, 265-6, 270
Balfour, Sir John, 232, 235, 238
Balfour Declaration, 31, 74, 77, 122-4, 125, 127, 132, 161, 172-3, 220, 230, 272, 278, 342, 347, 355, 378
Balfouria, 315
Balkans, 243, 380, 389
Ballarat, 185
Balliol College, 368
Banbury, 119
Bandoeng, 209
Baneth, Noemi, 65
Bank Leumi le-Israel, 81
Baptisms, 243-4, 389
Barcelona, 312-3, 394

Barnett, Canon, 36
Barnett, Richard, 52-3
Baron, Bernhard, 264-6
Basle, 42, 54, 277, 386
Basle Programme, 29, 272, 278
Batavia, 209, 210
Battle of the Nile, 52-3
Baudelaire, 107
Bearsted, Viscount, 329
Beaverbrook press, 221
Bechyne, M., 358
Belasco, David, 291
Belgians, 107, 108
Belgrade, 250-2
Belilios, E. R., 195
Ben-Gurion, David, 316, 317, 377, 384, 390
Bene Israel, 213, 215
Benn, W. Wedgwood, 36
Bennett, Sir Ernest, 355
Bensusan, S. L., 34
Bentinck, Lord Henry, 120
Bentwich, Herbert, 32, 73, 77
Bergelson, David, 375
Berlin, 62; author's residence in, 87-95, 113; meetings of Zionist General Council, 225, 240, 272, 278, 298, 328-9
Berlin Jewish Community, 102
Berlin University, 99
Berliner Tageblatt, 89
Berne, 134, 146, 281; University, 55
Bernstein (Braunstein), 247
Bessarabia, 242, 306
Bessborough, Earl of, 287
Beth Hamidrash, 6, 14, 254
Bethlehem, 315
Bethlen, Count, 250
Bevin, Ernest, 378, 383, 384, 391
Beyrut, 162
Bialik, Ch. N., 338
Bialystok, 241, 303
Bimetallism, 20
Bingen, 41
Birmingham, 371

Bishop of London, 120
"Black List" (Nazi), 328
Blackpool, 119
Blakeney, General, 355
Blau, Rabbi Dr. Joel, 266
Bloomsbury, 26
Blum, Leon, 268, 275, 334
Board of Deputies of British Jews, 123, 124, 158, 306, 361, 370, 373-4, 379, 380-1, 385
Bodenheimer, Dr. M., 80, 316
Boehm, Adolf, 323-4
Bohemia, 248
Bolsheviks, 152, 160, 247, 319
Bolshevism, 147, 154-160, 199, 348, 350, 355
Bombay, 213-5
Bonaparte, Napoleon, 139
Bonn, 41
Bookman, The, 280
Bottomley, Horatio, 118, 119
Bournemouth, 119
Bouverie Street, 58
Bradford, 200
Brailsford, H. N., 58, 60-1, 79, 147
Brainin, Reuben, 68-9
Brandeis, Judge L. D., 90, 168, 275, 335
Brandes, George, 51
Branting, Karl, 147
Bremen, 60
Brighton, 71
Brisbane, 191
Britain's Nameless Ally, 369
British Columbia, 291-3
British Government, negotiations with, 122
British Museum, 31, 39, 53, 64, 161, 273
British-Israelite theory, 191
Brixton Prison, 114-5
Brod, Max, 249
Brodetsky, Prof. S., 281, 317, 365, 381
Brondesbury, 113

Brooks, Collin, 372-3
Brotman, A. G., 381
Browne, E. G., 237
Browning, Robert, 70
Bruges, 41
Brunton, Chisholm D., 350
Brussels, 41
Brutzkus, Dr. J., 245-6
Bryan, W. Jennings, 90
Bryce, Viscount, 127
Buber, Martin, 44, 249
Bucharest, 234, 257, 306
Buckmaster, Lord, 150
Budapest, 173, 176-8, 232, 235-7, 249-250, 388
Budde, 237
Buenos Aires, 60, 388
Bukowina, 243
Bulgaria, 243, 244, 253-6, 380
Bund, 51, 52, 56, 58, 374
Bundists, 140, 202, 242, 246
Burmese, 211

Cabbala, 196; Cabbalists, 248, 315
Cable and Wireless, 322
Café des Westens, 94
Cairo, 179
Calcutta, 196, 212-3
Calgary, 289, 290
Cambridge, 48, 369; University, 226, 340, 382
Canada, 281-296, 367, 388
Canadian Jewish Congress, 285, 295
Canadian Pacific Railway, 289
"Candidus," 343
Canea, 253
Canetti, 253
Canton, 207
Cantors, 23
Capernaum, 315
Carcasonne, 394
Carl, King, 233
Carlsbad, 219-220, 225, 227
Carnegie Hall, 282
Carnival-tide, 87

Carpathian Ruthenia, 358
Carreras, Ltd., 265
Cassel, Sir Ernest, 171
Castleberg family, 190
Cecil, Lord, 173
Chamberlain, Sir Austen, 274
Champs Elysées, 384
Chancery Lane, 77, 122
Chassidim, 6, 245, 246, 286
Chatham House, 355, 361
Chatto and Windus, 38
Chaucer, 28
Chayes, Chief Rabbi, 176
Cheder, 9
Cheetham, 1
Cheltenham, 369
Chesterfield, Lady, 100
Chesterton, G. K., 180
Chicago, 295
Chichester Theological College, 48
China, 193-8
Chisinau, 257
Chovevei Zion, 18, 29, 32, 33
Christadelphians, 344, 353
Christchurch, 189-190
Chrzanow, 138
Churchill, Lady Randolph, 66
Churchill, Sir Winston, 66, 222, 328, 348
Claridge's Hotel, 363
Claxton, Brooke, 383
Clayton, Sir Gilbert, 341
Clerk, Sir George, 134, 220
Clerkenwell Town Hall, 32, 168
Cluj, 257
Codreanu, 257, 306
Cohen, Benjamin, V., 168, 169
Cohen, David, 131
Cohen, Rev. E. M. D., 212
Cohen, John J., 186
Cohen, Jonathan, 131, 368
Cohen, Lord Justice, 329, 366
Cohen, Tessie (author's wife), 131-2, holiday in Italy, 216; at Rapallo; 269; at Wiesbaden 272-3; at Rimini, 309; on Lake Garda, 322; at lunch to author, 365; opposed to flight to Canada, 367; war work, 368, 376; at W.I.Z.O. Conference, 386
Colleano, Bonar, 392
Collins, Churton, 36
Cologne, 41, 64, 80-87, 298
Colombo, 182
Colonial Office, 221, 222, 270, 343, 356
Committee of Jewish Delegations, 148, 163
Communists, 319, 392-3
Conference at St. James's Palace, 329-330
Congress, Zionist, 259-264. See also Zionist Congress
Conjoint Foreign Committee, 123
Conservatives, 58, 61
Constantinople, 76, 78, 83, 162, 241, 341
Contemporary Jewry, 242, 381, 391
Contemporary Review, 352, 360, 370, 373
Conway Hall, 354
Cordova, 312
Correspondence, in press, 352
County Forum, 20
Courland, 245
Courtney, W. L., 130
Cowen, Joseph, 61, 75, 81, 121, 166, 342
Cracow, 62-3, 135, 137, 138, 139, 145, 241, 303
Crane, Walter, 18
Cripps, Sir Stafford, 150, 328
Croatia, 251
Croll, David, 287
Cromwell, Oliver, 46
Crossman, R. H. S., 328
Crown Rabbi, 91
Crozier, W. P., 15
Crystal, Leon, 375
Cuba, 387

Cultural Zionism, 74
Current History, 352
Currie, Sir Arthur, 285
Cuza, Professor, 257
Czechoslovakia, 241, 326, 357-8
Czenstochau, 303
Czernowitz, 257

Dafoe, J. W., 288
Dagania, 181
Daily Chronicle, 51, 60
Daily Express, 348
Daily Graphic, 67, 123
Daily Mail, 221, 328, 348
Daily Mirror, 343
Daily News, 95
Dakotas, 292
Dalston, 35
Dalton, Hugh, 228
Damascus, 387
Daniel, Book, of, 327
Danzig, 141, 244, 248
Dark, Sidney, 343
Daszynski, I., 62-3, 136, 139
David, Reb, 9-12
David, Sir Sassoon, 214
Davidson, Sir Walter, 187
Davis, Israel, 75
Davis, Sir Mortimer, 284
Dead Sea, 315
Dead Sea Scrolls, 316
Death Camps, 374
Deedes, Sir Wyndham, 341
Delhi, 213, 382
Democratic Fraction, 44
Denikin, General, 158, 160
Denmark, 240, 378
Dent, J. M., 394
Detectives, 113
Detroit, 287
Dicey, A. V., 36
Dickens, Charles, 26
"Diplomaticus," 67
Disraeli, B., 200
Dizengoff, Meir, 316, 338

Djemal Pasba, 338
Dnystriansky, Prof., 146
Doeblinger Cemetery, 327
Dorpat, 247-8
"Dorshei Zion," 18
Dresden, 96
Dreyfus, Dr. C., 77
Droitwich, 367-8
"Dual nationality," 129
Dublin, 357
Dugdale, Mrs. Blanche, 342
Dugdale, T. C., 15
Duke's Place Synagogue, 30
Dukes, Sir Paul, 157
Duma, 91, 163
Dunedin, 190
Dunn, Nicol, 20
Duesseldorf, 45

East African scheme, 43-4, 54, 89, 201
East End, 28, 30, 59, 78. See also Whitechapel.
Easthampstead, 367
Ecuador, 116
Eden, Sir Anthony, 120
Eden, Sir Timothy, 120
Eder, Dr. M. D., 224, 227, 228
Edinburgh Review, 350
Edmonton, 289
Eichmann, 323
Einstein, Albert, 94, 268, 334-5
Eisner, Kurt, 147
El Arish scheme, 44, 121
Elbogen, Dr. I., 100
Eliash, Dr. Mordecai, 315
Elijah, *Gaon*, 304
Eliot, Sir Charles, 200
Embassy Theatre, 118
Emigration, from Bulgaria, 255; from Russia, 1, 283; from Poland, 389
Emissaries, 24
Empire House, 126, 161
Encyclopaedia Judaica, 298

English Review, 352
Erzberger, Dr. M., 99, 339
Espagnol, 252
Estonia, 247-8
Estoril, 312
Ethical Church, 354
Ettinger, Jacob, 124, 130
Evening Standard, 69, 88
Evian, Conference at, 362
Examination, University, 47
Exchange of prisoners, 110, 120
Executive, Zionist, 220-221
Eydtkuehnen, 244
Ezra, Sir David, 213
Ezra, Edward I., 197
Ezra, N. E. B., 198

Faitlovitch, Dr. J., 67
Falashas, 67
Farbstein, H., 139
Farm settlements, 292
Fascist régime, 277
Federation of Synagogues, 23
Feffer, Itzik, 375
Feisal, Emir (King), 168, 348
Ferdinand, King, 255, 339
Filderman, Dr. W., 257
Financial and Economic Committee, 220
Finland, 381
Fishman, Jacob, 297
Fledermaus, Die, 107
Florence, 216, 391
Flushing, 111
"Folkists," 140, 242
Forbes, Mrs. Rosita, 355
Foreign Affairs, 272
Foreign Office (British), 89, 113, 117, 134, 143, 149, 367, 378, 379, 383
Forester, Rev. O. St. M., 199-200
Fort William, 293
Fortnightly Review, 130, 347, 350, 352
Forum Magazine, 218
Foster, Dr. Gregory, 36

Frankfort, 41; City Library, 237
Frankfurter, Judge Felix, 168-9, 275, 348
Frankfurter Zeitung, 69, 334
Frankl, Dr. A., 249
Franklin, Lumby, 291
Franks, Jacob, 282
Freedman, Rev. D. I., 182-3
Freelance journalism, 53
Freiman, Aron, 237
Fremantle, 182
Freud, Sigmund, 362-3
Friedlaender, Dr. Michael, 26, 30, 31
Friedlaender, Mrs., 40
Friedmann, Desider, 326
Friends' House, 354
Fusan, 202

Gabriel, Col. Vivian, 350
Galicia, 62-3, 133, 137 seq., 303
Gallipoli, 341
Garvin, J. L., 70
Gas-chambers, 374
Gaster, Dr. Moses, 29, 30, 77, 126, 127
Gawler, Colonel, 184
Gaza, 179
Geddes, Prof. Patrick, 170, 180, 181, 214, 216
Geelong, 185
General Election, 378
General Secretary of Zionist Organisation, 220
Geneva, 52, 56, 330
Genoa, 269
Gentleman's Magazine, 38
German Embassy, 361
German Government, 110
German War Office, 114
German Zionist Federation, 89
Germany, persecution in, 305, 307, 313, 360-2
Gestapo, 325-6-7, 387
Ghent, 41

Ghetto, in Warsaw, 301; in Cracow, 303
Ghetto Gallery, A, 279
Gibbs, Philip, 58
Gibraltar, 312
Ginzberg, Asher, 74
Giurgiu, 256
Gladstone, Herbert, 61
Glasgow Herald, 88, 94, 118
Gleichen, Lord Edward, 354
Globe, The, 88
Goch, 111
Goebbels, 307, 325, 360
Goering, 305, 324-5
Goethe, 41
Goldberg, Boris, 163
Goldbloom, Rev. J. K., 121
Goldfaden, Abraham, 210
Goldmann, Dr. N., 298
Goldsmid, Col. Albert E., 19, 32
Goldstein, Dr. Angelo, 328, 357-8
Goldston, Edward, 279
Goldziher, Prof. I., 236
Goldziher, Prof. Karl, 236
Golem, 249
Goodman, Paul, 121, 394, 395
Gordon, Mrs. E. A., 201
Gordon, General, 205
Gorky, Maxim, 338
Grabski, M., 141
Graetz, 24, 185
Graham, Harry, 59
Grajevo, 3
Grasty, Mr., 230
Greece, 243, 252-3, 387, 389
Green, Rev. A. A., 31
Greenberg, Leopold J., 33, 35, 75, 76, 77, 201
Grossman, Chaya, 378
Gruenbaum, I., 139
Gubbay, Ezekiel, 212
Guedalla, Philip, 361
Guildhall Library, 36
Gumplowicz, Dr. L., 135

Haarlem, 46
Haas, Jacob de, 33, 168, 282
Habsburgs, 233
Hague, The, 46, 64, 124, 176, 216, 295, 340
Haifa, 181, 315
Haifa Technical Institute, 91
Haig, General D., 353
Hailsham, Lord, 274
Hakenkreuzler, 262-3
Haldimand, Sir Fredk., 282
Halevi, Judah, 311
Halevi, Samuel, 311
Halevy, Isaac, 24
Halifax (Canada), 283
Halifax, Viscount, 330
Hall, Marshall, 120
Halukah, 24
Halutzim, 178, 243
Hamburg, 18, 60, 82
Hamilton (Canada), 287, 293
Hammond, J. L., 58
Hampstead Conservatoire, 118
Hampstead Heath, 131
Hampstead Synagogue, 73
Hansard, 277
Haolam, 166, 318
Harbin, 176, 202-5, 290
Harden, Maximilian, 88
Harmsworth press, 221
Harrison, Frederic, 36
Hart, Aaron, 282
Hart, Mrs., 52
Hatikvah, 331
Hatzefirah, 64, 89
Haupt, Prof. P., 67
Hausmann, Dr. A., 136
Havazzelet, 24
Hawke, E. G., 57, 78
Hayehudi, 30, 31
Hearst press, 117
Hebrew authors, 24; Hebrew-speaking Society, 30.
Hebrew language, conflict about, 90; 216.

Hebrew schools, 9-13, 243; songs, 248
Hebrew University, 93, 171-2, 180, 253, 260, 315, 363
Hebrew University Library, 236
Hebron, 315
Hechler, Rev. W., 170
Heidelberg, 42
Heine, Heinrich, 41
Helena May Institute, 195
Hellman, 245
Henderson, Arthur, 147
Hendon Borough, 338
Henlein, Konrad, 362
Hereford, 369
Herskowitz, Mr., 202
Hertz, Rev. Dr. J. H., 33, 153, 157, 269
Herzl, Hans, 81
Herzl, Theodor, first meeting in London, 28; other meetings in London, 33; at Sixth Zionist Congress, 42-3; Weizmann's attitude to, 45; appointment of El Arish expedition, 121; in Vilna, 304; tomb of, 327
High Commissioner for Palestine, 216, 333
Hilfsverein, 90-1
Hill, William, 57
Hindustani, 212
Hirsch, Dr. S.A., 26, 31
Hirsch Institute, 284
Hirschfeld, Dr. H., 38
Hitler, 41, 240, 262, 288, 294, 298, 305, 306, 307, 310, 322, 323, 325, 331, 334, 359-60, 369, 374
Hobhouse, L. T., 58
Hohler, Thomas, 238
Holborn Restaurant, 126
Holland, 46, 114, 337
Hollier Hebrew Scholarship, 36
Holy Land, 23, 24
Homburg, 101
Hongkong, 193-5, 336

Hoofien, S., 80
Horowitz, Phineas, 121
Horthy Fund, 238
Hospital experiences, 393-4
House of Commons, 109, 120, 125, 149, 307, 357, 358, 361
Housman, A. E., 27
Hughes, W. M., 186
Hungary, outrages in, 176-8; mission concerning Zionist Federation, 231-3; 241, 243, 244, 249-50, 326; baptised Jews, 389
Hyde Park, 153, 356

Ignatius, Father, 30
Immigrants, 22, 60; in Canada, 288, 291; "illegal," 378
"Imprimerie Israélite," 56
India, 212-6; Government of, 69, 382
India Office, 70
Ingram, Dr. Winnington, 118
Intermarriage, 199
Iraq, 196, 205, 212, 348
Irish Times, 357
Iron Curtain, 393, 395
Iron Guard, 257, 306
Isaacs, Edward, 15
Isaacs, Sir Isaac, 185
Ish-Kishor, E., 29
Islam, 215
Israel, State of, 396
Israel in Italien, 65
Israel's Messenger, 198, 366
Israels, Josef, 46-7
Italian Government, 277
Italy, 65, 309-310
I.T.O., 76
Ivan Alexander, Czar, 254

Jabotinsky, V., 79, 122-3, 181, 223-6, 267, 278, 313, 341
Jacobs, Joseph, 37, 93
Jacobs, Tessie, 131
Jacobson, Dr. V., 76, 162

Jaffa, 314
Jahreskonferenz, 224
Jamal al Husseini, 355
Janina, 253
Janner, Barnett, 367, 381
Japan, 198-202
Jassy, 257, 258
Java, 209-210
Jerusalem, 179-181; Bishop of, 200
Jesus, 67
Jeune Turc, Le, 79
Jew-baiting, 234
Jewish Agency, 222-4, 266-9, 315, 335, 377, 388
Jewish Brigade Group, 370
Jewish Chronicle, 18, 33, 44, 53, 64, 75-6, 121, 201, 219, 337, 351, 355, 391
Jewish Colonial Trust, 86, 92, 121, 125, 260
Jewish Colonisation Association, 124, 292
Jewish Correspondence Bureau, 226
Jewish Encyclopedia, 368
Jewish Guardian, 352
Jewish Historical Society, 40
Jewish Life in Modern Times, 88, 94, 95, 104, 168, 241, 359, 391
Jewish National Fund, 80, 81, 86, 88, 92, 121, 124, 131, 176, 216, 228, 260
Jewish Publication Society, 296, 304, 366
Jewish Quarterly Review, 53
Jewish Standard, The, 287
Jewish State, 129
Jewish Telegraphic Agency, 226
Jewish Territorial Organisation, 56
Jewish Theological Seminary, 37, 92
Jewish Times, The, 225
Jewish World, The, 33, 38, 45, 53, 54, 65, 66-7
Jews' College, 10, 20-21, 25 *seq.*, 47-8, 391
Jews' Temporary Shelter, 59

Jezreel, Vale of, 339
Jodko, Dr., 63, 140
Johannesburg, 388
John Bull, 118
Joint Distribution Committee, 199, 301
Joseph, Henry, 282
Journal of a Jewish Traveller, 176
Journalism, 49-70, 116, 347 *seq.*, 352
Joyce, William, 373
Joynson-Hicks, W., 273
"Judaeans," 341
Juedische Rundschau, 89
"Judischer Verlag," 88, 162
Jury service, 385

Kaddish, 3
Kadoorie, Sir Ellis, 195, 336
Kadoorie, Sir Elly, 336
Kafka, Franz, 249
Kai-Feng-Fu, 196
Kalgoorlie, 183
Kalvariya, 1
Kandel, Isaac L., 15
Kann, J. H., 75, 79, 80, 84, 337
Kantara, 179
Kaplan, Dora, 155
Karaites, 304
Karminski, Justice, 270
Katzenelsohn, Dr. N., 75
Kellner, Prof. L., 67
Kenney, Rowland, 143
Kent, Duke of, 282
Ker, Prof. W. P., 27, 36
"Keren Hayesod," 218, 254, 310, 317, 366
Kessler, Leopold, 44, 75, 121
Kfar Kana, 181
Khachar Mansur Ala, 69
Kharkoff, 210
Kiddush, 6
Kilburn, 39, 70
Kiley, J. D., 150
Kilner, George W., 26
Kimens, Richard, 143

Kingsway Hall, 120
Kingsway Theatre, 124
King's Hall, 30
Kinross, Albert, 60
Kinnereth, 181
Kisch, F. H., 227
Kishinev, 257-8
Klatzkin, Dr. J., 298
Klaus, 304
Klebelsberg, Count von, 232, 249
Klee, Alfred, 337
"Knesset," 246
Kobe, 198, 201-2
Koenigsberg, 246
Kolu Li, 346
Kommers, 94
Kongress Zeitung, 260, 261
Korea, 202, 346
Kovno, 241, 244, 245
Kramer, Jacob, 153
Kropotkin, Prince, 52
Kruger, President, 33, 107
Kun, Bela, 178
Kyoto, 201

Labouchere, H., 373
Labour Government (Party), 378
Labrador, 295-6
Lamington, Earl of, 354
Lancing, 222
Landau, Herman, 150
Lane, John, 70
Langley, Sir Walter, 90
Laski, Prof. Harold, 66, 274, 275, 385-6
Laski, Nathan, 66
Laski, Neville, 66
Lasocki, Count, 136, 137
Lassalle, F., 52
Latvia, 242, 243, 246
Lauterbach, Dr. L., 340
Lauterpacht, Dr. H., 275, 340, 382
Lawrence, T. E., 348
Lazarus, Dayan H. M., 47
League of British Jews, 129

League of Nations, 221, 257, 277, 307, 321
Lectures, 371, 391
Leeds, 153; Conference at, 77
Leeds University, 281
Lemberg, 61, 135, 143-5
Lenin, 155
Lettish, 243
Letzte Nachrichten, 56
Levin, Dr. Shmarya, 91, 93, 162
Levine, Reb Mottel, 21, 23, 24
Levine, Rev. Ephraim, 367
Levy, Sir Daniel, 186, 191
Levy, Oscar, 272-3
Leyden, 46
Libau, 244, 246
Libel, law against, 294
Liberals, 58, 61, 65
Lichtheim, Richard, 305
Liebermann, Max, 46
Lilith, 2
Lipsky, Louis, 93, 229, 231, 297
Lipton (Canada), 290
Lipton, Sir Thomas, 120
Lisbon, 311-2, 339
Lithuania, 241, 242, 243, 244
Lithuanian Government, 223
Lloyd George, David, 122, 270, 271, 274
Locker, Berl, 281, 367
Lodz, 302-3
Loew, *Hohe* Rabbi, 248
Lomza, 1, 2, 3
London University, 39, 53
London Zionist League, 73
Lorelei, 41
Los Angeles, 291
Lottery, 12
Louvre, 49
Lubetkin, Zivia, 387
Lucerne, Congress at, 313-4, 317
Ludendorff, General, 362
Lugano, 381
Lullabies, 2
Luxembourg, 41

Lwow, 303. See also Lemberg.
Lydda, 179

Macao, 207
Maccabaean Club, 28
MacDonald, Malcolm, 277, 330
MacDonald, Ramsay, 61, 147, 231, 270-2, 276
MacDonogh, Sir George, 341
Macedonian Revolutionary Committee, 255
Maderoe, 210
Madrid, 164, 232, 310-11, 334
Magnus, Laurie, 76, 352
Magyars, 233
Maimonides, 304, 312
Malcolm, James A., 170
Manchester Courier, 14, 20
Manchester Evening Chronicle, 34
Manchester Examiner, 14
Manchester Free Trade Hall, 19
Manchester Grammar School, 15-17, 189
Manchester Guardian, 14, 15, 20, 51, 53, 54, 118, 122, 262, 279, 307, 322, 343, 355, 359, 371
Manchester Jews' School, 7-8
Manchester New Synagogue, 13
Manchester Reference Library, 17
Manchuria, 175, 290
Mandate for Palestine, 172, 221-3, 274, 275, 330
Mandatory Government, 300, 307, 321
Manila, 192-3
Manitoba Free Press, 288
Mann, Arthur H., 116
Manning, Mrs. Kathleen, 73
Maoriland, 188
Marble Arch, 356
Marchlevsky, Professor, 136
Markish, Peretz, 375
Marks, Rev. Prof. D. W., 36
Marmorek, Dr. Alexander, 65
Marriage, author's, 131

Marseillaise, 55
Marshall, Louis, 266-7, 268-9, 335
Martin, Kingsley, 274
Martini, Nino, 392
Marx, Karl, 51, 52
Masaryk, Jan, 305
Massacres, in Russia, 160
Massel, Joseph, 19
Massey, W. F., 189
Masterton, 190
Mazin's bookshop, 36, 51
McGill University, 285
McMahon correspondence, 348
McNeil, Hector, 383
Meina, 392
Meir, Chief Rabbi J., 253
Melammed, 9, 290
Melbourne, 184-6
Melchett, Lord, 125, 128, 253, 268, 269, 271, 274. See also Mond, Sir Alfred
Memel, 246
Menasce, Baron Felix de, 179
Menasseh ben Israel, 46
Merhavia, 339
Merriman, Sir F. B. (Lord), 270-1
Meshed, 215
Meshullochim, 24
Mesopotamia, 221, 350
Messiah, 208, 233, 396
Methuen, Sir Algernon, 78
Methuen & Co., 95, 118, 359
Mexico, 387
Meyer, Sir Menasseh, 207
Midrash, 11, 396
Mikhoels, Solomon, 375
Milan, 241
Millions Club, 187
Milner, Lord, 171, 173, 193
Ministry of Information, 131, 132
Minkoff (of Bulgaria), 255
Minorities Treaties, 148, 257, 359
Mizrachi, 278
Mocatta, Frederic D., 40
Mocatta Library, 40

Mommsen, 237
Monash, Sir John, 185
Mond, Sir Alfred, 125, 126, 127-8, 129, 173, 186, 222, 253. See also Melchett, Lord.
Montagu, Sir Samuel, 23, 29. See also Swaythling, Lord
Montefiore, Claude, 34, 124, 222, 266
Montefiore, Sir Francis, 32
Montefiore, Jacob, 184
Montefiore, Joseph, 186
Montefiore, Sir Moses, 184, 284, 304
Montreal, 282-5, 295-6
Montreux, 269, 392
More, Thomas, 38
Morgenthau, Henry, 154, 218
Morgenthau, Henry, Junior, 218
Morley, John, 19, 69-70
Morning Post, 20, 86, 151-2, 159
Morrison Plan, 384, 390-1
Moscow, 247
Moses, Dr. E., 213
Moslems, 214, 215
Mosque of Omar, 315
Motzkin, Leo, 56, 85, 163, 264, 343
Mount Carmel, 181
Mount Scopus, 180
Mourning, 3
Mowshowitch, Dr. D., 381
Mufti of Jerusalem, 356
Mukden, 202
Muller, Frederick, 369, 371
Mundy, A., 59
Murray, Capt. A. C., 89
Murray, Sir John, 306, 361
Musa Kazim Pasha, 221, 356
Musar, 245
Mussolini, 309, 310, 316, 322
"Mustermesse," 388
Myers, Asher I., 33, 35
Myers, Sir Michael, 189

Nablus, 315
Nagasaki, 81, 197
Nahalal, 315
Nalevki, 142
Nansen passports, 247
Naples, 316
Napoleon, 304
Naprzod, 136
Narbonne, 394
Nathan, Mrs. David, 188
Nathanson, Prof. W. 137
National Liberal Club, 167
Navy, English, 52-3
Nazis, 273, 294, 298, 306, 324-7, 338, 360, 361, 371, 387, 392
Near and Middle East Association, 354-5
Negev, 384
Nelson, Lord, 52
Ness-Zionah, 181
Neue Freie Presse, 67
Nevinson, Henry, 60
New Palestine, The, 231, 365
New South Wales, 186
New Statesman, The, 360, 362
New Testament, 23, 97
New Year, 6
New York, 282, 296-7
New York Times, 95, 229-231
New Zealand, 187-190, 388
Newcastle, 153, 191
Newton, Lord, 117
Niagara Falls, 287
Nichols, Beverley, 351-2
Nicolson, Sir Arthur, 89-90
Nietzsche, 273
Nineteenth Century, 350, 351, 352, 360
Noeldeke, 237
Nordau, Max, at Sixth Zionist Congress, 43; author's interview with, 49-51; at Seventh Congress, 54; message to Eleventh Congress, 93; life in London, 164-6; return to Paris and death, 167
Northcliffe, Lord, 132, 157-9, 221, 231

Norway, 240
Nova Scotia, 293
Novy Dziennik, 140
Numerus clausus, 137, 234, 235-6, 285
Nurock, Dr. Mordecai, 246
Nurock, Rabbi, 246

Oakeshott, W. F., 367
Observer, The, 280
Ochs, Adolph S., 229-231
O'Connor, T. P., 120
Olitzka, Rosa, 295
Onions, Oliver, 72
Onslow, Earl of, 90
Ontario, 283, 292
Oppenheimer, David, 291
Oppenheimer, Dr. Franz, 99, 339
Oradea Mare, 257
Order of Ancient Maccabaeans, 79, 83
Ospovat, Henry, 17-18, 35, 49, 70-72
Ostend, 40
Oswiecim, 146
Ottawa, 287
Ottoman régime, 125
Ouderkerk, 46
Outlook, The, 116
Oxford University, 151

Pacific Ocean, 288
Paderewski, Ignaz, 139, 141-2, 151
Padua, 216, 322
Palastina, 324
Palcor, 322
Pale of Settlement, 1, 13
Palestine, 24; 179-181, 216; visited in 1935, 314-6
Palestine (journal), 343
Palestine Electric Corporation, 271
Palestine Foundation Fund, 218, 362, 366
Palestine Land Development Co., 90
Palestine Restoration Fund, 129, 130, 171, 179, 217
Pall Mall Gazette, 51
Pamphlets, 130-131, 132, 348, 352-3, 361, 370
Paris, 49, 147-8, 229-231, 380
Parkes, Dr. James, 391
Parliament, Zionist members of, 242
Parmoor, Lord, 150
Parsees, 214
Partition (of Palestine), 321, 329
Pass, Herman L., 47-8
Passfield, Lord, 172, 271-2, 276. See also Webb, Sidney
Passfield White Paper, 273, 276-7, 278, 330
Passover, 5
Passport, 58, 308-9
Pasteina, Dr., 238
Patterson, Col. J. H., 341
Pavilion Theatre, 53
Peace Conference at Paris (1919), 146, 147-8, 152, 164, 168, 169, 172, 222, 227, 348; Conference of 1946, 381;
Peace Treaty (1919), 300-301
Peace Treaties (1946), 380, 383
Pedro the Cruel, 311
Peel Commission, 321
Peking, 197, 206
Penha, Joseph de la, 295
People's Palace, 153
Permanent Count of Justice, 275, 340
Permanenz-Ausschuss, 260
Perris, G. H., 57
Persia, 215
Perth (Australia), 182-3
Pester Lloyd, 250
Petach Tikvah, 180, 314
Petlura, General, 225
Petrograd, 204
Philby, H. St. J., 351, 352, 355
Philippopolis, 254
Phillips, Samuel, 53

Pile, Sir Thomas D., 120
Pilichowsky, L., 150
Pilsudski, Marshal, 135, 142-3
Pinsk, 152
Plaschkess, Dr., 326
Platt, J. A., 27
Plovdiv, 254, 256
Plunket nursing system, 188
Plymouth, 119, 200
Pogroms, 1; in Poland, 133; in Lemberg, 144-5; in Ukraine, 160, 225; in Rumania, 257-8; in Russia, 283, 289, 395
Poland, 3, 5, 135-147; propaganda in, 219, 241, 244; 299-305, 326, 362, 389-390
Polanga, 246
Polish Liquidation Commission, 136, 138, 139, 145
Polish Socialist Party, 62
Political Committee (London), 126
Political Quarterly, 360
Port Said, 182, 206, 215
Portugal, 311-2
Postan, Michael, 226
Potemkin, 52
Power, Eileen, 226
Prado, 311
Prag, Joseph, 32
Prager Presse, 362
Prague, 248-9, 305-9, 327-8, 362
Prato, Chief Rabbi, 316
Preaching, 39-40
Press Association, 128
Propaganda (in First World War), 132
Protocols of Elders of Zion, 294
Prussian War Office, 98
Psalms, 2, 16
Public Relations Officer, 217

Quarterly Review, The, 306, 360, 370, 371
Quebec, 283, 292, 294
Queen's Hall, 149, 153

Rabbinical Seminary, 100
Rabbinics, 38
Rabbis, 13, 14, 23, 42, 71, 103
Rabinowicz, Dr. O. K., 279
Rabinowitz, D., 60
Raczynski, Count Eduard, 363
Radicals, 278
Radio Athlone, 357
Radio talks, 285, 287
Rafa, 179
Rakovski, M., 232, 235
Ramath Gan, 314
Ramath Hashavim, 314
Rangoon, 196, 211
Rapallo, 269
Rappoport, Dr. A. S., 43, 45
Rashi, 45
Rathbone, Eleanor, 307
Ravenna, 309
Reading, Lady, 128
Reading, (first) Marquis of, 128-130, 149-150, 271, 275
Reading, (second) Marquis of, 128, 270, 329
Reform Synagogue (in London), 36, 266
Refugees, from Russia, 23, 52; from Germany 362; economic value of, 373
Regina, 289, 292
Regine Fountain, 206
Rehovot, 181, 314
Reich, Dr. Leon, 136
Religious education, 9-13
Rembrandt, 46, 47
Resistance Movement, 378, 387
Reuter, 128, 149
Reval, 248
Revisionist Party, 267, 278, 308, 313
Rhineland, 41
Richards, Bernard, 297
Richmond, E. T., 351, 355
Riga, 244-6, 247, 248
Rimini, 309
Rimutaka Gorge, 190

Ringel, Dr. Michael, 136
Rishon le-Zion, 180, 189, 314
"Ritual murder," 294
Riza Tewfik Bey, 78
Roc, Patricia, 392
Rockies, 291, 292
Rodin, 72
Rome, 216, 309
Roosevelt, President, 362
Rosenberg, Louis, 292
Rosenblatt, Judge Bernard, 230
Rotary Clubs, 354, 369
Rothschild, Alfred de, 117
Rothschild, Anthony de, 366
Rothschild, Charles de, 117
Rothschild, Baron Edmond de, 275, 287
Rothschild, James de, 329, 334
Rothschild, Lord (Walter), 158, 173
Rothschilds, in Frankfort, 41
Rothschilds, of London, 116
Rothstein, Theodore, 66
Rotorua, 188
Rotterdam, 46, 114
Royal Albert Hall, 269
Rozvadovsky, General, 143
Ruhleben Camp, 99-111, 151, 232, 273
Ruhleben Prison Camp, The, 118, 152
Ruhleben Prisoners' Release Committee, 130
Rumania, 24, 29, 233-5, 241, 243, 256-8, 306-7, 344
Runganhan, Sir Samuel, 382
Ruppin, Dr. A., 65, 85, 313, 334
Russell, Lord (Bertrand), 287
Russia, 1, 2, 17, 18; Zionists from, 55, 247; Zionist Central Committee, 88; persecution of Zionists, 319
Russische Korrespondenz, 56
Rustchuk, 256
Rutenberg, P., 271, 275, 336

Sabbath, observance of, 4-5, 286; neglect of, 244
Sacerdoti, Chief Rabbi, 309
Sadagora, 257
Sadler, Sir Michael, 153
Safed, 315
Salisbury, 353
Salonika, 252, 253
Salvation Army, 354, 368
Samaritans, 315
Samuel, Lady, 356
Samuel, Sir Stuart, 74, 124, 154, 158
Samuel, Viscount (formerly Sir Herbert), 29, 74; consultations with, 122; 126, 128, 130, 201, 222-3, 268, 274, 333-4, 350
Samuels, Sir Saul, 186
San Marino, 309
San Remo, 172
Sankey, Justice, 115
Sarah (Theodora, of Tirnova), 254
Sarona, 323
Saskatchewan, 292
Saskatoon, 290
Sassoon, David, 194
Sassoon, Elias, 194, 196
Sassoon, Haskell, 78
Sassoon, Sir Jacob, 194
Sassoon, Sir Philip, 353
Sassoons, 207
Saudi Arabia, 355
Scandinavia, 240
Schandau, 96, 98
Schechter, Prof. S., 37, 48, 92
Scheveningen, 46
Schmitz, Dr. Siegfried, 323-4
Schmorak, Dr. E., 135
Schubert, 41
Schuschnigg Fund, 326
Schwarzbart, Dr. I., 374
Scotland Yard, 113, 346
Scott, C. P., 51, 83, 122, 343
Scribe, Enoch, 34, 35
Scrutator, 343
Seattle, 292

Sebastopol Prison, 52
Seeley, Sir Charles, 102
Semarang, 210
Semitic languages, 39
Senators, Zionist, 243
Sephardic ritual, 194; synagogues, 251
Sephardim, 311-2
Serbia, 96
Seventh Dominion League, 342
Seville, 312
Shakespeare, 26, 70
Shanghai, 81, 196-8, 366
Sharett, M., 317, 384, 388
Shaw, G. Bernard, 68-9
Shaw, Sir Walter, 270
Shaw Commission, 270-1
Sheffield Conference, 76-7
Shekalim, 299
Shelichim, 388
Shellim, D., 213, 215
Shibly Jamal, 221, 356
Shiites, 215
Shiminoseki, 202
Shire, M. M., 121
Sholem Aleichem, 61, 67
Shuckburgh, Sir J., 270
Shulchan Aruch, 26
Shylock, 12
Siberia, 191, 197, 320
Sidebotham, H., 343
Sieff, Israel, 128
Siena, 391
Simon, Sir John (later Lord), 74, 274
Simon, Rev. Isidore, 21
Simon, Sir Leon, 15, 21, 371
Simpson, Sir J. Hope, 271, 273
Sinai Peninsula project, 44, 121
Singapore, 81, 196, 207-8, 210
Singer, Rev. S., 33
Skelton, Dr., 287
Slavinsky, 225
Slobodka, 245
Slovakia, 358
Smith, W. H., 70

"Smog," 12
Smuts, General, 270-1, 334
Smyllie, R. M., 357
Smyrna, 241, 252
Sneh, Moshe, 385
Snowman, Henry, 45, 65
Snowman, Isaac, 73
Socialism, 51, 52, 68
Socialists, 55
Socialist Conference, International, 147
Sofia, 254-5-6, 339
Sokolow, Nahum, Hebrew author, 64; Zionist General Secretary, 64, 76; in Constantinople, 78; in Berlin Executive, 89; political mission to England, 89; visit to America, 90; at Eleventh Congress, 93; in First World War, 122, 133; at Paris Peace Conference, 147; at Zionist headquarters, 161; relations with Weizmann, 172; President of Zionist Executive, 220; attitude to Jabotinsky, 225; attitude to Jewish Agency, 267-8; opens Congress of 1931, 277; President of Zionist Organisation, 279; in New York, 296; at Lucerne Congress, 313-4; President of Cultural Commission, 317; death of, 318; naturalisation of, 346
Solomon, Sassoon J., 196
Solomon, Solomon J., 46, 125
Solomon, V. C., 184
Solomon Islands, 211
Soloweitschik, Dr. M., 223
Sombart, Prof. W., 88
Sorbonne, 236
Soskice, Dr. David, 57-8
Soskice, Sir Frank, 57
Sourabaya, 210
South Africa, 97
South America, 373, 392
South Kensington School of Art, 18

Southampton, 282, 297
Soviet Union (Government), 160, 240, 258, 319-321, 350, 374, 380, 384, 393
Spaak, M., 382
Spain, 310-313
Spanish Embassy, 334
Speyer, 44
Srba, Deputy, 358
St. Catharine's, 287
St. James's Palace, 223
Stadtvogtei-Gefangnis, 97, 100, 106-8
Stalin, 331, 375
Stansgate, Viscount, 36
Star, The, 118
Steed, H. Wickham, 134
Stoll's Theatre, 124
Storm Troopers, 325
Stout, Sir Robert, 189
Stoyanovsky, Dr. J., 275
Strassburg, 44, 241
Strauss, Prof. A., 238, 339
Strauss, Richard, 87
Strick, M., 52
Stricker, Robert, 176, 326
Struck, Hermann, 46
Stubbs, Sir Reginald, 195
Students, in Rumania, 234; in Hungary, 235-6
Sueddeutsche Monatshefte, 352
Sudetenland, 328
Suez, 216
Sukenik, Prof. E., 316
Sully, Prof. James, 36
Sunday Times, 343
Suvalski, Isaac, 30
Swansea, 125
Swaythling, Dowager Lady, 19
Swaythling, Lord, 23
Sweden, 240, 378
Switzerland, 387
Sydenham, Lord, 350
Sydney, 186-7, 191
Sykes, Sir Mark, 126, 127, 170-1
Syria, 350

Szeptycki, Count, 140

Taj Mahal, 213
Talaat Bey, 78
Talmon, Dr. J. L., 381
Talmud, 11, 14
Talmud Torah school, 13, 344
Tavistock House, 20, 25
Teaching activity, 38-9
Technical Institute (Haifa), 91
Tel-Aviv, 180, 314, 338
Temesvar, 233, 257-8
Temple (London), 117
Tennenblatt, J., 136
Territorialists, 54
Teschen, 146
Tetragrammaton, 212
Theresienstadt, 377
Thomasson, F., 57, 65
Thon, Rabbi Dr. O., 135-137
Tiberias, 181, 315
Tientsin, 205
Tilbury, 115
Times, The, 56, 123, 134, 143, 147, 152, 154, 155, 156, 157-9, 270, 343, 385-6
Times Literary Supplement, 118, 279
Timisoara. See Temesvar
Tokyo, 200-201; University, 236
Toledo, 311
Toronto, 283, 284, 285-8
Torre, Senator della, 334
Toynbee Hall, 25, 36, 48, 354
Traill, H. D., 35
Transjordan, 348-9
Transvaal, 33
Transylvania, 233, 243, 306
Travels in Jewry, 65, 136, 144, 241, 244, 300, 392, 394-5
Tribune, The, 57 seq.
Trieste, 178, 241
Tripoli, 197
Trocadero Restaurant, 32
Troki, 304
Troon, 119

Truth, 372
Tsarist Russia, 3, 22, 58, 89
Tschlenow, Dr., 86, 91, 122
Tuby, M., 179
Tunisia, 227
Turkestan, 320
Turkey, Sultan of, 29, 78; deportation from, 78
Tzankoff (of Bulgaria), 254

Ukraine, massacres in, 160, 290
Ukraine delegation, 384
Ukrainians, 63, 140, 141, 144-5, 146, 303
Union of Jewish Literary Societies, 40
United Kingdom Delegation, 383
United Nations, 391, 393, 396
United States, 167, 282, 287, 342, 373, 374, 379, 383
Universities, in Rumania, 234-5; in Hungary, 235-6
University College, 26-8, 36, 37, 40, 68, 93
University societies, 354
Untermyer, Samuel, 218
Urga, 206
Ussishkin, Menachem, 86, 220, 237-8, 331
Utopia, 38

Vancouver, 289-291, 388
Vazsonyi, W., 233
Venice, 216
Venizelos, 167
Verona, 216
Veszi, Joseph, 249
Vevey, 56
Victoria (Canada), 283, 291-2
Victoria, Queen, 7, 20; Diamond Jubilee, 28, 282
Vienna, Congress in, 92-3, 262-4; 135, 146, 176, 178, 238, 309, 323-7

Vilna, 51, 88, 141, 152, 202, 244, 248, 304-5, 366; book on, 368-9, 389
Visser, Judge, 334
Vladivostok, 206
Voelkischer Beobachter, 307
Voevod, Vaida, 307
Vogel, Sir Julius, 189
"Volkshaus," 51-2, 56
Volos, 253
Vossische Zeitung, 89
Voynich, W. M., 62, 63, 141

Wade, Colonel, 139, 140, 145
Walko, Louis, 250
Wallace, General Lew., 24
War Office (British), 114
Warburg, Felix, 274, 275, 335
Warburg, Otto, 80, 84, 86
Warsaw, 57-8, 64, 88, 139-143, 241, 248, 299-302; Ghetto, 378, 387
Washington, 379
Wassilevsky, M., 140
Watts, G. F., 18
Webb, Beatrice, 171-2
Webb, Sidney, 171-2
Wedgwood, Col. Josiah, 269, 342
Weigall, Sir Archibald, 184
Weisgal, Meyer, 231, 287-8
Weissmann, Dr. M., 306
Weizmann, Chaim, author's first meeting with, 44; visits author in London, 45; lecturer at Manchester University, 61; at Hague Congress, 65; forms Political Committee, 75; kisses author, 77; at Hamburg Congress, 79; attitude to Wolffsohn, 82, in his University laboratory, 83; at Montreux, 84; Director of Admiralty Laboratories, 122; head of Palestine Commission, 126; entrusts author with mission to Poland, 133-4; at Zionist headquarters, 161, 217-8; pays tribute

to Nordau, 165; his Autobiography, 171, 228, 355; elected President of Zionist Organisation, 220; threatens resignation, 224; conflict with Zionist Executive, 226; advocacy of Jewish Agency, 266-9; views on Jewish State, 272; resigns Presidency, 274; end of Presidency, 279; absent from Prague Congress, 307; re-elected President, 313-4; at Geneva Congress, 330-331; convenes Economic Conference, 333; letter on author's retirement, 365; at 1945 Conference, 377; at 1946 Congress, 390; President of Jewish State, 390
Wellhausen, J., 237
Wellington, 188-9, 388
Welt, Die, 67, 81, 84, 88
Werfel, Franz, 249
Western Wall, 181
Westminster Hall, 165
White Paper, Churchill, 222-3
White Paper, Passfield, 276-8
White Paper, MacDonald, 330, 378
Whitechapel, 21, 22 seq., 290
Whitechapel Library, 36
Whitefield's Tabernacle, 354
Wiesbaden, 101, 272-3
William III, 295
Wilson, Gen. Sir Chas., 32
Wilson, President, 154
Winchester, 376
Windsor (Canada), 287
Windsor, Duke of, 201
Winnipeg, 283, 284, 288-9
Winterton, Earl, 357-9
Wise, Dr. Stephen, 267, 282
Wissotzki, 74
Wolf, Prof. A., 48
Wolf, Lucien, 30, 54, 66, 123
Wolffsohn, David, attends London Conference, 32; elected President of Zionist Organisation, 56, 64; addresses meeting in Holborn, 76; appoints author Secretary at Zionist Central Office, 80; tour in England, 82; visit to South Africa, 85; at Vienna Congress, 92-4; opposed by Weizmann, 228
Woman suffrage, 109
Women's International Zionist Organisation, 188
Woodhead Commission, 329
World's Work, The, 218
World Jewish Congress, 298, 380, 392-3
World War, First, 96 *seq.*, 359, 395
World War, Second, 322, 364 *seq.*, 389, 395
Worms, 44-5
Wronchinski, Col., 140
Wronski, Alex, 62

Yeshivah, 1, 245
Yevsektzia, 319
Yiddish, 2, 13, 22, 29; operatic society, 35; plays, 53; in Japan, 199; in Lithuania, 241; schools, 243; folksong, 245; theatre, 286; in Canada, 293; in Soviet Russia, 375; in Mexico, 387
Yokohama, 198-200
Yorkshire Post, 118
Young, Sir Alban, 252
Young Israel, 35
Young Turks, 78
Young Zion Institute, 32
Yugoslavia, 243, 250-2, 387, 389

Zagreb, 250-1, 387
Zaleski, August, 64, 135, 146-7, 363
Zamenhof, Dr. L., 303
Zangwill, Israel, 19, 28, 32, 34, 36, 53-4, 55-6, 61, 67, 76, 95, 117
Zemiroth, 245
Zichron, Jacob, 315
Ziegelbaum, S., 374

Zimmern, Alfred E., 339
Zion Mule Corps, 341
Zione Zion, 54
Zionism, 28-31; Cultural and Spiritual, 74-5
Zionist Bureau (London), 126, 133, 149
Zionist Congress, First (1897), 29
Zionist Congress, Sixth (1903), 42
Zionist Congress, Seventh (1905), 54
Zionist Congress, Eighth (1907), 64-5
Zionist Congress, Ninth (1909), 79-80
Zionist Congress, Tenth (1911), 86
Zionist Congress, Eleventh (1913), 92-94
Zionist Congress, Twelfth (1921), 219
Zionist Congress, Thirteenth (1923), 227-8
Zionist Congress, Fourteenth (1925), 262-4
Zionist Congress, Sixteenth (1929), 268
Zionist Congress, Seventeenth (1931), 277-9
Zionist Congress, Eighteenth 1933), 305, 307-8
Zionist Congress, Nineteenth (1935), 313-4
Zionist Congress, Twentieth (1937), 321-2
Zionist Congress, Twenty-First (1939), 330-2
Zionist Congress, Twenty-Second (1946), 386-390
Zionist Correspondence, 33
Zionist Federation, of England, 32, 33, 78, 79, 121, 123, 126, 164, 172, 371; of Canada, 285; of Germany, 298; of Austria, 262; of Hungary, 232, 239, 249-250; of Czechoslovakia, 328; of Yugoslavia, 387, 389
Zionist Movement, The, 371
Zionist Organisation (World), in Cologne, 64, 76-7; in Berlin, 87-95; in London, 122, 158.
Zionist Record, The, (S. Africa), 366
Zionist Review, The, 343
Zionist Work in Palestine, 82
Zionists, Political and Practical, 65, 92, 164; in Galicia, 145; in Soviet Russia, 319-321
Zollschan, Dr. Ignaz, 85
Zuk, M., 136
Zurich, 135, 238-9, 268, 321, 335